An introductiṅ... ...y.

theory of statistics

G. Udny Yule

Alpha Editions

This edition published in 2019

ISBN : 9789353897796

Design and Setting By
Alpha Editions
email - alphaedis@gmail.com

AN INTRODUCTION TO THE
THEORY OF STATISTICS

BY

G. UDNY YULE, C.B.E., M.A., F.R.S.,

UNIVERSITY LECTURER IN STATISTICS, CAMBRIDGE;
FELLOW AND SOMETIME HONORARY SECRETARY OF THE ROYAL STATISTICAL
SOCIETY OF LONDON;
MEMBER OF THE INTERNATIONAL STATISTICAL INSTITUTE;
FELLOW OF THE ROYAL ANTHROPOLOGICAL INSTITUTE,

With 53 Figures and Diagrams.

SIXTH EDITION, ENLARGED.

LONDON:

CHARLES GRIFFIN AND COMPANY, LIMITED,

EXETER STREET, STRAND, W.C. 2.

1922.

PREFACE TO THE SIXTH EDITION.

THAT the large Fifth Edition of the *Introduction*, printed just after the close of the War, has been exhausted in three years is gratifying evidence that, after ten years of service, the volume still continues to hold its own.

The present edition has been enlarged by a considerable addition to the Supplement on testing Goodness of Fit, dealing with the application of this method to Association and Contingency Tables, and including results only recently published. A brief. Supplement has also been inserted, giving the deduction of the regressions by the use of the differential calculus, and the Supplementary List of References has been extended and brought up to date. Opportunity has also been taken to correct some minor errors in the text and the answers to questions.

In view of the high costs of printing and composition still ruling, it was thought better to maintain the present form, with the additional matter as Supplements, rather than to revise the text, since the latter course would inevitably have necessitated a heavy increase in the selling price. The Index has been revised to cover all new matter

G. U. Y.

June 1922.

PREFACE TO THE FIFTH EDITION.

THE rapid exhaustion of the Fourth Edition, by the end of last year, is evidence that, in spite of the slight revision which has been possible in the last few years, the *Introduction to the Theory of Statistics* has continued to be of service.

The present edition has been enlarged by the inclusion of two supplementary notes, on the Law of Small Chances and on the test of Goodness of Fit of an observed to a theoretical distribution respectively, and also of an extensive list of additional references.

Owing to a serious impairment of vision, reading and writing are at present difficult to me, and I have to express my great indebtedness to my friend and frequent collaborator, Captain M. Greenwood, R.A.M.C.T., of the Lister Institute, for the drafting of these notes and the compilation of the list of references. Their inclusion as supplements, instead of the incorporation of the matter in the text, was decided on as any extensive revision of the text, owing to post-war conditions, would have been disproportionately slow and costly. As the index has been revised to cover all the new matter, it is hoped that this will cause little inconvenience.

G. U. Y.

April 1919.

PREFACE TO THE FIRST EDITION.

THE following chapters are based on the courses of instruction given during my tenure of the Newmarch Lectureship in Statistics at University College, London, in the sessions 1902–1909. The variety of illustrations and examples has, however, been increased to render the book more suitable for the use of biologists and others besides those interested in economic and vital statistics, and some of the more difficult parts of the subject have been treated in greater detail than was possible in a sessional course of some thirty lectures. For the rest, the chapters follow closely the arrangement of the course, the three parts into which the volume is divided corresponding approximately to the work of the three terms. To enable the student to proceed further with the subject, fairly detailed lists of references to the original memoirs have been given at the end of each chapter: exercises have also been added for the benefit, more especially, of the student who is working without the assistance of a teacher.

The volume represents an attempt to work out a systematic introductory course on statistical methods—the methods available for discussing, as distinct from collecting, statistical data—suited to those who possess only a limited knowledge of mathematics : an acquaintance with algebra up to the binomial theorem, together with such elements of co-ordinate geometry as are now generally included therewith, is all that is assumed. I hope that it may prove of some service to the students of the diverse sciences in which statistical methods are now employed.

My most grateful thanks are due to Mr R. H. Hooker not only

for reading the greater part of the manuscript, and the proofs, and for making many criticisms and suggestions which have been of the greatest service, but also for much friendly help and encouragement without which the preparation of the volume, often delayed and interrupted by the pressure of other work, might never have been completed : my debt to Mr Hooker is indeed greater than can well be expressed in a formal preface. My thanks are also due to Mr H. D. Vigor for some assistance in checking the arithmetic, and my acknowledgments to Professor Edgeworth for the example used in § 5 of Chap. XVII. to illustrate the influence of the form of the frequency distribution on the probable error of the median.

I can hardly hope that all errors in the text or in the mass of arithmetic involved in examples and exercises have been eliminated, and will feel indebted to any reader who directs my attention to any such mistakes, or to any omissions, ambiguities, or obscurities.

G. U. Y.

December 1910.

CONTENTS.

INTRODUCTION.

PART I.—THE THEORY OF ATTRIBUTES.

CHAPTER I.

NOTATION AND TERMINOLOGY.

CHAPTER II.

CONSISTENCE.

CHAPTER III.

ASSOCIATION.

CHAPTER IV.

PARTIAL ASSOCIATION.

CHAPTER V.

MANIFOLD CLASSIFICATION.

PART II.—THE THEORY OF VARIABLES.

CHAPTER VI.

THE FREQUENCY-DISTRIBUTION.

CHAPTER VII.

AVERAGES.

CHAPTER VIII.

MEASURES OF DISPERSION, ETC.

CHAPTER IX.

CORRELATION.

CHAPTER X.

CORRELATION: ILLUSTRATIONS AND PRACTICAL METHODS.

CHAPTER XI.

MISCELLANEOUS THEOREMS INVOLVING THE USE OF THE CORRELATION-COEFFICIENT.

CHAPTER XII.

PARTIAL CORRELATION.

PART III.—THEORY OF SAMPLING.

CHAPTER XIII.

SIMPLE SAMPLING OF ATTRIBUTES.

CHAPTER XIV.

SIMPLE SAMPLING CONTINUED: EFFECT OF REMOVING THE LIMITATIONS OF SIMPLE SAMPLING.

CHAPTER XV.

THE BINOMIAL DISTRIBUTION AND THE NORMAL CURVE.

CHAPTER XVII.

THE SIMPLER CASES OF SAMPLING FOR VARIABLES : PERCENTILES AND MEAN.

THEORY OF STATISTICS.

INTRODUCTION.

1. THE words "statist," "statistics," "statistical," appear to be all derived, more or less indirectly, from the Latin *status*, in the sense that it acquired in mediæval Latin of a political *state*.

2. The first term is, however, of much earlier date than the two others. The word "statist" is found, for instance, in *Hamlet* (1602),[1] *Cymbeline* (1610 or 1611),[2] and in *Paradise Regained* (1671).[3] The earliest occurrence of the word "statistics" yet noted is in *The Elements of Universal Erudition*, by Baron J. F. von Bielfeld, translated by W. Hooper, M.D. (3 vols., London, 1770). One of its chapters is entitled *Statistics*, and contains a definition of the subject as "The science that teaches us what is the political arrangement of all the modern states of the known world."[4] "Statistics" occurs again with a rather wider definition in the preface to *A Political Survey of the Present State of Europe*, by E. A. W. Zimmermann,[5] issued in 1787. "It is about forty years ago," says Zimmermann, "that that branch of political knowledge, which has for its object the actual and relative power of the several modern states, the power arising from their natural advantages, the industry and civilisation of their inhabitants, and the wisdom of their governments, has been formed, chiefly by German writers, into a separate science. . . . By the more convenient form it has now received . . . . this science, distinguished by the new-coined name of *statistics*, is become a favourite study in Germany" (p. ii); and the adjective is also given (p. v), "To the several articles contained in this work, some respectable

---

[1] Act v., sc. 2.   [2] Act ii., sc. 4.   [3] Bk. iv.

[4] I cite from Dr W. F. Willcox, *Quarterly Publications of the American Statistical Association*, vol. xiv., 1914, p. 287.

[5] Zimmermann's work appears to have been written in English, though he was a German, Professor of Natural Philosophy at Brunswick.

1

statistical writers have added a view of the principal epochs of the
history of each country."

3. Within the next few years the words were adopted by several
writers, notably by Sir John Sinclair, the editor and organiser of the
first *Statistical Account of Scotland*,[1] to whom, indeed, their introduction has been frequently ascribed. In the circular letter to the
Clergy of the Church of Scotland issued in May 1790,[2] he states
that in Germany "'Statistical Inquiries,' as they are called, have
been carried to a very great extent," and adds an explanatory
footnote to the phrase "Statistical Inquiries"—"or inquiries
respecting the population, the political circumstances, the pro-
ductions of a country, and other matters of state." In the
"History of the Origin and Progress"[3] of the work, he tells us,
"Many people were at first surprised at my using the new words,
Statistics and *Statistical*, as it was supposed that some term in our
own language might have expressed the same meaning. But in
the course of a very extensive tour, through the northern parts of
Europe, which I happened to take in 1786, I found that in
Germany they were engaged in a species of political enquiry,
to which they had given the name of *Statistics*;[4] .... as I
thought that a new word might attract more public attention,
I resolved on adopting it, and I hope that it is now completely
naturalised and incorporated with our language." This hope
was certainly justified, but the meaning of the word underwent
rapid development during the half century or so following its
introduction.

4. "Statistics" (statistik), as the term is used by German
writers of the eighteenth century, by Zimmermann and by Sir
John Sinclair, meant simply the exposition of the noteworthy
characteristics of a state, the mode of exposition being—almost
inevitably at that time—preponderantly verbal. The conciseness
and definite character of numerical data were recognised at a
comparatively early period—more particularly by English writers
—but trustworthy figures were scarce. After the commencement
of the nineteenth century, however, the growth of official data
was continuous, and numerical statements, accordingly, began
more and more to displace the verbal descriptions of earlier days.
"Statistics" thus insensibly acquired a narrower signification, viz.,

[1] Twenty-one vols., 1791–99.
[2] *Statistical Account*, vol. xx., Appendix to "The History of the Origin and
Progress . . . ." given at the end of the volume.
[3] *Loc. cit.*, p. xiii.
[4] The *Abriss der Statswissenschaft der Europäischen Reiche* (1749) of Gottfried
Achenwall, Professor of Politics at Göttingen, is the volume in which the word
"statistik" appears to be first employed, but the adjective "statisticus"
occurs at a somewhat earlier date in works written in Latin.

the exposition of the characteristics of a State by *numerical* methods. It is difficult to say at what epoch the word came definitely to bear this quantitative meaning, but the transition appears to have been only half accomplished even after the foundation of the Royal Statistical Society in 1834. The articles in the first volume of the *Journal*, issued in 1838–9, are for the most part of a numerical character, but the official definition has no reference to method. "Statistics," we read, "may be said, in the words of the prospectus of this Society, to be the ascertaining and bringing together of those facts which are calculated to illustrate the condition and prospects of society."[1] It is, however, admitted that "the statist commonly prefers to employ figures and tabular exhibitions."

5. Once, however, the first change of meaning was accomplished, further changes followed. From the name of a science or art of state-description by numerical methods, the word was transferred to those series of figures with which it operated, as we speak of vital statistics, poor-law statistics, and so forth. But similar data occur in many connections ; in meteorology, for instance, in anthropology, etc. Such collections of numerical data were also termed "statistics," and consequently, at the present day, the word is held to cover a collection of numerical data, analogous to those which were originally formed for the study of the state, on almost any subject whatever. We not only read of rainfall "statistics," but of "statistics" showing the growth of an organisation for recording rainfall.[2] We find a chapter headed "Statistics" in a book on psychology,[3] and the author, writing of "statistics concerning the mental characteristics of man," "statistics of children, under the headings bright—average—dull."[4] We are informed that, in a book on Latin verse, the characteristics of the Virgilian hexameter "are examined carefully with statistics."[5]

6. The development in meaning of the adjective "statistical" was naturally similar. The methods applied to the study of numerical data concerning the state were still termed "statistical methods," even when applied to data from other sources. Thus we read of the inheritance of genius being treated "in a statistical manner,"[6] and we have now "a journal for the statistical study of biological problems."[7] Such phrases as "the statistical

---

[1] *Jour. Stat. Soc.*, vol. i. p. 1.
[2] Symons' *British Rainfall* for 1899, p. 15.
[3] E. W. Scripture, *The New Psychology*, 1897, chap. ii.
[4] *Op. cit.* p. 18.
[5] *Athenæum*, Oct. 3, 1903.
[6] Francis Galton, *Hereditary Genius* (Macmillan, 1869), preface.
[7] *Biometrika*, Cambridge Univ. Press, the first number issued in 1901

investigation of the motion of molecules"[1] have become part of the ordinary language of physicists. We find a work entitled "the principles of statistical mechanics,"[2] and the Bakerian lecture for 1909, by Sir J. Larmor, was on "the statistical and thermodynamical relations of radiant energy."

7. It is unnecessary to multiply such instances to show that the words "statistics," "statistical," no longer bear any necessary reference to "matters of state." They are applied indifferently in physics, biology, anthropology, and meteorology, as well as in the social sciences. Diverse though these cases are, there must be some community of character between them, or the same terms and the same methods would not be applied. What, then, is this common character?

8. Let us turn to social science, as the parent of the methods termed "statistical," for a moment, and consider its characteristics as compared, say, with physics or chemistry. One characteristic stands out so markedly that attention has been repeatedly directed to it by "statistical" writers as the source of the peculiar difficulties of their science—*the observer of social facts cannot experiment, but must deal with circumstances as they occur, apart from his control.* Now the object of experiment is to replace the complex systems of causation usually occurring in nature by simple systems in which only one causal circumstance is permitted to vary at a time. This simplification being impossible, the observer has, in general, to deal with highly complicated cases of multiple causation—cases in which a given result may be due to any one of a number of alternative causes or to a number of different causes acting conjointly.

9. A little consideration will show, however, that this is also precisely the characteristic of the observations in other fields to which *statistical methods* are applied. The meteorologist, for example, is in almost precisely the same position as the student of social science. He can experiment on minor points, but the records of the barometer, thermometer, and rain gauge have to be treated as they stand. With the biologist, matters are in somewhat better case. He can and does apply experimental methods to a very large extent, but frequently cannot approximate closely to the experimental ideal; the internal circumstances of animals and plants too easily evade complete control. Hence a large field (notably the study of variation and heredity) is left, in which statistical methods have either to aid or to replace the methods of experiment. The physicist and chemist, finally,

[1] Clerk Maxwell, "Theory of Heat" (1871), and "On Boltzmann's Theorem" (1878), *Camb. Phil. Trans.*, vol. xii.
[2] By J. Willard Gibbs (Macmillan, 1902).

stand at the other extremity of the scale. Theirs are the sciences in which experiment has been brought to its greatest perfection. But even so, statistical methods still find application. In the first place, the methods available for eliminating the effect of disturbing circumstances, though continually improved, are not, and cannot be, absolutely perfect. The observer himself, as well as the observing instrument, is a source of error; the effects of changes of temperature, or of moisture, of pressure, draughts, vibration, cannot be completely eliminated. Further, in the problems of molecular physics, referred to in the last sentences of § 6, multiplicity of causes is of the essence of the case. The motion of an atom or of a molecule in the middle of a swarm is dependent on that of every other atom or molecule in the swarm.

10. In the light of this discussion, we may accordingly give the following definitions :—

By **statistics** we mean quantitative data affected to a marked extent by a multiplicity of causes.

By **statistical** methods we mean methods specially adapted to the elucidation of quantitative data affected by a multiplicity of causes.

By **theory of statistics** we mean the exposition of statistical methods.

The insertion in the first definition of some such words as "to a marked extent" is necessary, since the term "statistics" is not usually applied to data, like those of the physicist, which are affected only by a relatively small residuum of disturbing causes. At the same time, "statistical methods" are applicable to all such cases, whether the influence of many causes be large or not.

REFERENCES.

The History of the Words "Statistics," "Statistical."

(1) John, V., *Der. Name Statistik*; Weiss, Berne, 1883. A translation in *Jour. Roy. Stat. Soc.* for same year.
(2) Yule, G. U., "The Introduction of the Words 'Statistics,' 'Statistical,' into the English Language," *Jour. Roy. Stat. Soc.*, vol. lxviii., 1905, p. 391.

The History of Statistics in General.

(3) John, V., *Geschichte der Statistik*, 1te Teil, bis auf Quetelet; Enke, Stuttgart, 1884. (All published; the author died in 1900. By far the best history of statistics down to the early years of the nineteenth century.)
(4) Mohl, Robert von, *Geschichte und Litteratur der Staatswissenschaften*, 3 vols.; Enke, Erlangen, 1855–58. (For history of statistics see principally latter half of vol. iii.)

(5) GABAGLIO, ANTONIO, *Teoria generale della statistica*, 2 vols.; Hoepli, Milano, 2nd edn., 1888. (Vol. i., *Parte storica*.)

Several works on theory of statistics include short histories, *e.g.* H. Westergaard's *Die Grundzüge der Theorie der Statistik* (Fischer, Jena, 1890), and P. A. Meitzen's *Geschichte, Theorie und Technik der Statistik* (new edn., 1903; American translation by R. P. Falkner, 1891). There is no detailed history in English, but the article "Statistics" in the *Encyclopædia Britannica* (11th edn.) gives a very slight sketch, and the biographical articles in Palgrave's *Dictionary of Political Economy* are useful. For its importance as regards the English school of political arithmetic, reference may also be made to—

(6) HULL, C. H., *The Economic Writings of Sir William Petty, together with the Observations on the Bills of Mortality more probably by Captain John Graunt*, Cambridge University Press, 2 vols., 1899.

History of Theory of Statistics.

Somewhat slight information is given in the general works cited. From the purely mathematical side the following is important:—

(7) TODHUNTER, I., *A History of the Mathematical Theory of Probability from the time of Pascal to that of Laplace*; Macmillan, 1865.

History of Official Statistics.

(8) BERTILLON, J., *Cours élémentaire de statistique*; Société d'éditions scientifiques, 1895. (Gives an exceedingly useful outline of the history of official statistics in different countries.)

PART I.—THE THEORY OF ATTRIBUTES.

CHAPTER I.

NOTATION AND TERMINOLOGY.

1. THE methods of statistics, as defined in the Introduction, deal with quantitative data alone. The quantitative character may, however, arise in two different ways.

In the first place, the observer may note only the *presence* or *absence* of some attribute in a series of objects or individuals, and count how many do or do not possess it. Thus, in a given population, we may count the number of the blind and seeing, the dumb and speaking, or the insane and sane. The quantitative character, in such cases, arises solely in the counting.

In the second place, the observer may note or measure the actual magnitude of some variable character for each of the objects or individuals observed. He may record, for instance, the ages of persons at death, the prices of different samples of a commodity, the statures of men, the numbers of petals in flowers. The observations in these cases are quantitative *ab initio*.

2. The methods applicable to the former kind of observations, which may be termed **statistics of attributes,** are also applicable to the latter, or **statistics of variables.** A record of statures of men, for example, may be treated by simply counting all measurements as *tall* that exceed a certain limit, neglecting the magnitude of excess or defect, and stating the numbers of *tall* and *short* (or

more strictly not-tall) on the basis of this classification. Similarly, the methods that are specially adapted to the treatment of statistics of variables, making use of each value recorded, are available to a greater extent than might at first sight seem possible for dealing with statistics of attributes. For example, we may treat the presence or absence of the attribute as corresponding to the changes of a variable which can only possess two values, say 0 and 1. Or, we may assume that we have really to do with a variable character which has been crudely classified, as suggested above, and we may be able, by auxiliary hypotheses as to the nature of this variable, to draw further conclusions. But the methods and principles developed for the case in which the observer only notes the presence or absence of attributes are the simplest and most fundamental, and are best considered first. This and the next three chapters (Chapters I.–IV.) are accordingly devoted to the Theory of Attributes.

3. The objects or individuals that possess the attribute, and those that do not possess it, may be said to be members of two distinct classes, the observer classifying the objects or individuals observed. In the simplest case, where attention is paid to one attribute alone, only two mutually exclusive classes are formed. If several attributes are noted, the process of classification may, however, be continued indefinitely. Those that do and do not possess the first attribute may be reclassified according as they do or do not possess the second, the members of each of the sub-classes so formed according as they do or do not possess the third, and so on, every class being divided into two at each step. Thus the members of the population of any district may be classified into males and females; the members of each sex into sane and insane; the insane males, sane males, insane females, and sane females into blind and seeing. If we were dealing with a number of peas (*Pisum sativum*) of different varieties, they might be classified as tall or dwarf, with green seeds or yellow seeds, with wrinkled seeds or round seeds, so that we would have eight classes—tall with round green seeds, tall with round yellow seeds, tall with wrinkled green seeds, tall with wrinkled yellow seeds, and four similar classes of dwarf plants.

4. It may be noticed that the fact of classification does not necessarily imply the existence of either a natural or a clearly defined boundary between the two classes. The boundary may be wholly arbitrary, *e.g.* where prices are classified as above or below some special value, barometer readings as above or below some particular height. The division may also be vague and uncertain: sanity and insanity, sight and blindness, pass into each other by such fine gradations that judgments may

differ as to the class in which a given individual should be entered. The possibility of uncertainties of this kind should always be borne in mind in considering statistics of attributes: whatever the nature of the classification, however, natural or artificial, definite or uncertain, the final judgment must be decisive; any one object or individual must be held either to possess the given attribute or not.

5. A classification of the simple kind considered, in which each class is divided into two sub-classes and no more, has been termed by logicians **classification**, or, to use the more strictly applicable term, **division by dichotomy** (cutting in two). The classifications of most statistics are not dichotomous, for most usually a class is divided into more than two sub-classes, but dichotomy is the fundamental case. In Chapter V. the relation of dichotomy to more elaborate (**manifold**, instead of twofold or dichotomous) processes of classification, and the methods applicable to some such cases, are dealt with briefly.

6. For theoretical purposes it is necessary to have some simple notation for the classes formed, and for the numbers of observations assigned to each.

The capitals A, B, C, ... will be used to denote the several attributes. An object or individual possessing the attribute A will be termed simply A. The class, all the members of which possess the attribute A, will be termed *the class A*. It is convenient to use single symbols also to denote the *absence* of the attributes A, B, C, ... We shall employ the Greek letters, a, β, γ, ... Thus if A represents the attribute *blindness*, a represents *sight*, *i.e.* non-blindness; if B stands for *deafness*, β stands for *hearing*. Generally "a" is equivalent to "non-A," or *an object or individual not possessing the attribute A* ; *the class a is equivalent to the class none of the members of which possess the attribute A*.

7. Combinations of attributes will be represented by juxtapositions of letters. Thus if, as above, A represents *blindness*, B *deafness*, AB represents the combination *blindness and deafness*. If the presence and absence of these attributes be noted, the four classes so formed, viz. AB, $A\beta$, aB, $a\beta$, include respectively the *blind and deaf*, the *blind but not-deaf*, *the deaf but not-blind*, and the *neither blind nor deaf*. If a third attribute be noted, *e.g.* insanity, denoted say by C, the class ABC, includes those who are at once *deaf, blind, and insane*, $AB\gamma$ those who are *deaf and blind but not insane*, and so on.

Any letter or combination of letters like A, AB, aB, $AB\gamma$, by means of which we specify the characters of the members of a class, may be termed a class symbol.

8. The number of observations assigned to any class is termed, for brevity, the **frequency** of the class, or the **class-frequency**. Class-frequencies will be denoted by enclosing the corresponding class-symbols in brackets. Thus—

(A)	denotes number of A's,			*i.e.* objects possessing attribute A
(a)	,,	,,	a's,	,, not ,, ,, A
(AB)	,,	,,	AB's,	,, possessing attributes A and B
(aB)	,,	,,	aB's,	,, ,, ,, B but not A
(ABC)	,,	,,	ABC's,	,, ,, ,, A, B, and C
(aBC)	,,	,,	aBC's,	,, ,, ,, B and C but not A
$(a\beta C)$	,,	,,	$a\beta C$'s,	,, ,, ,, C but neither A nor B

and so on for any number of attributes. If A represent, as in the illustration above, blindness, B deafness, C insanity, the symbols given stand for the numbers of the *blind*, the *not-blind*, the *blind and deaf*, the *deaf but not blind*, the *blind, deaf, and insane*, the *deaf and insane but not blind*, and the *insane but neither blind nor deaf*, respectively.

9. The attributes denoted by capitals ABC, . , . may be termed **positive** attributes, and their *contraries* denoted by Greek letters **negative** attributes. If a class-symbol include only capital letters, the class may be termed a positive class; if only Greek letters, a negative class. Thus the classes A, AB, ABC are positive classes; the classes a, $a\beta$, $a\beta\gamma$, negative classes.

If two classes are such that every attribute in the symbol for the one is the negative or contrary of the corresponding attribute in the symbol for the other, they may be termed **contrary classes** and their frequencies **contrary frequencies**; *e.g.* AB and $a\beta$, $A\beta$ and aB, $A\beta C$ and $aB\gamma$, are pairs of **contraries**.

10. The classes obtained by noting say n attributes fall into natural groups according to the numbers of attributes used to specify the respective classes, and these natural groups should be borne in mind in tabulating the class-frequencies. A class specified by r attributes may be spoken of as a class of the rth **order** and its frequency as a frequency of the rth order. Thus AB, AC, BC are classes of the second order; (A), $(A\beta)$, (aBC), $(AB\gamma D)$, class-frequencies of the first, second, third, and fourth orders respectively.

11. The classes of one and the same order fall into further groups according to the actual attributes specified. Thus if three attributes A, B, C have been noted, the classes of the second order may be specified by any one of the pairs of attributes AB, AC, or BC (and their contraries). The series of classes or class-frequencies given by any one positive class and the classes whose symbols are derived therefrom by substituting Greek letters for one or more of the italic capital letters in every possible way will be termed an aggregate. Thus (AB) $(A\beta)$ (aB) $(a\beta)$ form an aggre-

gate of frequencies of the second order, and the twelve classes of
the second order which can be formed where three attributes
have been noted may be grouped into three such aggregates.

12. Class-frequencies should, in tabulating, be arranged so that
frequencies of the same order and frequencies belonging to the
same aggregate are kept together. Thus the frequencies for the
case of three attributes should be grouped as given below; the
whole number of observations denoted by the letter N being
reckoned as a frequency of order zero, since no attributes are
specified :—

$$
\left.
\begin{array}{llll}
\text{Order 0.} & N & & \\
\text{Order 1.} & (A) & (B) & (C) \\
& (a) & (\beta) & (\gamma) \\
\text{Order 2.} & (AB) & (AC) & (BC) \\
& (A\beta) & (A\gamma) & (B\gamma) \\
& (aB) & (aC) & (\beta C) \\
& (a\beta) & (a\gamma) & (\beta\gamma) \\
\text{Order 3.} & (ABC) & (aBC) & \\
& (AB\gamma) & (aB\gamma) & \\
& (A\beta C) & (a\beta C) & \\
& (A\beta\gamma) & (a\beta\gamma) &
\end{array}
\right\} \quad . \quad . \quad (1)
$$

13. In such a complete table for the case of three attributes,
twenty-seven distinct frequencies are given :—1 of order zero, 6
of the first order, 12 of the second, and 8 of the third. It
is, however, in no case necessary to give such a complete
statement.

The whole number of observations must clearly be equal to the
number of A's together with the number of a's, the number of
A's to the number of A's that are B together with the number of
A's that are not B ; and so on,—i.e. any class-frequency can always
be expressed in terms of class-frequencies of higher order. Thus—

$$
\left.
\begin{aligned}
N &= (A) + (a) = (B) + (\beta) = \text{etc.} \\
&= (AB) + (A\beta) + (aB) + (a\beta) = \text{etc.} \\
(A) &= (AB) + (A\beta) = (AC) + (A\gamma) = \text{etc.} \\
(AB) &= (ABC) + (AB\gamma) = \text{etc.}
\end{aligned}
\right\} \quad . \quad . \quad (2)
$$

Hence, instead of enumerating all the frequencies as under (1),
no more need be given, for the case of three attributes, than
the eight frequencies of the third order. If four attributes had
been noted it would be sufficient to give the sixteen frequencies of
the fourth order.

The classes specified by all the attributes noted in any case,
i.e. classes of the nth order in the case of n attributes, may be

termed the **ultimate classes** and their frequencies the **ultimate frequencies.** Hence we may say that *it is never necessary to enumerate more than the ultimate frequencies.* All the others can be obtained from these by simple addition.

Example i.—(See reference 5 at the end of the chapter.) A number of school children were examined for the presence or absence of certain defects of which three chief descriptions were noted, *A* development defects, *B* nerve signs, *C* low nutrition.

Given the following ultimate frequencies, find the frequencies of the positive classes, including the whole number of observations N.

(ABC)	57	(aBC)	78
$(AB\gamma)$	281	$(aB\gamma)$	670
$(A\beta C)$	86	$(a\beta C)$	65
$(A\beta\gamma)$	453	$(a\beta\gamma)$	8310

The whole number of observations N is equal to the grand total : $N = 10,000$.

The frequency of any first-order class, *e.g.* (A) is given by the total of the four third-order frequencies, the class-symbols for which contain the same letter—

$$(ABC) + (AB\gamma) + (A\beta C) + (A\beta\gamma) = (A) = 877.$$

Similarly, the frequency of any second-order class, *e.g.* (AB), is given by the total of the two third-order frequencies, the class-symbols for which both contain the same pair of letters—

$$(ABC) + (AB\gamma) = (AB) = 338.$$

The complete results are—

N	10,000	(AB)	338
(A)	877	(AC)	143
(B)	1,086	(BC)	135
(C)	286	(ABC)	57

14. The number of ultimate frequencies in the general case of n attributes, or the number of classes in an aggregate of the nth order, is given by considering that each letter of the class-symbol may be written in two ways (A or a, B or β, C or γ), and that either way of writing one letter may be combined with either way of writing another. Hence the whole number of ways in which the class-symbol may be written, *i.e.* the number of classes, is—

$$2 \times 2 \times 2 \times 2 \ldots \ldots = 2^n.$$

The ultimate frequencies form one natural set in terms of which the data are completely given, but any other set containing the same number of algebraically independent frequencies, viz. 2^n, may be chosen instead.

15. The **positive class-frequencies**, including under this head the total number of observations N, form one such set. They are algebraically independent; no one positive class-frequency can be expressed wholly in terms of the others. Their number is, moreover, 2^n, as may be readily seen from the fact that if the Greek letters are struck out of the symbols for the ultimate classes, they become the symbols for the positive classes, with the exception of $\alpha\beta\gamma$ .... for which N must be substituted. Otherwise the number is made up as follows :—

Order 0. (The whole number of observations)   .   .   .   1
Order 1. (The number of attributes noted) .   .   .   . n
Order 2. (The number of combinations of n things 2 together) $\dfrac{n(n-1)}{1.2}$
Order 3. (The number of combinations of n things 3 together) $\dfrac{n(n-1)(n-2)}{1.2.3}$

and so on. But the series

$$1 + n + \frac{n(n-1)}{1.2} + \frac{n(n-1)(n-2)}{1.2.3} + \ldots$$

is the binomial expansion of $(1+1)^n$ or 2^n, therefore the total number of positive classes is 2^n.

16. The set of positive class-frequencies is a most convenient one for both theoretical and practical purposes.

Compare, for instance, the two forms of statement, in terms of the ultimate and the positive classes respectively, as given in Example i., § 13. The latter gives directly the whole number of observations and the totals of A's, B's, and C's. The former gives none of those fundamentally important figures without the performance of more or less lengthy additions. Further, the latter gives the second-order frequencies (AB), (AC), and (BC), which are necessary for discussing the relations subsisting between A, B, and C, but are only indirectly given by the frequencies of the ultimate classes.

17. The expression of any class-frequency in terms of the positive frequencies is most easily obtained by a process of step-by-step substitution; thus—

$$
\begin{aligned}
(\alpha\beta) &= (\alpha) - (\alpha B)\\
&= N - (A) - (B) + (AB) \quad . \quad . \quad . \quad . \quad . \quad (3)\\
(\alpha\beta\gamma) &= (\alpha\beta) - (\alpha\beta C)\\
&= N - (A) - (B) + (AB) - (\alpha C) + (\alpha BC)\\
&= N - (A) - (B) - (C) + (AB) + (AC) + (BC) - (ABC) \quad (4)
\end{aligned}
$$

Arithmetical work, however, should be executed from first principles, and not by quoting formulæ like the above.

Example ii.—Check the work of Example i., § 13, by finding the frequencies of the ultimate classes from the frequencies of the positive classes.

$$(AB\gamma) = (AB) - (ABC) = 338 - 57 = 281$$
$$(A\beta\gamma) = (A\gamma) - (AB\gamma) = (A) - (AC) - (AB\gamma)$$
$$= 877 - 143 - 281 = 453$$
$$(\alpha\beta\gamma) = (\beta\gamma) - (A\beta\gamma) = N - (B) - (C) + (BC) - (A\beta\gamma)$$
$$= 10,000 - 1086 - 286 + 135 - 453$$
$$= 10,135 - 1825 = 8310$$

and so on.

18. Examples of statistics of precisely the kind now under consideration are afforded by the census returns, *e.g.*, of 1891 or 1901, for England and Wales, of persons suffering from different "infirmities," any individual who is deaf and dumb, blind or mentally deranged (lunatic, imbecile, or idiot) being required to be returned as such on the schedule. The classes chosen for tabulation are, however, neither the positive nor the ultimate classes, but the following (neglecting minor distinctions amongst the mentally deranged and the returns of persons who are deaf but not dumb):—Dumb, blind, mentally deranged; dumb and blind but not deranged; dumb and deranged but not blind; blind and deranged but not dumb; blind, dumb, and deranged. If, in the symbolic notation, deaf-mutism be denoted by A, blindness by B, and mental derangement by C, the class-frequencies thus given are (A), (B), (C), $(AB\gamma)$, $(A\beta C)$, (αBC), (ABC) (cf. *Census of England and Wales, 1891*, vol. iii., tables 15 and 16, p. lvii. *Census of 1901, Summary Tables*, table xlix.). This set of frequencies does not appear to possess any special advantages.

19. The symbols of our notation are, it should be remarked, used in an inclusive sense, the symbol A, for example, signifying an object or individual possessing the attribute A with or without others. This seems to be the only natural use of the symbol, but at least one notation has been constructed on an *exclusive* basis (*cf.* ref. 5), the symbol A denoting that the object or individual possesses the attribute A, but not B or C or D, or whatever other attributes have been noted. An exclusive notation is apt to be relatively cumbrous and also ambiguous, for the reader cannot know what attributes a given symbol excludes until he has seen the whole list of attributes of which note has been taken, and this list he must bear in mind. The statement that the symbol A is used exclusively cannot mean, obviously, that the object referred to possesses only the attribute A and no others

whatever; it merely excludes the other attributes noted in the particular investigation. Adjectives, as well as the symbols which may represent them, are naturally used in an inclusive sense, and care should therefore be taken, when classes are verbally described, that the description is complete, and states what, if anything, is excluded as well as what is included, in the same way as our notation. The terminology of the English census has not, in this respect, been quite clear. The "Blind" includes those who are "Blind and Dumb," or "Blind, Dumb, and Lunatic," and so forth. But the heading "Blind and Dumb," in the table relating to "combined infirmities," is used in the sense "Blind and Dumb, but not Lunatic or Imbecile," etc., and so on for the others. In the first table the headings are inclusive, in the second exclusive.

REFERENCES.

(1) JEVONS, W. STANLEY, "On a General System of Numerically Definite Reasoning," *Memoirs of the Manchester Lit. and Phil. Soc.*, 1870. Reprinted in *Pure Logic and other Minor Works*; Macmillan, 1890. (The method used in these chapters is that of Jevons, with the notation slightly modified to that employed in the next three memoirs cited.)

(2) YULE, G. U., "On the Association of Attributes in Statistics, etc.," *Phil. Trans. Roy. Soc.*, Series A, vol. cxciv., 1900, p. 257.

(3) YULE, G. U., "On the Theory of Consistence of Logical Class-frequencies and its Geometrical Representation," *Phil. Trans. Roy. Soc.*, Series A, vol. cxcvii., 1901, p. 91.

(4) YULE, G. U., "Notes on the Theory of Association of Attributes in Statistics," *Biometrika*, vol. ii., 1903, p. 121. (The first three sections of (4) are an abstract of (2) and (3). The remarks made as regards the tabulation of class-frequencies at the end of (2) should be read in connection with the remarks made at the beginning of (3) and in this chapter: cf. *footnote* on p. 94 of (3).)

Material has been cited from, and reference made to the notation used in—

(5) WARNER, F., and others, "Report on the Scientific Study of the Mental and Physical Conditions of Childhood"; published by the Committee, Parkes Museum, 1895.

(6) WARNER, F., "Mental and Physical Conditions among Fifty Thousand Children, etc.," *Jour. Roy. Stat. Soc.*, vol. lix., 1896, p. 125.

EXERCISES.

1. (Figures from ref. (5).) The following are the numbers of boys observed with certain classes of defects amongst a number of school-children. A, denotes development defects; B, nerve signs; C, low nutrition.

(ABC)	149	(aBC)	204
$(AB\gamma)$	738	$(aB\gamma)$	1,762
$(A\beta C)$	225	$(a\beta C)$	171
$(A\beta\gamma)$	1,196	$(a\beta\gamma)$	21,842

Find the frequencies of the *positive* classes.

2. (Figures from ref. (5).) The following are the frequencies of the positive classes for the girls in the same investigation :—

N	23,713	(AB)	587
(A)	1,618	(AC)	428
(B)	2,015	(BC)	335
(C)	770	(ABC)	156

Find the frequencies of the ultimate classes.

3. (Figures from *Census, England and Wales, 1891*, vol. iii.) Convert the census statement as below into a statement in terms of (a) the positive, (b) the ultimate class-frequencies. A = blindness, B = deaf-mutism, C = mental derangement.

N	29,002,525	$(AB\gamma)$	82
(A)	23,467	$(A\beta C)$	380
(B)	14,192	(aBC)	500
(C)	97,383	(ABC)	25

4. (*Cf.* Mill's *Logic*, bk. iii., ch. xvii., and ref. (1).) Show that if A occurs in a larger proportion of the cases where B is than where B is not, then will B occur in a larger proportion of the cases where A is than where A is not : *i.e.* given $(AB)/(B) > (A\beta)/(\beta)$, show that $(AB)/(A) > (aB)/(a)$.

5. (*Cf.* De Morgan, *Formal Logic*, p. 163, and ref. (1).) Most B's are A's, most B's are C's : find the least number of A's that are C's, *i.e.* the lowest possible value of (AC).

6. Given that

$$(A) = (a) = (B) = (\beta) = \tfrac{1}{2}N,$$

show that

$$(AB) = (a\beta), \ (A\beta) = (aB).$$

7. (*Cf.* ref. (2), § 9, "Case of equality of contraries.") Given that

$$(A) = (a) = (B) = (\beta) = (C) = (\gamma) = \tfrac{1}{2}N,$$

and also that

$$(ABC) = (a\beta\gamma),$$

show that

$$2 (ABC) = (AB) + (AC) + (BC) - \tfrac{1}{2}N.$$

8. Measurements are made on a thousand husbands and a thousand wives. If the measurements of the husbands exceed the measurements of the wives in 800 cases for one measurement, in 700 cases for another, and in 660 cases for both measurements, in how many cases will both measurements on the wife exceed the measurements on the husband ?

CHAPTER II.

CONSISTENCE.

1-3. The field of observation or universe and its specification by symbols—4. Derivation of complex from simple relations by specifying the universe—5-6. Consistence—7-10. Conditions of consistence for one and for two attributes—11-14. Conditions of consistence for three attributes.

1. ANY statistical inquiry is necessarily confined to a certain time, space, or material. An investigation on the prevalence of insanity, for instance, may be limited to England, to England in 1901, to English males in 1901, or even to English males over 60 years of age in 1901, and so on.

For actual work on any given subject, no term is required to denote the material to which the work is so confined : the limits are specified, and that is sufficient. But for theoretical purposes some term is almost essential to avoid circumlocution. The expression the **universe of discourse**, or simply the **universe**, used in this sense by writers on logic, may be adopted as familiar and convenient.

2. The **universe**, like any **class**, may be considered as specified by an enumeration of the attributes common to all its members, *e.g.* to take the illustration of § 1, those implied by the predicates *English, male, over* 60 *years of age, living in* 1901. It is not, in general, necessary to introduce a special letter into the class-symbols to denote the attributes common to all members of the universe. We know that such attributes must exist, and the common symbol can be understood.

In strictness, however, the symbol ought to be written : if, say, U denote the combination of attributes, English—male—over 60 —living in 1901, A insanity, B blindness, we should strictly use the symbols—

(U) = Number of English males over 60 living in 1901,
(UA) = ,, insane English males over 60 living in 1901,
(UB) = ,, blind ,, ,, ,, ,,
(UAB) = , blind and insane English males over 60 living in 1901,

instead of the simpler symbols N (A) (B) (AB). Similarly, the general relations (2), § 13, Chap. I., using U to denote the common attributes of all the members of the universe and (U) consequently the total number of observations N, should in strictness be written in the form—

$$(U) \quad = (UA) + (Ua) = (UB) + (U\beta) = \text{etc.}$$
$$= (UAB) + (UA\beta) + (UaB) + (Ua\beta) = \text{etc.}$$
$$(UA) \quad = (UAB) + (UA\beta) = (UAC) + (UA\gamma) = \text{etc.}$$
$$(UAB) = (UABC) + (UAB\gamma) = \text{etc.}$$

3. Clearly, however, we might have used any other symbol instead of U to denote the attributes common to all the members of the universe, *e.g.* A or B or AB or ABC, writing in the latter case—

$$(ABC) = (ABCD) + (ABC\delta)$$

and so on. Hence *any attribute or combination of attributes common to all the class-symbols in an equation may be regarded as specifying the universe within which the equation holds good.* Thus the equation just written may be read in words : " The number of objects or individuals in the universe ABC is equal to the number of D's together with the number of not-D's within the same universe." The equation

$$(AC) = (ABC) + (A\beta C)$$

may be read : " The number of A's is equal to the number of A's that are B together with the number of A's that are not-B *within the universe C.*"

4. The more complex may be derived from the simpler relations between class-frequencies very readily by the process of *specifying the universe.* Thus starting from the simple equation

$$(a) = N - (A),$$

we have, by specifying the universe as β,

$$(a\beta) = (\beta) - (A\beta)$$
$$= N - (A) - (B) + (AB).$$

Specifying the universe, again, as γ, we have

$$(a\beta\gamma) = (\gamma) - (A\gamma) - (B\gamma) + (AB\gamma)$$
$$= N - (A) - (B) - (C) + (AB) + (AC) + (BC) - (ABC).$$

5. Any class-frequencies which have been or might have been observed within one and the same universe may be said to be

consistent with one another. They conform with one another, and do not in any way conflict.

The conditions of consistence are some of them simple, but others are by no means of an intuitive character. Suppose, for instance, the data are given—

N	1000	(AB)	42
(A)	525	(AC)	147
(B)	312	(BC)	86
(C)	470	(ABC)	25

—there is nothing obviously wrong with the figures. Yet they are certainly inconsistent. They might have been observed at different times, in different places or on different material, but they cannot have been observed in one and the same universe. They imply, in fact, a negative value for $(\alpha\beta\gamma)$—

$$(\alpha\beta\gamma) = 1000 - 525 - 312 - 470 + 42 + 147 + 86 - 25.$$
$$= 1000 - 1307 + 275 - 25.$$
$$= -57.$$

Clearly no class-frequency can be negative. If the figures, consequently, are alleged to be the result of an actual inquiry in a definite universe, there must have been some miscount or misprint.

6. Generally, then, we may say that any given class-frequencies are inconsistent if they imply negative values for any of the unstated frequencies. Otherwise they are consistent. To test the consistence of any set of 2^n algebraically independent frequencies, for the case of n attributes, we should accordingly calculate the values of all the unstated frequencies, and so verify the fact that they are positive. This procedure may, however, be limited by a simple consideration. If the ultimate class-frequencies are positive, all others must be so, being derived from the ultimate frequencies by simple addition. Hence we need only calculate the values of the ultimate class-frequencies in terms of those given, and verify the fact that they exceed zero.

7. As we saw in the last chapter, there are two sets of 2^n algebraically independent frequencies of practical importance, viz. (1) the ultimate, (2) the positive class-frequencies.

It follows from what we have just said that there is only one condition of consistence for the ultimate frequencies, viz. that they must all exceed zero. Apart from this, any one frequency of the set may vary anywhere between 0 and ∞ without becoming inconsistent with the others.

For the positive class-frequencies, the conditions may be

expressed symbolically by expanding the ultimate in terms of the positive frequencies, and writing each such expansion not less than zero. We will consider the cases of one, two, and three attributes in turn.

8. If only one attribute be noted, say A, the positive frequencies are N and (A). The ultimate frequencies are (A) and (a), where

$$(a) = N - (A).$$

The conditions of consistence are therefore simply

$$(A) \not< 0 \qquad N - (A) \not< 0$$

or, more conveniently expressed,

$$(a) \quad (A) \not< 0 \qquad (b) \quad (A) \not> N \quad . \qquad . \qquad . \quad (1)$$

These conditions are obvious: the number of A's cannot be less than zero, nor exceed the whole number of observations.

9. If two attributes be noted there are four ultimate frequencies (AB), $(A\beta)$, (aB), $(a\beta)$. The following conditions are given by expanding each in terms of the frequencies of positive classes—

$$\left. \begin{array}{llll} (a) & (AB) \not< 0 & \text{or } (AB) \text{ would be negative} \\ (b) & (AB) \not< (A) + (B) - N & \text{,, } (a\beta) \quad \text{,,} \quad \text{,,} \\ (c) & (AB) \not> (A) & \text{,, } (A\beta) \quad \text{,,} \quad \text{,,} \\ (d) & (AB) \not> (B) & \text{,, } (aB) \quad \text{,,} \quad \text{,,} \end{array} \right\} \quad (2)$$

(a), (c), and (d) are obvious; (b) is perhaps a little less obvious, and is occasionally forgotten. It is, however, of precisely the same type as the other three. None of these conditions are really of a new form, but may be derived at once from (1) (a) and (1) (b) by specifying the universe as B or as β respectively. The conditions (2) are therefore really covered by (1).

10. But a further point arises as regards such a system of limits as is given by (2). The conditions (a) and (b) give lower or minor limits to the value of (AB); (c) and (d) give upper or major limits. If either major limit be less than either minor limit the conditions are impossible, and it is necessary to see whether (A) and (B) can take such values that this may be the case.

Expressing the condition that the major limits must be not less than the minor, we have—

$$\left. \begin{array}{l} (A) \not< 0 \\ (A) \not> N \end{array} \right\} \qquad \left. \begin{array}{l} (B) \not< 0 \\ (B) \not> N \end{array} \right\}$$

These are simply the conditions of the form (1). If, therefore, (A) and (B) fulfil the conditions (1), the conditions (2) must be possible. The conditions (1) and (2) therefore give all the conditions of consistence for the case of two attributes, conditions of an extremely simple and obvious kind.

11. Now consider the case of three attributes. There are eight ultimate frequencies. Expanding the ultimate in terms of the positive frequencies, and expressing the condition that each expansion is not less than zero, we have—

or the frequency given below will be negative.

$$
\begin{array}{lll}
(a) & (ABC) \not< 0 & (ABC) \\
(b) & \not< (AB) + (AC) - (A) & (A\beta\gamma) \\
(c) & \not< (AB) + (BC) - (B) & (\alpha B\gamma) \\
(d) & \not< (AC) + (BC) - (C) & (\alpha\beta C) \\
(e) & \not> (AB) & (AB\gamma) \\
(f) & \not> (AC) & (A\beta C) \\
(g) & \not> (BC) & (\alpha BC) \\
(h) & \not> (AB) + (AC) + (BC) - (A) - (B) - (C) + N & (\alpha\beta\gamma)
\end{array} \right\} (3)
$$

These, again, are not conditions of a new form. We leave it as an exercise for the student to show that they may be derived from (1) (a) and (1) (b) by specifying the universe in turn as BC, $B\gamma$, βC, and $\beta\gamma$. The *two* conditions holding in *four* universes give the eight inequalities above.

12. As in the last case, however, these conditions will be impossible to fulfil if any one of the major limits (e)–(h) be less than any one of the minor limits (a)–(d). The values on the right must be such as to make no major limit less than a minor.

There are four major and four minor limits, or sixteen comparisons in all to be made. But twelve of these, the student will find, only lead back to conditions of the form (2) for (AB), (AC), and (BC) respectively. The four comparisons of expansions due to contrary frequencies ((a) and (h), (b) and (g), (c) and (f), (d) and (e)) alone lead to new conditions, viz.—

$$
\begin{array}{ll}
(a) & (AB) + (AC) + (BC) \not< (A) + (B) + (C) - N \\
(b) & (AB) + (AC) - (BC) \not> (A) \\
(c) & (AB) - (AC) + (BC) \not> (B) \\
(d) & -(AB) + (AC) + (BC) \not> (C)
\end{array} \right\} \quad . \quad (4)
$$

13. These are conditions of a wholly new type, not derivable in any way from those given under (1) and (2). They are conditions for the consistence of the second-order frequencies *with each other*, whilst the inequalities of the form (2) are only conditions for the consistence of the second-order frequencies with those of lower orders. Given any two of the second-order frequencies, *e.g.*

(AB) and (AC), the conditions (4) give limits for the third, viz. (BC). They thus replace, for statistical purposes, the ordinary rules of syllogistic inference. From data of the syllogistic form, they would, of course, lead to the same conclusion, though in a somewhat cumbrous fashion; one or two cases are suggested as exercises for the student (Questions 6 and 7). The following will serve as illustrations of the statistical uses of the conditions :—

Example i.—Given that $(A)=(B)=(C)=\frac{1}{2}N$ and 80 per cent. of the A's are B, 75 per cent. of A's are C, find the limits to the percentage of B's that are C. The data are—

$$\frac{2(AB)}{N}=0.8 \qquad \frac{2(AC)}{N}=0.75$$

and the conditions give—

(a) $\quad \dfrac{2(BC)}{N} \not< 1 \quad -0.8 \ -0.75$

(b) $\qquad\qquad \not< 0.8 + 0.75 - 1$

(c) $\qquad\qquad \not> 1 \ -0.8 \ +0.75$

(d) $\qquad\qquad \not> 1 \ +0.8 \ -0.75$

(a) gives a negative limit and (d) a limit greater than unity; hence they may be disregarded. From (b) and (c) we have—

$$\frac{2(BC)}{N} \not< 0.55 \qquad \frac{2(BC)}{N} \not> 0.95$$

—that is to say, not less than 55 per cent. nor more than 95 per cent. of the B's can be C.

Example ii.—If a report give the following frequencies as actually observed, show that there must be a misprint or mistake of some sort, and that possibly the misprint consists in the dropping of a 1 before the 85 given as the frequency (BC).

N 1000

(A)	510	(AB)	189
(B)	490	(AC)	140
(C)	427	(BC)	85

From (4) (a) we have—

$$(BC) \not< 510 + 490 + 427 - 1000 - 189 - 140$$
$$\not< 98.$$

But $85 < 98$, therefore it cannot be the correct value of (BC). If we read 185 for 85 all the conditions are fulfilled.

Example iii.—In a certain set of 1000 observations $(A) = 45$, $(B) = 23$, $(C) = 14$. Show that whatever the percentages of B's that are A and of C's that are A, it cannot be inferred that any B's are C.

The conditions (a) and (b) give the lower limit of (BC), which is required. We find—

$$(a) \quad \frac{(BC)}{N} \not< - \frac{(AB)}{N} - \frac{(AC)}{N} - \cdot 918.$$

$$(b) \quad \frac{(BC)}{N} \not< \frac{(AB)}{N} + \frac{(AC)}{N} - \cdot 045.$$

The first limit is clearly negative. The second must also be negative, since $(AB)/N$ cannot exceed ·023 nor $(AC)/N$ ·014. Hence we cannot conclude that there is any limit to (BC) greater than 0. This result is indeed immediately obvious when we consider that, even if all the B's were A, and of the remaining 22 A's 14 were C's, there would still be 8 A's that were neither B nor C.

14. The student should note the result of the last example, as it illustrates the sort of result at which one may often arrive by applying the conditions (4) to practical statistics. For given values of N, (A), (B), (C), (AB), and (AC), it will often happen that *any* value of (BC) not less than zero (or, more generally, not less than either of the lower limits (2) (a) and (2) (b)) will satisfy the conditions (4), and hence no true inference of a lower limit is possible. The argument of the type "So many A's are B and so many B's are C that we must expect some A's to be C" must be used with caution.

REFERENCES.

(1) MORGAN, A. DE, *Formal Logic*, 1847 (chapter viii., "On the Numerically Definite Syllogism").
(2) BOOLE, G., *Laws of Thought*, 1854 (chapter xix., "Of Statistical Conditions").
The above are the classical works with respect to the general theory of numerical consistence. The student will find both difficult to follow on account of their special notation, and, in the case of Boole's work, the special method employed.
(3) YULE, G. U., "On the Theory of Consistence of Logical Class-frequencies and its Geometrical Representation," *Phil. Trans.*, A, vol. cxcvii. (1901), p. 91. (Deals at length with the theory of consistence for any number of attributes, using the notation of the present chapters.)

EXERCISES.

1. (For this and similar estimates *cf.* "Report, by Miss Collet on the Statistics of Employment of Women and Girls" [C.—7564] 1894). If, in the urban district of Bury, 817 per thousand of the women between 20 and 25 years of age were returned as "occupied" at the census of 1891, and 263 per thousand as married or widowed, what is the lowest proportion per thousand of the married or widowed that must have been occupied ?

2. If, in a series of houses actually invaded by small-pox, 70 per cent. of the inhabitants are attacked and 85 per cent. have been vaccinated, what is the lowest percentage of the vaccinated that must have been attacked ?

3. Given that 50 per cent. of the inmates of a workhouse are men, 60 per cent. are "aged" (over 60), 80 per cent. non-able-bodied, 35 per cent. aged men, 45 per cent. non-able-bodied men, and 42 per cent. non-able-bodied and aged, find the greatest and least possible proportions of non-able-bodied aged men.

4. (Material from ref. 5 of Chap. I.) The following are the proportions per 10,000 of boys observed, with certain classes of defects amongst a number of school-children. A=development defects, B=nerve signs, D=mental dulness.

$$N = 10,000 \qquad (D) = 789$$
$$(A) = 877 \qquad (AB) = 338$$
$$(B) = 1,086 \qquad (BD) = 455$$

Show that some dull boys do not exhibit development defects, and state how many at least do not do so.

5. The following are the corresponding figures for girls:—

$$N = 10,000 \qquad (D) = 689$$
$$(A) = 682 \qquad (AB) = 248$$
$$(B) = 850 \qquad (BD) = 363$$

Show that some defectively developed girls are not dull, and state how many at least must be so.

6. Take the syllogism "All A's are B, all B's are C, therefore all A's are C," express the premises in terms of the notation of the preceding chapters, and deduce the conclusion by the use of the general conditions of consistence.

7. Do the same for the syllogism "All A's are B, no B's are C, therefore no A's are C."

8. Given that $(A)=(B)=(C)=\frac{1}{2}N$, and that $(AB)/N=(AC)/N=p$, find what must be the greatest or least values of p in order that we may infer that $(BC)/N$ exceeds any given value, say q.

9. Show that if

$$\frac{(A)}{N} = x \qquad \frac{(B)}{N} = 2x \qquad \frac{(C)}{N} = 3x$$

and

$$\frac{(AB)}{N} = \frac{(AC)}{N} = \frac{(BC)}{N} = y,$$

the value of neither x nor y can exceed $\frac{1}{4}$.

CHAPTER III.

ASSOCIATION.

1. If there is no sort of relationship, of any kind, between two attributes A and B, we expect to find the same proportion of A's amongst the B's as amongst the non-B's. We may anticipate, for instance, the same proportion of abnormally wet seasons in leap years as in ordinary years, the same proportion of male to total births when the moon is waxing as when it is waning, the same proportion of heads whether a coin be tossed with the right hand or the left.

Two such unrelated attributes may be termed independent, and we have accordingly as the criterion of independence for A and B—

$$\frac{(AB)}{(B)} = \frac{(A\beta)}{(\beta)} \quad . \quad . \quad . \quad . \quad . \quad (1)$$

If this relation hold good, the corresponding relations

$$\frac{(aB)}{(B)} = \frac{(a\beta)}{(\beta)}$$

$$\frac{(AB)}{(A)} = \frac{(aB)}{(a)}$$

$$\frac{(A\beta)}{(A)} = \frac{(a\beta)}{(a)}.$$

must also hold. For it follows at once from (1) that—

$$\frac{(B)-(AB)}{(B)} = \frac{(\beta)-(A\beta)}{(\beta)},$$

that is
$$\frac{(aB)}{(B)} = \frac{(a\beta)}{(\beta)},$$

and the other two identities may be similarly deduced.

2. The criterion may, however, be put into a somewhat different and theoretically more convenient form. The equation (1) expresses (AB) in terms of (B), (β), and a second-order frequency $(A\beta)$; eliminating this second-order frequency we have—

$$\frac{(AB)}{(B)} = \frac{(AB)+(A\beta)}{(B) + (\beta)} = \frac{(A)}{N},$$

i.e. in words, "the proportion of A's amongst the B's is the same as in the universe at large." The student should learn to recognise this equation at sight in any of the forms—

$$\begin{aligned} \frac{(AB)}{(B)} &= \frac{(A)}{N} \qquad &(a) \\[2mm] \frac{(AB)}{(A)} &= \frac{(B)}{N} \qquad &(b) \\[2mm] (AB) &= \frac{(A)(B)}{N} \qquad &(c) \\[2mm] \frac{(AB)}{N} &= \frac{(A)}{N}\ \frac{(B)}{N} \qquad &(d) \end{aligned} \qquad \cdots \quad (2)$$

The equation (d) gives the important fundamental rule: *If the attributes A and B are independent, the proportion of AB's in the universe is equal to the proportion of A's multiplied by the proportion of B's.*

The advantage of the forms (2) over the form (1) is that they give expressions for the second-order frequency in terms of the frequencies of the first order and the whole number of observations alone; the form (1) does not.

Example i.— If there are 144 A's and 384 B's in 1024 observations, how many AB's will there be, A and B being independent?

$$\frac{144 \times 384}{1024} = 54.$$

There will therefore be 54 AB's.

Example ii.—If the A's are 60 per cent., the B's 35 per cent., of the whole number of observations, what must be the percentage of AB's in order that we may conclude that A and B are independent?

$$\frac{60 \times 35}{100} = 21,$$

and therefore there must be 21 per cent. (more or less closely, *cf.* §§ 7, 8 below) of AB's in the universe to justify the conclusion that A and B are independent.

3. It follows from § 1 that if the relation (2) holds for any one of the four second-order frequencies, *e.g.* (AB), similar relations must hold for the remaining three. Thus we have directly from (1)—

$$\frac{(A\beta)}{(\beta)} = \frac{(AB)+(A\beta)}{(B)+(\beta)} = \frac{(A)}{N},$$

giving

$$(A\beta) = \frac{(A)(\beta)}{N}.$$

And again,

$$\frac{(aB)}{(B)} = \frac{(a\beta)}{(\beta)} = \frac{(aB)+(a\beta)}{(B)+(\beta)} = \frac{(a)}{N},$$

which gives

$$(aB) = \frac{(a)(B)}{N}, \qquad (a\beta) = \frac{(a)(\beta)}{N}.$$

Example iii.—In Example i. above, what would be the number of $a\beta$'s, A and B being independent?

$$(a) = 1024 - 144 = 880$$
$$(\beta) = 1024 - 384 = 640$$
$$\therefore \quad (a\beta) = \frac{880 \times 640}{1024} = 550.$$

The theorem is an important one, and the result may be deduced more directly from first principles, replacing (AB) by its value $(A)(B)/N$ in the expansions—

$$(aB) = (B) - (AB).$$
$$(A\beta) = (A) - (AB).$$
$$(a\beta) = (N) - (A) - (B) + (AB).$$

This is left as an exercise for the student.

4. Finally, the criterion of independence may be expressed in yet a third form, viz. in terms of the second-order frequencies alone. If A and B are independent, it follows at once from equation (2) and the work of the preceding section that—

$$(AB)(a\beta) = \frac{(A)(B)(a)(\beta)}{N^2}.$$

And evidently $(aB)(A\beta)$ is equal to the same fraction.

Therefore—

$$(AB)(a\beta) = (aB)(A\beta) \quad (a)$$

$$\frac{(AB)}{(aB)} = \frac{(A\beta)}{(a\beta)} \quad (b)$$

$$\frac{(AB)}{(A\beta)} = \frac{(aB)}{(a\beta)} \quad (c)$$

$$\tag{3}$$

The equation (b) may be read "The ratio of A's to a's amongst the B's is equal to the ratio of A's to a's amongst the β's," and (c) similarly.

This form of criterion is a convenient one if all the four second-order frequencies are given, enabling one to recognise almost at a glance whether or not the two attributes are independent.

Example iv.—If the second-order frequencies have the following values, are A and B independent or not?

$$(AB) = 110 \qquad (aB) = 90 \qquad (A\beta) = 290 \qquad (a\beta) = 510.$$

Clearly $$(AB)(a\beta) > (aB)(A\beta),$$

so A and B are not independent.

5. Suppose now that A and B are not independent, but related in some way or other, however complicated.

Then if $$(AB) > \frac{(A)(B)}{N},$$

A and B are said to be positively **associated**, or sometimes simply associated. If, on the other hand,

$$(AB) < \frac{(A)(B)}{N},$$

A and B are said to be negatively **associated** or, more briefly, disassociated.

The student should notice that these words are not used exactly in their ordinary senses, but in a technical sense. When A and B are said to be associated, it is not meant merely that *some A's are B's,* but that *the number of A's which are B's exceeds the number to be expected if A and B are independent.* Similarly, when A and B are said to be negatively associated or disassociated, it is not meant that *no A's are B's,* but that *the number of A's which are B's falls short of the number to be expected if A and B are independent.* "Association" cannot be inferred from the mere fact that *some* A's are B's, however great that proportion; this principle is fundamental, and should be always borne in mind.

6. The greatest possible value of (AB) for given values of N, (A), and (B) is either (A) or (B) (whichever is the less). When (AB) attains either of these values, A and B may be said to be *completely* or *perfectly* associated. The lowest possible value of (AB), on the other hand, is either zero or $(A) + (B) - N$ (whichever is the greater). When (AB) falls to either of these values, A and B may be said to be *completely* disassociated. Complete association is generally understood to correspond to one or other of the cases, "All A's are B" or "All B's are A," or it may be more narrowly defined as corresponding only to the case when both these statements were true. Complete disassociation may be similarly taken as corresponding to one or other of the cases. "No A's are B," or "no a's are β," or more narrowly to the case when both these statements are true. The greater the divergence of (AB) from the value $(A)(B)/N$ towards the limiting value in either direction, the greater, we may say, is the *intensity* of association or of disassociation, so that we may speak of attributes being *more* or *less*, *highly* or *slightly* associated. This conception of *degrees* of association, degrees which may in fact be measured by certain formulæ (*cf.* § 13), is important.

7. When the association is very slight, *i.e.* where (AB) only differs from $(A)(B)/N$ by a few units or by a small proportion, it may be that such association is not really significant of any definite relationship. To give an illustration, suppose that a coin is tossed a number of times, and the tosses noted in pairs; then 100 pairs may give such results as the following (taken from an actual record) :—

First toss heads and second heads . . 26
,, ,, ,, tails . . . 18
First toss tails and second heads . 27
,, ,, ,, tails . . . 29

If we use A to denote "heads" in the first toss, B "heads" in the second, we have from the above $(A) = 44$, $(B) = 53$. Hence $(A)(B)/N = \dfrac{44 \times 53}{100} = 23\cdot32$, while actually (AB) is 26. Hence there is a positive association, in the given record, between the result of the first throw and the result of the second. But it is fairly certain, from the nature of the case, that such association cannot indicate any real connection between the results of the two throws; it must therefore be due merely to such a complex system of causes, impossible to analyse, as leads, for example, to differences between small samples drawn from the same material. The conclusion is confirmed by the fact that, of a number of such records, some give a positive association (like the above), but others a negative association.

8. An event due, like the above occurrence of positive association, to an extremely complex system of causes of the general nature of which we are aware, but of the detailed operation of which we are ignorant, is sometimes said to be due to *chance*, or better to the chances or fluctuations of sampling.

A little consideration will suggest that such associations due to the fluctuations of sampling must be met with in all classes of statistics. To quote, for instance, from § 1, the two illustrations there given of independent attributes, we know that in any *actual* record we would not be likely to find *exactly* the same proportion of abnormally wet seasons in leap years as in ordinary years, nor *exactly* the same proportion of male births when the moon is waxing as when it is waning. But so long as the divergence from independence is not well-marked we must regard such attributes as practically independent, or dependence as at least unproved.

The discussion of the question, how great the divergence must be before we can consider it as "well-marked," must be postponed to the chapters dealing with the theory of sampling. At present the attention of the student can only be directed to the existence of the difficulty, and to the serious risk of interpreting a "chance association" as physically significant.

9. The definition of § 5 suggests that we are to test the existence or the intensity of association between two attributes by a comparison of the actual value of (AB) with its independence-value (as it may be termed) $(A)(B)/N$. The procedure is from the theoretical standpoint perhaps the most natural, but it is usual, in practice, to adopt a method of comparing *proportions*, e.g. the proportion of A's amongst the B's with the proportion in the universe at large. Such proportions are usually expressed in the form of percentages or proportions per thousand.

A large number of such comparisons are available for the purpose, as indicated by the inequalities (4) below, which all hold good for the case of *positive* association between A and B. The first two, (a) and (b), follow at once from the definition of § 5, (c) and (d) follow from (a) and (b), on multiplying across and expanding (A) and N in the first case, (B) and N in the second. The deduction of the remainder is left to the student.

$$\frac{(AB)}{(B)} > \frac{(A)}{N} \quad (a) \qquad\qquad \frac{(AB)}{(A)} > \frac{(B)}{N} \quad (b)$$

$$\frac{(AB)}{(B)} > \frac{(A\beta)}{(\beta)} \quad (c) \qquad\qquad \frac{(AB)}{(A)} > \frac{(aB)}{(a)} \quad (d)$$

$$\frac{(A\beta)}{(\beta)} < \frac{(A)}{N} \quad (e) \qquad\qquad \frac{(A\beta)}{(A)} < \frac{(\beta)}{N} \quad (f)$$

$$\frac{(aB)}{(B)} < \frac{(a)}{N} \quad (g) \qquad\qquad \frac{(aB)}{(a)} < \frac{(B)}{N} \quad (h)$$

$$\frac{(a\beta)}{(\beta)} > \frac{(a)}{N} \quad (j) \qquad\qquad \frac{(a\beta)}{(a)} > \frac{(\beta)}{N} \quad (k)$$

$$\frac{(a\beta)}{(\beta)} > \frac{(aB)}{(B)} \quad (l) \qquad\qquad \frac{(a\beta)}{(a)} > \frac{(A\beta)}{(A)} \quad (m)$$

$$\Bigg\} \qquad \bullet \quad (4)$$

The question arises then, which is the best comparison to adopt?

10. Two principles should decide this point: (1) of any two comparisons, that is the better which brings out the more clearly the degree of association; (2) of any two comparisons, that is the better which illustrates the more important aspect of the problem under discussion.

The second condition will generally exclude all the comparisons (e)–(m), for the capital letters will naturally be used to denote the important aspect of the character. We will generally be concerned, for instance, with the proportion of A's amongst the B's as compared with the β's (as in (c)), and not with the proportion of the a's in those two universes (as in (l)); or with the proportion of A's amongst the B's as compared with the whole universe (a), and not with the proportion of a's amongst the β's as compared with the whole universe (j). That is simply the natural method of using the notation. We may confine our attention accordingly to the comparisons (a)–(d). Of these four, (c) or (d) is generally to be preferred to (a) or (b), for the reason that either of the latter may give a misleading impression as to the intensity of the association. We have in fact—

$$\frac{(A)}{N} = \frac{(AB)}{(B)} \cdot \frac{(B)}{N} + \frac{(A\beta)}{(\beta)} \cdot \frac{(\beta)}{N}.$$

Hence if $(B)/N$ be large compared with $(\beta)/N$, $(A)/N$ will approach the value $(AB)/(B)$ and the association will appear to be very small, even though $(AB)/(B)$ and $(A\beta)/(\beta)$ differ considerably. Suppose, for example, in some given case, for a considerable number of observations—

$$(AB)/(B) = \cdot70 \qquad (A\beta)/(\beta) = \cdot40$$

this would mean a considerable positive association between
A and B. But if it were only stated that—

$$(AB)/(B) = \cdot70 \qquad (A)/N = \cdot67$$

the association would *appear* to be small. Yet the two statements are equivalent if $(B)/N = 0\cdot9$, for then we have—

$$(A)/N = \cdot7 \times \cdot9 + \cdot4 \times \cdot1 = \cdot67$$

The *meaning* of (a) or (b), in fact, cannot be fully realised
unless the value of $(B)/N$ (or $(A)/N$ in the second case) is known,
and therefore (c) is to be preferred to (a), and (d) to (b). An
exception may, however, be made in cases where the proportion
of B's (or A's) in the universe is very small, so that $(A)/N$
approaches closely to $(A\beta)/(\beta)$ or $(B)/N$ to $(aB)/(a)$ (*cf.* Example
vi. below).

There still remains the choice between (a) and (b), or between
(c) and (d). This must be decided with reference to the second
principle, *i.e.* with regard to the more important aspect of the
problem under discussion, the exact question to be answered,
or the hypothesis to be tested, as illustrated by the examples
below. Where no *definite* question has to be answered or
hypothesis tested both pairs of proportions may be tabulated,
as in Example vi. again.

Example v.—Association between sex and death. (Material
from 64th Annual Report Reg. General. [Cd. 1230] 1903.)

Males in England and Wales, 1901 . . 15,773,000
Females   ,,   ,,   ,,   . . 16,848,000
Of the Males died 285,618
Of the Females died 265,967

We may denote the number of males by (A), the number of
deaths by (B); then the natural comparison is between $(AB)/(A)$
and $(aB)/(a)$, *i.e.* the proportion of males that died and the
proportion of females. We find—

$$\frac{(AB)}{(A)} = \frac{285,618}{15,773,000} = \cdot0181.$$

$$\frac{(aB)}{(a)} = \frac{265,967}{16,848,000} = \cdot0158.$$

Therefore $(AB)/(A) > (aB)/(a)$, and there is positive association
between *male-sex* and *death*. It is usual to express proportions

of deaths, births, marriages, etc., to the population as rates per thousand ; so that the above figures would be written—

Death-rate among Males . . 18·1 per thousand.
  „   „   Females .   . 15·8   „

A comparison of the death-rate among males with the death-rate for the whole population would be equally valid, but it should be remembered that the latter depends on the sex-ratio as well as on the causes that determine the death-rates amongst males and females. The above figures give— ,

Death-rate among males . . 18·1 per thousand.
  „   for whole population . 16·9   „

This brings out the difference between the death-rates of males and of the *whole population*, but is not so clear an indication of the difference between males and *females*, which is the point to be investigated.

A comparison of the form (4) (*c*) is again *valid* for testing the association, but the form is not desirable, illustrating very well the remarks on the opposite page. Statisticians are concerned with death-rates, and not with the sex-ratios of the living and the dead. The student should learn, however, to recognise such forms of statement as the following, as equivalent to the above :—

Proportion of males amongst those } 518 per thousand.
  that died in the year . . . }

Proportion of males amongst those } 483   „
  that did not die in the year . }

Since $(AB)/(B) > (A\beta)/(\beta)$, it follows, as before, that there is positive association between A and B.

Example vi.—Deaf-mutism and Imbecility. (Material from Census of 1901. Summary Tables. [Cd. 1523.])

Total population of England and Wales . . 32,528,000
Number of the imbecile (or feeble-minded) . 48,882
Number of deaf-mutes 15,246
Number of imbecile deaf-mutes . . . 451

Required, to find whether deaf-mutism is associated with imbecility.

We may denote the number of the imbecile by (A), of deaf-mutes by (B). One of the comparisons (*a*) or (*b*) may very well be used in this case, seeing that $(A)/N$ and $(B)/N$ differ very little from $(A\beta)/(\beta)$ and $(aB)/(a)$ respectively. The question

3

whether to give the preference to (a) or to (b) depends on the nature of the investigation we wish to make. If it is desired to exhibit the conditions among deaf-mutes (a) may be used :—

Proportion of imbeciles among deaf-mutes $= (AB)/(B)$ . . . } 29·6 per thousand.

Proportion of imbeciles in the whole population $= (A)/N$ . . . } 1·5 ,,

If, on the other hand, it is desired to exhibit the conditions amongst the imbecile, (b) will be preferable.

Proportion of deaf-mutes amongst the imbecile $(AB)/(A)$ . . } 9·2 per thousand.

Proportion of deaf-mutes in the whole population $(B)/N$ . . } 0·5 ,,

Either comparison exhibits very clearly the high degree of association between the attributes. It may be pointed out, however, that census data as to such infirmities are very untrustworthy.

Example vii.—Eye-colour of father and son (material due to Sir Francis Galton, as given by Professor Karl Pearson, *Phil. Trans.*, A, vol. cxcv. (1900), p. 138; the classes 1, 2, and 3 of the memoir treated as light).

Fathers with light eyes and sons with light eyes (AB) . 471
,, ,, ,, not light ,, $(A\beta)$. 151
,, not light ,, light ,, (aB) . 148
,, ,, ,, not light ,, $(a\beta)$. 230

Required to find whether the colour of the son's eyes is associated with that of the father's. In cases of this kind the father is reckoned once for each son; *e.g.* a family in which the father was light-eyed, two sons light-eyed and one not, would be reckoned as giving two to the class AB and one to the class $A\beta$.
The best comparison here is—

Percentage of light-eyed amongst the sons of light-eyed fathers . . . . } 76 per cent.

Percentage of light-eyed amongst the sons of not-light-eyed fathers . . . } 39 ,,

But the following is equally valid—

Percentage of light-eyed amongst the fathers of light-eyed sons . . } 76 per cent.

Percentage of light-eyed amongst the fathers of not-light-eyed sons . . } 40 ,,

The reason why the former comparison is preferable is, that we usually wish to estimate the character of offspring from that of the parents, and define heredity in terms of the resemblance of offspring to parents. We do not, as a rule, want to make use of the power of estimating the character of parents from that of their offspring, nor do we define heredity in terms of the resemblance of parents to offspring. Both modes of statement, however, indicate equally clearly the tendency to resemblance between father and son.

11. The values that the four second-order frequencies take in the case of independence, viz.—

$$\frac{(A)(B)}{N}, \quad \frac{(a)(B)}{N}, \quad \frac{(A)(\beta)}{N}, \quad \frac{(a)(\beta)}{N},$$

are of such great theoretical importance, and of so much use as reference-values for comparing with the actual values of the frequencies (AB) (aB) $(A\beta)$ and $(a\beta)$, that it is often desirable to employ single symbols to denote them. We shall use the symbols—

$$(AB)_0 = \frac{(A)(B)}{N} \qquad (a\beta)_0 = \frac{(a)(\beta)}{N}$$

$$(aB)_0 = \frac{(a)(B)}{N} \qquad (A\beta)_0 = \frac{(A)(\beta)}{N}.$$

If δ denote the excess of (AB) over $(AB)_0$, then we have—

$$(aB) = (B) - (AB) = (B) - (AB)_0 - \delta$$

$$= \frac{[N - (A)](B)}{N} - \delta$$

$$= (aB)_0 - \delta.$$

$$\therefore \quad (AB) - (AB)_0 = (aB)_0 - (aB).$$

Similarly it may be shown that—

$$(A\beta) = (A\beta)_0 - \delta.$$
$$(a\beta) = (a\beta)_0 + \delta.$$

Therefore, quite generally we have—

$$(AB) - (AB)_0 = (a\beta) - (a\beta)_0 = (A\beta)_0 - (A\beta) = (aB)_0 - (aB).$$

Supposing, for example,

$$N = 100 \qquad (A) = 60 \qquad (B) = 45$$

then

$$(AB)_0 = 27 \qquad (aB)_0 = 18 \qquad (A\beta)_0 = 33 \qquad (a\beta)_0 = 22.$$

If, now, A and B are positively associated, and $(AB) =$ say 35, then $(aB) = 45 - 35 = 10$, $(A\beta) = 60 - 35 = 25$, $(a\beta) = 100 - 60 - 45 + 35 = 30$, and we have—

$$35 - 27 = 30 - 22 = 18 - 10 = 33 - 25 = 8.$$

Similarly, if A and B be disassociated and $(AB) =$ say 19, the student will find that—

$$(AB) = 19 \qquad (aB) = 26 \qquad (A\beta) = 41 \qquad (a\beta) = 14$$
and $\qquad 19 - 27 = 14 - 22 = 18 - 26 = 33 - 41 = -8.$

12. The value of this common difference δ may be expressed in a form that it is useful to note. We have by definition—

$$\delta = (AB) - (AB)_0 = (AB) - \frac{(A)(B)}{N}.$$

Bring the terms on the right to a common denominator, and express all the frequencies of the numerator in terms of those of the second order; then we have—

$$\delta = \frac{1}{N} \left\{ \begin{array}{l} (AB)[(AB) + (aB) + (A\beta) + (a\beta)] \\ - [(AB) + (A\beta)][(AB) + (aB)] \end{array} \right\}$$
$$= \frac{1}{N} \left\{ (AB)(a\beta) - (aB)(A\beta) \right\}.$$

That is to say, the common difference is equal to $1/N$th of the difference of the "cross products" $(AB)(a\beta)$ and $(aB)(A\beta)$; e.g. taking the examples of § 11, we have

$$\delta = \frac{1}{100} \left\{ 35 \times 30 - 25 \times 10 \right\} = 8$$
and $\qquad \delta = \frac{1}{100} \left\{ 19 \times 14 - 26 \times 41 \right\} = -8.$

It is evident that the difference of the cross-products may be very large if N be large, although δ is really very small. In using the difference of the cross-products to test mentally the sign of the association in a case where all the four second-order frequencies are given, this should be remembered: the difference should be compared with N, or it will be liable to suggest a higher degree of association than actually exists.

Example viii.—The following data were observed for hybrids of

Datura (W. Bateson and Miss Saunders, Report to the Evolution Committee of the Royal Society, 1902) :—

Flowers violet,	fruits	prickly (AB)	.	. 47
,,	,,	smooth $(A\beta)$	.	. 12
Flowers white,	,,	prickly (aB)	.	. 21
,,	,,	smooth $(a\beta)$	.	. 3

Investigate the association between colour of flower and character of fruit.

Since $3 \times 47 = 141$, $12 \times 21 = 252$, *i.e.* $(AB) (a\beta) < (aB) (A\beta)$, there is clearly a negative association ; $252 - 141 = 111$, and at first sight this considerable difference is apt to suggest a considerable association. But $\delta = 111/83 = 1\cdot3$ only, so that in point of fact the association is small, so small that no stress can be laid on it as indicating anything but a fluctuation of sampling. Working out the percentages we have—

Percentage of violet-flowered plants with prickly fruits . . . . . } 80 per cent.

Percentage of white-flowered plants with prickly fruits . . . . . } 87 ,,

13. While the methods used in the preceding pages suffice for most practical purposes, it is often very convenient to measure the intensities of association in different cases by means of some formula or "coefficient," so devised as to be zero when the attributes are independent, $+1$ when they are completely associated, and -1 when they are completely disassociated, in the sense of §6. If we use the term "complete association" in the wider sense there defined, we have, grouping the frequencies in a small table in a way that is sometimes convenient, the three cases of complete association :—

(1)

(AB)	0	(A)
(aB)	$(a\beta)$	(a)
(B)	(β)	N

(2)

(AB)	$(A\beta)$	(A)
0	$(a\beta)$	(a)
(B)	(β)	N

(3)

(AB)	0	(A)
0	$(a\beta)$	(a)
(B)	(β)	N

In the first case all A's are B, and so $(A\beta) = 0$; in the second all B's are A and so $(aB) = 0$; and in the third case we have $(A) =$

$(B) = (AB)$, so that all A's are B and also all B's are A. The three corresponding cases of complete disassociation are—

(4)

0	$(A\beta)$	(A)
(aB)	$(a\beta)$	(a)
(B)	(β)	N

(5)

(AB)	$(A\beta)$	(A)
(aB)	0	(a)
(B)	(β)	N

(6)

0	$(A\beta)$	(A)
(aB)	0	(a)
(B)	(β)	N

It is required to devise some formula which shall give the value $+1$ in the first three cases, -1 in the second three, and shall also be zero where the attributes are independent. Many such formulæ may be devised, but perhaps the simplest possible (though not necessarily the most advantageous) is the expression—

$$Q = \frac{(AB)(a\beta) - (A\beta)(aB)}{(AB)(a\beta) + (A\beta)(aB)}$$
$$= \frac{N\delta}{(AB)(a\beta) + (A\beta)(aB)}$$

—where δ is the symbol used in the two last sections for the difference $(AB) - (AB)_0$. It is evident that Q is zero when the attributes are independent, for then δ is zero: it takes the value $+1$ when there is complete association, for then the second term in both numerator and denominator of the first form of the expression is zero: similarly it is -1 where there is complete disassociation, for then the first term in both numerator and denominator is zero. Q may accordingly be termed a *coefficient of association*. As illustrations of the values it will take in certain cases, the association between deaf-mutism and imbecility, on the basis of the English census figures (Example vi.) is $+0.91$; between light eye colour in father and in son (Example vii.) $+0.66$; between colour of flower and prickliness of fruit in *Datura* (Example viii.) -0.28, an association which, however, as already stated, is probably of no practical significance and due to mere fluctuations of sampling.

The student should note that the value of Q for a given table is unaltered by multiplying either a row or a column by any arbitrary number, *i.e.* the value is independent of the relative proportions of A's and a's included in the table. This property is of importance, and renders such a measure of association specially adapted to cases (*e.g.* experiments) in which the proportions are arbitrary. A form possessing the same property but certain marked advantages over Q is suggested in ref. (3).

The coefficient is only mentioned here to direct the attention of the student to the possibility of forming such a measure of association, a measure which serves a similar purpose in the case of attributes to that served by certain other coefficients in the cases of manifold classification (*cf.* Chap. V.) and of variables (*cf.* Chap. IX., and the references to Chaps. X. and XVI.). For further illustrations of the use of this coefficient the reader is referred to the reference (1) at the end of this chapter; for the modified form of the coefficient, possessing the same properties but certain advantages, to ref. (3); and for a mode of deducing another coefficient, based on theorems in the theory of variables, which has come into more general use, though in the opinion of the present writer its use is of doubtful advantage, to ref. (4). Reference should also be made to the coefficient described in § 10 of Chap. XI. The question of the best coefficient to use as a measure of association is still the subject of controversy : for a discussion the student is referred to refs. (3), (5), and (6).

14. In concluding this chapter, it may be well to repeat, for the sake of emphasis, that (*cf.* § 5) the mere fact of 80, 90, or 99 per cent. of A's being B implies nothing as to the association of A with B; in the absence of information, we can but assume that 80, 90, or 99 per cent. of a's may also be B. In order to apply the criterion of independence for two attributes A and B, it is necessary to have information concerning a's and β's as well as A's and B's, or concerning a universe that includes both a's and A's, β's and B's. Hence an investigation as to the causal relations of an attribute A must not be confined to A's, but must be extended to a's (unless, of course, the necessary information as to a's is already obtainable): no *comparison* is otherwise possible. It would be no use to obtain with great pains the result (*cf.* Example vi.) that 29·6 per thousand of deaf-mutes were imbecile unless we knew that the proportion of imbeciles in the whole population was only 1·5 per thousand ; nor would it contribute anything to our knowledge of the heredity of deaf-mutism to find out the proportion of deaf-mutes amongst the offspring of deaf-mutes unless the proportions amongst the offspring of normal individuals were also investigated or known.

REFERENCES.

(1) YULE, G. U., "On the Association of Attributes in Statistics," *Phil. Trans. Roy. Soc.*, Series A, vol. cxciv., 1900, p. 257. (Deals fully with the theory of association : the association coefficient of § 13 suggested.)

(2) YULE, G. U., "Notes on the Theory of Association of Attributes in Statistics," *Biometrika*, vol. ii., 1903, p. 121. (Contains an abstract of the principal portions of (1) and other matter.)

(3) YULE, G. U., "On the Methods of Measuring the Association between Two Attributes," *Jour. Roy. Stat. Soc.*, vol. lxxv., 1912, pp. 579–642. (A critical survey of the various coefficients that have been suggested for measuring association and their properties : a modified form of the coefficient of § 13 given which possesses marked advantages.)

(4) PEARSON, KARL, "On the Correlation of Characters not Quantitatively Measurable," *Phil. Trans. Roy. Soc.*, Series A, vol. cxcv., 1900, p. 1. (Deals with the problem of measurement of intensity of association from the standpoint of the theory of variables, giving a method which has since been largely used : only the advanced student will be able to follow the work. For a criticism see ref. 3.)

(5) PEARSON, KARL, and DAVID HERON, "On Theories of Association," *Biometrika*, vol. ix., 1913, pp. 159–332. (A reply to criticisms in ref. 3.)

(6) GREENWOOD, M., and G. U. YULE, "The Statistics of Anti-typhoid and Anti-cholera Inoculations, and the interpretation of such statistics in general," *Proc. Roy. Soc. of Medicine*, vol. viii., 1915, p. 113. (Cited for the discussion of association coefficients in § 4, and the conclusion that none of these coefficients are of much value for comparative purposes in interpreting statistics of the type considered.)

(7) LIPPS, G. F., "Die Bestimmung der Abhängigkeit zwischen den Merkmalen eines Gegenstandes," *Berichte d. math.-phys. Klasse d. kgl. sächsischen Gesellschaft d. Wissenschaften*, Leipzig, Feb. 1905. (Deals with the general theory of the dependence between two characters, however classified ; the coefficient of association of § 13 is again suggested independently.)

EXERCISES.

1. At the census of England and Wales in 1901 there were (to the nearest 1000) 15,729,000 males and 16,799,000 females ; 3497 males were returned as deaf-mutes from childhood, and 3072 females.

State proportions exhibiting the association between deaf-mutism from childhood and sex. How many of each sex for the same total number would have been deaf-mutes if there had been no association ?

2. Show, as briefly as possible, whether A and B are independent, positively associated, or negatively associated in each of the following cases :—

(a)	$N = 5000$	$(A) = 2350$	$(B) = 3100$	$(AB) = 1600$
(b)	$(A) = 490$	$(AB) = 294$	$(a) = 570$	$(aB) = 380$
(c)	$(AB) = 256$	$(aB) = 768$	$(A\beta) = 48$	$(a\beta) = 144$

3. (Figures derived from Darwin's *Cross- and Self-fertilisation of Plants*, *cf.* ref. 1, p. 294.) The table below gives the numbers of plants of certain species that were above or below the average height, stating separately those that were derived from cross-fertilised and from self-fertilised parentage. Investigate the association between height and cross-fertilisation of parentage, and draw attention to any special points you notice.

Species.	Parentage Cross-fertilised. Height—		Parentage Self-fertilised. Height—	
	Above Average.	Below Average.	Above Average.	Below Average.
Ipomœa purpurea . . .	63	10	18	55
Petunia violacea . . .	61	16	13	64
Reseda lutea	25	7	11	21
Reseda odorata . . .	39	16	25	30
Lobelia fulgens . . .	17	17	12	22

4. (Figures from same source as Example vii. p. 34, but material differently grouped; classes 7 and 8 of the memoir treated as "dark.") Investigate the association between darkness of eye-colour in father and son from the following data:—

Fathers with dark eyes and sons with dark eyes (AB) .   50
   ,,   ,,   ,,   not-dark eyes $(A\beta)$.   79
Fathers with not-dark eyes and sons with dark eyes (aB) .   89
   ,,   ,,   ,,   not-dark eyes $(a\beta)$. 782

Also tabulate for comparison the frequencies that would have been observed had there been no heredity, i.e. the values of $(AB)_0$, $(A\beta)_0$, etc. (§ 11).

5. (Figures from same source as above.) Investigate the association between eye colour of husband and eye colour of wife ("assortative mating") from the data given below.

Husbands with light eyes and wives with light eyes (AB) . 309
   ,,   ,,   ,,   not-light eyes $(A\beta)$. 214
Husbands with not-light eyes and wives with light eyes (aB) . 132
   ,,   ,,   ,,   not-light eyes $(a\beta)$. 119

Also tabulate for comparison the frequencies that would have been observed had there been strict independence between eye colour of husband and eye colour of wife, i.e. the values of $(AB)_0$, etc., as in question 4.

6. (Figures from the *Census of England and Wales,* 1891, vol. iii. : the data cannot be regarded as trustworthy.) The figures given below show the number of males in successive age groups, together with the number of the blind (A), of the mentally-deranged (B), and the blind mentally-deranged (AB). Trace the association between blindness and mental derangement from childhood to old age, tabulating the proportions of insane amongst the whole population and amongst the blind, and also the association coefficient Q of § 13. Give a short verbal statement of your results.

	5–	15–	25–	35–	45–	55–	65–	75 and upwards.
N	3,304,230	2,712,521	2,089,010	1,611,077	1,191,789	770,124	444,896	161,692
(A)	844	1,184	1,165	1,501	1752	1,905	1,932	1,701
(B)	2,820	6,225	8,482	9,214	8,187	5,799	3,412	1,098
(AB)	17	19	19	31	32	34	22	9

7. Show that if

$$(AB)_1 \quad (aB)_1 \quad (A\beta)_1 \quad (a\beta)_1$$
$$(AB)_2 \quad (aB)_2 \quad (A\beta)_2 \quad (a\beta)_2$$

be two aggregates corresponding to the same values of (A), (B), (a), and (β),

$$(AB)_1 - (AB)_2 = (aB)_2 - (aB)_1 = (A\beta)_2 - (A\beta)_1 = (a\beta)_1 - (a\beta)_2.$$

8. Show that if

$$\delta = (AB) - (AB)_0$$
$$(AB)^2 + (a\beta)^2 - (aB)^2 - (A\beta)^2 = [(A) - (a)][(B) - (\beta)] + 2N.\ \delta.$$

9. The existence of association may be tested either by comparison of proportions (e.g. $(AB)/(B)$ with $(A\beta)/(\beta)$), as in §§ 9, 10, or by the value of δ, as in §§ 11, 12. Show that

$$\delta = \frac{(B)(\beta)}{N}\left\{\frac{(AB)}{(B)} - \frac{(A\beta)}{(\beta)}\right\}$$
$$= \frac{(A)(a)}{(N)}\left\{\frac{(AB)}{(A)} - \frac{(aB)}{(a)}\right\}$$

CHAPTER IV.

PARTIAL ASSOCIATION.

1. If we find that in any given case

$$(AB) > \text{ or } < \frac{(A)(B)}{N},$$

all that is known is that there is a relation of some sort or kind between A and B. The result by itself cannot tell us whether the relation is direct, whether possibly it is only due to "fluctuations of sampling" (cf. Chap. III. §§ 7-8), or whether it is of any other particular kind that we may happen to have in our minds at the moment. Any interpretation of the meaning of the association is necessarily hypothetical, and the number of possible alternative hypotheses is in general considerable.

2. The commonest of all forms of alternative hypothesis is of this kind: it is argued that the relation between the two attributes A and B is not direct, but due, in some way, to the association of A with C and of B with C. An illustration or two will make the matter clearer:—

(1) An association is observed between "vaccination" and "exemption from attack by small-pox," i.e. more of the vaccinated than of the unvaccinated are exempt from attack. It is argued that this does not imply a protective effect of vaccination, but is wholly due to the fact that most of the unvaccinated are drawn from the lowest classes, living in very unhygienic conditions. Denoting *vaccination* by A, *exemption from attack* by B, *hygienic conditions* by C, the argument is that the observed association between A and B is due to the associations of both with C

(2) It is observed, at a general election, that a greater proportion of the candidates who spent more money than their opponents won their elections than of those who spent less. It is argued that this does not mean an influence of expenditure on the result of elections, but is due to the fact that Conservative principles generally carried the day, and that the Conservatives generally spent more than the Liberals. Denoting *winning* by A, *spending more than the opponent* by B, and *Conservative* by C, the argument is the same as the above (*cf.* Question 9 at the end of the chapter).

(3) An association is observed between the presence of some attribute in the father and its presence in the son; and also between the presence of the attribute in the grandfather and its presence in the grandson. Denoting the presence of the attribute in son, father, and grandfather by A, B, and C, the question arises whether the association between A and C may not be due solely to the associations between A and B, B and C, respectively.

3. The ambiguity in such cases evidently arises from the fact that the universe of observation, in each case, contains not merely objects possessing the third attribute alone, or objects not possessing it, but both.

If the universe were restricted to *either class alone* the given ambiguity would not arise, though of course others might remain.

Thus, in the first illustration, if the statistics of vaccination and attack were drawn from one narrow section of the population living under approximately the same hygienic conditions, and an association were still observed between vaccination and exemption from attack, the supposed argument would be refuted. The fact would prove that the association between *vaccination* and *exemption* could not be wholly due to the association of both with *hygienic conditions*.

Again, in the second illustration, if we confine our attention to the "universe" of Conservatives (instead of dealing with candidates of both parties together), and compare the percentages of *Conservatives* winning elections when they spend more than their opponents and when they spend less, we shall avoid the possible fallacy. If the percentage is greater in the former case than in the latter, it cannot be for the reasons suggested in § 2.

The biological case of the third illustration should be similarly treated. If the association between A and C be observed for those cases in which all the parents, say, possess the attribute, or else all do not, and it is still sensible, then the association first observed between A and C for the whole universe cannot have been due solely to the observed associations between A and B, B and C.

4. The associations observed between the attributes A and B in the universe of C's and the universe of γ's may be termed **partial** associations, to distinguish them from the **total** associations observed between A and B in the universe at large. In terms of the definition of § 5 of Chap. III., A and B will be said to be positively associated in the universe of C's (cf. § 4 of Chap. II.) when

$$(ABC) > \frac{(AC)(BC)}{(C)} \qquad \cdots \qquad (1)$$

and negatively associated in the converse case.

As in the simpler case, the association is most simply tested by a comparison of percentages or proportions (§ 9, Chap. III.), although for some purposes a "coefficient of association" of some kind may be useful. Confining our attention to the more fundamental method, if A and B are positively associated within the universe of C's, we must have, to quote only the four most convenient comparisons (cf. (4) (a)-(d), Chap. III. p. 31),

$$\left. \begin{array}{ll} \dfrac{(ABC)}{(BC)} > \dfrac{(AC)}{(C)} \quad (a) & \dfrac{(ABC)}{(AC)} > \dfrac{(BC)}{(C)} \quad (b) \\[2ex] \dfrac{(ABC)}{(BC)} > \dfrac{(A\beta C)}{(\beta C)} \quad (c) & \dfrac{(ABC)}{(AC)} > \dfrac{(aBC)}{(aC)} \quad (d) \end{array} \right\} \qquad (2)$$

These inequalities may easily be rewritten for any other case by making the proper substitutions in the symbols; thus to obtain the inequalities for testing the association between A and C in the universe of B's, B must be written for C, β for γ, and *vice versâ*, throughout; it being remembered that the order of the letters in the class-symbol is immaterial. The remarks of § 10, Chap. III., as to the choice of the comparison to be used, apply of course equally to the present case.

5. Though we shall confine ourselves in the present work to the detailed discussion of the case of three attributes, it should be noticed that precisely similar conceptions and formulæ to the above apply in the general case where more than three attributes have been noted, or where the relations of more than three have to be taken into account. If, when it is observed that A and B are still associated within the universe of C's, it is argued that this is due to the association of both A and B with D, the argument may be tested by still further limiting the field of observation to the universe CD. If

$$(ABCD) > \frac{(ACD)(BCD)}{(CD)},$$

A and B are positively associated within the universe of CD's, and the association cannot be wholly ascribed to the presence and absence of D as suggested, nor to the presence and absence of C and D conjointly. If it be then argued that the presence and absence of E is the source of association, the process may be repeated as before, the association of A and B being tested for the universe CDE, and so on as far as practicable.

Partial associations thus form the basis of discussion for any case, however complicated. The two following examples will serve as illustrations for the case of three attributes.

Example i.—(Material from ref. 5 of Chap. I.)

The following are the proportions per 10,000 of boys observed with certain classes of defects, amongst a number of school children. (A) denotes the number with development defects, (B) with nerve-signs, (D) the number of the "dull."

N	10,000	(AB)	338
(A)	877	(AD)	338
(B)	1,086	(BD)	455
(D)	789	(ABD)	153

The *Report* from which the figures are drawn concludes that "the connecting link between defects of body and mental dulness is the coincident defect of brain which may be known by observation of abnormal nerve-signs." Discuss this conclusion.

The phrase "connecting link" is a little vague, but it may mean that the mental defects indicated by nerve-signs B may give rise to development-defects A, and also to mental-dulness D; A and D being thus common effects of the same cause B (or another attribute necessarily indicated by B), and not directly influencing each other. The case is thus similar to that of the first illustration of § 2 (liability to small-pox and to non-vaccination being held to be common effects of the same circumstances), and may be similarly treated by investigation of the partial associations between A and D for the universes B and β. As the ratios $(A)/N$, $(B)/N$, $(D)/N$ are small, comparisons of the form (4) (a) or (b) of Chap. III. (p. 31), or (2) (a) (b) above, may very well be used (*cf.* the remarks in § 10 of the same chapter, pp. 31–2).

The following figures illustrate, then, the association between A and D for the whole universe, the B-universe and the β-universe :—

For the entire material :—

Proportion of the dull $= (D)/N$ . . . $= \dfrac{789}{10,000} = 7\cdot9$ per cent.

,, ,, defectively developed who who were dull $= (AD)/(A)$ . . . . $\Big\} = \dfrac{338}{877} = 38\cdot5$,,

For those exhibiting nerve signs :—

Proportion of the dull $=(BD/(B)$ . . $=\dfrac{455}{1,086}=41\cdot9$ per cent.

,, ,, defectively developed who $\Big\}$ were dull $=(ABD)/(AB)$ . . . $\Big\}=\dfrac{153}{338}=45\cdot3$,,

For those not exhibiting nerve signs :—

Proportion of the dull $=(\beta D)/(\beta)$ . . $=\dfrac{334}{8,914}=3\cdot7$,,

,, ,, defectively developed who $\Big\}$ were dull $=(A\beta D)/(A\beta)$ . . . $\Big\}=\dfrac{185}{539}=34\cdot3$,,

The results are extremely striking; the association between A and D is very high indeed both for the material as a whole (the universe at large) and for those not exhibiting nerve-signs (the β-universe), but it is *very small* for those who do exhibit nerve-signs (the B-universe).

This result does not appear to be in accord with the conclusion of the *Report*, as we have interpreted it, for the association between A and D in the β-universe should in that case have been very low instead of very high.

Example ii.—Eye-colour of grandparent, parent and child. (Material from Sir Francis Galton's *Natural Inheritance* (1889), table 20, p. 216. The table only gives particulars for 78 large families with not less than 6 brothers or sisters, so that the material is hardly entirely representative, but serves as a good illustration of the method.) The original data are treated as in Example vii. of the last chapter (p. 34). Denoting a light-eyed child by A, parent by B, grandparent by C, every possible line of descent is taken into account. Thus, taking the following two lines of the table,

Children		Parents		Grandparents	
A. Light-eyed.	*a.* Not-Light-eyed.	*B.* Light-eyed.	*β.* Not-Light-eyed.	*C.* Light-eyed.	*γ.* Not-Light-eyed
4	5	1	1	1	3
3	4	1	1	4	0

the first would give $4 \times 1 \times 1 = 4$ to the class ABC, $4 \times 1 \times 3 = 12$ to the class $AB\gamma$, 4 to $A\beta C$, 12 to $A\beta\gamma$, 5 to aBC, 15 to $aB\gamma$, 5 to $a\beta C$, and 15 to $a\beta\gamma$; the second would give $3 \times 1 \times 4 = 12$ to the class ABC, 12 to $A\beta C$, 16 to aBC, 16 to $a\beta C$, and none to the remainder. The class-frequencies so derived from the whole table are,

(ABC)	1928	(aBC)	303
$(AB\gamma)$	596	$(aB\gamma)$	225
$(A\beta C)$	552	$(a\beta C)$	395
$(A\beta\gamma)$	508	$(a\beta\gamma)$	501

The following comparisons indicate the association between grandparents and parents, parents and children, and grandparents and grandchildren, respectively :—

Grandparents and Parents.

Proportion of light-eyed amongst the children of light-eyed grandparents $\left.\right\} = \dfrac{(BC)}{(C)} = \dfrac{2231}{3178} = 70 \cdot 2$ per cent.

Proportion of light-eyed amongst the children of not-light-eyed grandparents . . . . . $\left.\right\} = \dfrac{(B\gamma)}{(\gamma)} = \dfrac{821}{1830} = 44 \cdot 9$,,

Parents and Children.

Proportion of light-eyed amongst the children of light-eyed parents $\left.\right\} = \dfrac{(AB)}{(B)} = \dfrac{2524}{3052} = 82 \cdot 7$ per cent.

Proportion of light-eyed amongst the children of not-light-eyed parents. $\left.\right\} = \dfrac{(A\beta)}{(\beta)} = \dfrac{1060}{1956} = 54 \cdot 2$,,

In both the above cases we are really dealing with the association between parent and offspring, and consequently the intensity of association is, as might be expected, approximately the same ; in the next case it is naturally lower :—

Grandparents and Grandchildren.

Proportion of light-eyed amongst the grandchildren of light-eyed grandparents . . . . . $\left.\right\} = \dfrac{(AC)}{(C)} = \dfrac{2480}{3178} = 78 \cdot 0$ per cent.

Proportion of light-eyed amongst the grandchildren of not-light-eyed grandparents . . . . $\left.\right\} = \dfrac{(A\gamma)}{(\gamma)} = \dfrac{1104}{1830} = 60 \cdot 3$,,

We proceed now to test the *partial associations* between grandparents and grandchildren, as distinct from the total associations given above, in order to throw light on the real nature of the resemblance. There are two such partial associations to be tested : (1) where the parents are light-eyed, (2) where they are not-light-eyed. The following are the comparisons :—

Grandparents and Grandchildren : Parents light-eyed.

Proportion of light-eyed amongst the grandchildren of light-eyed grandparents . . . . . $\left.\right\} = \dfrac{(ABC)}{(BC)} = \dfrac{1928}{2231} = 86 \cdot 4$ per cent.

Proportion of light-eyed amongst the grandchildren of not-light-eyed grandparents . . . . $\left.\right\} = \dfrac{(AB\gamma)}{(B\gamma)} = \dfrac{596}{821} = 72 \cdot 6$,,

Grandparents and Grandchildren : Parents not-light-eyed.

$$\left.\begin{array}{l}\text{Proportion of light-eyed amongst the}\\\text{grandchildren of light-eyed grand-}\\\text{parents}\end{array}\right\} = \frac{(A\beta C)}{(\beta C)} = \frac{552}{947} = 58\cdot3 \text{ per cent.}$$

$$\left.\begin{array}{l}\text{Proportion of light-eyed amongst the}\\\text{grandchildren of not-light-eyed}\\\text{grandparents}\end{array}\right\} = \frac{(A\beta\gamma)}{(\beta\gamma)} = \frac{508}{1009} = 50\cdot3 \quad ,,$$

In both cases the partial association is quite well-marked and positive ; the total association between grandparents and grandchildren cannot, then, be due wholly to the total associations between grandparents and parents, parents and children, respectively. There is an *ancestral heredity*, as it is termed, as well as a parental heredity.

We need not discuss the partial association between children and parents, as it is comparatively of little consequence. It may be noted, however, as regards the above results, that the most important feature may be brought out by stating three ratios only.

If A and B are positively associated, $(AB)/(B) > (A)/N$.

If A and C are positively associated in the universe of B's, $(ABC)/(BC) > (AB)/(B)$. Hence $(A)/N$, $(AB)/(B)$, and $(ABC)/(BC)$ form an ascending series. Thus we have from the given data—

$$\left.\begin{array}{l}\text{Proportion of light-eyed amongst}\\\text{children in general}\end{array}\right\} = (A)/N = 71\cdot6 \text{ per cent.}$$

$$\left.\begin{array}{l}\text{Proportion of light-eyed amongst the}\\\text{children of light-eyed parents}\end{array}\right\} = (AB)/(B) = 82\cdot7 \quad ,,$$

$$\left.\begin{array}{l}\text{Proportion of light-eyed amongst the}\\\text{children of light-eyed parents and}\\\text{grandparents}\end{array}\right\} = (ABC)/(BC) = 86\cdot4 \quad ,,$$

If the great-grandparents, etc., etc., were also known, the series might be continued, giving $(ABCD)/(BCD)$, $(ABCDE)/(BCDE)$, and so forth. The series would probably ascend continuously though with smaller intervals, A and D being positively associated in the universe of BC's, A and E in the universe of BCD's, etc.

6. The above examples will serve to illustrate the practical application of partial associations to concrete cases. The general nature of the fallacies involved in interpreting associations between two attributes as if they were necessarily due to the most obvious form of direct causation is more clearly exhibited by the following theorem :—

If A and B are independent within the universe of C's and also within the universe of γ's, they will nevertheless be associated within the universe at large, unless C is independent of either A or B or both.

The two data give—

$$(ABC) = \frac{(AC)(BC)}{(C)}$$
$$(AB\gamma) = \frac{(A\gamma)(B\gamma)}{(\gamma)} = \frac{[(A)-(AC)][(B)-(BC)]}{(\gamma)}$$.   (3)

Adding them together we have—

$$(AB) = \frac{1}{(C)(\gamma)}\left\{ N(AC)(BC) - (A)(C)(BC) - (B)(C)(AC) + (A)(B)(C) \right\}$$

Write, as in § 11 of Chap. III. (p. 35)—

$$(AB)_0 = \frac{(A)(B)}{N}, \quad (AC)_0 = \frac{(A)(C)}{N}, \quad (BC)_0 = \frac{(B)(C)}{N},$$

subtract $(AB)_0$ from both sides of the above equation, simplify, and we have

$$(AB) - (AB)_0 = \frac{N}{(C)(\gamma)}[(AC) - (AC)_0][(BC) - (BC)_0]$$.   (4)

This proves the theorem; for the right-hand side will not be zero unless either $(AC) = (AC)_0$ or $(BC) = (BC)_0$.

7. The result indicates that, while no degree of heterogeneity in the universe can influence the association between A and B if all other attributes are independent of either A or B or both, an illusory or misleading association may arise in any case where there exists in the given universe a third attribute C with which both A and B are associated (positively or negatively). If both associations are of the same sign, the resulting illusory association between A and B will be positive ; if of opposite sign, negative. The three illustrations of § 2 are all of the first kind. In (1) it is argued that the positive associations between *vaccination* and *hygienic conditions, exemption from attack* and *hygienic conditions,* give rise to an illusory positive association between *vaccination* and *exemption from attack.* In (2) it is argued that the positive associations between *conservative* and *winning, conservative* and *spending more,* give rise to an illusory positive association between *winning* and *spending more.* In (3) the question is raised whether the positive association between *grandparent* and *grandchild* may not be due solely to the positive associations between *grandparent* and *parent, parent* and *child.*

Misleading associations of this kind may easily arise through

4

the mingling of records, *e.g.* respecting the two sexes, which a careful worker would keep distinct.

Take the following case, for example. Suppose there have been 200 patients in a hospital, 100 males and 100 females, suffering from some disease. Suppose, further, that the death-rate for males (the case mortality) has been 30 per cent., for females 60 per cent. A new treatment is tried on 80 per cent. of the males and 40 per cent. of the females, and the results published without distinction of sex. The three attributes, with the relations of which we are here concerned, are *death*, *treatment* and *male sex*. The data show that more males were treated than females, and more females died than males; therefore the first attribute is associated negatively, the second positively, with the third. It follows that there will be an illusory negative association between the first two—*death* and *treatment*. If the treatment were completely inefficient we would, in fact, have the following results :—

	Males.	Females.	Total.
Treated and died . . .	24	24	48
„ and did not die .	56	16	72
Not treated and died . .	6	36	42
„ and did not die .	14	24	38

i.e. of the treated, only $48/120 = 40$ per cent. died, while of those not treated $42/80 = 52\cdot5$ per cent. died. If this result were stated without any reference to the fact of the mixture of the sexes, to the different proportions of the two that were treated and to the different death-rates under normal treatment, then some value in the new treatment would appear to be suggested. To make a fair return, either the results for the two sexes should be stated separately, or the same proportion of the two* sexes must receive the experimental treatment. Further, care would have to be taken in such a case to see that there was no selection (perhaps unconscious) of the less severe cases for treatment, thus introducing another source of fallacy (*death* positively associated with *severity*, *treatment* negatively associated with *severity*, giving rise to illusory negative association between *treatment* and *death*).

A misleading association between the characters of parent and offspring might similarly be created if the records for male-male and female-female lines of descent were mixed. Thus suppose 50 per cent. of males and 10 per cent. of females exhibit some attribute for which there is no association in either line, then we would have for each line and for a mixed record of equal numbers—

	Male line.	Female line.	Mixed record.
Parents with attribute and children with . .	25 per cent.	1 per cent.	13 per cent.
Parents with attribute and children without . .	25 ,,	9 ,,	17 ,,
Parents without attribute and children with .	25 ,,	9 ,,	17 ,,
Parents without attribute and children without .	25 ,,	81 ,,	53 ,,

Here $13/30 = 43$ per cent. of the offspring of parents with the attribute possess the attribute themselves, but only $17/70 = 24$ per cent. of the offspring of parents without the attribute. The association between *attribute in parent* and *attribute in offspring* is, however, due solely to the association of both with *male sex*. The student will see that if records for male-female and female-male lines were mixed, the illusory association would be negative, and that if all four lines were combined there would be no illusory association at all.

8. Illusory associations may also arise in a different way through the personality of the observer or observers. If the observer's attention fluctuates, he may be more likely to notice the presence of A when he notices the presence of B, and *vice versâ*; in such a case A and B (so far as the record goes) will both be associated with the observer's attention C, and consequently an illusory association will be created. Again, if the attributes are not well defined, one observer may be more generous than another in deciding when to record the presence of A and also the presence of B, and even one observer may fluctuate in the generosity of his marking. In this case the recording of A and the recording of B will both be associated with the generosity of the observer in recording their presence, C, and an illusory association between A and B will consequently arise, as before.

9. It is important to notice that, though we cannot actually determine the partial associations unless the third-order frequency (ABC) is given, we can make some conjecture as to their sign from the values of the second-order frequencies.

Suppose, for instance, that—

$$
\left.
\begin{aligned}
(ABC) &= \frac{(AC)(BC)}{(C)} + \delta_1 \\
(AB\gamma) &= \frac{(A\gamma)(B\gamma)}{(\gamma)} + \delta_2
\end{aligned}
\right\} \qquad . \qquad . \qquad . \quad (5)
$$

so that δ_1 and δ_2 are positive or negative according as A and B are positively or negatively associated in the universes of C and γ respectively. Then we have by addition—

$$(AB) = \frac{(AC)(BC)}{(C)} + \frac{(A\gamma)(B\gamma)}{(\gamma)} + \delta_1 + \delta_2 \quad . \quad . \quad (6)$$

Hence if the value of (AB) exceed the value given by the first two terms (*i.e.* if $\delta_1 + \delta_2$ be positive), A and B must be positively associated either in the universe of C's, the universe of γ's, or both. If, on the other hand, (AB) fall short of the value given by the first two terms, A and B must be negatively associated in the universe of C's, the universe of γ's, or both. Finally, if (AB) be equal to the value of the first two terms, A and B must be positively associated in the one partial universe and negatively in the other, or else independent in both.

The expression (6) may often be used in the following form, obtained by dividing through by, say, (B)—

$$\frac{(AB)}{(B)} = \frac{(AC)}{(C)} \cdot \frac{(BC)}{(B)} + \frac{(A\gamma)}{(\gamma)} \cdot \frac{(B\gamma)}{(B)} + \frac{\delta_1 + \delta_2}{(B)} \quad . \quad . \quad (7)$$

In using this expression we make use solely of proportions or percentages, and judge of the sign of the partial associations between A and B accordingly. A concrete case, as in Example iii. below, is perhaps clearer than the general formula.

Example iii.—(Figures compiled from *Supplement to the Fifty-fifth Annual Report of the Registrar-General* [C.—8503], 1897.) The following are the death-rates per thousand per annum, and the proportions over 65 years of age, of occupied males in general, farmers, textile workers, and glass workers (over 15 years of age in each case) during the decade 1891–1900 in England and Wales.

	Death-rate per thousand.	Proportion per thousand over 65 Years of Age.
Occupied males over 15 .	15·8	46
Farmers ,, ,, . .	19·6	132
Textile workers, males over 15 .	15·9	34
Glass workers ,, ,, .	16·6	16

Would farming, textile working, and glass working seem to be relatively healthy or unhealthy occupations, given that the death-rates among occupied males from 15–65 and over 65 years of age are 11·5 and 102·3 per thousand respectively?

If A denote *death*, B the given *occupation*, C *old age*, we have to apply the principle of equation (7). Calculate what would be the death-rate for each occupation on the supposition that the death-rates for occupied males in general (11·5, 102·3) apply to each of its separate age-groups (under 65, over 65), and see whether the total death-rate so calculated exceeds or falls short of the actual death-rate. If it exceeds the actual rate, the occupation must on the whole be healthy; if it falls short, unhealthy. Thus we have the following calculated death-rates :—

Farmers .	.	.	$11 \cdot 5 \times \cdot 868 + 102 \cdot 3 \times \cdot 132 = 23 \cdot 5.$
Textile workers		.	$11 \cdot 5 \times \cdot 966 + 102 \cdot 3 \times \cdot 034 = 14 \cdot 6.$
Glass workers .		.	$11 \cdot 5 \times \cdot 984 + 102 \cdot 3 \times \cdot 016 = 13 \cdot 0.$

The calculated rate for farmers largely exceeds the actual rate; farming, then, must on the whole, as one would expect, be a healthy occupation. The death-rate for either young farmers or old farmers, or both, must be less than for occupied males in general (the last is actually the case); the high death-rate observed is due solely to the large proportion of the aged. Textile working, on the other hand, appears to be unhealthy ($14 \cdot 6 < 15 \cdot 9$), and glass working still more so ($13 \cdot 0 < 16 \cdot 6$); the actual low total death-rates are due merely to low proportions of the aged.

It is evident that age-distributions vary so largely from one occupation to another that total death-rates are liable to be very misleading—so misleading, in fact, that they are not tabulated at all by the Registrar-General; only death-rates for narrow limits of age (5 or 10 year age-classes) are worked out. Similar fallacies are liable to occur in comparisons of local death-rates, owing to variations not only in the relative proportions of the old, but also in the relative proportions of the two sexes.

It is hardly necessary to observe that as *age* is a variable quantity, the above procedure for calculating the comparative death-rates is extremely rough. The death-rate of those engaged in any occupation depends not only on the mere proportions over and under 65, but on the relative numbers at every single year of age. The simpler procedure brings out, however, better than a more complex one, the nature of the fallacy involved in assuming that crude death-rates are measures of healthiness. [See also Chap. XI. §§ 17–19.]

Example iv.—Eye-colour in grandparent, parent and child. (The figures are those of Example ii.)

A, light-eyed child; B, light-eyed parent; C, light-eyed grandparent.

$N = 5008$	$(AB) = 2524$
$(A) = 3584$	$(AC) = 2480$
$(B) = 3052$	$(BC) = 2231$
$(C) = 3178$	

Given only the above data, investigate whether there is probably a partial association between child and grandparent.

If there were no partial association we would have—

$$(AC) = \frac{(AB)(BC)}{(B)} + \frac{(A\beta)(\beta C)}{(\beta)}$$

$$= \frac{2524 \times 2231}{3052} + \frac{1060 \times 947}{1956}$$

$$= 1845 \cdot 0 + 513 \cdot 2$$

$$= 2358 \cdot 2.$$

Actually $(AC) = 2480$; there must, then, be partial association either in the B-universe, the β-universe, or both. In the absence of any reason to the contrary, it would be natural to suppose there is a partial association in both; *i.e.* that there is a partial association with the grandparent whether the line of descent passes through "light-eyed" or "not-light-eyed" parents, but this could not be *proved* without a knowledge of the class-frequency (ABC).

10. The total possible number of associations to be derived from n attributes grows so rapidly with the value of n that the evaluation of them all for any case in which n is greater than four becomes almost unmanageable. For three attributes there are 9 possible associations—three totals, three partials in positive universes, and three partials in negative universes. For four attributes, the number of possible associations rises to 54, for there are 6 pairs to be formed from four attributes, and we can find 9 associations for each pair (1 total, 4 partials with the universe specified by one attribute, and 4 partials with the universe specified by two). For five attributes the student will find that there are no less than 270, and for six attributes 1215 associations.

As suggested by Examples i. and ii. above, however, it is not necessary in any actual case to investigate all the associations that are theoretically possible; the nature of the problem indicates those that are required.

In Example i., for instance, the total and partial associations between A and D were alone investigated; the associations between A and B, B and D were not essential for answering the question that was asked. In Example ii., again, the three total associations and the partial association between A and C were worked out, but the partial associations between A and B, B and C were omitted as unnecessary. Practical considerations of this kind will always lessen the amount of necessary labour.

11. It might appear, at first sight, that theoretical considerations would enable us to lessen it still further. As we saw in Chapter I., all class-frequencies can be expressed in terms of those of the *positive* classes, of which there are 2^n in the case of n attributes. For given values of the $\overline{n+1}$ frequencies N, (A), (B), (C), . . . of order lower than the second, assigned values of the positive class-frequencies of the second and higher orders must therefore correspond to determinate values of *all* the possible associations. But the number of these positive class-frequencies of the second and higher orders is only $2^n - \overline{n+1}$; therefore the number of *algebraically independent associations* that can be derived from n attributes is only $2^n - \overline{n+1}$. For successive values of n this gives—

n	$2^n - \overline{n+1}$
2	1
3	4
4	11
5	26
6	57

Hence if we give data, in any form, that determine *four* associations in the case of three attributes, *eleven* in the case of four attributes, and so on, in addition to N and the class-frequencies of the first order, we have done all that is theoretically necessary. The remaining associations can be deduced.

12. Practically, however, the mere fact that they *can be* deduced is of little help unless such deduction can be effected simply, indeed almost directly, by mere mental arithmetic almost, and this is not the case. The relations that exist between the ratios or differences, such as $(AB) - (AB)_0$, that indicate the associations are, in fact, so complex that an unknown association cannot be determined from those that are given without more or less lengthy work ; it is not possible to infer even its sign by any simple process of inspection. We have, for instance, from (5), by the process used in obtaining (4) for the special case of § 6—

$$\left[(AB\gamma) - \frac{(A\gamma)(B\gamma)}{(\gamma)} \right] = [(AB) - (AB)_0] - \frac{(N)}{(C)(\gamma)}[(AC) - (AC)_0][(BC) - (BC)_0]$$
$$- \left[(ABC) - \frac{(AC)(BC)}{(C)} \right],$$

which gives us the difference of $(AB\gamma)$ from the value it would have if A and B were independent in the universe of γ's in terms of the difference of (ABC) from the value it would have if A and

B were independent in the universe of C's, and the corresponding differences for the frequencies (AB), (AC), and (BC). The four quantities in the brackets on the right represent, say, the four known associations, the bracket on the left the unknown association. Clearly, the relation is not of such a simple kind that the term on the left can be, in general, mentally evaluated. Hence, in considering the choice and number of associations to be actually tabulated, regard must be had to practical considerations rather than to theoretical relations.

13. The particular case in which all the $2^n - n + 1$ given associations are zero is worth some special investigation.

It follows, in the first place, that all other possible associations must be zero, $i.e.$ that a state of **complete independence**, as we may term it, exists. Suppose, for instance, that we are given—

$$(AB) = \frac{(A)(B)}{N} \qquad\qquad (AC) = \frac{(A)(C)}{N}$$

$$(BC) = \frac{(B)(C)}{N} \qquad\qquad (ABC) = \frac{(AC)(BC)}{(C)} = \frac{(A)(B)(C)}{N^2}.$$

Then it follows at once that we have also—

$$(ABC) = \frac{(AB)(BC)}{(B)} = \frac{(AB)(AC)}{(A)},$$

$i.e.$ A and C are independent in the universe of B's, and B and C in the universe of A's. Again,

$$(AB\gamma) = (AB) - (ABC) = \frac{(A)(B)}{N} - \frac{(A)(B)(C)}{N^2}$$

$$= \frac{(A)(B)(\gamma)}{N^2} = \frac{(A\gamma)(B\gamma)}{(\gamma)}.$$

Therefore A and B are independent in the universe of γ's. Similarly, it may be shown that A and C are independent in the universe of β's, B and C in the universe of α's.

In the next place it is evident from the above that relations of the general form (to write the equation symmetrically)

$$\frac{(ABC)}{N} = \frac{(A)}{N} \cdot \frac{(B)}{N} \cdot \frac{(C)}{N} \qquad \cdot \qquad \cdot \qquad \cdot \quad (8)$$

must hold for every class-frequency. This relation is the general form of the equation of independence, (2) (d), Chap. III. (p. 26).

14. It must be noted, however, that (8) is not a *criterion* for the

complete independence of *A*, *B*, and *C* in the sense that the equation

$$\frac{(AB)}{N} = \frac{(A)}{N} \cdot \frac{(B)}{N}$$

is a criterion for the complete independence of *A* and *B*. If we are given *N*, *(A)*, and *(B)*, and the last relation quoted holds good, we know that similar relations must hold for *(Aβ)*, *(aB)*, and *(aβ)*. If *N*, *(A)*, *(B)*, and *(C)* be given, however, and the equation (8) hold good, we can draw no conclusion without further information; the data are insufficient. There are *eight* algebraically independent class-frequencies in the case of three attributes, while *N*, *(A)*, *(B)*, *(C)* are only four: the equation (8) must therefore be shown to hold good for *four* frequencies of the third order before the conclusion can be drawn that it holds good for the remainder, *i.e.* that a state of complete independence subsists. The direct verification of this result is left for the student.

Quite generally, if *N*, *(A)*, *(B)*, *(C)*, ... be given, the relation

$$\frac{(ABC \ldots)}{N} = \frac{(A)}{N} \cdot \frac{(B)}{N} \cdot \frac{(C)}{N} \cdots \qquad \cdot \quad (9)$$

must be shown to hold good for $2^n - \overline{n+1}$ of the *n*th order classes before it may be assumed to hold good for the remainder. It is only because

$$2^n - \overline{n+1} = 1$$

when $n = 2$ that the relation

$$\frac{(AB)}{N} = \frac{(A)}{N} \cdot \frac{(B)}{N},$$

may be treated as a *criterion* for the independence of *A* and *B*. *If* all the *n* $(n > 2)$ attributes are completely independent, the relation (9) holds good; but it does not follow that if the relation (9) hold good they are all independent.

REFERENCES.

(1) Yule, G. U., "On the Association of Attributes in Statistics," *Phil. Trans. Roy. Soc.*, Series A, vol. cxciv., 1900, p. 257. (Deals fully with the theory of partial as well as of total association, with numerous illustrations : a notation suggested for the partial coefficients.)

(2) Yule, G. U., "Notes on the Theory of Association of Attributes in Statistics," *Biometrika*, vol. ii., 1903, p. 121. (*Cf.* especially §§ 4 and 5, on the theory of complete independence, and the fallacies due to mixing of records.)

EXERCISES.

1. Take the following figures for girls corresponding to those for boys in Example i., p. 45, and discuss them similarly, but not necessarily using exactly the same comparisons, to see whether the conclusion that "the connecting link between defects of body and mental dulness is the coincident defect of brain which may be known by observation of abnormal nerve signs" seems to hold good.

A, development defects.　B, nerve signs.　D, mental dulness

N	10,000	(AB)	248
(A)	682	(AD)	307
(B)	850	(BD)	363
(D)	689	(ABD)	128

2. (Material from *Census of England and Wales*, 1891, vol. iii.) The following figures give the numbers of those suffering from single or combined infirmities : (1) for all males, (2) for males of 55 years of age and over.

A, Blindness.　B, Mental derangement.　C, Deaf-mutism.

	(1) All Males.	(2) Males 55–		(1) All Males.	(2) Males 55–
N	14,053,000	1,377,000	(AB)	183	65
(A)	12,281	5,538	(AC)	51	14
(B)	45,392	10,309	(BC)	299	47
(C)	7,707	746	(ABC)	11	3

Tabulate proportions per thousand, exhibiting the total association between blindness and mental derangement, and the partial association between the same two infirmities among deaf-mutes, (1) for males in general, (2) for those of 55 years of age or over. Give a short verbal statement of the results, and contrast them with those of Question 1.

3. (Material from supplement to 55th Annual Report Reg.-Genl.)
The death-rate from cancer for occupied males in general (over 15) is 0·685 per thousand per annum, and for farmers 1·20.
The death-rates from cancer for occupied males under and over 45 respectively are 0·13 and 2·25 respectively. Of the farmers 46·1 per cent. are over 45.
Would you say that farmers were peculiarly liable to cancer?

4. A population of males over 15 years of age consists of 7 per cent. over 65 years of age and 93 per cent. under. The death-rates are 12 per thousand per annum in the younger class and 110 in the older, or 18·86 in the whole population. The death-rate of males (over 15) engaged in a certain industry is 26·7 per thousand.
If the industry be not unhealthy, what must be the approximate proportion of those over 65 engaged in it (neglecting minor differences of age distribution)?

5. Show that if A and B are independent, while A and C, B and C are associated, A and B must be disassociated either in the universe of C's, the universe of γ's, or both.

6. As an illustration of Question 5, show that if the following were actual data, there would be a slight disassociation between the eye-colours of husband and wife (father and mother) for the parents either of light-eyed sons or not-light-eyed sons, or both, although there is a slight positive association for parents at large.

A light-eye colour in husband, B in wife, C in son—

N	1000	(AB)	358
(A)	622	(AC)	471
(B)	558	(BC)	419
(C)	617		

7. Show that if $(ABC)=(a\beta\gamma)$, $(aBC)=(A\beta\gamma)$, and so on (the case of "complete equality of contrary frequencies" of Question 7, Chap. I.), A, B, and C are completely independent if A and B, A and C, B and C are independent pair and pair.

8. If, in the same case of complete equality of contraries,

$$(AB) - N/4 = \delta_1$$
$$(AC) - N/4 = \delta_2$$
$$(BC) - N/4 = \delta_3$$

show that

$$2\left[(ABC) - \frac{(AC)(BC)}{(C)}\right] = 2\left[(AB\gamma) - \frac{(A\gamma)(B\gamma)}{(\gamma)}\right] = \delta_1 - \frac{4\delta_2\delta_3}{N}$$

so that the partial associations between A and B in the universes C and γ are positive or negative according as

$$\delta_1 \gtrless \frac{4\delta_2\delta_3}{N}.$$

9. In the simple contests of a general election (contests in which one Conservative opposed one Liberal and there were no other candidates) 66 per cent. of the winning candidates (according to the returns) spent more money than their opponents. Given that 63 per cent. of the winners were Conservatives, and that the Conservative expenditure exceeded the Liberal in 80 per cent. of the contests, find the percentages of elections won by Conservatives (1) when they spent more and (2) when they spent less than their opponents, and hence say whether you consider the above figures evidence of the influence of expenditure on election results or no. (*Note* that if the one candidate in a contest be a *Conservative-winner-who spends more than his opponent*—the other must necessarily be a *Liberal-loser-who spends less* — and so forth. Hence the case is one of complete equality of contraries.)

10. Given that $(A)/N=(B)/N=(C)/N=x$, and that $(AB)/N=(AC)/N=y$, find the major and minor limits to y that enable one to infer positive association between B and C, i.e. $(BC)/N>x^2$.

Draw a diagram on squared paper to illustrate your answer, taking x and y as co-ordinates, and shading the limits within which y must lie in order to permit of the above inference. Point out the peculiarities in the case of inferring a positive association from two negative associations.

11. Discuss similarly the more complex case $(A)/N=x$, $(B)/N=2x$, $(C)/N=3x$:—

(1) for inferring positive association between B and C given $(AB)/N=(AC)/N=y$.
(2) for inferring positive association between A and C given $(AB)/N=(BC)/N=y$.
(3) for inferring positive association between A and B given $(AC)/N=(BC)/N=y$.

CHAPTER V.

MANIFOLD CLASSIFICATION.

1. The general principle of a manifold classification—2-4. The table of
double-entry or contingency table and its treatment by fundamental
methods—5-8. The coefficient of contingency—9-10. Analysis of
a contingency table by tetrads—11-13. Isotropic and anisotropic
distributions—14-15. Homogeneity of the classifications dealt with
in this and the preceding chapters: heterogeneous classifications.

1. CLASSIFICATION by dichotomy is, as was briefly pointed out in
Chap. I. § 5, a simpler form of classification than usually occurs
in the tabulation of practical statistics. It may be regarded as
a special case of a more general form in which the individuals or
objects observed are first divided under, say, s heads, $A_1 A_2 \ldots$
A_s, each of the classes so obtained then subdivided under t heads,
$B_1, B_2 \ldots B_t$, each of these under u heads, $C_1, C_2 \ldots C_u$, and
so on, thus giving rise to $s \cdot t \cdot u \ldots$ ultimate classes altogether.

2. The general theory of such a manifold as distinct from a
twofold or dichotomous classification, in the case of n attributes
or characters $ABC \ldots N$, would be extremely complex: in the
present chapter the discussion will be confined to the case of two
characters, A and B, only. If the classification of the A's be s-
fold and of the B's t-fold, the frequencies of the st classes of the
second order may be most simply given by forming a table with
s columns headed A_1 to A_s and t rows headed B_1 to B_t. The
number of the objects or individuals possessing any combination
of the two characters, say A_m and B_n, *i.e.* the frequency of the
class $A_m B_n$, is entered in the compartment common to the mth
column and the nth row, the st compartments thus giving all
the second-order frequencies. The totals at the ends of rows
and the feet of columns give the first-order frequencies, *i.e.* the
numbers of A_m's and B_n's, and finally the grand total at the
right-hand bottom corner gives the whole number of observations.
Tables I. and II. below will serve as illustrations of such tables
of double-entry or contingency tables, as they have been termed
by Professor Pearson (ref. 1).

3. In Table I. the division is 3 × 3-fold : the houses in England and Wales are divided into those which are in (1) London, (2) other urban districts, (3) rural districts, and the houses in each of these divisions are again classified into (1) inhabited houses, (2) uninhabited but completed houses, (3) houses that are "building," *i.e.* in course of erection. Thus from the first row we see that there were in London, in round numbers, 616,000 houses, of which 571,000 were inhabited, 40,000 uninhabited, and 5000 in course of erection : from the first column, there were 6,260,000 inhabited houses in England and Wales, of which 571,000 were in London, 4,064,000 in other urban districts, and 1,625,000 in rural districts.

TABLE I.—*Houses in England and Wales.* (*Census of* 1901. *Summary Table X.*) (000's *omitted.*)

	Inhabited.	Unin-habited.	Building.	Total.
Adm. County of London .	571	40	5	616
Other urban districts . .	4064	285	45	4394
Rural districts . . .	1625	124	12	1761
Total for England and Wales	6260	449	62	6771

In Table II., on the other hand, the classification is 3 × 4-fold : the eye-colours are classed under the three heads "blue," "grey or green," and "brown," while the hair-colours are classed under four heads, "fair," "brown," "black," and "red." The table is

TABLE II.—*Hair- and Eye-Colours of* 6800 *Males in Baden.* (*Ammon, Zur Anthropologie der Badener.*)

Eye-colour.	Hair-colour.				Total.
	Fair.	Brown.	Black.	Red.	
Blue	1768	807	189	47	2811
Grey or Green .	946	1387	746	53	3132
Brown . . .	115	438	288	16	857
Total .	2829	2632	1223	116	6800

read similarly to the last. Taking the first row, it tells us that there were 2811 men with blue eyes noted, of whom 1768 had fair hair, 807 brown hair, 189 black hair, and 47 red hair. Similarly, from the first column, there were 2829 men with fair hair, of whom 1768 had blue eyes, 946 grey or green eyes, and 115 brown eyes. The tables are a generalised form of the four-fold (2×2-fold) tables in § 13, Chap. III.

4. For the purpose of discussing the nature of the relation between the A's and the B's, any such table may be treated on the principles of the preceding chapters by reducing it in different ways to 2×2-fold form. It then becomes possible to trace the association between any one or more of the A's and any one or more of the B's, either in the universe at large or in universes limited by the omission of one or more of the A's, of the B's, or of both. Taking Table I., for example, trace the association between the erection of houses and the urban character of a district. Adding together the first two rows—*i.e.* pooling London and the other urban districts together—and similarly adding the first two columns, so as to make no distinction between inhabited and uninhabited houses as long as they are completed, we find—

Proportion of all houses which are in course of erection in urban districts . . . $50/5010 = 10$ per thousand.

Proportion of all houses which are in course of erection in rural districts . . . $12/1761 = 7$,,

There is therefore, as might be expected, a distinct positive association, a larger proportion of houses being in course of erection in urban than in rural districts.

If, as another illustration, it be desired to trace the association between the "uninhabitedness" of houses and the urban character of the district, the procedure will be rather different. Rows 1 and 2 may be added together as before, but column 3 may be omitted altogether, as the houses which are only in course of erection do not enter into the question. We then have—

Proportion of all houses which are uninhabited in urban districts . . . . $325/4960 = 66$ per thousand.

Proportion of all houses which are uninhabited in rural districts . . . . $124/1749 = 71$,,

The association is therefore negative, the proportion of houses uninhabited being greater in rural than in urban districts.

The eye- and hair-colour data of Table II. may be treated in a precisely similar fashion. If, *e.g.*, we desire to trace the association between a lack of pigmentation in eyes and in hair, rows 1 and 2 may be pooled together as representing the least pigmentation of the eyes, and columns 2, 3, and 4 may be pooled together as representing hair with a more or less marked degree of pigmentation. We then have—

Proportion of light-eyed with fair hair . . . . $2714/5943 = 46$ per cent.

Proportion of brown-eyed with fair hair . . . . $115/857 = 13$ „

The association is therefore well-marked. For comparison we may trace the corresponding association between the most marked degree of pigmentation in eyes and hair, *i.e.* brown eyes and black hair. Here we must add together rows 1 and 2 as before, and columns 1, 2, and 4—the column for red being really misplaced, as red represents a comparatively slight degree of pigmentation. The figures are—

Proportion of brown-eyed with black hair . . . . $288/857 = 34$ per cent.

Proportion of light-eyed with black hair . . . . $935/5943 = 16$ „

The association is again positive and well-marked, but the difference between the two percentages is rather less than in the last case.

5. The mode of treatment adopted in the preceding section rests on first principles, and, if fully carried out, it gives the most detailed information possible with regard to the relations of the two attributes. At the same time a distinct need is felt in practical work for some more summary method—a method which will enable a single and definite answer to be given to such a question as—Are the A's on the whole distinctly dependent on the B's; and if so, is this dependence very close, or the reverse? The subject of coefficients of association, which affords the answer to this question in the case of a dichotomous classification, was only dealt with briefly and incidentally, for it is still the subject of some controversy: further, where there are only four classes of the second order to be considered the matter is not nearly so complex as where the number is, say, twenty-five or more, and the need for any summary coefficient is not so often nor so keenly felt. The ideas on which Professor Pearson's general measure of dependence, the "coefficient of contingency," is based, are, moreover, quite simple and fundamental, and the mode of calculation

is therefore given in full in the following section. The advanced student should refer to the original memoir (ref. 1) for a completer treatment of the theory of the coefficient, and of its relation to the theory of variables.

6. Generalising slightly the notation of the preceding chapters, let the frequency of A_m's be denoted by (A_m), the frequency of B_n's by (B_n), and the frequency of objects or individuals possessing both characters by $(A_m B_n)$. Then, if the A's and B's be completely independent in the universe at large, we must have for all values of m and n—

$$(A_m B_n) = \frac{(A_m)(B_n)}{N} = (A_m B_n)_0 \quad . \quad . \quad . \quad (1)$$

If, however, A and B are not completely independent, $(A_m B_n)$ and $(A_m B_n)_0$ will not be identical for all values of m and n. Let the difference be given by

$$\delta_{mn} = (A_m B_n) - (A_m B_n)_0 \quad . \quad . \quad . \quad (2)$$

A coefficient such as we are seeking may evidently be based in some way on these values of δ. It will not do, however, simply to add them together, for the sum of all the values of δ, some of which are negative and others positive, must be zero in any case, the sum of both the (AB)'s and the $(AB)_0$'s being equal to the whole number of observations N. It is necessary, therefore, to get rid of the signs, and this may be done in two simple ways: (1) by neglecting them and forming the arithmetical instead of the algebraical sum of the differences δ, or (2) by squaring the differences and then summing the squares. The first process is the shorter, but the second the better, as it leads to a coefficient easily treated by algebraical methods, which the first process does not: as the student will see later, squaring is very usefully and very frequently employed for the purpose of eliminating algebraical signs. Suppose, then, that every δ is calculated, and also the ratio of its square to the corresponding value of $(AB)_0$, and that the sum of all such ratios is, say, χ^2; or, in symbols, using Σ to denote " the sum of all quantities like " :—

$$\chi^2 = \Sigma \left(\frac{\delta_{mn}^2}{(A_m B_n)_0} \right) \quad . \quad . \quad . \quad (3)$$

Being the sum of a series of squares, χ^2 is necessarily positive, and if A and B be independent it is zero, because every δ is zero. If, then, we form a coefficient C given by the relation

$$C = \sqrt{\frac{\chi^2}{N + \chi^2}} \quad . \quad . \quad . \quad (4)$$

this coefficient is zero if the characters A and B are completely independent, and approaches more and more nearly towards unity as χ^2 increases. In general, no sign should be attached to the root, for the coefficient simply shows whether the two characters are or are not independent, and nothing more, but in some cases a conventional sign may be used. Thus in Table II. slight pigmentation of eyes and of hair appear to go together, and the contingency may be regarded as definitely positive. If slight pigmentation of eyes had been associated with marked pigmentation of hair, the contingency might have been regarded as negative. C is Professor Pearson's mean square contingency coefficient.[1]

7. The coefficient, in the simple form (4), has one disadvantage, viz. that coefficients calculated on different systems of classification are not comparable with each other. It is clearly desirable for practical purposes that two coefficients calculated from the same data classified in two different ways should be, at least approximately, identical. With the present coefficient this is not the case : if certain data be classified in, say, (1) 6 × 6-fold, (2) 3 × 3-fold form, the coefficient in the latter form tends to be the least. The greatest possible value of the coefficient is, in fact, only unity if the number of classes be infinitely great; for any finite number of classes the limiting value of C is the smaller the smaller the number of classes. This may be briefly illustrated as follows. Replacing δ_{mn} in equation (3) by its value in terms of $(A_m B_n)$ and $(A_m B_n)_0$ we have—

$$\chi^2 = \Sigma \left\{ \frac{(A_m B_n)^2}{(A_m B_n)_0} \right\} - N \qquad . \qquad . \qquad . \quad (5)$$

and therefore, denoting the expression in brackets by S,

$$C = \sqrt{\frac{S - N}{S}} \qquad . \qquad . \qquad . \quad (6)$$

Now suppose we have to deal with a $t \times t$-fold classification in which $(A_m) = (B_m)$ for all values of m; and suppose, further, that the association between A_m and B_m is perfect, so that $(A_m B_m) = (A_m) = (B_m)$ for all values of m, the remaining frequencies of the second order being zero ; all the frequency is then concentrated in the diagonal compartments of the table, and each contributes

---

[1] Professor Pearson (ref. 1) terms δ a sub-contingency ; χ^2 the square contingency ; the ratio χ^2/N, which he denotes by ϕ^2, the mean square contingency ; and the sum of all the δ's of one sign only, on which a different coefficient can be based, the mean contingency.

N to the sum S. The total value of S is accordingly tN, and the value of C—

$$C = \sqrt{\frac{t-1}{t}}.$$

This is the greatest possible value of C for a symmetrical $t \times t$-fold classification, and therefore, in such a table, for—

$$
\begin{array}{lllll}
t = & 2 & C \text{ cannot exceed } & 0.707 \\
t = & 3 & \text{,,} & \text{,,} & 0.816 \\
t = & 4 & \text{,,} & \text{,,} & 0.866 \\
t = & 5 & \text{,,} & \text{,,} & 0.894 \\
t = & 6 & \text{,,} & \text{,,} & 0.913 \\
t = & 7 & \text{,,} & \text{,,} & 0.926 \\
t = & 8 & \text{,,} & \text{,,} & 0.935 \\
t = & 9 & \text{,,} & \text{,,} & 0.943 \\
t = & 10 & \text{,,} & \text{,,} & 0.949 \\
\end{array}
$$

It is as well, therefore, to restrict the use of the " coefficient of contingency " to 5 × 5-fold or finer classifications. At the same time the classification must not be made too fine, or else the value of the coefficient is largely affected by casual irregularities of no physical significance in the class-frequencies (cf. the remarks in Chap. III. §§ 7–8).

TABLE III.—*Independence-Values of the Frequencies for Table II.*

Eye-colour.	Fair.	Brown.	Black.	Red.
Blue	1169	1088	506	48·0
Grey or Green	1303	1212	563	53·4
Brown	357	332	154	14·6

8. As the classification of Table II. is only 3 × 4-fold, it is rather crude for the purpose of calculating the coefficient, but will serve simply as an illustration of the form of the arithmetic. In Table III. are given the values of the independence frequencies, 2829 × 2811/6800 = 1169 and so on. The value of χ^2 is more readily calculated from equation (5) than from (3) :—

$(1768)^2/1169$ 2673·9
$(946)^2/1303$ 686·8
$(115)^2/357$ 37·0
$(807)^2/1088$ *   598·6
$(1387)^2/1212$ 1587·3
$(438)^2/332$ 577·8
$(189)^2/506$ 70·6
$(746)^2/563$ 988·5
$(288)^2/154$ 538·6
$(47)^2/48·0$ 46·0
$(53)^2/53·4$ 52·6
$(16)^2/14·6$ 17·5

Total $= S =$ 7875·2
$N =$ 6800

$S - N =$ 1075·2

$$\therefore \quad C = \sqrt{\frac{1075·2}{7875·2}} = \sqrt{·1365} = 0·37$$

The squares in such work may conveniently be taken from Barlow's *Tables of Squares, Cubes, etc.* (see list of tables on p. 356), or logarithms may be used throughout—five-figure logarithms are quite sufficient.

9. While such a coefficient of contingency, in some form or other, is a great convenience in many fields of work, its use should not lead to a neglect of those details which a treatment by the elementary methods of § 4 would have revealed. Whether the coefficient be calculated or no, every table should always be examined with care to see if it exhibit any apparently significant peculiarities in the distribution of frequency, *e.g.* in the associations subsisting between A_m and B_n in limited universes. A good deal of caution must be used in order not to be misled by casual irregularities due to paucity of observations in some compartments of the table, but important points that would otherwise be overlooked will often be revealed by such a detailed examination.

10. Suppose, for example, that any four adjacent frequencies, say—

$$(A_m B_n) \qquad (A_{m+1} B_n)$$
$$(A_m B_{n+1}) \qquad (A_{m+1} B_{n+1})$$

are extracted from the general contingency table. Considering these as a table exhibiting the association between A_m and B_n in a universe limited to $A_m A_{m+1} B_n B_{n+1}$ alone, the association is positive, negative, or zero according as $(A_m B_n)/(A_{m+1} B_n)$ is greater than, less than, or equal to the ratio $(A_mB_{n+1})/(A_{m+1}B_{n+1})$. The whole of the contingency table can be analysed into a series of elementary groups of four frequencies like the above, each one overlapping its neighbours so that an rs-fold table contains $(r-1)(s-1)$ such "tétrads," and the associations in them all can be very quickly determined by simply tabulating the ratios like $(A_mB_n)/(A_{m+1}B_n)$, $(A_mB_{n+1})/(A_{m+1}B_{n+1})$, etc., or perhaps better, the proportions $(A_mB_n)/\{(A_mB_n)+(A_{m+1}B_n)\}$, etc., for every pair of columns or of rows, as may be most convenient. Taking the figures of Table II. as an illustration, and working from the rows, the proportions run as follows :—

For rows 1 and 2.		For rows 2 and 3.	
1768/2714	0·651	946/1061	0·892
807/2194	0·368	1387/1825	0·760
189/935	0·202	746/1034	0·721
47/100	0·470	53/69	0·768

In both cases the first three ratios form descending series, but the fourth ratio is greater than the second. The signs of the associations in the six tetrads are accordingly—

$$+ \quad + \quad -$$
$$+ \quad + \quad -$$

The negative sign in the two tetrads on the right is striking, the more so as other tables for hair- and eye-colour, arranged in the same way, exhibit just the same characteristic. But the peculiarity will be removed at once if the fourth column be placed immediately after the first: if this be done, i.e. if "red" be placed between "fair" and "brown" instead of at the end of the colour-series, the sign of the association in all the elementary tetrads will be the same. The colours will then run fair, red, brown, black, and this would seem to be the more natural order, considering the depth of the pigmentation.

11. A distribution of frequency of such a kind that the association in every elementary tetrad is of the same sign possesses several useful and interesting properties, as shown in the following theorems. It will be termed an **isotropic distribution.**

(1) *In an isotropic distribution the sign of the association is the same not only for every elementary tetrad of adjacent frequencies, but for every set of four frequencies in the compartments common to two rows and two columns, e.g.* (A_mB_n), $(A_{m+p}B_n)$, (A_mB_{n+q}), $(A_{m+p}B_{n+q})$.

For suppose that the sign of association in the elementary tetrads is positive, so that—

$$(A_mB_n)(A_{m+1}B_{n+1}) > (A_{m+1}B_n)(A_mB_{n+1}) \qquad . \qquad . \quad (1)$$

and similarly,

$$(A_{m+1}B_n)(A_{m+2}B_{n+1}) > (A_{m+2}B_n)(A_{m+1}B_{n+1}) \qquad . \quad (2)$$

Then multiplying up and cancelling we have

$$(A_mB_n)(A_{m+2}B_{n+1}) > (A_{m+2}B_n)(A_mB_{n+1}) \qquad . \qquad . \quad (3)$$

That is to say, the association is still positive though the two columns A_m and A_{m+2} are no longer adjacent.

(2) *An isotropic distribution remains isotropic in whatever way it may be condensed by grouping together adjacent rows or columns.*

Thus from (1) and (3) we have, adding—

$$(A_mB_n)[(A_{m+1}B_{n+1}) + (A_{m+2}B_{n+1})] > (A_mB_{n+1})[(A_{m+1}B_n) + (A_{m+2}B_n)],$$

that is to say, the sign of the elementary association is unaffected by throwing the $(m+1)$th and $(m+2)$th columns into one.

(3) As the extreme case of the preceding theorem, we may suppose both rows and columns grouped and regrouped until only a 2×2-fold table is left; we then have the theorem—

If an isotropic distribution be reduced to a fourfold distribution in any way whatever, by addition of adjacent rows and columns, the sign of the association in such fourfold table is the same as in the elementary tetrads of the original table.

The case of complete independence is a special case of isotropy. For if

$$(A_mB_n) = (A_m)(B_n)/N$$

for all values of m and n, the association is evidently zero for every tetrad. Therefore the distribution remains independent in whatever way the table be grouped, or in whatever way the universe be limited by the omission of rows or columns. The expression "complete independence" is therefore justified.

From the work of the preceding section we may say that Table II. is not isotropic as it stands, but may be regarded as a disarrangement of an isotropic distribution. It is best to rearrange such a table in isotropic order, as otherwise different reductions to fourfold form may lead to associations of different sign, though of course they need not necessarily do so.

12. The following will serve as an illustration of a table that is not isotropic, and cannot be rendered isotropic by any rearrangement of the order of rows and columns.

TABLE IV.—*Showing the Frequencies of Different Combinations of Eye-colours in Father and Son.*

(Data of Sir F. Galton, from Karl Pearson, *Phil. Trans.*, A, vol. cxcv. (1900), p. 138 ; classification condensed.)

1. Blue. 2. Blue-green, grey. 3. Dark grey, hazel. 4. Brown.

FATHER'S EYE-COLOUR.

Son's Eye-colour.	1.	2.	3.	4.	Total.
1	194	70	41	30	335
2	83	124	41	36	284
3	25	34	55	23	137
4	56	36	43	109	244
Total	358	264	180	198	1000

The following are the ratios of the frequency in column m to the sum of the frequencies in columns m and $m+1$:—

COLUMNS

1 and 2.	2 and 3.	3 and 4.
0·735	0·631	0·577
0·401	0·752	0·532
0·424	0·382	0·705
0·609	0·456	0·283

The order in which the ratios run is different for each pair of columns, and it is accordingly impossible to make the table isotropic. The distribution of signs of association in the several tetrads is—

+	−	+
−	+	−
−	−	+

The distribution is a curious one, the associations in tetrads round the diagonal of the whole table being so markedly positive and those in the immediately adjacent tetrads equally markedly negative. Neglecting the other signs, this is the effect that would be produced by taking an isotropic distribution and then increasing the frequencies in the diagonal compartments by a sufficient percentage. Comparison of the given table with others from the same source shows that the peculiarity is common to the great majority of the tables, and accordingly its origin demands explanation. Were such a table treated by the method of the contingency coefficient, or a similar summary method, alone, the peculiarity might not be remarked.

13. It may be noted, in concluding this part of the subject, that in the case of complete independence the distribution of frequency in every row is similar to the distribution in the row of totals, and the distribution in every column similar to that in the column of totals ; for in, say, the column A_n the frequencies are given by the relations —

$$(A_n B_1) = \frac{(A_n)}{N}(B_1), \ (A_n B_2) = \frac{(A_n)}{N}(B_2), \ (A_n B_3) = \frac{(A_n)}{N}(B)_3,$$

and so on. This property is of special importance in the theory of variables.

14. The classifications both of this and of the preceding chapters have one important characteristic in common, viz. that they are, so to speak, "homogeneous"—the principle of division being the same for all the sub-classes of any one class. Thus A's and a's are both subdivided into B's and β's, A_1's, A_2's . . . . A_s's into B_1's, B_2's . . . . B_t's, and so on. Clearly this is necessary in order to render possible those comparisons on which the discussions of associations and contingencies depend. If we only know that amongst the A's there is a certain percentage of B's, and amongst the a's a certain percentage of C's, there are no data for any conclusion.

Many classifications are, however, essentially of a heterogeneous character, e.g. biological classifications into orders, genera, and species; the classifications of the causes of death in vital statistics, and of occupations in the census. To take the last case as an illustration, the first "order" in the list of occupations is "General or Local Government of the Country," subdivided under the headings (1) National Government, (2) Local Government. The next order is "Defence of the Country," with the sub-headings (1) Army, (2) Navy and Marines—not (1) National and (2) Local Government again—the sub-heads are necessarily distinct. Similarly, the third order is "Professional Occupations and their Subordinate Services," with the fresh sub-heads (1) Clerical, (2) Legal, (3) Medical, (4) Teaching, (5) Literary and Scientific, (6) Engineers and Surveyors, (7) Art, Music, Drama, (8) Exhibitions, Games, etc. The number of sub-heads under each main heading is, in such a case, arbitrary and variable, and different for each main heading ; but so long as the classification remains purely heterogeneous, however complex it may become, there is no opportunity for any discussion of causation within the limits of the matter so derived. It is only when a homogeneous division is in some way introduced that we can begin to speak of associations and contingencies.

15. This may be done in various ways according to the nature of the case. Thus the relative frequencies of different botanical families, genera, or species may be discussed in connection with the topographical characters of their habitats— desert, marsh, or moor—and we may observe statistical associations between given genera and situations of a given topographical type. The causes of death may be classified according to sex, or age, or occupation, and it then becomes possible to discuss the association of a given cause of death with one or other of the two sexes, with a given age-group, or with a given occupation. Again, the classifications of deaths and of occupations are repeated at successive intervals of time; and if they have remained strictly the same, it is also possible to discuss the association of a given occupation or a given cause of death with the earlier or later year of observation—*i.e.* to see whether the numbers of those engaged in the given occupation or succumbing to the given cause of death have increased or decreased. But in such circumstances the greatest care must be taken to see that the necessary condition as to the identity of the classifications at the two periods is fulfilled, and unfortunately it very seldom is fulfilled. All practical schemes of classification are subject to alteration and improvement from time to time, and these alterations, however desirable in themselves, render a certain number of comparisons impossible. Even where a classification has remained verbally the same, it is not necessarily really the same; thus, in the case of the causes of death, improved methods of diagnosis may transfer many deaths from one heading to another without any change in the incidence of the disease, and so bring about a virtual change in the classification. In any case, heterogeneous classification should be regarded only as a partial process, incomplete until a homogeneous division is introduced either directly or indirectly, *e.g.* by repetition.

REFERENCES.

Contingency.

(1) PEARSON, KARL, "On the Theory of Contingency and its Relation to Association and Normal Correlation," *Drapers' Company Research Memoirs, Biometric Series* i. ; Dulau & Co., London, 1904. (The memoir in which the coefficient of contingency is proposed.)

(2) Lipps, G. F., "Die Bestimmung der Abhängigkeit zwischen den Merkmalen eines Gegenstandes," *Berichte der math.-phys. Klasse der kgl. Sächsischen Gesellschaft der Wissenschaften*; Leipzig, 1905. (A general discussion of the problems of association and contingency.)

(3) Pearson, Karl, "On a Coefficient of Class Heterogeneity or Divergence," *Biometrika*, vol. v. p. 198, 1906. (An application of the contingency coefficient to the measurement of heterogeneity, *e.g.* in different districts of a country, by treating the observed frequencies of some quality $A_1, A_2 \ldots \ldots A_n$ in the different districts as rows of a contingency table and working out the coefficient: the same principle is also applicable to the comparison of a single district with the rest of the country.)

Isotropy.

(4) Yule, G. U., "On a Property which holds good for all Groupings of a Normal Distribution of Frequency for Two Variables, with applications to the Study of Contingency Tables for the Inheritance of Unmeasured Qualities," *Proc. Roy. Soc.*, Series A, vol. lxxvii., 1906, p. 324. (On the property of isotropy and some applications.)

(5) Yule, G. U., "On the Influence of Bias and of Personal Equation in Statistics of Ill-defined Qualities," *Jour. Anthrop. Inst.*, vol. xxxvi., 1906, p. 325. (Includes an investigation as to the influence of bias and of personal equation in creating divergences from isotropy in contingency tables.)

Contingency Tables of two Rows only.

(6) Pearson, Karl, "On a New Method of Determining Correlation between a Measured Character A and a Character B of which only the Percentage of Cases wherein B exceeds (or falls short of) a given Intensity is recorded for each Grade of A," *Biometrika*, vol. vii., 1909, p. 96. (Deals with a measure of dependence for a common type of table, *e.g.* a table showing the numbers of candidates who passed or failed at an examination, for each year of age. The table of such a type stands between the contingency tables for unmeasured characters and the correlation table (chap. ix.) for variables. Pearson's method is based on that adopted for the correlation table, and assumes a normal distribution of frequency (chap. xv.) for B.)

(7) Pearson, Karl, "On a New Method of Determining Correlation, when one Variable is given by Alternative and the other by Multiple Categories," *Biometrika*, vol. vii., 1910, p. 248. (The similar problem for the case in which the variable is replaced by an unmeasured quality.)

EXERCISES.

(1) (Data from Karl Pearson, "On the Inheritance of the Mental and Moral Characters in Man." *Jour. of the Anthrop. Inst.*, vol. xxxiii., and *Biometrika*, vol. iii.) Find the coefficient of contingency (coefficient of mean square contingency) for the two tables below, showing the resemblance between brothers for athletic capacity and between sisters for temper. Show that neither table is even remotely isotropic. (As stated in § 7, the coefficient of contingency should not as a rule be used for tables smaller than 5 × 5-fold: these small tables are given to illustrate the method, while avoiding lengthy arithmetic.)

A. ATHLETIC CAPACITY.

First Brother.

		Athletic.	Betwixt.	Non-athletic.	Total.
	Athletic . . .	906	20	140	1066
Second Brother.	Betwixt . . .	20	76	9	105
	Non-athletic . . .	140	9	370	519
	Total .	1066	105	519	1690

B. TEMPER.

First Sister.

		Quick.	Good-natured.	Sullen.	Total.
	Quick . . .	198	177	77	452
Second Sister.	Good-natured . .	177	996	165	1338
	Sullen . . .	77	165	120	362
	Total .	452	1338	362	2152

PART II.—THE THEORY OF VARIABLES.

CHAPTER VI.

THE FREQUENCY-DISTRIBUTION.

1. THE methods described in Chaps. I.-V. are applicable to all observations, whether qualitative or quantitative ; we have now to proceed to the consideration of specialised processes, definitely adapted to the treatment of quantitative measurements, but not as a rule available (with some important exceptions, as suggested by Chap. I. § 2) for the discussion of purely qualitative observations. Since numerical measurement is applied only in the case of a quantity that can present more than one numerical value, that is, a varying quantity, or more shortly a variable, this section of the work may be termed the theory of variables. As common examples of such variables that are subject to statistical treatment may be cited birth- or death-rates, prices, wages, barometer readings, rainfall records, and measurements or enumerations (*e.g.* of glands, spines, or petals) on animals or plants.

2. If some hundreds or thousands of values of a variable have been noted merely in the arbitrary order in which they happened to occur, the mind cannot properly grasp the significance of the record : the observations must be ranked or classified in some way before the characteristics of the series can be comprehended, and those comparisons, on which arguments as to causation depend, can be made with other series. The dichotomous classi-

fication, considered in Chaps. I.–IV., is too crude : if the values are merely classified as A's or a's according as they exceed or fall short of some fixed value, a large part of the information given by the original record is lost. A manifold classification, however (*cf.* Chap. V.), avoids the crudity of the dichotomous form, since the classes may be made as numerous as we please, and numerical measurements lend themselves with peculiar readiness to a manifold classification, for the class limits can be conveniently and precisely defined by assigned values of the variable. For convenience, the values of the variable chosen to define the successive classes should be equidistant, so that the numbers of observations in the different classes (the class-frequencies) may be comparable. Thus for measurements of stature the interval chosen for classifying (the class-interval, as it may be termed) might be 1 inch, or 2 centimetres, the numbers of individuals being counted whose statures fall within each successive inch, or each successive 2 centimetres, of the scale ; returns of birth- or death-rates might be grouped to the nearest unit per thousand of the population ; returns of wages might be classified to the nearest shilling, or, if desired to obtain a more condensed table, by intervals of five shillings or ten shillings, and so on. When the variation is discontinuous, as for example in enumerations of numbers of children in families or of petals on flowers, the unit is naturally taken as the class-interval unless the range of variation is very great. The manner in which the observations are distributed over the successive equal intervals of the scale is spoken of as the frequency-distribution of the variable.

3. A few illustrations will make clearer the nature of such frequency-distributions, and the service which they render in summarising a long and complex record :—

(*a*) Table I. In this illustration the mean annual death-rates, expressed as proportions per thousand of the population per annum, of the 632 registration districts of England and Wales, for the decade 1881–90, have been classified to the nearest unit ; *i.e.* the numbers of districts have been counted in which the death-rate was over 12·5 but under 13·5, over 13·5 but under 14·5, and so on. The frequency-distribution is shown by the following table.

[TABLE I.

TABLE I.—*Showing the Numbers of Registration Districts in England and Wales with Different mean Death-rates per Thousand of the Population per Annum for the Ten Years 1881-90.* (Material from the *Supplement to the* 55*th Annual Report of the Registrar-General for England and Wales* [*C.*—7769] 1895.)

Mean Annual Death-rate.	Number of Districts with Death-rate between Limits stated.	Mean Annual Death-rate.	Number of Districts with Death-rate between Limits stated.
12·5–13·5	5	23·5–24·5	5
13·5–14·5	16	24·5–25·5	3
14·5–15·5	61	25·5–26·5	1
15·5–16·5	112	26·5–27·5	1
16·5–17·5	159	27·5–28·5	2
17·5–18·5	104	28·5–29·5	...
18·5–19·5	67	29·5–30·5	...
19·5–20·5	42	30·5–31·5	2
20·5–21·5	25	31·5–32·5	...·
21·5–22·5	18	32·5–33·5	1
22·5–23·5	8		
		Total	632

Whilst a glance through the original returns fails to convey any very definite impression, owing to the large and erratic differences between the death-rates in successive districts, a brief inspection of the above table brings out a number of important points. Thus we see that the death-rates range, in round numbers, from 13 to 33 per thousand per annum, but in the great majority of districts lie nearer the lower limit than the upper; that the death-rates in some 60 per cent. of the districts lie within the narrow limits 15·5 to 18·5, the rates being most frequent near 17 per thousand, and so forth.

(b) Table II. The ages at death, in years, of the married women in certain Quaker families were recorded and classified in 5-year groups according as they were over 17·5 but under 22·5, over 22·5 but under 27·5, and so on. The frequency-distribution was as follows:—

[TABLE II.

TABLE II.—*Showing the Numbers of Married Women, in certain Quaker Families, Dying at Different Ages.* (Cited from *Proc. Roy. Soc.*, vol. lxvii. (1900), p. 172. *On the Correlation between Duration of Life and Number of Offspring,* by Miss M. Beeton, Karl Pearson, and G. U. Yule.)

Age at Death, Years.	Number of Women Dying between said Years of Age.	Age at Death, Years.	Number of Women Dying between said Years of Age.
17·5–22·5	29	62·5– 67·5	73
22·5–27·5	87	67·5– 72·5	83
27·5–32·5	99	72·5– 77·5	77
32·5–37·5	109	77·5– 82·5	78
37·5–42·5	90	82·5– 87·5	59
42·5–47·5	87	87·5– 92·5	26
47·5–52·5	64	92·5– 97·5	7
52·5–57·5	54	97·5–102·5	4
57·5–62·5	69		
		Total	1095

The distribution is somewhat more irregular than in the last case; the commencement is abrupt; a maximum frequency is attained in the fourth class (age at death 32·5 to 37·5), and then there is a slow fall to the age-class 52·5–57·5. After this class the frequency rises again and attains a secondary maximum in the age-class 67·5–72·5.

(c) Table III. The numbers of stigmatic rays on a number of Shirley poppies were counted. As the range of variation is not great, the unit is taken as the class-interval. The frequency-distribution is given by the following table.

TABLE III.—*Showing the Frequencies of Seed Capsules on certain Shirley Poppies, with Different Numbers of Stigmatic Rays.* (Cited from *Biometrika,* ii. p. 89, 1902.)

Number of Stigmatic Rays.	Number of Capsules with said Number of Stigmatic Rays.	Number of Stigmatic Rays.	Number of Capsules with said Number of Stigmatic Rays.
6	3	14	302
7	11	15	234
8	38	16	128
9	106	17	50
10	152	18	19
11	238	19	3
12	305	20	1
13	315		
		Total	1905

The numbers of rays range from 6 to 20,—12, 13, or 14 rays being the most usual.

4. To expand slightly the brief description given in §.2, tables like the preceding are formed in the following way :—(1) The magnitude of the class-interval, *i.e.* the number of units to each interval, is first fixed ; one unit was chosen in the case of Tables I. and III., five units in the case of Table II. (2) The position or origin of the intervals must then be determined, *e.g.* in Table I. we must decide whether to take as intervals 12–13, 13–14, 14–15, etc., or 12·5–13·5, 13·5–14·5, 14·5–15·5, etc. (3) This choice having been made, the complete scale of intervals is fixed, and the observations are classified accordingly. (4) The process of classification being finished, a table is drawn up on the general lines of Tables I.–III., showing the total numbers of observations in each class-interval. Some remarks may be made on each of these heads.

5. *Magnitude of Class-Interval.*—As already remarked, in cases where the variation proceeds by discrete steps of considerable magnitude as compared with the range of variation, there is very little choice as regards the magnitude of the class-interval. The unit will in general have to serve. But if the variation be continuous, or at least take place by discrete steps which are small in comparison with the whole range of variation, there is no such natural class-interval, and its choice is a matter for judgment.

The two conditions which guide the choice are these : (*a*) we desire to be able to treat all the values assigned to any one class, without serious error, as if they were equal to the mid-value of the class-interval, *e.g.* as if the death-rate of every district in the first class of Table I. were exactly 13·0, the death-rate of every district in the second class 14·0, and so on ; (*b*) for convenience and brevity we desire to make the interval as large as possible, subject to the first condition. These conditions will generally be fulfilled if the interval be so chosen that the whole number of classes lies between 15 and 25. A number of classes less than, say, ten leads in general to very appreciable inaccuracy, and a number over, say, thirty makes a somewhat unwieldy table. A preliminary inspection of the record should accordingly be made and the highest and lowest values be picked out. Dividing the difference between these by, say, five and twenty, we have an approximate value for the interval. The actual value should be the nearest integer or simple fraction.

6. *Position of Intervals.*—The position or starting-point of the intervals is, as a rule, more or less indifferent, but in general it is fixed either so that the limits of intervals are integers, or, as in Tables I. and II., so that the mid-values are integers. It may,

however, be chosen, for simplicity in classification, so that no limit corresponds exactly to any recorded value (*cf.* § 8 below). In some exceptional cases, moreover, the observations exhibit a marked clustering round certain values, *e.g.* tens, or tens and fives. This is generally the case, for instance, in age returns, owing to the tendency to state a round number where the true age is unknown. Under such circumstances, the values round which there is a marked tendency to cluster should preferably be made mid-values of intervals, in order to avoid sensible error in the assumption that the mid-value is approximately representative of the values in the class. Thus, in the case of ages, since the clustering is chiefly round tens, " 25 and under 35," " 35 and under 45," etc., the classification of the English census, is a better grouping than " 20 and under 30," " 30 and under 40," and so on (*cf.* the *Census of England and Wales*, 1911, vol. vii., and also ref. 5, in which a different view is taken). When there is any probability of a clustering of this kind occurring, it is as well to subject the raw material to a close examination before finally fixing the classification.

7. *Classification.*—The scale of intervals having been fixed, the observations may be classified. If the number of observations is not large, it will be sufficient to mark the limits of successive intervals in a column down the left-hand side of a sheet of paper, and transfer the entries of the original record to this sheet by marking a 1 on the line corresponding to any class for each entry assigned thereto. It saves time in subsequent totalling if each fifth entry in a class is marked by a diagonal across the preceding four, or by leaving a space.

The disadvantage in this process is that it offers no facilities for checking : if a repetition of the classification leads to a different result, there is no means of tracing the error. If the number of observations is at all considerable and accuracy is essential, it is accordingly better to enter the values observed on cards, one to each observation. These are then dealt out into packs according to their classes, and the whole work checked by running through the pack corresponding to each class, and verifying that no cards have been wrongly sorted.

8. In some cases difficulties may arise in classifying, owing to the occurrence of observed values corresponding to class-limits. Thus, in compiling Table I., some districts will have been noted with death-rates entered in the Registrar-General's returns as 16·5, 17·5, or 18·5, any one of which might at first sight have been apparently assigned indifferently to either of two adjacent classes. In such a case, however, where the original figures for numbers of deaths and population are available, the difficulty may be readily surmounted by working out the rate to another place

of decimals: if the rate stated to be 16·50 proves to be 16·502, it will be sorted to the class 16·5–17·5; if 16·498, to the class 15·5–16·5. Death-rates that work out to half-units exactly do not occur in this example, and so there is no real difficulty. In the case of Table II., again, there is no difficulty : if the year of birth and death alone are given, the age at death is only calculable to the nearest unit; if the actual day of birth and death be cited, half-years still cannot occur in the age at death, because there is an odd number of days in the year. The difficulty may always be avoided if it be borne in mind in fixing the limits to class-intervals, these being carried to a further place of decimals, or a smaller fraction, than the values in the original record. Thus if statures are measured to the nearest centimetre, the class-intervals may be taken as 150·5–151·5, 151·5–152·5, etc. ; if to the nearest eighth of an inch, the intervals may be $59\frac{15}{16}$–$60\frac{15}{16}$, $60\frac{15}{16}$–$61\frac{15}{16}$, and so on.

If the difficulty is not evaded in any of these ways, it is usual to assign one-half of an intermediate observation to each adjacent class, with the result that half-units occur in the class-frequencies (cf. Tables VII., p. 90, X., p. 96, and XI., p. 96). The procedure is rough, but probably good enough for practical purposes ; it would be slightly better, but a good deal more laborious, to assign the intermediate observations to the adjacent classes in proportion to the numbers of other observations falling into the two classes.

9. *Tabulation.*—As regards the actual drafting of the final table, there is little to be said, except that care should be taken to express the class-limits clearly, and, if necessary, to state the manner in which the difficulty of intermediate values has been met or evaded. The class-limits are perhaps best given as in Tables I. and II., but may be more briefly indicated by the mid-values of the class-intervals. Thus Table I. might have been given in the form—

Death-rate per 1000 per annum to the Nearest Unit.	Number of Districts with said Death-rate.
13	5
14	16
15	61
16	112
etc.	etc.

A common mode of defining the class-intervals is to state the limits in the form "*x* and less than *y*." In the case of measurements of stature, for example, the table might run—

Stature in Inches.	Number of Observations.
57 and less than 58	2
58 ,, ,, 59	4
59 ,, ,, 60	14
etc.	etc.

—the statement "57 and less than 58," etc., being often abbreviated to 57–, 58–, 59–, etc. (cf. Table VI., p. 88). The mode of grouping is, in effect, that described in the last paragraph as of service in avoiding intermediate observations, but it should be noted that the form of statement leaves the class-limits uncertain unless the degree of accuracy of the measurements is also given. Thus, if measurements were taken to the nearest eighth of an inch, the class-limits are really $56\frac{15}{16}$–$57\frac{15}{16}$, $57\frac{15}{16}$–$58\frac{15}{16}$, etc. ; if they were only taken to the nearest quarter of an inch, the limits are $56\frac{7}{8}$–$57\frac{7}{8}$, $57\frac{7}{8}$–$58\frac{7}{8}$, etc. With such a form of tabulation a statement as to the number of significant figures in the original record is therefore essential. It is better, perhaps, to state the true class-limits and avoid ambiguity.

10. The rule that class-intervals should be all equal is one that is very frequently broken in official statistical publications, principally in order to condense an otherwise unwieldy table, thus not only saving space in printing but also considerable expense in compilation, or possibly, in the case of confidential figures, to avoid giving a class which would contain only one or two observations, the identity of which might be guessed. It would hardly be legitimate, for example, to give a return of incomes relating to a limited district in such a form that the income of the two or three wealthiest men in the district would be clear to any intelligent reader with local knowledge. If the intervals be made unequal, the application of many statistical methods is rendered awkward, or even impossible, and the relative values of the frequencies are at first sight misleading, so that the table is not perspicuous. Thus, consider the first two columns of Table IV., showing the numbers of dwelling-houses of different annual values, assessed to inhabited house duty. On running the eye down the column headed "number of houses" it is at once caught by the two striking irregularities at the classes "£60 and under £80," and "£100 and under £150." But these have no real significance; they are merely due to changes from a £10 to a £20, and then to a £50 interval. Moreover, the intervals after £150 go on continuously increasing, but attention is not directed thereto by any marked changes in the frequencies. To make the latter really comparable *inter se*, they must first be

TABLE IV.—*Showing the Annual Value and Number of Dwelling-houses in Great Britain assessed to Inhabited House Duty in* 1885–6. (Cited from *Jour. Roy. Stat. Soc.*, vol. L., 1887, p. 610.)

Annual Value in £'s.			Number of Houses.	Frequency per £10 Interval.
£20 and under		£30	306,408	306,408
30	,,	40	182,972	182.972
40	,,	50	105,407	105,407
50	,,	60	63,096	63,096
60	,,	80	71,436	35,718
80	,,	100	32,365	16,182
100	,,	150	41,336	8,267
150	,,	300	26,732	1,782
300	,,	500	6,198	310
500	,,	1000	2,098	42
1000 and upwards			644	?
Total number of houses			838,692	—

reduced to a common interval as basis, *e.g.* £10, by dividing the fifth and sixth numbers by 2, the seventh by 5, the eighth by 15, and so on. This gives the mean frequencies per £10 interval tabulated in the third column of Table IV. The reduction is, however, impossible in the case of the last class, for we are only told the number of houses of £1000 annual value and upwards: the magnitude of the class is indefinite. Such an indefinite class is in many respects a great inconvenience, and should always be avoided in work not subject to the necessary limitations of official publications.

The general rule that intervals should be equal must not be held to bar the analysis by smaller equal intervals of some portion of the range over which the frequency varies very rapidly. In Table XII., p. 98, for example, giving the numbers of deaths from diphtheria at successive ages, a five-year interval might be substituted with advantage for the irregular intervals after the fifth year of age, but it would still be desirable to give the numbers of deaths in each year for the first five years, so as to bring out the rapid rise to the maximum in the fourth year of life.

11. When the table has been completed, it is often convenient to represent the frequency-distribution by means of a diagram which conveys the general run of the observations to the eye better than a column of figures. The following short table,

giving the distribution of head-breadths for 1000 men, will serve as an example.

Table V.—*Showing the Frequency-distribution of Head-breadths for Students at Cambridge. Measurements taken to the nearest tenth of an inch.* (Cited from W. R. Macdonell, *Biometrika*, i., 1902, p. 220.)

Head-breadth in Inches.	Number of Men with said Head-breadth.	Head-breadth in Inches.	Number of Men with said Head-breadth.
5·5	3	6·3	99
5·6	12	6·4	37
5·7	43	6·5	15
5·8	80	6·6	12
5·9	131	6·7	3
6·0	236	6·8	2
6·1	185		
6·2	142	Total	1000

Taking a piece of squared paper ruled, say, in inches and tenths, mark off along a horizontal base-line a scale representing class-intervals; a half-inch to the class-interval would be suitable. Then choose a vertical scale for the class-frequencies, say 50 observations per interval to the inch, and mark off, on the verticals or *ordinates* through the points marked 5·5, 5·6, 5·7 . . . . at the centres of the class-intervals on the base-line, heights representing on this scale the class-frequencies 3, 12, 43. . . . The diagram may then be completed in one of two ways: (1) as a **frequency-polygon**, by joining up the marks on the verticals by straight lines, the last points at each end being joined down to the base at the centre of the next class-interval (fig. 1); or (2) as a column diagram or **histogram** (to use a term suggested by Professor Pearson, ref. 1), short horizontals being drawn through the marks on the verticals (fig. 2), which now form the central axes of a series of rectangles representing the class-frequencies. The student should note that in any such diagram, of either form, a certain *area* represents a given number of observations. On the scales suggested, 1 inch on the horizontal represents 2 intervals, and 1 inch on the vertical represents 50 observations per interval: 1 square inch therefore represents $50 \times 2 = 100$ observations. The diagrams are, however, conventional: the whole area of the figure is correct in either case, but the area over each interval is not correct in the case of the frequency-polygon, and the frequency of each fraction of any

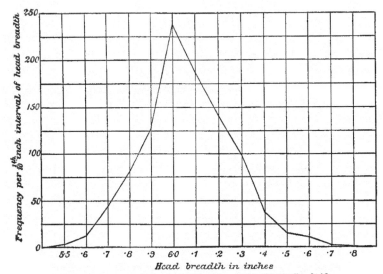

Fig. 1.—Frequency-Polygon for Head-breadths of 1000 Cambridge Students. (Table V.)

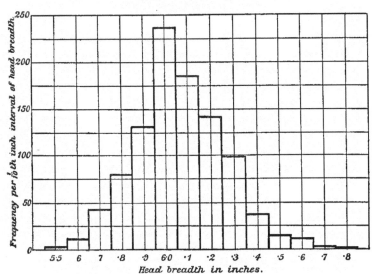

Fig. 2.—Histogram for the same data as Fig. 1.

interval is not the same, as suggested by the histogram. The area shown by the frequency-polygon over any interval with an ordinate y_2 (fig. 3) is only correct if the tops of the three

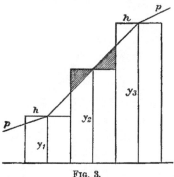

FIG. 3.

successive ordinates y_1, y_2, y_3 lie on a line, *i.e.* if $y_2 = \frac{1}{2}(y_1 + y_3)$, the areas of the two little triangles shaded in the figure being equal. If y_2 fall short of this value, the area shown by the

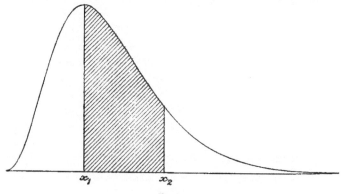

FIG. 4.

polygon is too great; if y_2 exceed it, the area shown by the polygon is too small; and if, for this reason, the frequency-polygon tends to become very misleading at any part of the range, it is better to use the histogram. In the mortality distribution of Table I., for instance, the frequency rises so sharply

to the maximum that a histogram is, on the whole, the better representation of the distribution of frequency, and in such a
distribution as that of Table IV. the use of the histogram is
almost imperative.

12. If the class-interval be made smaller and smaller, and at
the same time the number of observations be proportionately increased, so that the class-frequencies may remain finite, the
polygon and the histogram will approach more and more closely
to a smooth curve. Such an ideal limit to the frequency-polygon
or histogram is termed a frequency-curve. In this ideal frequency-
curve the area between any two ordinates whatever is strictly
proportional to the number of observations falling between the
corresponding values of the variable. Thus the number of
observations falling between the values x_1 and x_2 of the variable
in fig. 4 will be proportional to the area of the shaded strip in the
figure; the number of observed values greater than x_2 will
similarly be given by the area of the curve to the right of the
ordinate through x_2, and so on. When, in any actual case, the
number of observations is considerable—say a thousand at least
—the run of the class-frequencies is generally sufficiently
smooth to give a good notion of the form of the ideal distribution; with small numbers the frequencies may present all
kinds of irregularities, which, most probably, have very little
significance (cf. Chap. XV. § 15, and § 18, Ex. iv.). The forms
presented by smoothly running sets of numerous observations
present an almost endless variety, but amongst these we notice
a small number of comparatively simple types, from which many
at least of the more complex distributions may be conceived as
compounded. For elementary purposes it is sufficient to consider
these fundamental simple types as four in number, the symmetrical distribution, the moderately asymmetrical distribution, the
extremely asymmetrical or J-shaped distribution, and the U-shaped
distribution.

13. *The symmetrical distribution*, the class-frequencies decreasing to zero symmetrically on either side of a central maximum.
Fig. 5 illustrates the ideal form of the distribution.

Being a special case of the more general type described under
the second heading, this form of distribution is comparatively rare
under any circumstances, and very exceptional indeed in economic
statistics. It occurs more frequently in the case of biometric, more
especially anthropometric, measurements, from which the following
illustrations are drawn, and is important in much theoretical work.
Table VI. shows the frequency-distribution of statures for adult
males in the British Isles, from data published by a British
Association Committee in 1883, the figures being given separately

TABLE VI.—*Showing the Frequency-distributions of Statures for Adult Males born in England, Ireland, Scotland, and Wales. Final Report of the Anthropometric Committee to the British Association.* (*Report*, 1883, p. 256.) *As Measurements are stated to have been taken to the nearest* $\frac{1}{8}$th *of an Inch, the Class-Intervals are here presumably* $56\frac{15}{16}$–$57\frac{15}{16}$, $57\frac{15}{16}$–$58\frac{15}{16}$, *and so on* (*cf.* § 9). See Fig. 6.

Height without shoes, Inches.	Number of Men within said Limits of Height. Place of Birth—				Total.
	England.	Scotland.	Wales.	Ireland.	
57–	1	—	1	—	2
58–	3	1	—	—	4
59–	12	—	1	1	14
60–	39	2	—	—	41
61–	70	2	9	2	83
62–	128	9	30	2	169
63–	320	19	48	7	394
64–	524	47	83	15	669
65–	740	109	108	33	990
66–	881	139	145	58	1223
67–	918	210	128	73	1329
68–	886	210	72	62	1230
69–	753	218	52	40	1063
70–	473	115	33	25	646
71–	254	102	21	15	392
72–	117	69	6	10	202
73–	48	26	2	3	79
74–	16	15	1	—	32
75–	9	6	1	—	16
76–	1	4	—	—	5
77–	1	1	—	—	2
Total	6194	1304	741	346	8585

for persons born in England, Scotland, Wales, and Ireland, and totalled in the last column. These frequency-distributions are approximately of the symmetrical type. The frequency-polygon for the totals given by the last column of the table is shown in fig. 6. The student will notice that an error of $\frac{1}{16}$ inch, scarcely appreciable in the diagram on its reduced scale, is neglected in the scale shown on the base-line, the intervals being treated as if they were 57–58, 58–59, etc. Diagrams should be drawn for comparison showing, to a good open scale, the separate distributions for England, Scotland, Wales, and Ireland.

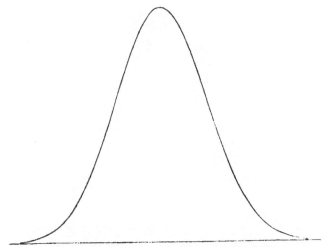

FIG. 5.—An ideal symmetrical Frequency-distribution.

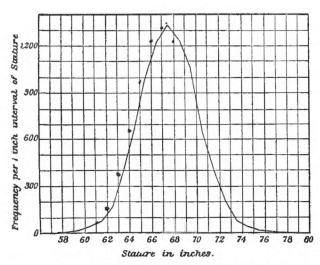

FIG. 6.—Frequency-distribution of Stature for 8585 Adult Males born in
the British Isles. (Table VI.)

Table VII. gives two similar distributions from more recent investigations, relating respectively to sons over 18 years of age, with parents living, in Great Britain, and to students at Cambridge. The polygons are shown in figs. 7 and 8. Both these distributions are more irregular than that of fig. 6, but, roughly speaking, they may all be held to be approximately symmetrical.

14. *The moderately asymmetrical distribution*, the class-frequencies decreasing with markedly greater rapidity on one side of the maximum than on the other, as in fig. 9 (a) or (b). This is the most common of all smooth forms of frequency-distribution, illustrations occurring in statistics from almost every source. The distribution of death-rates in the registration districts of England

TABLE VII.—*Showing the Frequency-distribution of Statures for* (1) 1078 *English Sons* (Karl Pearson, *Biometrika*, ii., 1903, p. 415) ; (2) *for* 1000 *Male Students at Cambridge* (W. R. Macdonell, *Biometrika*, i., 1902, p. 220). See Figs. 7 and 8.

Stature in Inches.	Number of Men within said Limits of Stature.	
	(1) English Sons.	(2) Cambridge Students.
59·5–60·5	2·0	—
60·5–61·5	1·5	—
61·5–62·5	3·5	4·0
62·5–63·5	20·5	19·0
63·5–64·5	38·5	24·5
64·5–65·5	61·5	40·5
65·5–66·5	89·5	84·5
66·5–67·5	148·0	123·5
67·5–68·5	173·5	139·0
68·5–69·5	149·5	179·0
69·5–70·5	128·0	138·5
70·5–71·5	108·0	108·0
71·5–72·5	63·0	53·5
72·5–73·5	42·0	47·5
73·5–74·5	29·0	21·0
74·5–75·5	8·5	12·0
75·5–76·5	4·0	5·0
76·5–77·5	4·0	0·5
77·5–78·5	3·0	—
78·5–79·5	0·5	—
Total	1078	1000

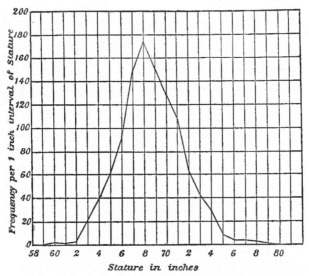

Fig. 7.—Frequency-distribution of Stature for 1078 " English Sons."
(Table VII.)

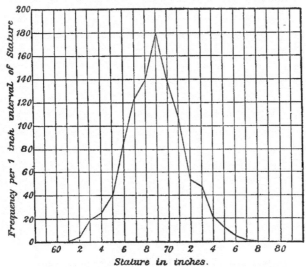

Fig. 8.—Frequency-distribution of Stature for 1000 Cambridge
Students. (Table VII.)

and Wales, given in Table I., p. 77, is a somewhat rough example of the type. The distribution of rates of pauperism in the same

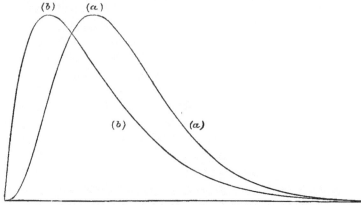

Fig 9.—Ideal distributions of the moderately asymmetrical form.

districts (Table VIII. and fig. 10) is smoother and more like the type (a) of fig 9. The frequency attains a maximum for

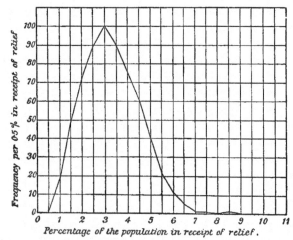

Fig. 10.—Frequency-distribution of Pauperism (Percentage of the Population in Receipt of Poor-law Relief) on 1st January 1891 in the Registration Districts of England and Wales: 632 Districts. (Table VIII.)

districts with $2\frac{3}{4}$ to $3\frac{1}{4}$ per cent. of the population in receipt of relief, and then tails off slowly to unions with 6, 7, and 8 per cent. of pauperism.

TABLE VIII.—*Showing the Number of Registration Districts in England and Wales with Different Percentages of the Population in receipt of Poor-law Relief on the 1st January* 1891. (Yule, *Jour. Roy. Stat. Soc.*, vol. lix., 1896, p. 347, *q.v.* for distributions for earlier years.) See Fig. 10.

Percentage of the Population in receipt of Relief.	Number of Unions with given Percentage in receipt of Relief.
0·75–1·25	18
1·25–1·75	48
1·75–2·25	72
2·25–2·75	89
2·75–3·25	100
3·25–3·75	90
3·75–4·25	75
4·25–4·75	60
4·75–5·25	40
5·25–5 75	21
5·75–6·25	11
6·25–6·75	5
6·75–7·25	1
7·25–7·75	1
7·75–8·25	0
8·25–8·75	1
Total	632

While the distribution of stature is in general symmetrical, that of weight is asymmetrical or *skew*, the greater frequencies lying towards the lower end of the range. This is shown very well by the data (Table IX. and fig. 11) collected by the same British Association Committee, from the Report of which the data as to stature were cited in the last section. As in the case of the stature diagram (fig. 6), the small error of $\frac{1}{2}$ lb. has been neglected, for the sake of brevity, in lettering the base-line of fig. 11, the classes being treated as if they were 90 lb.–100 lb., 100 lb.–110 lb., and so on.

Table X. and fig. 12 give a biological illustration, viz. the distribution of fecundity (ratio of yearling foals produced to coverings) in mares. The student should notice the difficulty

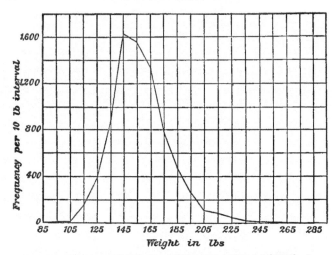

FIG. 11.—Frequeucy-distribution of Weight for 7749 Adult Males in
the British Isles. (Table IX.)

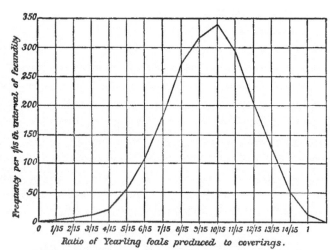

FIG. 12.—Frequency-distribution of Fecundity for Brood-mares :
2000 observations. (Table X.)

TABLE IX. —*Showing the Frequency-distribution of Weights for Adult Males born in England, Ireland, Scotland, and Wales.* (*Loc. cit., Table VI.*) *Weights were taken to the nearest pound, consequently the true Class-Intervals are* 89·5–99·5, 99·5–109·5, *etc.* (§ 9).

Weight in lbs.	Number of Men within given Limits of Weight. Place of Birth—				Total.
	England.	Scotland.	Wales.	Ireland.	
90–	2	—	—	—	2
100–	26	1	2	5	34
110–	133	8	10	1	152
120–	338	22	23	7	390
130–	694	63	68	42	867
140–	1240	173	153	57	1623
150–	1075	255	178	51	1559
160–	881	275	134	36	1326
170–	492	168	102	25	787
180–	304	125	34	13	476
190–	174	67	14	8	263
200–	75	24	7	1	107
210–	62	14	8	1	85
220–	33	7	1	—	41
230–	10	4	2	—	16
240–	9	2	—	—	11
250–	3	4	1	—	8
260–	1	—	—	—	1
270–	—	—	—	—	—
280–	—	—	1	—	1
Total	5552	1212	738	247	7749

of classification in this case : the class-interval chosen throughout the middle of the range is 1/15th, but the last interval is " 29/30–1." This is not a whole interval, but it is more than a half, for all the cases of complete fecundity are reckoned into the class. In the diagram (fig. 12) it has been reckoned as a whole class, and this gives a smooth distribution.

To take an illustration from meteorology, the distribution of barometer heights at any one station over a period of time is, in general, asymmetrical, the most frequent heights lying towards the upper end of the range for stations in England and Wales. Table XI. and fig. 13 show the distribution for daily observations at Southampton during the years 1878–90 inclusive.

The distributions of Tables VIII.–XI. all follow more or less the type of fig. 9 (*a*), the frequency tailing off, at the steeper end of

TABLE X.—*Showing the Frequency-distribution of Fecundity*, i.e. *the Ratio of the Number of Yearling Foals produced to the Number of Coverings, for Brood-mares (Race-horses) Covered Eight Times at Least.* (Pearson, Lee, and Moore, *Phil. Trans.*, A, vol. cxcii. (1899), p. 303.) See Fig. 12.

Fecundity.	Number of Mares with Fecundity between the Given Limits.	Fecundity.	Number of Mares with Fecundity between the Given Limits.
1/30– 3/30	2	17/30–19/30	315
3/30– 5/30	7·5	19/30–21/30	337
5/30– 7/30	11·5	21/30–23/30	293·5
7/30– 9/30	21·5	23/30–25/30	204
9/30–11/30	55	25/30–27/30	127
11/30–13/30	104·5	27/30–29/30	49
13/30–15/30	182	29/30–1	19
15/30–17/30	271·5		
		Total	2000·0

TABLE XI. — *Showing the Frequency-distribution of Barometer Heights for Daily Observations during the Thirteen Years* 1878–1890 *at Southampton.* (Karl Pearson and A. Lee, *Phil. Trans.*, A, vol. cxc. (1897), p. 428, *q.v.* for numerous other distributions.) See Fig. 13.

Height of Barometer in Inches.	Number of Days on which Height was observed between the Given Limits.	Height of Barometer in Inches.	Number of Days on which Height was observed between the Given Limits.
28·45–28·55	1	29·85– ·95	548·5
·55– ·65	2	·95–30·05	602·5
·65– ·75	2	30·05– ·15	619·5
·75– ·85	4	·15– ·25	500
·85– ·95	8·5	·25– ·35	382
·95–29·05	13·5	·35– ·45	237·5
29·05– ·15	21·5	·45– ·55	189·5
·15– ·25	37	·55– ·65	88·5
·25– ·35	79	·65– ·75	43·5
·35– ·45	108	·75– ·85	7
·45– ·55	181·5	·85– ·95	4
·55– ·65	254·5	30·95–31·05	1
·65– ·75	348·5		
·75– ·85	463·5	Total	4748

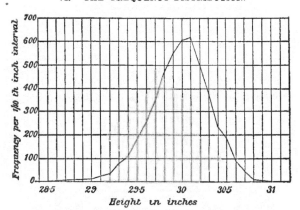

FIG. 13.—Frequency-distribution of Barometer Heights at
Southampton : 4748 observations.   (Table XI.)

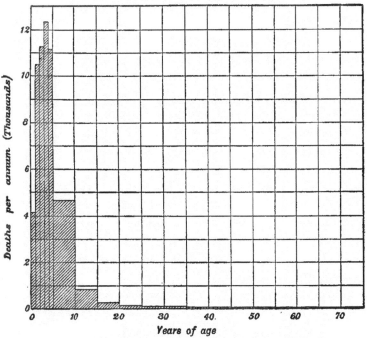

FIG. 14.—Frequency-distribution of Deaths from Diphtheria at different Ages
in England and Wales, 1891–1900.   (Table XII.)

7

the distribution, in such a way as to suggest that the ideal curve is tangential to the base. Cases of greater asymmetry, suggesting an ideal curve that meets the base (at one end) at a finite angle, even a right angle, as in fig. 9 (b), are less frequent, but occur occasionally. The distribution of deaths from diphtheria, according to age, affords one such example of a more asymmetrical kind. The actual figures for this case are given in Table XII., and illustrated by fig. 14; and it will be seen that the frequency of deaths reaches a maximum for children aged "3 and under 4," the number rising very rapidly to the maximum, and thence falling so slowly that there is still an appreciable frequency for persons over 60 or 70 years of age.

TABLE XII.—*Showing the Numbers of Deaths from Diphtheria at Different Ages in England and Wales during the Ten Years 1891-1900. (Supplement to 65th Annual Report of the Registrar-General, 1891-1900, p. 3.) See Fig. 14.*

Age in Years.	Number of Deaths between Given Limits of Age.	Number per Annum.
Under 1 year	4,186	4,186
1–	10,491	10,491
2–	11,218	11,218
3–	12,390	12,390
4–	11,194	11,194
5–	23,348	4,670
10–	4,092	818
15–	1,123	225
20–	585	117
25–	786	79
35–	512	51
45–	324	32
55–	260	26
65–	127	13
75 and upwards	35	?
Total	80,671	—

15. *The extremely asymmetrical, or "J-shaped," distribution*, the class-frequencies running up to a maximum at one end of the range, as in fig. 15.

This may be regarded as the extreme form of the last distribution, from which it cannot always be distinguished by elementary methods if the original data are not available. If, for instance, the frequencies of Table XII. had been given by five-year intervals only, they would have run 49,479, 23,348, 4,092, and so on, thus suggesting a maximum number of deaths at the beginning of life, *i.e.* a distribution of the present type. It is only the analysis of the deaths in the earlier years of life by one-year intervals which shows that the frequency reaches a true maximum in the fourth year, and therefore the distribution is of the moderately asymmetrical type. In practical cases no hard and

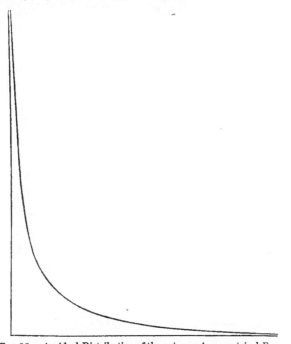

FIG. 15.—An ideal Distribution of the extreme Asymmetrical Form.

fast line can always be drawn between the moderately and extremely asymmetrical types, any more than between the moderately asymmetrical and the symmetrical type.

In economic statistics this form of distribution is particularly characteristic of the distribution of wealth in the population at large, as illustrated, *e.g.*, by income tax and house valuation returns, by returns of the size of agricultural holdings, and so on (*cf.* ref. 4). The distributions may possibly be a very extreme case of the last type ; but if the maximum is not absolutely at the lower end of the range, it is very close indeed thereto. Official returns do not usually give the necessary analysis of the frequencies at the lower end of the range to enable the exact position of the maximum to be determined; and for this reason the data on which Table XIII. is founded, though of course very unreliable, are of some interest. It will be seen from the table and fig. 16 that with the given classification the distribution appears clearly assignable to the present type, the number of estates between zero and £100 in annual value being more than six times as great as the number between £100 and £200 in annual value, and the frequency continuously falling as the value increases. A close analysis of the first class suggests, however, that the greatest frequency does not occur actually at zero, but that there is a true maximum frequency for estates of about £1 15 0 in annual value. The distribution might therefore be more correctly assigned to the second type, but the position of the greatest frequency indicates a

TABLE XIII.—*Showing the Numbers and Annual Values of the Estates of those who had taken part in the Jacobite Rising of* 1715. (Compiled from Cosin's *Names of the Roman Catholics, Nonjurors, and others who refused to take the Oaths to his late Majesty King George, etc.* ; London, 1745. Figures of very doubtful absolute value. See a note in Southey's *Commonplace Book*, vol. i. p. 573, quoted from the Memoirs of T. Hollis.) See Fig. 16.

Annual Value in £100.	Number of Estates.	Annual Value in £100.	Number of Estates.
0– 1	1726·5	17–18	1
1– 2	280	—	—
2– 3	140·5	20–21	4
3– 4	87	21–22	1
4– 5	46·5	22–23	1
5– 6	42·5	23–24	1
6– 7	29·5	—	—
7– 8	25·5	27–28	2
8– 9	18·5	—	—
9–10	21	31–32	1
10–11	11·5	—	—
11–12	9·5	39–40	1
12–13	4	—	—
13–14	3·5	45–46	1
14–15	8	—	—
15–16	3	48–49	1
16–17	5	Total	2476

degree of asymmetry that is high even compared with the asymmetry of fig. 14 : the distribution of numbers of deaths from

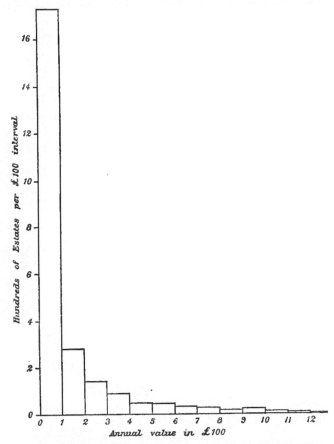

FIG. 16.—Frequency-distribution of the Annual Values of certain Estates in England in 1715 : 2476 Estates. (Table XIII.)

diphtheria would more closely resemble the distribution of estate-values if the maximum occurred in the fourth and fifth weeks of life instead of in the fourth year. The figures of Table IV., p. 83, showing the annual value and number of dwelling-houses, afford a good illustration of this form of distribution, but marred by the unequal intervals so common in official returns.

TABLE XIV.—*Showing the Frequencies of Different Numbers of Petals for Three Series of* Ranunculus bulbosus. (H. de Vries, *Ber. dtsch. bot. Ges.*, Bd. xii., 1894, *q.v.* for details.) See Fig. 17.

Number of Petals.	Frequency.		
	Series A.	Series B.	Series C.
5	312	345	133
6	17	24	55
7	4	7	23
8	2	—	7
9	2	2	2
10	—	—	2
11	—	2	—
Total	337	380	222

The type is not very frequent in other classes of material, but instances occur here and there. Table XIV. and fig. 17 show

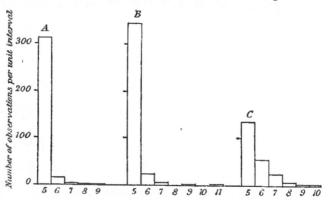

Fig. 17.—Frequency-distributions of Numbers of Petals for Three Series of *Ranunculus bulbosus*: A 337, B 380, C 222 observations. (Table XIV.)

distributions of this form for the petals of the buttercup, *Ranunculus bulbosus*.

16. *The U-shaped distribution*, exhibiting a maximum frequency

at the ends of the range and a minimum towards the centre.
The ideal form of the distribution is illustrated by fig. 18.

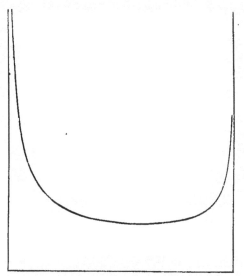

Fig. 18.—An ideal Distribution of the U-shaped Form.

This is a rare but interesting form of distribution, as it stands
in somewhat marked contrast to the preceding forms.   Table XV.
and fig. 19 illustrate an example based on a considerable number
of observations, viz. the distribution of degrees of cloudiness, or
estimated percentage of the sky covered by cloud, at Breslau

TABLE XV.—*Showing the Frequencies of Estimated Intensities of Cloudiness
at Breslau during the Ten Years* 1876-85.   (See ref. 2.)   See Fig. 19.

Cloudiness.	Frequency.	Cloudiness.	Frequency.
0	751	6	21
1	179	7	71
2	107	8	194
3	69	9	117
4	46	10	2089
5	9		
		Total	3653

during the years 1876–85. A sky completely, or almost completely, overcast at the time of observation is the most common, a practically clear sky comes next, and intermediates are more rare.

This form of distribution appears to be sometimes exhibited by the percentages of offspring possessing a certain attribute when one at least of the parents also possesses the attribute. The remarks

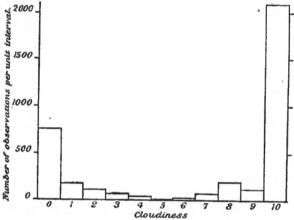

Fig. 19.—Frequeney-distribution of Degrees of Cloudiness at Breslau 1876–85 : 3653 observations. (Table XV.)

of Sir Francis Galton in *Natural Inheritance* suggest such a form for the distribution of "consumptivity" amongst the offspring of consumptives, but the figures are not in a decisive shape. Table XVI. gives the distribution for an analogous case, viz. the

TABLE XVI.—*Showing the Percentages of Deaf-mutes among Children of Parents one of whom at least was a Deaf-mute, for Marriages producing Five Children or more.* (Compiled from material in *Marriages of the Deaf in America*, ed. E. A. Fay, Volta Bureau, Washington, 1898.)

Percentage of Deaf-mutes.	Number of Families.	Percentage of Deaf-mutes.	Number of Families.
0–20	220	60–80	5·5
20–40	20·5	80–100	15
40–60	12		
		Total	273

distribution of deaf-mutism amongst the offspring of parents one of whom at least was a deaf-mute. In general less than one-fifth of the children are deaf-mutes : at the other end of the range the cases in which over 80 per cent. of the children are deaf-mutes are nearly three times as many as those in which the percentage lies between 60 and 80. The numbers are, however, too small to form a very satisfactory illustration.

REFERENCES.

(1) PEARSON, KARL, "Skew Variation in Homogeneous Material," *Phil. Trans. Roy. Soc.*, Series A, vol. clxxxvi. (1895), pp. 343–414.

(2) PEARSON, KARL, "Cloudiness: Note on a Novel Case of Frequency," *Proc. Roy. Soc.*, vol. lxii. (1897), p. 287.

(3) PEARSON, KARL, "Supplement to a Memoir on Skew Variation," *Phil. Trans. Roy. Soc.*, Series A, vol. cxcvii. (1901), pp. 443–459.

(4) PARETO, VILFREDO, *Cours d'économie politique*; 2 vols., Lausanne, 1896–7. See especially tome ii., livre iii., chap. i., "La courbe des revenus."

The first three memoirs above are mathematical memoirs on the theory of ideal frequency-curves, the first being the fundamental memoir, and the second and third supplementary. The elementary student may, however, refer to them with advantage, on account of the large collection of frequency-distributions which is given, and from which some of the illustrations in the preceding chapter have been cited. Without attempting to follow the mathematics, he may also note that each of our rough empirical types may be divided into several sub-types, the theoretical division into types being made on different grounds.

The fourth work is cited on account of the author's discussion of the distribution of wealth in a community, to which reference was made in § 15.

In connection with the remarks in § 6, on the grouping of ages, reference may be made to the following in which a different conclusion is drawn as to the best grouping :—

(5) YOUNG, ALLYN A., "A Discussion of Age Statistics," *Census Bulletin 13*, Bureau of the Census, Washington, U.S.A., 1904.

Reference should also be made to the *Census of England and Wales*, 1911, vol. vii., "Ages and Condition as to Marriage," especially the Report by Mr George King on the graduation of ages.

EXERCISES.

1. If the diagram fig. 6 is redrawn to scales of 300 observations per interval to the inch and 4 inches of stature to the inch, what is the scale of observations to the square inch ?

If the scales are 100 observations per interval to the centimetre and 2 inches of stature to the centimetre, what is the scale of observations to the square centimetre ?

2. If fig. 10 is redrawn to scales of 25 observations per interval to the inch and 2 per cent. to the inch, what is the scale of observations to the square inch ?

If the scales are ten observations per interval to the centimetre and 1 per cent. to the centimetre, what is the scale of observations to the square centimetre ?

3. If a frequency-polygon be drawn to represent the data of Table I., what number of observations will the polygon show between death-rates of 16·5 and 17·5 per thousand, instead of the true number 159 ?

4. If a frequency-polygon be drawn to represent the data of Table V., what number of observations will the polygon show between head-breadths 5·95 and 6·05, instead of the true number 236 ?

CHAPTER VII.

AVERAGES.

1. In § 2 of the last chapter it was pointed out that a classification of the observations in any long series is the first step necessary to make the observations comprehensible, and to render possible those comparisons with other series which are essential for any discussion of causation. Very little experience, however, would show that classification alone is not an adequate method, seeing that it only enables qualitative or verbal comparisons to be made. The next step that it is desirable to take is the quantitative definition of the characters of the frequency-distribution, so that quantitative comparisons may be made between the corresponding characters of two or more series. It might seem at first sight that very difficult cases of comparison could arise in which, for example, we had to contrast a symmetrical distribution with a "J-shaped" distribution. As a matter of practice, however, we seldom have to deal with such a case; distributions drawn from similar material are, in general, of similar form. When we have to compare the frequency-distributions of stature in two races of man, of the death-rates in English registration districts in two successive decades, of the numbers of petals in two races of the same species of *Ranunculus*, we have only to compare with each other two distributions of the same or nearly the same type.

2. Confining our attention, then, to this simple case, there are two fundamental characteristics in which such distributions may

differ : (1) they may differ markedly in position, *i.e.* in the values of the variable round which they centre, as in fig. 20, *A*, or (2) they may centre round the same value, but differ in the range of variation or *dispersion*, as it is termed, as in fig. 20, *B*. Of course the distributions may differ in both characters at once, as in fig 20, *C*, but the two properties may be considered independently. Measures of the first character, *position*, are generally known as averages ; measures of the second are termed measures of dispersion. In addition to these two principal and fundamental characters, we may also take a third of some interest but of much less importance, viz. the degree of asymmetry of the distribution.

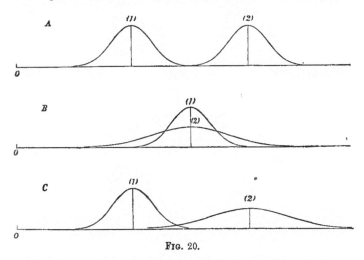

Fig. 20.

The present chapter deals only with averages; measures of dispersion are considered in Chapter VIII. and measures of asymmetry are also briefly discussed at the end of that chapter.

3. In whatever way an average is defined, it may be as well to note, it is merely a certain value of the variable, and is therefore necessarily of the same *dimensions* as the variable : *i.e.* if the variable be a length, its average is a length ; if the variable be a percentage, its average is a percentage, and so on. But there are several different ways of approximately defining the position of a frequency-distribution, that is, there are several different forms of average, and the question therefore arises, By what criteria are we to judge the relative merits of different forms ? What are, in fact, the desirable properties for an average to possess ?

4. (a) In the first place, it almost goes without saying that an average should be rigidly defined, and not left to the mere estimation of the observer. An average that was merely estimated would depend too largely on the observer as well as the data. (b) An average should be based on all the observations made. If not, it is not really a characteristic of the whole distribution. (c) It is desirable that the average should possess some simple and obvious properties to render its general nature readily comprehensible : an average should not be of too abstract a mathematical character. (d) It is, of course, desirable that an average should be calculated with reasonable ease and rapidity. Other things being equal, the easier calculated is the better of two forms of average. At the same time too great weight must not be attached to mere ease of calculation, to the neglect of other factors. (e) It is desirable that the average should be as little affected as may be possible by what we have termed *fluctuations of sampling*. If different samples be drawn from the same material, however carefully they may be taken, the averages of the different samples will rarely be quite the same, but one form of average may show much greater differences than another. Of the two forms, the more stable is the better. The full discussion of this condition must, however, be postponed to a later section of this work (Chap. XVII.). (f) Finally, by far the most important desideratum is this, that the measure chosen shall lend itself readily to algebraical treatment. If, *e.g.*, two or more series of observations on similar material are given, the average of the combined series should be readily expressed in terms of the averages of the component series : if a variable may be expressed as the sum of two or more others, the average of the whole should be readily expressed in terms of the averages of its parts. A measure for which simple relations of this kind cannot be readily determined is likely to prove of somewhat limited application.

5. There are three forms of average in common use, the arithmetic mean, the median, and the mode, the first named being by far the most widely used in general statistical work. To these may be added the geometric mean and the harmonic mean, more rarely used, but of service in special cases. We will consider these in the order named.

6. *The arithmetic mean.*—The arithmetic mean of a series of values of a variable X_1, X_2, X_3, . . . X_n, N in number, is the quotient of the sum of the values by their number. That is to say, if M be the arithmetic mean,

$$M = \frac{1}{N}(X_1 + X_2 + X_3 + \ldots + X_n),$$

or, to express it more briefly by using the symbol Σ to denote "the sum of all quantities like,"

$$M = \frac{1}{N}\Sigma(X) \qquad . \qquad . \qquad . \qquad . \quad (1)$$

The word *mean* or *average* alone, without qualification, is very generally used to denote this particular form of average : that is to say, when anyone speaks of "the mean " or "the average " of a series of observations, it may, as a rule, be assumed that the arithmetic mean is meant. It is evident that the arithmetic mean fulfils the conditions laid down in (*a*) and (*b*) of § 4, for it is rigidly defined and based on all the observations made. Further, it fulfils condition (*c*), for its general nature is readily comprehensible. If the wages-bill for N workmen is £P, the arithmetic mean wage, P/N pounds, is the amount that each would receive if the whole sum available were divided equally between them : conversely, if we are told that the mean wage is £M, we know this means that the wages-bill is $N.M$ pounds. Similarly, if N families possess a total of C children, the mean number of children per family is C/N—the number that each family would possess if the children were shared uniformly. Conversely, if the mean number of children per family is M, the total number of children in N families is $N.M$. The arithmetic mean expresses, in fact, a simple relation between the whole and its parts.

7. As regards simplicity of calculation, the mean takes a high position. In the cases just cited, it will be noted that the mean is actually determined without even the necessity of determining or noting all the individual values of the variable : to get the mean wage we need not know the wages of every hand, but only the wages-bill ; to get the mean number of children per family we need not know the number in each family, but only the total. If this total is not given, but we have to deal with a moderate number of observations—so few (say 30 or 40) that it is hardly worth while compiling the frequency-distribution—the arithmetic mean is calculated directly as suggested by the definition, *i.e.* all the values observed are added together and the total divided by the number of observations. But if the number of observations be large, this direct process becomes a little lengthy. It may be shortened considerably by forming the frequency-table and treating all the values in each class as if they were identical with the mid-value of the class-interval, a process which in general gives an approximation that is quite sufficiently exact for practical purposes if the class-interval has been taken moderately

small (*cf.* Chap. VI. § 5). In this process each class-frequency is multiplied by the mid-value of the interval, the products added together, and the total divided by the number of observations. If f denote the frequency of any class, X the mid-value of the corresponding class-interval, the value of the mean so obtained may be written—

$$M = \frac{1}{N}\Sigma(f.X) \quad . \quad . \quad . \quad . \quad (2)$$

8. But this procedure is still further abbreviated in practice by the following artifices :—(1) The class-interval is treated as the unit of measurement throughout the arithmetic ; (2) the difference between the mean and the mid-value of some arbitrarily chosen class-interval is computed instead of the absolute value of the mean.

If A be the arbitrarily chosen value and

$$X = A + \xi. \quad . \quad . \quad . \quad (3)$$

then

$$\Sigma(fX) = \Sigma(f.A) + \Sigma(f.\xi),$$

or, since A is a constant,

$$M = A + \frac{1}{N}\Sigma(f.\xi) \quad . \quad . \quad . \quad (4)$$

The calculation of $\Sigma(f.X)$ is therefore replaced by the calculation of $\Sigma(f.\xi)$. The advantage of this is that the class-frequencies need only be multiplied by small integral numbers ; for A being the mid-value of a class-interval, and X the mid-value of another, and the class-interval being treated as a unit, the ξ's must be a series of integers proceeding from zero at the arbitrary origin A. To keep the values of ξ as small as possible, A should be chosen near the middle of the range.

It may be mentioned here that $\Sigma(\xi)$, or $\Sigma(f.\xi)$ for the grouped distribution, is sometimes termed the *first moment* of the distribution about the arbitrary origin A : we shall not, however, make use of this term.

9. The process is illustrated by the following example, using the frequency-distribution of Table VIII., Chap. VI. The arbitrary origin A is taken at 3·5 per cent., the middle of the sixth class-interval from the top of the table, and a little nearer than the middle of the range to the estimated position of the mean. The consequent values of ξ are then written down as in column (3) of the table, against the corresponding frequencies, the values starting, of course, from zero opposite 3·5 per cent. Each frequency f is then multiplied by its ξ and the products entered

in another column (4). The positive and negative products are totalled separately, giving totals -776 and $+509$ respectively, whence $\Sigma(f.\xi) = -267$. Dividing this by N, viz. 632, we have the difference of M from A in class-intervals, viz. 0.42 intervals, that is 0.21 per cent. Hence the mean is $3.5 - 0.21 = 3.29$ per cent.

CALCULATION OF THE MEAN : *Example i.—Calculation of the Arithmetic Mean of the Percentages of the Population in receipt of Relief, from the Figures of Table VIII., Chap. VI., p. 93.*

(1) Mid-values of the Class-intervals (Percentage in receipt of Relief).	(2) Frequency f.	(3) Deviation from Arbitrary Value A ξ.	(4) Product $f\xi$.
1	18	-5	90
1·5	48	-4	192
2	72	-3	216
2·5	89	-2	178
3	100	-1	100
3·5	90	0	-776
4	75	$+1$	75
4·5	60	$+2$	120
5	40	$+3$	120
5·5	21	$+4$	84
6	11	$+5$	55
6·5	5	$+6$	30
7	1	$+7$	7
7·5	1	$+8$	8
8·	—	$+9$	—
8·5	1	$+10$	10
Total	632	—	$+509$

$$\Sigma(f\xi) = +509 - 776 = -267$$
$$M - A = -\frac{267}{632} \text{ class-intervals} = -0.42 \text{ class-intervals}$$
$$= -0.21 \text{ units}$$
$$\therefore \quad \text{mean } M = 3.5 - 0.21 = 3.29 \text{ per cent.}$$

It must always be remembered that $\Sigma(f.\xi)/N$ gives the value of $M - A$ in class-intervals, and must not be added directly to A unless the interval is also a unit. In the present illustration the interval is half a unit, and accordingly the quotient 267/632 is halved in order to obtain an answer in units. Care must also be taken to give the right sign to the quotient.

10. As the process is an important one we give a second illustration from the figures of Table VI., Chap. VI. In this case the class-interval is a unit (1 inch), so the value of $M - A$ is given directly by dividing $\Sigma(f.\xi)$ by N. The student must notice that, measures having been made to the nearest eighth of an inch, the mid-values of the intervals are $57\frac{7}{16}$, $58\frac{7}{16}$, etc., and not $57\cdot5$, $58\cdot5$, etc.

CALCULATION OF THE MEAN : *Example* ii.—*Calculation of the Arithmetic Mean Stature of Male Adults in the British Isles from the Figures of Chap. VI., Table VI., p. 88.*

(1) Height, Inches.	(2) Frequency *f.*	(3) Deviation from Arbitrary Value *A* ξ.	(4) Product *fξ.*
57–	2	– 10	20
58–	4	– 9	36
59–	14	– 8	112
60–	41	– 7	287
61–	83	– 6	498
62–	169	– 5	845
63–	394	– 4	1576
64–	669	– 3	2007
65–	990	– 2	1980
66–	1223	– 1	1223
67–	1329	0	– 8584
68–	1230	+ 1	1230
69–	1063	+ 2	2126
70–	646	+ 3	1938
71–	392	+ 4	1568
72–	202	+ 5	1010
73–	79	+ 6	474
74–	32	+ 7	224
75–	16	+ 8	128
76–	5	+ 9	45
77–	2	+10	20
Total	8585	–	+ 8763

$$\Sigma(f\xi) = +8763 - 8584 = +179$$

$$M - A = +\frac{179}{8585} = +\cdot02 \text{ class-intervals or inches.}$$

$$\therefore \quad M = 67\tfrac{7}{16} + \cdot02 = 67\cdot46 \text{ inches.}$$

It is evident that an absolute check on the arithmetic of any
such calculation may be effected by taking a different arbitrary
origin for the deviations : all the figures of col. (4) will be changed,
but the value ultimately obtained for the mean must be the
same. The student should note that a classification by unequal
intervals is, at best, a hindrance to this simple form of calculation,
and the use of an indefinite interval for the extremity of the
distribution renders the exact calculation of the mean impossible
(*cf.* Chap. VI. § 10).

11. We return again below (§ 13) to the question of the

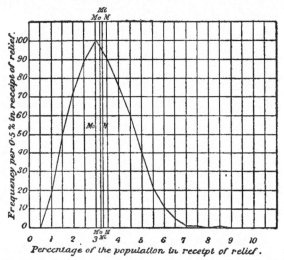

FIG. 21.—Showing the Arithmetic Mean M, the Median Mi, and the Mode Mo,
by verticals drawn through the corresponding points on the base, for the
distribution of pauperism of fig. 10, p. 92.

errors caused by the assumption that all values within the same
interval may be treated as approximately the mid-value of the
interval. It is sufficient to say here that the error is in general
very small and of uncertain sign for a distribution of the
symmetrical or only moderately asymmetrical type, provided of
course the class-interval is not large (Chap. VI. § 5). In the case
of the "J-shaped" or extremely asymmetrical distribution, however, the error is evidently of definite sign, for in all the intervals
the frequency is piled up at the limit lying towards the greatest
frequency, *i.e.* the lower end of the range in the case of the illustrations given in Chap. VI., and is not evenly distributed over the

8

interval. In distributions of such a type the intervals must be made very small indeed to secure an approximately accurate value for the mean. The student should test for himself the effect of different groupings in two or three different cases, so as to get some idea of the degree of inaccuracy to be expected.

12. If a diagram has been drawn representing the frequency-distribution, the position of the mean may conveniently be indicated by a vertical through the corresponding point on the base. Thus fig. 21 (a reproduction of fig. 10) shows the frequency-polygon for our first illustration, and the vertical MM indicates the mean. In a moderately asymmetrical distribution at all of this form the mean lies, as in the present example, on the side of the greatest frequency towards the longer "tail" of the distribu-

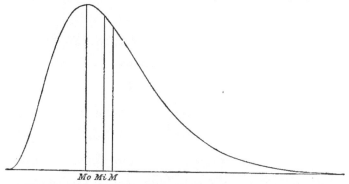

Mo Mi M

Fig. 22.—Mean M, Median Mi, and Mode Mo, of the ideal moderately asymmetrical distribution.

tion: M in fig. 22 shows similarly the position of the mean in an ideal distribution. In a symmetrical distribution the mean coincides with the centre of symmetry. The student should mark the position of the mean in the diagram of every frequency distribution that he draws, and so accustom himself to thinking of the mean, not as an abstraction, but always in relation to the frequency-distribution of the variable concerned.

13. The following examples give important properties of the arithmetic mean, and at the same time illustrate the facility of its algebraic treatment :—

(a) The sum of the deviations from the mean, taken with their proper signs, is zero.

This follows at once from equation (4): for if M and A are identical, evidently $\Sigma(f.\xi)$ must be zero.

(b) If a series of N observations of a variable X consist of, say, two component series, the mean of the whole series can be readily expressed in terms of the means of the two components. For if we denote the values in the first series by X_1 and in the second series by X_2,

$$\Sigma(X) = \Sigma(X_1) + \Sigma(X_2),$$

that is, if there be N_1 observations in the first series and N_2 in the second, and the means of the two series be M_1, M_2 respectively,

$$N.M = N_1.M_1 + N_2.M_2 \qquad . \qquad . \qquad . \quad (5)$$

For example, we find from the data of Table VI., Chap. VI.,

Mean stature of the 346 men born in Ireland $= 67\cdot78$ in.
,, ,, ,, 741 ,, ,, Wales $= 66\cdot62$ in.

Hence the mean stature of the 1087 men born in the two countries is given by the equation—

$$1087.M = (346 \times 67\cdot78) + (741 \times 66\cdot62).$$

That is, $M = 66\cdot99$ inches. It is evident that the form of the relation (5) is quite general : if there are r series of observations $X_1, X_2 \ldots X_r$, the mean M of the whole series is related to the means $M_1, M_2 \ldots M_r$, of the component series by the equation

$$N.M = N_1.M_1 + N_2.M_2 + \ldots + N_r.M_r \quad . \qquad . \quad (6)$$

For the convenient checking of arithmetic, it is useful to note that, if the same arbitrary origin A for the deviations ξ be taken in each case, we must have, denoting the component series by the subscripts 1, 2, $\ldots$ r as before,

$$\Sigma(f.\xi) = \Sigma(f_1.\xi_1) + \Sigma(f_2.\xi_2) + \ldots + \Sigma(f_r.\xi_r) \qquad . \quad (7)$$

The agreement of these totals accordingly checks the work.

As an important corollary to the general relation (6), it may be noted that the approximate value for the mean obtained from any frequency distribution is the same whether we assume (1) that all the values in any class are identical with the mid-value of the class-interval, or (2) that the mean of the values in the class is identical with the mid-value of the class-interval.

(c) The mean of all the sums or differences of corresponding observations in two series (of equal numbers of observations) is equal to the sum or difference of the means of the two series.

This follows almost at once. For if

$$X = X_1 \pm X_2,$$
$$\Sigma(X) = \Sigma(X_1) \pm \Sigma(X_2).$$

That is, if M, M_1, M_2 be the respective means,

$$M = M_1 \pm M_2 \quad . \quad . \quad . \quad . \quad (8)$$

Evidently the form of this result is again quite general, so that if

$$X = X_1 \pm X_2 \pm \ldots \pm X_n$$
$$M = M_1 \pm M_2 \pm \ldots \pm M_r \quad . \quad . \quad . \quad (9)$$

As a useful illustration of equation (8), consider the case of measurements of any kind that are subject (as indeed all measures must be) to greater or less errors. The actual measurement X in any such case is the algebraic sum of the true measurement X_1 and an error X_2. The mean of the actual measurements M is therefore the sum of the true mean M_1, and the arithmetic mean of the errors M_2. If, and only if, the latter be zero, will the observed mean be identical with the true mean. Errors of grouping (§ 11) are a case in point.

14. *The median.*—The median may be defined as the middlemost or central value of the variable when the values are ranged in order of magnitude, or as the value such that greater and smaller values occur with equal frequency. In the case of a frequency-curve, the median may be defined as that value of the variable the vertical through which divides the area of the curve into two equal parts, as the vertical through Mi in fig. 22.

The median, like the mean, fulfils the conditions (*b*) and (*c*) of § 4, seeing that it is based on all the observations made, and that it possesses the simple property of being the central or middlemost value, so that its nature is obvious. But the definition does not necessarily lead in all cases to a determinate value. If there be an odd number of different values of X observed, say $2n + 1$, the $(n + 1)$th in order of magnitude is the only value fulfilling the definition. But if there be an even number, say $2n$ different values, any value between the nth and $(n + 1)$th fulfils the conditions. In such a case it appears to be usual to take the mean of the nth and $(n + 1)$th values as the median, but this is a convention supplementary to the definition. It should also be noted that in the case of a discontinuous variable the second form of the definition in general breaks down: if we range the values in order there is always a middlemost value (provided the number of observations be odd), but there is not, as a rule, any value such that greater and less values occur with equal frequency. Thus in Table III., § 3 of Chap. VI., we see that 45 per cent. of the poppy capsules had 12 or fewer stigmatic rays, 55 per cent. had 13 or more; similarly 61 per cent. had 13 or fewer rays, 39 per cent. had 14 or more. There is no number of rays such that the frequencies in excess and defect are equal. In the case of the buttercups of Table XIV. (Chap. VI. § 15) there is no number of petals that even remotely fulfils the required condition. An analogous difficulty may arise, it may be remarked, even in the case of an odd number of observations of a continuous variable if the number of observations be small and several of the observed values identical. The median is therefore a form of average of most uncertain meaning in cases of strictly discontinuous variation, for it may be exceeded by 5, 10, 15, or 20 per cent. only of the observed values, instead of by 50 per cent.: its use in such cases is to be deprecated, and is perhaps best avoided in any case, whether the variation be continuous or discontinuous, in which small series of observations have to be dealt with.

15. When a table showing the frequency-distribution for a long series of observations of a continuous variable is given, no difficulty arises, as a sufficiently approximate value of the median can be readily determined by simple interpolation on the hypothesis that the values in each class are uniformly distributed throughout the interval. Thus, taking the figures in our first illustration of the method of calculating the mean, the total number of observations (registration districts) is 632, of which the half is 316. Looking down the table, we see that there are 227 districts with not more than 2·75 per cent. of the population in receipt of relief, and 100 more with between 2·75 and 3·25 per cent. But only 89 are required to make up the total of 316 ; hence the value of the median is taken as

$$2 \cdot 75 + \frac{89}{100} \cdot \tfrac{1}{2} = 2 \cdot 75 + 0 \cdot 445$$
$$= 3 \cdot 195 \text{ per cent.}$$

The mean being 3·29, the median is slightly less ; its position is indicated by Mi in fig. 21.

The value of the median stature of males may be similarly calculated from the data of the second illustration. The work may be indicated thus :—

Half the total number of observations (8585) $= 4292 \cdot 5$
Total frequency under $66\tfrac{15}{16}$ inches . . $= 3589$

Difference . . . . . $= 703 \cdot 5$
Frequency in next interval . . $= 1329$
Therefore median $= 66\tfrac{15}{16} + \dfrac{703 \cdot 5}{1329}$
$= 67 \cdot 47$ inches.

The difference between median and mean in this case is therefore only about one-hundredth of an inch, the smallness of the difference arising from the approximate symmetry of the distribution. In an absolutely symmetrical distribution it is evident that mean and median must coincide.

16. Graphical interpolation may, if desired, be substituted, for arithmetical interpolation. Taking, again, the figures of Example i., the number of districts with pauperism not exceeding 2·25 is 138; not exceeding 2·75, 227; not exceeding 3·25, 327; and not exceeding 3·75, 417. Plot the numbers of districts with pauperism not exceeding each value X to the corresponding

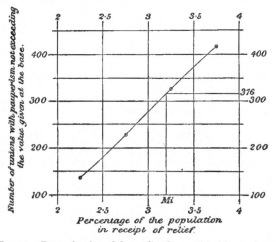

FIG. 23.—Determination of the median by graphical interpolation.

value of X on squared paper, to a good large scale, as in fig. 23, and draw a smooth curve through the points thus obtained, preferably with the aid of one of the "curves," splines, or flexible curves sold by instrument-makers for the purpose. The point in which the smooth curve so obtained cuts the horizontal line corresponding to a total frequency $N/2 = 316$ gives the median. In general the curve is so flat that the value obtained by this graphical method does not differ appreciably from that calculated arithmetically (the arithmetical process assuming that the curve is a straight line between the points on either side of the median); if the curvature is considerable, the graphical value—assuming, of course, careful and accurate draughtsmanship —is to be preferred to the arithmetical value, as it does not involve the crude assumption that the frequency is *uniformly* distributed over the interval in which the median lies.

17. A comparison of the calculations for the mean and for the median respectively will show that on the score of brevity of calculation the median has a distinct advantage. When, however, the ease of algebraical treatment of the two forms of average is compared, the superiority lies wholly on the side of the mean. As was shown in § 13, when several series of observations are combined into a single series, the mean of the resultant distribution can be simply expressed in terms of the means of the components. The expression of the median of the resultant distribution in terms of the medians of the components is, however, not merely complex and difficult, but impossible: the value of the resultant median depends on the forms of the component distributions, and not on their medians alone. If two symmetrical distributions of the same form and with the same numbers of observations, but with different medians, be combined, the resultant median must evidently (from symmetry) coincide with the resultant mean, *i.e.* lie halfway between the means of the components. But if the two components be asymmetrical, or (whatever their form) if the degrees of dispersion or numbers of observations in the two series be different, the resultant median will not coincide with the resultant mean, nor with any other simply assignable value. It is impossible, therefore, to give any theorem for medians analogous to equations (5) and (6) for means. It is equally impossible to give any theorem analogous to equations (8) and (9) of § 13. The median of the sum or difference of pairs of corresponding observations in two series is not, in general, equal to the sum or difference of the medians of the two series ; the median value of a measurement subject to error is not necessarily identical with the true median, even if the median error be zero, *i.e.* if positive and negative errors be equally frequent.

18. These limitations render the applications of the median in any work in which theoretical considerations are necessary comparatively circumscribed. On the other hand, the median may have an advantage over the mean for special reasons. (*a*) It is very readily calculated ; a factor to which, however, as already stated, too much weight ought not to be attached. (*b*) It is readily obtained, without the necessity of measuring all the objects to be observed, in any case in which they can be arranged by eye in order of magnitude. If, for instance, a number of men be ranked in order of stature, the stature of the middlemost is the median, and he alone need be measured. (On the other hand

it is useless in the cases cited at the end of § 6 ; the median wage
cannot be found from the total of the wages-bill, and the total
of the wages-bill is not known when the median is given.) (c) It
is sometimes useful as a makeshift, when the observations are so
given that the calculation of the mean is impossible, owing, *e.g.*, to
a final indefinite class, as in Table IV. (Chap. VI. § 10). (d) The
median *may* sometimes be preferable to the mean, owing to its
being less affected by abnormally large or small values of the
variable. The stature of a giant would have no more influence
on the median stature of a number of men than the stature of
any other man whose height is only just greater than the median.
If a number of men enjoy incomes closely clustering round a
median of £500 a year, the median will be no more affected by
the addition to the group of a man with the income of £50,000
than by the addition of a man with an income of £5000, or even
£600. If observations of any kind are liable to present occasional
greatly outlying values of this sort (whether real, or due to
errors or blunders), the median will be more stable and less
affected by fluctuations of sampling than the arithmetic mean.
(In general the mean is the less affected.) The point is discussed
more fully later (Chap. XVII.). (e) It may be added that the
median is, in a certain sense, a particularly real and natural
form of average, for the object or individual that is the median
object or individual on any one system of measuring the character
with which we are concerned will remain the median on any
other method of measurement which leaves the objects in the
same relative order. Thus a batch of eggs representing eggs
of the median price, when prices are reckoned at so much per
dozen, will remain a batch representing the median 'price when
prices are reckoned at so many eggs to the shilling.

19. *The Mode.*—The mode is the value of the variable corresponding to the maximum of the ideal frequency-curve which
gives the closest possible fit to the actual distribution.

It is evident that in an ideal symmetrical distribution mean,
median and mode coincide with the centre of symmetry. If,
however, the distribution be asymmetrical, as in fig. 22, the three
forms of average are distinct, Mo being the mode, Mi the median,
and M the mean. Clearly, the mode is an important form of
average in the cases of skew distributions, though the term is of
recent introduction (Pearson, ref. 11). It represents the value
which is most frequent or typical, the value which is in fact the
fashion (*la mode*). But a difficulty at once arises on attempting
to determine this value for such distributions as occur in practice.
It is no use giving merely the mid value of the class-interval into
which the greatest frequency falls, for this is entirely dependent

on the choice of the scale of class-intervals. It is no use making the class-intervals very small to avoid error on that account, for the class-frequencies will then become small and the distribution irregular. What we want to arrive at is the mid-value of the interval for which the frequency would be a maximum, if the intervals could be made indefinitely small and at the same time the number of observations be so increased that the class-frequencies should run smoothly. As the observations cannot, in a practical case, be indefinitely increased, it is evident that some process of smoothing out the irregularities that occur in the actual distribution must be adopted, in order to ascertain the approximate value of the mode. But there is only one smoothing process that is really satisfactory, in so far as every observation can be taken into account in the determination, and that is the method of fitting an ideal frequency-curve of given equation to the actual figures. The value of the variable corresponding to the maximum of the fitted curve is then taken as the mode, in accordance with our definition. Mo in fig. 21 is the value of the mode so determined for the distribution of pauperism, the value 2·99 being, as it happens, very nearly coincident with the centre of the interval in which the greatest frequency lies. The determination of the mode by this—the only strictly satisfactory—method must, however, be left to the more advanced student.

20. At the same time there is an approximate relation between mean, median, and mode that appears to hold good with surprising closeness for moderately asymmetrical distributions, approaching the ideal type of fig. 9, and it is one that should be borne in mind as giving—roughly, at all events—the relative values of these three averages for a great many cases with which the student will have to deal. It is expressed by the equation—

$$\text{Mode} = \text{Mean} - 3(\text{Mean} - \text{Median}).$$

That is to say, the median lies one-third of the distance from the mean towards the mode (compare figs. 21 and 22). For the distribution of pauperism we have, taking the mean to three places of decimals,—

Mean	3·289
Median	3·195
Difference	0·094

Hence approximate mode $= 3·289 - 3 \times 0·094$
$$= 3·007,$$

or 3·01 to the second place of decimals, which is sufficient accuracy for the final result, though three decimal places must be retained for the calculation. The true mode, found by fitting an ideal distribution, is 2·99. As further illustrations of the closeness with which the relation may be expected to hold in different cases, we give below the results for the distributions of pauperism in the unions of England and Wales in the years 1850, 1860, 1870, 1881, and 1891 (the last being the illustration taken above), and also the results for the distribution of barometer heights at Southampton (Table XI., Chap. VI. § 14), and similar distributions at four other stations.

Comparison of the Approximate and True Modes in the Case of Five Distributions of Pauperism (Percentages of the Population in receipt of Relief) in the Unions of England and Wales. (Yule, *Jour. Roy. Stat. Soc.*, vol. lix., 1896.)

Year.	Mean.	Median.	Approximate Mode.	True Mode.
1850	6·508	6·261	5·767	5·815
1860	5·195	5·000	4·610	4·657
1870	5·451	5·380	5·238	5·038
1881	3·676	3·523	3·217	3·240
1891	3·289	3·195	3·007	2·987

Comparison of the Approximate and True Modes in the Case of Five Distributions of the Height of the Barometer for Daily Observations at the Stations named. (Distributions given by Karl Pearson and Alice Lee, *Phil. Trans.*, A, vol. cxc. (1897), p. 423.)

Station.	Mean.	Median.	Approximate Mode.	True Mode.
Southampton .	29·981	30·000	30·038	30·039
Londonderry .	29·891	29·915	29·963	29·960
Carmarthen .	29·952	29·974	30·018	30·013
Glasgow .	29·886	29·906	29·946	29·967
Dundee . .	29·870	29·890	29·930	29·951 .

It will be seen that in the case of the pauperism figures the approximate mode only diverges markedly from the true value in the year 1870, a year in which the frequency-distribution was very irregular. In all the other years the difference between the true and approximate values of the mode is hardly greater than the alteration that might be caused in the true mode itself by slight variations in the method of fitting the curve to the actual distribution. Similar remarks apply to the second series of illustrations; the true and approximate values are extremely close, except in the case of Dundee and Glasgow, where the divergence reaches two-hundredths of an inch.

21. Summing up the preceding paragraphs, we may say that the mean is the form of average to use for all general purposes;

it is simply calculated, its value is always determinate, its algebraic treatment is particularly easy, and in most cases it is rather less affected than the median by errors of sampling. The median is, it is true, somewhat more easily calculated from a given frequency-distribution than is the mean ; it is sometimes a useful makeshift, and in a certain class of cases it is more and not less stable than the mean ; but its use is undesirable in cases of discontinuous variation, its value may be indeterminate, and its algebraic treatment is difficult and often impossible. The mode, finally, is a form of average hardly suitable for elementary use, owing to the difficulty of its determination, but at the same time it represents an important value of the variable. The arithmetic mean should invariably be employed unless there is some very definite reason for the choice of another form of average, and the elementary student will do very well if he limits himself to its use. Objection is sometimes taken to the use of the mean in the case of asymmetrical frequency-distributions, on the ground that the mean is not the mode, and that its value is consequently misleading. But no one in the least degree familiar with the manifold forms taken by frequency-distributions would regard the two as in general identical ; and while the importance of the mode is a good reason for stating its value in addition to that of the mean, it cannot replace the latter. The objection, it may be noted, would apply with almost equal force to the median, for, as we have seen (§ 20), the difference between mode and median is usually about two-thirds of the difference between mode and mean.

22. *The Geometric Mean.*—The geometric mean G of a series of values $X_1, X_2, X_3, \ldots \ldots X_n$, is defined by the relation

$$G = (X_1 . X_2 . X_3 \ldots X_n)^{\frac{1}{n}} . \qquad . \qquad . \quad (10)$$

The definition may also be expressed in terms of logarithms,

$$\log G = \frac{1}{N} \Sigma (\log X) \qquad . \qquad . \quad (11)$$

that is to say, the logarithm of the geometric mean of a series of values is the arithmetic mean of their logarithms.

The geometric mean of a given series of quantities is always less than their arithmetic mean ; the student will find a proof in most text-books of algebra, and in ref. 10. The magnitude of the difference depends largely on the amount of dispersion of the variable in proportion to the magnitude of the mean (*cf.* Chap. VIII., Question 8). It is necessarily zero, it should be noticed, if even a single value of X is zero, and it may become imaginary if negative values occur. Excluding these cases, the value of the geometric mean is always determinate and is rigidly defined. The computation is a little long, owing to the necessity of taking logarithms : ,it is hardly necessary to give an example, as the method is simply that of finding the arithmetic mean of the *logarithms* of X (instead of the values of X) in accordance with equation (11). If there are many observations, a table should be drawn up giving the frequency-distribution of log X, and the mean should be calculated as in Examples i. and ii. of §§ 9 and 10. The geometric mean has never come into general use as a representative average, partly, no doubt, on account of its rather troublesome computation, but principally on account of its somewhat abstract mathematical character (*cf.* § 4 (*c*)) : the geometric mean does not possess any simple and obvious properties which render its general nature readily comprehensible.

23. At the same time, as the following examples show, the mean possesses some important properties, and is readily treated algebraically in certain cases.

(*a*) If the series of observations X consist of r component series, there being N_1 observations in the first, N_2 in the second, and so on, the geometric mean G of the whole series can be readily expressed in terms of the geometric means G_1, G_2, etc., of the component series. For evidently we have at once (as in § 13 (*b*))—

$$N . \log G = N_1 . \log G_1 + N_2 . \log G_2 + \ldots . + N_r . \log G_r . \quad (12)$$

(*b*) The geometric mean of the ratios of corresponding observations in two series is equal to the ratio of their geometric means. For if

$$X = X_1 / X_2,$$
$$\log X = \log X_1 - \log X_2,$$

then summing for all pairs of X_1's and X_2's,

$$G = G_1 / G_2 \quad . \quad . \quad . \quad . \quad (13)$$

(*c*) Similarly, if a variable X is given as the product of any number of others, *i.e.* if

$$X = X_1 . X_2 . X_3 \ldots . X_r$$

X_1, X_2, $\ldots . X_r$ denoting corresponding observations in r different series, the geometric mean G of X is expressed in terms of the geometric means G_1, G_2, $\ldots . G_r$ of X_1, X_2, $\ldots . X_r$, by the relation

$$G = G_1 . G_2 . G_3 \ldots . G_r \quad . \quad . \quad . \quad (14)$$

That is to say, the geometric mean of the product is the product of the geometric means.

24. The use of the geometric mean finds its simplest application in estimating the numbers of a population midway between two epochs (say two census years) at which the population is known. If nothing is known concerning the increase of the population save that the numbers recorded at the first census were P_0 and at the second census n years later P_n, the most reasonable assump-

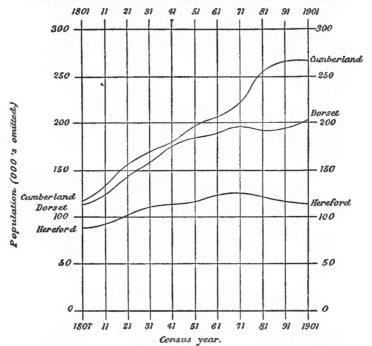

FIG. 24.—Showing the Populations of certain rural counties of England for each Census year from 1801 to 1901.

tion to make is that the percentage increase in each year has been the same, so that the populations in successive years form a geometric series, $P_0 r$ being the population a year after the first census, $P_0 r^2$ two years after the first census, and so on, and

$$P_n = P_0 \cdot r^n \qquad \cdots \qquad (15)$$

The population midway between the two censuses is therefore

$$P_{n/2} = P_0 \cdot r^{n/2} = (P_0 \cdot P_n)^{\frac{1}{2}} \qquad \cdots \qquad (16)$$

i.e. the geometric mean of the numbers given by the two censuses. This result must, however, be used with discretion. The rate of increase of population is not necessarily, or even usually, constant over any considerable period of time : if it were so, a curve representing the growth of population as in fig. 24 would be continuously convex to the base, whether the population were increasing or decreasing. In the diagram it will be seen that the curves are frequently concave towards the base, and similar results will often be found for districts in which the population is not increasing very rapidly, and from which there is much emigration. Further, the assumption is not self-consistent in any case in which the rate of increase is not uniform over the entire area—and almost any area can be analysed into parts which are not similar in this respect. For if in one part of the area considered the initial population is P_0 and the common ratio R, and in the remainder of the area the initial population is p_0 and the common ratio r, the population in year n is given by

$$P_n + p_n = P_0.R^n + p_0.r^n.$$

This does not represent a constant rate of increase unless $R = r$. If then, for example, a constant percentage rate of increase be assumed for England and Wales as a whole, it cannot be assumed for the Counties : if it be assumed for the Counties, it cannot be assumed for the country as a whole. The student is referred to refs. 14, 15 for a discussion of methods that may be used for the consistent estimation of populations under such circumstances.

25. The property of the geometric mean illustrated by equation (13) renders it, in some respects, a peculiarly convenient form of average in dealing with ratios, *i.e.* "index-numbers," as they are termed, of prices. Let

$$X'_0, X''_0, X'''_0, \ldots X^n_0$$
$$X'_1, X''_1, X'''_1, \ldots X^n_1$$
$$X'_2, X''_2, X'''_2, \ldots X^n_2$$
$$. \quad . \quad . \quad . \quad .$$

denote the prices of N commodities in the years $0, 1, 2 \ldots$. Further, let $Y_{10} = X_1/X_0$, and so on, so that

$$Y'_{10}, Y''_{10}, Y'''_{10}, \ldots Y^n_{10}$$
$$Y'_{20}, Y''_{20}, Y'''_{20}, \ldots Y^n_{20}$$
$$. \quad . \quad . \quad . \quad .$$

represent the ratios of the prices of the several commodities in years $1, 2, \ldots$ to their prices in year 0. These ratios, in practice multiplied by 100, are termed *index-numbers* of the prices of the several commodities, on the year 0 as base. Evidently some form of average of the Y's for any given year will afford an indication of the general level of prices for that year, provided the commodities chosen are sufficiently numerous and representative. The question is, what form of average to choose. If the geometric mean be chosen, and G_{10}, G_{20} denote the geometric means of the Y's for the years 1 and 2 respectively, we have

$$
\begin{aligned}
\frac{G_{20}}{G_{10}} &= \left(\frac{Y'_{20}}{Y'_{10}} \cdot \frac{Y''_{20}}{Y''_{10}} \cdot \frac{Y'''_{20}}{Y'''_{10}} \cdots \cdots \frac{Y^n_{20}}{Y^n_{10}}\right)^{\frac{1}{N}} \\
&= \left(\frac{X'_2}{X'_1} \cdot \frac{X''_2}{X''_1} \cdot \frac{X'''_2}{X'''_1} \cdots \cdots \frac{X^n_2}{X^n_1}\right)^{\frac{1}{N}} \\
&= \left(Y'_{21} \cdot Y''_{21} \cdot Y'''_{21} \cdots \cdots Y^n_{21}\right)^{\frac{1}{N}}
\end{aligned}
\qquad . \quad (17)
$$

From the first form of this equation we see that the ratio of the geometric mean index-number in year 2 to that in year 1 is identical with the geometric mean of the ratios for the index-numbers of the several commodities. A similar property does not hold for any other form of average: the ratio of the arithmetic mean index-numbers is not the same as the arithmetic mean of the ratios, nor is the ratio of the medians the median of the ratios. From the second and third forms of the equation it appears further that the ratio of the geometric mean index-number in year 2 to that in year 1 is independent of the prices in the year first chosen as base (*i.e.* year 0), and is identical with the geometric mean of the index-numbers for year 2, on year 1 as base. Again, a similar property does not hold for any other form of average. If arithmetic means of the index-numbers be taken, for example, the ratio of the mean in year 2 to the mean in year 1 will vary with the year taken as base, and will differ more or less from the arithmetic mean ratio of the prices in year 2 to the prices of the same commodities in year 1; the same statement is true if medians be used. The results given by the use of the geometric mean possess, therefore, a certain consistency that is not exhibited if other forms of average are employed. It was used in a classical paper by Jevons (ref. 4), though not on quite the same grounds, but has never been at all generally employed.

26. The general use of the geometric mean has been suggested on another ground, namely, that the magnitudes of deviations appear, as a rule, to be dependent in some degree on the magnitude of the average; thus the length of a mouse varies less than the stature of a man, and the height of a shrub less than that of a tree. Hence, it is argued, variations in such cases should be measured rather by their ratio to, than their difference from, the average; and if this is done, the geometric mean is the natural average to use. If deviations be measured in this way, a

deviation G/r will be regarded as the equivalent of a deviation $r.G$, instead of a deviation $-x$ as the equivalent of a deviation $+x$. If a distribution take the simplest possible form when *relative* deviations are regarded as equivalents, the frequency of deviations between G/s and G/r will be equal to the frequency of deviations between $r.G$ and $s.G$. The frequency-curve will then be symmetrical round log G if plotted to log X as base, and if there be a single mode, log G will be that mode—a *logarithmic* or *geometric mode*, as it might be termed : G will not be the mode if the distribution be plotted in the ordinary way to values of X as base. The theory of such a distribution has been discussed by more than one author (refs. 2, 8, 9). The general applicability of the assumption made does not, however, appear to have been very widely tested, and the reasons assigned have not sufficed to bring the geometric mean into common use. It may be noted that, as the geometric mean is always less than the arithmetic mean, the fundamental assumption which would justify the use of the former clearly does not hold where the (arithmetic) mode is greater than the arithmetic mean, as in Tables X. and XI. of the last chapter.

27. *The Harmonic Mean.*—The harmonic mean of a series of quantities is the reciprocal of the arithmetic mean of their reciprocals, that is, if H be the harmonic mean,

$$\frac{1}{H} = \frac{1}{N}\Sigma\left(\frac{1}{X}\right) \quad . \quad . \quad . \quad . \quad (18)$$

The following illustration, the result of which is required for an example in a later chapter (Chap. XIII. § 11), will serve to show the method of calculation.

The table gives the number of litters of mice, in certain breeding experiments, with given numbers (X) in the litter. (Data from A. D. Darbishire, *Biometrika*, iii. pp. 30, 31.)

Number in Litter. X.	Number of Litters. f.	f/X.
1	7	7·000
2	11	5·500
3	16	5·333
4	17	4·250
5	26	5·200
6	31	5·167
7	11	1·571
8	1	0·125
9	1	0·111
—	121	34·257

Whence, $1/H = 0.2831$, $H = 3.532$. The arithmetic mean is 4.587, or more than a unit greater.

If the prices of a commodity at different places or times are stated in the form "so much for a unit of money," and an average price obtained by taking the arithmetic mean of the quantities sold for a unit of money, the result is equivalent to the harmonic mean of prices stated in the ordinary way. Thus retail prices of eggs were quoted before the War as "so many to the shilling." Supposing we had 100 returns of retail prices of eggs, 50 returns showing twelve eggs to the shilling, 30 fourteen to the shilling, and 20 ten to the shilling; then the mean number per shilling would be 12·2, equivalent to a price of 0·984d. per egg. But if the prices had been quoted in the form usual for other commodities, we should have had 50 returns showing a price of 1d. per egg, 30 showing a price of 0·857d., and 20 a price of 1·2d.: arithmetic mean 0·997d., a slightly greater value than the harmonic mean of 0·984. The official returns of prices in India were, until 1907, given in the form of "Sers (2·057 lbs.) per rupee." The average annual price of a commodity was based on half-monthly prices stated in this form, and "index-numbers" were calculated from such annual averages. In the issues of "Prices and Wages in India" for 1908 and later years the prices have been stated in terms of "rupees per maund (82·286 lbs.)." The change, it will be seen, amounts to a replacement of the harmonic by the arithmetic mean price.

The harmonic mean of a series of quantities is always lower than the geometric mean of the same quantities, and, à fortiori, lower than the arithmetic mean, the amount of difference depending largely on the magnitude of the dispersion relatively to the magnitude of the mean. (Cf. Question 9, Chap. VIII.)

REFERENCES.

General.

(1) FECHNER, G. T. "Ueber den Ausgangswerth der kleinsten Abweichungssumme, dessen Bestimmung, Verwendung und Verallgemeinerung," *Abh. d. kgl. sächsischen Gesellschaft d. Wissenschaften*, vol. xviii. (also numbered xi. of the *Abh. d. math.-phys. Classe*); Leipzig (1878), p. 1. (The average defined as the origin from which the dispersion, measured in one way or another, is a minimum: geometric mean dealt with incidentally, pp. 13-16.)

(2) FECHNER, G. T., *Kollektivmasslehre*, herausgegeben von G. F. Lipps; Engelmann, Leipzig, 1897. (Posthumously published: deals with frequency-distributions, their forms, averages, and measures of dispersion in general: includes much of the matter of (1).)

(3) ZIZEK, FRANZ, *Die statistischen Mittelwerthe*; Duncker und Humblot, Leipzig, 1908: English translation, *Statistical Averages*, translated with additional notes, etc., by W. M. Persons, Holt & Co., New York, 1913. (Non-mathematical, but useful to the economic student for references cited.)

9

The Geometric Mean.

(4) JEVONS, W. STANLEY, *A Serious Fall in the Value of Gold ascertained and its Social Effects set forth*; Stanford, London, 1863. Reprinted in *Investigations in Currency and Finance*; Macmillan, London, 1884. (The geometric mean applied to the measurement of price changes.)

(5) JEVONS, W. STANLEY, "On the Variation of Prices and the Value of the Currency since 1782," *Jour. Roy. Stat. Soc.*, vol. xxviii., 1865. Also reprinted in volume cited above.

(6) EDGEWORTH, F. Y., "On the Method of ascertaining a Change in the Value of Gold," *Jour. Roy. Stat. Soc.*, vol. xlvi., 1883, p. 714. (Some criticism of the reasons assigned by Jevons for the use of the geometric mean.)

(7) GALTON, FRANCIS, "The Geometric Mean in Vital and Social Statistics," *Proc. Roy. Soc.*, vol. xxix., 1879, p. 365.

(8) McALISTER, DONALD, "The Law of the Geometric Mean," *ibid.*, p. 367. (The law of frequency to which the use of the geometric mean would be appropriate.)

(9) KAPTEYN, J. C., *Skew Frequency-curves in Biology and Statistics*; Noordhoff, Gröningen, and Wm. Dawson, London, 1903. (Contains, amongst other forms, a generalisation of McAlister's law.)

(10) CRAWFORD, G. E., "An Elementary Proof that the Arithmetic Mean of any number of Positive Quantities is greater than the Geometric Mean," *Proc. Edin. Math. Soc.*, vol. xviii., 1899–1900. See also refs. 1 and 2.

The Mode.

(11) PEARSON, KARL, "Skew Variation in Homogeneous Material," *Phil. Trans. Roy. Soc.*, Series A, vol. clxxxvi., 1895, p. 343. (Definition of mode, p. 345.)

(12) YULE, G. U., "Notes on the History of Pauperism in England and Wales, etc. : Supplementary Note on the Determination of the Mode," *Jour. Roy. Stat. Soc.*, vol. lix., 1896, p. 343. (The note deals with elementary methods of approximately determining the mode : the one-third rule and one other.)

(13) PEARSON, KARL, "On the Modal Value of an Organ or Character," *Biometrika*, vol. i., 1902, p. 260. (A warning as to the inadequacy of mere inspection for determining the mode.)

Estimates of Population.

(14) WATERS, A. C., "A Method for estimating Mean Populations in the last Intercensal Period," *Jour. Roy. Stat. Soc.*, vol. lxiv., 1901, p. 293.

(15) WATERS, A. C., *Estimates of Population : Supplement to Annual Report of the Registrar-General for England and Wales* (Cd. 2618, 1907, p. cxvii.) For the methods actually used, see the *Reports of the Registrar-General of England and Wales* for 1907, pp. cxxxii–cxxxiv, and for 1910, pp. xi–xii. *Cf.* SNOW, ref. 11, Chap. XII., for a different method based on the symptoms of growth such as numbers of births or of houses.

Index-numbers.

These were incidentally referred to in § 25.' The general theory of index-numbers and the different methods in which they may be formed are not considered in the present work. The student will find copious references to the literature in the following :—

(16) EDGEWORTH, E. Y., "Reports of the Committee appointed for the

purpoee of investigating the best methods of ascertaining and measuring Variations in the Value of the Monetary Standard," *British Association Reports*, 1887 (p. 247), 1888 (p. 181), 1889 (p. 133), and 1890 (p. 485).
(17) EDGEWORTH, F. Y., Article "Index-numbers" in Palgrave's *Dictionary of Political Economy*, vol. ii.; Macmillan, 1896.
(18) FOUNTAIN, H., "Memorandum on the Construction of Index-numbers of Prices," in the Board of Trade *Report on Wholesale and Retail Prices in the United Kingdom*, 1903.

EXERCISES,

1. Verify the following means and medians from the data of Table VI., Chap. VI., p. 88.

Stature in Inches for Adult Males in—

	England.	Scotland.	Wales.	Ireland.
Mean . . .	67·31	68·55	66·62	67·78
Median . . .	67·35	68·48	66·56	67·69

In the calculation of the means, use the same arbitrary origin as in Example ii., and check your work by the method of § 13 (*b*).

2. Find the mean weight of adult males in the United Kingdom from the data in the last column of Table IX., Chap VI., p. 95. Also find the median weight, and hence the approximate mode, by the method of § 20.

3. Similarly, find the mean, median, and approximate value of the mode for the distribution of fecundity in race-horses, Table X., Chap. VI., p. 96.

4. Using a graphical method, find the median annual value of houses assessed to inhabited house duty in the financial year 1885-6 from the data of Table IV., Chap. VI., p. 83.

5. (Data from Sauerbeck, *Jour. Roy. Stat. Soc.*, March 1909.) The figures in columns 1 and 2 of the small table below show the index-numbers (or percentages) of prices of certain animal foods in the years 1898 and 1908, on their average prices during the years 1867-77. In column 3 have been added the ratios of the index-numbers in 1908 to the index-numbers in 1898, the latter being taken as 100.

Find the average ratio of prices in 1908 to prices in 1898, taken as 100:—
(1) From the arithmetic mean of the ratios in col. 3.
(2) From the ratio of the arithmetic means of cols. 1 and 2.
(3) From the ratio of the geometric means of cols. 1 and 2.
(4) From the geometric mean of the ratios in col. 3.
Note that, by § 25, the last two methods must give the same result.

Commodity.	Index- number of price in		Ratio
	1898.	1908.	08/98.
	1.	2.	3.
1. Beef, primo . . .	78	88	112·8
2. Beef, middling . . .	72	90	125·0
3. Mutton, prime . . .	84	92	109·5
4. Mutton, middling .	67	95	141·8
5. Pork	87	83	95·4
6. Bacon	78	84	107·7
7. Butter	76	91	119·7

6. (Data from census of 1901.) The table below shows the population of the rural sanitary districts of Essex, the urban sanitary districts (other than the borough of West Ham), and the borough of West Ham, at the censuses of 1891 and 1901. Estimate the total population of the county at a date midway between the two censuses, (1) on the assumption that the percentage rate of increase is constant for the county as a whole, (2) on the assumption that the percentage rate of increase is constant in each group of districts and the borough of West Ham.

Essex.	Population.	
	1891.	1901.
Rural districts . . .	232,867	240,776
West Ham	204,903	267,358
Other urban districts . .	345,604	575,864
Total .	783,374	1,083,998

7. (Data from *Agricultural Statistics* for 1905, Cd. 3061, 1906.) The following statement shows the monthly average prices of eggs in Great Britain in 1905, as compiled from the weekly returns of market prices for first and second quality British eggs, per 120 :—

Month.	First Quality.	Second Quality.
	s. d.	s. d.
January . . .	13 0	11 0
February . .	11 0	9 0
March	8 0	6 0
April . , .	7 6	6 6
May . . .	8 0	7 6
June . . .	8 6	8 0
July . . .	9 6	8 6
August . . .	11 0	10 0
September . . .	11 6	10 6
October	14 0	12 6
November . . .	18 0	16 0
December . . .	17 6	15 0
Mean for year .	11 5½	10 0½

What would have been the mean price for the year in each case if the wholesale prices had been recorded in the same way as retail prices, *i.e.* at so many eggs per shilling ? State your answer in the form of the equivalent price per 120, and obtain it in the shortest way by taking the harmonic mean of the above prices (*cf.* § 27).

8. Supposing the frequencies of values 0, 1, 2, . . . of a variable to be given by the terms of the binomial series

$$q^n, \; n.q^{n-1}.p, \; \frac{n(n-1)}{1.2}q^{n-2}.p^2, \; \ldots .$$

where $p + q = 1$, find the mean.

CHAPTER VIII.

MEASURES OF DISPERSION, ETC.

1. THE simplest possible measure of the dispersion of a series of values of a variable is the actual range, *i.e.* the difference between the greatest and least values observed. While this is frequently quoted, it is as a rule the worst of all possible measures for any serious purpose. There are seldom real upper and lower limits to the possible values of the variable, very large or very small values being only more or less infrequent : the range is therefore subject to meaningless fluctuations of considerable magnitude according as values of greater or less infrequency happen to have been actually observed. Note, for instance, the figures of Table IX., Chap. VI. p. 95, showing the frequency distributions of weights of adult males in the several parts of the United Kingdom. In Wales, one individual was observed with a weight of over 280 lbs., the next heaviest being under 260 lbs. The addition of the one very exceptional individual has increased the range by some 30 lbs., or about one-fifth. A measure subject to erratic alterations by casual influences in this way is clearly not of much use for comparative purposes. Moreover, the measure takes no account of the form of the distribution within the limits of the range ; it might well happen that, of two distributions covering precisely the same range of variation, the one showed the observations for the most part closely clustered round the average, while the other exhibited an almost even distribution of frequency over the whole range. Clearly we should not regard two such distributions as exhibiting the same *dispersion*, though they exhibit the same *range*. Some sort of measure of dispersion is therefore required, based, like the averages discussed in the last

chapter, on all the observations made, so that no single observation can have an unduly preponderant effect on its magnitude ; indeed, the measure should possess all the properties laid down as desirable for an *average* in § 4 of Chap. VII. There are three such measures in common use—the **standard deviation**, the **mean deviation**, and the **quartile deviation** or **semi-interquartile range**, of which the first is the most important.

2. *The Standard Deviation.*—The standard deviation is the square root of the arithmetic mean of the squares of all deviations, deviations being measured from the arithmetic mean of the observations. If the standard deviation be denoted by σ, and a deviation from the arithmetic mean by x, as in the last chapter, then the standard deviation is given by the equation

$$\sigma^2 = \frac{1}{N}\Sigma(x^2) \qquad . \quad . \quad . \quad . \quad (1)$$

To square all the deviations may seem at first sight an artificial procedure, but it must be remembered that it would be useless to take the mere sum of the deviations, in order to obtain a measure of dispersion, since this sum is necessarily zero if deviations be taken from the mean. In order to obtain some quantity that shall vary with the dispersion it is necessary to average the deviations by a process that treats them as if they were all of the same sign, and *squaring* is the simplest process for eliminating signs which leads to results of algebraical convenience.

3. A quantity analogous to the standard deviation may be defined in more general terms. Let A be any arbitrary value of X, and let ξ (as in Chap. VII. § 8) denote the deviation of X from A ; *i.e.* let

$$\xi = X - A.$$

Then we may define the root-mean-square deviation s from the origin A by the equation

$$s^2 = \frac{1}{N}\Sigma(\xi^2) \quad . \qquad . \quad . \quad . \qquad (2)$$

In terms of this definition the standard deviation is the root-mean-square deviation from the mean. There is a very simple relation between the standard deviation and the root-mean-square deviation from any other origin. Let

$$M - A = d. \qquad . \qquad . \qquad . \qquad (3)$$

so that $\xi = x + d.$

Then $\xi^2 = x^2 + 2x.d + d^2,$

$$\Sigma(\xi^2) = \Sigma(x^2) + 2d.\Sigma(x) + N.d^2.$$

But the sum of the deviations from the mean is zero, therefore the second term vanishes, and accordingly

$$s^2 = \sigma^2 + d^2 . \quad . \quad . \quad . \quad (4)$$

Hence the root-mean-square deviation is least when deviations are measured from the mean, *i.e.* the standard deviation is the least possible root-mean-square deviation.

$\Sigma(\xi^2)$, or $\Sigma(f.\xi^2)$ if we are dealing with a grouped distribution and f is the frequency of ξ, is sometimes termed the *second moment* of the distribution about A, just as $\Sigma(\xi)$ or $\Sigma(f.\xi)$ is termed the first moment (*cf.* Chap. VII. § 8): we shall not make use of the term in the present work. Generally, $\Sigma(f.\xi^n)$ is termed the nth moment.

4. If σ and d are the two sides of a right-angled triangle, s is

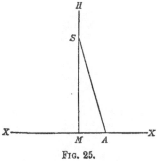

FIG. 25.

the hypotenuse. If, then, MH be the vertical through the mean of a frequency-distribution (fig. 25), and MS be set off equal to the standard deviation (on the same scale in which the variable X is plotted along the base), SA will be the root-mean-square deviation from the point A. This construction gives a concrete idea of the way in which the root-mean-square deviation depends on the origin from which deviations are measured. It will be seen that for small values of d the difference of s from σ will be very minute, since A will lie very nearly on the circle drawn through M with centre S and radius SM: slight errors in the mean due to approximations in calculation will not, therefore, appreciably affect the value of the standard deviation.

5. If we have to deal with relatively few, say thirty or forty, ungrouped observations, the method of calculating the standard deviation is perfectly straightforward. It is illustrated by the figures given below for the estimated average earnings of

agricultural labourers in 38 rural unions. The values (earnings) are first of all totalled and the total divided by N to give the arithmetic mean M, viz. 15s. $11\frac{10}{38}$d., or 15s. 11d. to the nearest penny. The earnings being estimates, it is not necessary to take the average to any higher degree of accuracy. Having found the mean, the difference of each observation from the mean is next written down as in col. 3, one penny being taken as the unit : the signs are not entered, as they are not wanted, but the work should be checked by totalling the positive and negative differences separately. [The positive total is 300 and the negative 290, thus checking the value for the mean, viz. 15s. 11d. + 10/38.]

Finally, each difference is squared, and the squares entered in col. 4,—tables of squares are useful for such work if any of the differences to be squared are large (see list of Tables, p. 356). The sum of the squares is 16,018. Treating the value taken for the mean as sensibly accurate, we have—

$$\sigma^2 = \frac{16018}{38} = 421\cdot5$$

$$\sigma = 20\cdot5d.$$

If we wish to be more precise we can reduce to the true mean by the use of equation (4), as follows :—

$$s^2 = \frac{16,018}{38} = 421\cdot5263$$

$$d = \frac{10}{38} = 0\cdot2632 ; \quad d^2 = 0\cdot0693$$

Hence

$$\sigma^2 = s^2 - d^2 = 421\cdot4570$$
$$\sigma = 20\cdot529d.$$

Evidently this reduction, in the given case, is unnecessary, illustrating the fact mentioned at the end of § 4, that small errors in the mean have little effect on the value found for the standard deviation. The first value is correct within a very small fraction of a penny.

CALCULATION OF THE STANDARD DEVIATION: *Example* i.—*Calculation of Mean and Standard Deviation for a Short Series of Observations ungrouped. Estimated Average Weekly Earnings of Agricultural Labourers in Thirty-eight Rural Unions, in 1892-3.* (W. Little: *Labour Commission; Report,* vol. v., part i., 1894.)

1.	2.	3.	4.
Union.	Earnings (Shillings and Pence).	Difference ξ (Pence).	(Difference)^2 ξ^2.
	s.　d.		
1. Glendale	20　9	58	3,364
2. Wigton	20　3	52	2,704
3. Garstang	19　8	45	2,025
4. Belper	18　6	31	961
5. Nantwich	17　8	21	441
6. Atcham	17　6	19	361
7. Driffield	17　1	14	196
8. Uttoxeter	17　0	13	169
9. Wetherby	17　0	13	169
10. Easingwold . . .	16　11	12	144
11. Southwell	16　6	7	49
12. Hollingbourn . .	16　4	5	25
13. Melton Mowbray . .	16　3	4	16
14. Truro . . .	16　3	4	16
15. Godstone . . .	16　0	1	1
16. Louth	16　0	1	1
17. Brixworth	15　9	2	4
18. Crediton	15　8	3	9
19. Holbeach	15　6	5	25
20. Maldon	15　6	5	25
21. Monmouth . . .	15　4	7	49
22. St Neots	15　3	8	64
23. Swaffham	15　0	11	121
24. Thakeham	15　0	11	121
25. Thame . . .	15　0	11	121
26. Thingoe	15　0	11	121
27. Basingstoke . . .	15　0	11	121
28. Cirencester . . .	15　0	11	121
29. N.Witchford . .	14　10	13	169
30. Pewsey	14　9	14	196
31. Bromyard	14　9	14	196
32. Wantage	14　9	14	196
33. Stratford-on-Avon . .	14　7	16	256
34. Dorchester . . .	14　6	17	289
35. Woburn	14　6	17	289
36. Buntingford . . .	14　4	19	361
37. Pershore . . .	13　6	29	841
38. Langport	12　6	41	1,681
Total .	605　8 ⎰	+300 ⎱	⎰ 16,018 ⎱
		−290	

The figures dealt with in this illustration are estimates of the weekly *earnings* of the agricultural labourers, *i.e.* they include allowances for gifts in kind, such as coal, potatoes, cider, etc. The estimated weekly money wages are, however, also given in the same Report, and we are thus enabled to make an interesting comparison of the dispersions of the two. It might be expected that earnings would vary less than wages, as his earnings and not the mere money wages he receives are the important matter to the labourer, and as a fact we find

Standard deviation of weekly earnings . . 20·5d.
  „   „   „   wages . 26·0d.

The arithmetic mean wage is 13s. 5d.

6. If we have to deal with a grouped frequency-distribution, the same artifices and approximations are used as in the calculation of the mean (Chap. VII. §§ 8, 9, 10). The mid-value of one of the class-intervals is chosen as the arbitrary origin A from which to measure the deviations ξ, the class-interval is treated as a unit throughout the arithmetic, and all the observations within any one class-interval are treated as if they were identical with the mid-value of the interval. If, as before, we denote the frequency in any one interval by f, these f observations contribute $f\xi^2$ to the sum of the squares of deviations and we have—

$$s^2 = \frac{1}{N}\Sigma(f\xi^2).$$

The standard deviation is then calculated from equation (4).

7. The whole of the work proceeds naturally as an extension of that necessary for calculating the mean, and we accordingly use the same illustrations as in the last chapter. Thus in Example ii. below, cols. 1, 2, 3, and 4 are the same as those we have already given in Example i. of Chap. VII. for the calculation of the mean. Column 5 gives the figures necessary for calculating the standard deviation, and is derived directly from col. 4 by multiplying the figures of that column again by ξ. Thus $90 \times 5 = 450$, $192 \times 4 = 768$, and so on. The work is therefore done very rapidly. The remaining steps of the arithmetic are given below the table; the student must be careful to remember the final conversion, if necessary, from the class-interval as unit to the natural unit of measurement. In this case the value found is 2·48 class-intervals, and the class-interval being half a unit, that is 1·24 per cent.

CALCULATION OF THE STANDARD DEVIATION : *Example* ii.—*Calculation of the Standard Deviation of the Percentages of the Population in receipt of Relief, in addition to the Mean, from the figures of Table VIII. of Chap. VI.* (*Cf.* the work for the mean alone, p. 111.)

(1) Percentage in receipt of Relief.	(2) Frequency. f.	(3) Deviation from Value A. ξ.	(4) Product. $f\xi$.	(5) Product. $f\xi^2$.
1	18	− 5	90	450
1·5	48	− 4	192	768
2	72	− 3	216	648
2·5	89	− 2	178	356
3	100	− 1	100	100
3·5	90	0	− 776	—
4	75	+ 1	75	75
4·5	60	+ 2	120	240
5	40	+ 3	120	360
5·5	21	+ 4	84	336
6	11	+ 5	55	275
6·5	5	+ 6	30	180
7	1	+ 7	7	49
7·5	1	+ 8	8	64
8	...	+ 9	—	—
8·5	1	+10	10	100
Total	632	—	+509	4001

From previous work, p. 111, $M - A = d = - 0\cdot4225$ class-intervals.

$$\frac{\Sigma(f\xi^2)}{N} = \frac{4001}{632} = 6\cdot3307.$$

$$\therefore \quad \sigma^2 = 6\cdot3307 - (\cdot4225)^2$$
$$= 6\cdot1522.$$

$$\therefore \quad \sigma = 2\cdot48 \text{ intervals} = 1\cdot24 \text{ per cent.}$$

To illustrate again the value of the standard deviation for purposes of comparison, figures are given below showing the means and standard deviations of similar distributions for a series of years from·1850. It will be seen that not only did the mean decrease during the period, but the standard deviation decreased to an equally marked extent, having been halved between 1850 and 1891 ; the average was lowered, and at the same time the percentages of the population in receipt of relief clustered much more closely round the lower average.

Means and Standard Deviations of the Distributions of Pauperism (Percentage of the Population in receipt of Poor-law Relief) in the Unions of England and Wales since 1850. (From Yule, *Jour. Roy. Stat. Soc.*, vol. lix., 1896, figures slightly amended.)

Year.	Percentage of the Population in receipt of Relief.	
	Arithmetic Mean.	Standard Deviation.
1850	6·51	2·50
1860	5·20	2·07
1870	5·45	2·02
1881	3·68	1·36
1891	3·29	1·24

8. In the table given on p. 141 (Example iii.), the calculation of the standard deviation is similarly shown for the distribution of the statures of adult males in the British Isles, the work being continued from the stage which it reached for the calculation of the mean in Example ii. of Chap. VII. The steps of the arithmetic hardly call for further explanation, but it may be noted that the class-interval being a unit in this case, no conversion of the standard deviation from class-intervals to units is required.

9. The student must remember, as in the case of the calculation of the mean, that the treatment of all values within each class-interval as if they were identical with the mid-value of the interval is an approximation and no more (*cf.* Chap. VII. § 11), though, for a distribution of the symmetrical or moderately asymmetrical type with a class-interval not greater than one-twentieth or so of the range, the approximation may be a very close one. But while the value of the arithmetic mean may be either increased or decreased by grouping, in the case of distributions which are not more than slightly asymmetrical, the standard deviation of such distributions tends to be increased, and the increase is the greater the cruder the grouping. We give an approximate correction for this effect later (Chap. XI. § 4). The student is recommended to test for himself the effect of grouping in two or three cases.

10. It is a useful empirical rule to remember that a range of six times the standard deviation usually includes 99 per cent. or more of all the observations in the case of distributions of the symmetrical or moderately asymmetrical type. Thus in Example

CALCULATION OF THE STANDARD DEVIATION : *Example* iii.—*Calculation of the Standard Deviation of Stature of Male Adults in the British Isles from the figures of Table VI., p. 88. (Cf. p. 112 for the calculation of mean alone.)*

(1) Height. Inches.	(2) Frequency. f.	(3) Deviation from Value A. ξ.	(4) Product. $f.\xi$.	(5) Product $f.\xi^2$.
57–	2	–10	20	200
58–	4	– 9	36	324
59–	14	– 8	112	896
60–	41	– 7	287	2,009
61–	83	– 6	498	2,988
62–	169	– 5	845	4,225
63–	394	– 4	1576	6,304
64–	669	– 3	2007	6,021
65–	990	– 2	1980	3,960
66–	1223	– 1	1223	1,223
67–	1329	0	– 8584	—
68–	1230	+ 1	1230	1,230
69–	1063	+ 2	2126	4,252
70–	646	+ 3	1938	5,814
71–	392	+ 4	1568	6,272
72–	202	+ 5	1010	5,050
73–	79	+ 6	474	2,844
74–	32	+ 7	224	1,568
75–	16	+ 8	128	1,024
76–	5	+ 9	45	405
77–	2	+10	20	200
Total	8585	—	+8763	56,809

From previous work, $M - A = d = + \cdot 0209$ class-intervals or inches.

$$\frac{\Sigma(f.\xi^2)}{N} = \frac{56809}{8585} = 6 \cdot 6172.$$

$$\sigma^2 = 6 \cdot 6172 - (\cdot 0209)^2$$
$$= 6 \cdot 6168.$$

$$\therefore \quad \sigma = 2 \cdot 57 \text{ class-intervals or inches.}$$

ii. the standard deviation is 1·24 per cent. ; six times this is 7·44 per cent., and a range from 0·75 to 8·19 per cent. includes all but one observation out of 632. In Example iii. the standard deviation is 2·57 in., six times this is 15·42 in., and a range from, say, 60 in. to 75·4 in. includes all but some 37 out of 8585 individuals, *i.e.* about 99·6 per cent. This rough rule serves to give a more definite and concrete meaning to the standard deviation, and also to check arithmetical work to some extent—sufficiently, that is to say, to guard against very gross blunders. It must not be expected to hold for short series of observations : in Example i., for instance, the actual range is a good deal less than six times the standard deviation.

11. The standard deviation is the measure of dispersion which it is most easy to treat by algebraical methods, resembling in this respect the arithmetic mean amongst measures of position. The majority of illustrations of its treatment must be postponed to a later stage (Chap. XI.), but the work of § 3 has already served as one example, and we may take another by continuing the work of § 13 (b), Chap. VII. In that section it was shown that if a series of observations of which the mean is M consist of two component series, of which the means are M_1 and M_2 respectively,

$$N.M = N_1.M_1 + N_2 M_2,$$

N_1 and N_2 being the numbers of observations in the two component series, and $N = N_1 + N_2$ the number in the entire series. Similarly, the standard deviation σ of the whole series may be expressed in terms of the standard deviations σ_1 and σ_2 of the components and their respective means. Let

$$M_1 - M = d_1$$
$$M_2 - M = d_2.$$

Then the mean-square deviations of the component series about the mean M are, by equation (4), $\sigma_1^2 + d_1^2$ and $\sigma_2^2 + d_2^2$ respectively. Therefore, for the whole series,

$$N.\sigma^2 = N_1(\sigma_1^2 + d_1^2) + N_2(\sigma_2^2 + d_2^2) \quad . \quad . \quad (5)$$

If the numbers of observations in the component series be equal and the means be coincident, we have as a special case—

$$\sigma^2 = \tfrac{1}{2}(\sigma_1^2 + \sigma_2^2) \quad . \quad . \quad . \quad . \quad (6)$$

so that in this case the square of the standard deviation of the whole series is the arithmetic mean of the squares of the standard deviations of its components.

It is evident that the form of the relation (5) is quite general : if a series of observations consists of r component series with standard deviations $\sigma_1, \sigma_2, \ldots \sigma_r$, and means diverging from the general mean of the whole series by $d_1, d_2, \ldots d_r$, the standard deviation σ of the whole series is given (using m to denote any subscript) by the equation—

$$N.\sigma^2 = \Sigma(N_m.\sigma_m^2) + \Sigma(N_m.d_m^2) \quad . \quad . \quad . \quad (7)$$

Again, as in § 13 of Chap. VII., it is convenient to note, for the checking of arithmetic, that if the same arbitrary origin be used for the calculation of the standard deviations in a number of component distributions we must have

$$\Sigma(f.\xi^2) = \Sigma(f_1.\xi_1^2) + \Sigma(f_2.\xi_2^2) + \ldots + \Sigma(f_r.\xi_r^2) \qquad (8)$$

12. As another useful illustration, let us find the standard deviation of the first N natural numbers. The mean in this case is evidently $(N+1)/2$. Further, as is shown in any elementary Algebra, the sum of the squares of the first N natural numbers is

$$\frac{N(N+1)(2N+1)}{6}.$$

The standard deviation σ is therefore given by the equation—

$$\sigma^2 = \tfrac{1}{6}(N+1)(2N+1) - \tfrac{1}{4}(N+1)^2,$$

that is, $\qquad\qquad \sigma^2 = \tfrac{1}{12}(N^2 - 1) \qquad . \qquad . \qquad . \qquad . \quad (9)$

This result is of service if the relative merit of, or the relative intensity of some character in, the different individuals of a series is recorded not by means of measurements, *e.g.* marks awarded on some system of examination, but merely by means of their respective positions when ranked in order as regards the character, in the same way as boys are numbered in a class. With N individuals there are always N *ranks*, as they are termed, whatever the character, and the standard deviation is therefore always that given by equation (9).

Another useful result follows at once from equation (9), namely, the standard deviation of a frequency-distribution in which all values of X within a range $\pm l/2$ on either side of the mean are equally frequent, values outside these limits not occurring, so that the frequency-distribution may be represented by a rectangle. The base l may be supposed divided into a very large number N of equal elements, and the standard deviation reduces to that of the first N natural numbers when N is made indefinitely large. The single unit then becomes negligible compared with N, and consequently

$$\sigma^2 = \frac{l^2}{12} \qquad . \qquad . \qquad . \qquad . \quad (10)$$

13. It will be seen from the preceding paragraphs that the standard deviation possesses the majority at least of the properties which are desirable in a measure of dispersion as in an average (Chap. VII. § 4). It is rigidly defined; it is based on all the observations made; it is calculated with reasonable ease; it lends itself readily to algebraical treatment; and we may add, though the student will have to take the statement on trust for the present, that it is, as a rule, the measure least affected by fluctuations of

sampling. On the other hand, it may be said that its general nature is not very readily comprehended, and that the process of squaring deviations and then taking the square root of the mean seems a little involved. The student will, however, soon surmount this feeling after a little practice in the calculation and use of the constant, and will realise, as he advances further, the advantages that it possesses. Such root-mean-square quantities, it may be added, frequently occur in other branches of science. The standard deviation should always be used as the measure of dispersion, unless there is some very definite reason for preferring another measure, just as the arithmetic mean should be used as the measure of position. It may be added here that the student will meet with the standard deviation under many different names, of which we have adopted the most recent (due to Pearson, ref. 2): many of the earlier names are hardly adapted to general use, as they bear evidence of their derivation from the theory of errors of observation. Thus the terms "mean error" (Gauss), "error of mean square" (Airy), and "mean square error" have all been used in the same sense. The square of the standard deviation, and also twice the square, have been termed the "fluctuation" (Edgeworth): the standard deviation multiplied by the square root of 2, the "modulus" (Airy),—the student will see later the reason for the adoption of the factor. The reciprocal of the modulus has been termed the "precision" (Lexis).

14. *The Mean Deviation.*—The mean deviation of a series of values of a variable is the arithmetic mean of their deviations from some average, taken without regard to their sign. The deviations may be measured either from the arithmetic mean or from the median, but the latter is the natural origin to use. Just as the root-mean-square deviation is least when deviations are measured from the arithmetic mean, so the mean deviation is least when deviations are measured from the median. For suppose that, for some origin exceeded by m values out of N, the mean deviation has a value Δ. Let the origin be displaced by an amount c until it is just exceeded by $m - 1$ of the values only, *i.e.* until it coincides with the mth value from the upper end of the series. By this displacement of the origin the sum of deviations in excess of the mean is reduced by $m.c$, while the sum of deviations in defect of the mean is increased by $(N - m)c$. The new mean deviation is therefore

$$\Delta + \frac{(N - m)c - mc}{N}$$

$$= \Delta + \frac{1}{N}(N - 2m)c.$$

The new mean deviation is accordingly less than the old so long as

$$m > \tfrac{1}{2}N.$$

That is to say, if N be even, the mean deviation is constant for all origins within the range between the $N/2$th and the $(N/2 + 1)$th observations, and this value is the least : if N be odd, the mean deviation is lowest when the origin coincides with the $(N+1)/2$th observation. The mean deviation is therefore a minimum when deviations are measured from the median or, if the latter be indeterminate, from an origin within the range in which it lies.

15. The calculation of the mean deviation either from the mean or from the median for a series of ungrouped observations is very simple. Take the figures of Example i. (p. 137) as an illustration. We have already found the mean (15s. 11d. to the nearest penny), and the deviations from the mean are written down in column 3. Adding up this column without respect to the sign of the deviations we find a total of 590. The mean deviation from the mean is therefore $590/38 = 15\cdot53$d. The mean deviation from the median is calculated in precisely the same way, but the median replaces the mean as the origin from which deviations are measured. The median is 15s. 6d. The deviations in pence run 63, 57, 50, 36, and so on; their sum is 570; and, accordingly, the mean deviation from the median is 15d. exactly.

16. In the case of a grouped frequency-distribution, the sum of deviations should be calculated first from the centre of the class-interval in which the mean (or median) lies, and then reduced to the mean as origin. Thus in the case of Example ii. the mean is $3\cdot29$ per cent. and lies in the class-interval centring round $3\cdot5$ per cent. We have already found that the sum of deviations in defect of $3\cdot5$ per cent. is 776, and of deviations in excess 509 : total (without regard to sign) 1285,—the unit of measurement being, of course, as it is necessary to remember, the class-interval. If the number of observations below the mean is N_1 and above the mean N_2, and $M - A = d$, as before, we have to add $N_1.d$ to the sum found and subtract $N_2.d$. In the present case $N_1 = 327$ and $N_2 = 305$, while $d = -0\cdot42$ class-intervals, therefore

$$d(N_1 - N_2) = -0\cdot42 \times 22 = -9\cdot2,$$

and the sum of deviations from the mean is $1285 - 9\cdot2 = 1275\cdot8$. Hence the mean deviation from the mean is $1275\cdot8/632 = 2\cdot019$ class-intervals, or $1\cdot01$ per cent.

17. The mean deviation from the median should be found in precisely similar fashion, but the mid-value of the interval in which the median (instead of the mean) lies should, for con-

10

venience, be taken as origin. Thus in Example ii. the median is (Chap. VII. § 15) 3·195 per cent. Hence 3·0 per cent. should be taken as the origin, $d = +0·39$ intervals, $N_1 = 327$, $N_2 = 305$. The deviation-sum with 3·0 as origin is found to be 1263, and the correction is $+0·39 \times 22 = +8·6$. Hence the mean deviation from the median is 2·012 intervals, or again 1·01 per cent. The value is really smaller than that of the mean deviation from the arithmetic mean, but the difference is too slight to affect the second place of decimals.

It should be noted that, as in the case of the standard deviation, this method of calculation implies the assumption that all the values of X within any one class-interval may be treated as if they were the mid-value of that interval. This is, of course, an approximation, but as a rule gives results of amply sufficient accuracy for practice if the class-interval be kept reasonably small (cf. again Chap. VI. § 5). We have left it as an exercise to the student to find the correction to be applied if the values in each interval are treated as if they were evenly distributed over the interval, instead of concentrated at its centre (Question 7).

18. The mean deviation, it will be seen, can be calculated rather more rapidly than the standard deviation, though in the case of a grouped distribution the difference in ease of calculation is not great. It is not, on the other hand, a convenient magnitude for algebraical treatment; for example, the mean deviation of a distribution obtained by combining several others cannot in general be expressed in terms of the mean deviations of the component distributions, but depends upon their forms. As a rule, it is more affected by fluctuations of sampling than is the standard deviation, but may be less affected if large and erratic deviations lying somewhat beyond the bulk of the distribution are liable to occur. This may happen, for example, in some forms of experimental work, and in such cases the use of the mean deviation may be slightly preferable to that of the standard deviation.

19. It is a useful empirical rule for the student to remember that for symmetrical or only moderately asymmetrical distributions, approaching the ideal forms of figs. 5 and 9, the mean deviation is usually very nearly four-fifths of the standard deviation. Thus for the distribution of pauperism we have

$$\frac{\text{mean deviation}}{\text{standard deviation}} = \frac{1·01}{1·24} = 0·81.$$

In the case of the distribution of male statures in the British Isles, Example iii., the ratio found is 0·80. For a short series of observations like the wage statistics of Example i. a regular result could hardly be expected: the actual ratio is $15·0/20·5 = 0·73$.

We pointed out in § 10 that in distributions of the simple forms referred to, a range of six times the standard deviation contains over 99 per cent. of all the observations. If the mean deviation be employed as the measure of dispersion, we must substitute a range of $7\frac{1}{2}$ times this measure.

20. *The Quartile Deviation or Semi-interquartile Range.*—If a value Q_1 of the variable be determined of such magnitude that one-quarter of all the values observed are less than Q_1 and three-quarters greater, then Q_1 is termed the lower quartile. Similarly, if a value Q_3 be determined such that three-quarters of all the values observed are less than Q_3 and one-quarter only greater, then Q_3 is termed the upper quartile. The two quartiles and the median divide the observed values of the variable into four classes of equal frequency. If Mi be the value of the median, in a symmetrical distribution ·

$$Mi - Q_1 = Q_3 - Mi,$$

and the difference may be taken as a measure of dispersion. But as no distribution is rigidly symmetrical, it is usual to take as the measure

$$Q = \frac{Q_3 - Q_1}{2},$$

and Q is termed the quartile deviation, or better, the semi-interquartile range—it is not a measure of the deviation from any particular average : the old name *probable error* should be confined to the theory of sampling (Chap. XV. § 17).

21. In the case of a short series of ungrouped observations the quartiles are determined, like the median, by inspection. In the wage statistics of Example i., for instance, there are 38 observations, and $38/4 = 9\cdot5$: What is the lower quartile ? The student may be tempted to take it halfway between the ninth and tenth observations from the bottom of the list ; but this would be wrong, for then there would be nine observations only below the value chosen instead of $9\cdot5$. The quartile must be taken as given by the tenth observation itself, which may be regarded as divided by the quartile, and falling half above it and half below. Therefore

Lower quartile $Q_1 = 14$s. 10d.

Upper quartile $Q_3 = 16$s. 11d.

and $Q = \frac{Q_3 - Q_1}{2} = 12\cdot5d.$

22. In the case of a grouped distribution, the quartiles, like the median, are determined by simple arithmetical or by

graphical interpolation (*cf.* Chap. VII. §§ 15, 16). Thus for the distribution of pauperism, Example ii., we have

$$632 \div 4 = 158$$

Total frequency under 2·25 per cent. $= 138$

	Difference =	20
Frequency in interval 2·25 – 2·75	=	89

Whence $Q_1 = 2 \cdot 25 + \dfrac{20}{89} \times 0 \cdot 5$ $\qquad = 2 \cdot 362$ per cent.

Similarly we find Q_3 $\qquad\qquad\qquad = 4 \cdot 130$,,

Hence $\qquad\qquad Q = \dfrac{Q_3 - Q_1}{2} = 0 \cdot 884$,,

It is left to the student to check the value by graphical interpolation.

23. For distributions approaching the ideal forms of figs. 5 and 9, the semi-interquartile range is usually about two-thirds of the standard deviation. Thus for Example ii. we find

$$\frac{Q}{\sigma} = \frac{0 \cdot 884}{1 \cdot 24} = 0 \cdot 71.$$

The distribution of statures, Example iii., gives the ratio 0·68. The short series of wage statistics in Example i. could not be expected to give a result in very strict conformity with the rule, but the actual ratio, viz. 0·61, does not diverge greatly. It follows from this ratio that a range of nine times the semi-interquartile range, approximately, is required to cover the same proportion of the total frequency (99 per cent. or more) as a range of six times the standard deviation.

24. Of the three measures of dispersion, the semi-interquartile range has the most clear and simple meaning. It is calculated, like the median, with great ease, and the quartiles may be found, if necessary, by measuring two individuals only. If, *e.g.*, the dispersion as well as the average stature of a group of men is required to be determined with the least possible expenditure of time, they may be simply ranked in order of height, and the three men picked out for measurement who stand in the centre and one-quarter from either end of the rank. This measure of dispersion may also be useful as a makeshift if the calculation of the standard deviation has been rendered difficult or impossible owing to the employment of an irregular classification of the frequency or of an indefinite terminal class. Such uses are, however, a little exceptional, and, generally speaking, the

semi-interquartile range as a measure of dispersion is not to be recommended, unless simplicity of meaning is of primary importance, owing to the lack of algebraical convenience which it shares with the median. Further, it is obvious that the quartile, like the median, may become indeterminate, and that the use of this measure of dispersion is undesirable in cases of discontinuous variation : the student should refer again to the discussion of the similar disadvantage in the case of the median, Chap. VII. § 14. It has, however, been largely used in the past, particularly for anthropometric work.

25. *Measures of Relative Dispersion.*—As was pointed out in Chapter VII. § 26, if relative size is regarded as influencing not only the average, but also deviations from the average, the geometric mean seems the natural form of average to use, and deviations should be measured by their ratios to the geometric mean. As already stated, however, this method of measuring deviations, with its accompanying employment of the geometric mean, has never come into general use. It is a much more simple matter to allow for the influence of size by taking the ratio of the measure of absolute dispersion (*e.g.* standard deviation, mean deviation, or quartile deviation) to the average (mean or median) from which the deviations were measured. Pearson has termed the quantity

$$v = 100 \cdot \frac{\sigma}{M},$$

i.e. the percentage ratio of the standard deviation to the arithmetic mean, the **coefficient of variation** (ref. 7), and has used it, for example, in comparing the relative variations of corresponding organs or characters in the two sexes : the ratio of the quartile deviation to the median has also been suggested (Verschaeffelt, ref. 8). Such a measure of relative dispersion is evidently a mere number, and its magnitude is independent of the units of measurement employed.

26. *Measures of Asymmetry or Skewness.*—If we have to compare a series of distributions of varying degrees of asymmetry, or skewness, as Pearson has termed it, some numerical measure of this character is desirable. Such a measure of skewness should obviously be independent of the units in which we measure the variable—*e.g.* the skewness of the distribution of the weights of a given set of men should not be dependent on our choice of the pound, the stone, or the kilogramme as the unit of weight—and the measure should accordingly be a mere number. Thus the difference between the deviations of the two quartiles on either side of the median *indicates* the existence of skewness, but to measure the degree of skewness we should take the ratio of this

difference to some quantity of the same dimensions, *e.g.* the semi-interquartile range. Our measure would then be, taking the skewness to be positive if the longer tail of the distribution runs in the direction of high values of X,

$$\text{skewness} = \frac{(Q_3 - Mi) - (Mi - Q_1)}{Q} = \frac{Q_1 + Q_3 - 2Mi}{Q} \qquad (11)$$

This would not be a bad measure if we were using the quartile deviation as a measure of dispersion : its lowest value is zero, when the distribution is symmetrical ; and while its highest possible value is 2, it would rarely in practice attain higher numerical values than ± 1. A similar measure might be based on the mean deviations in excess and in defect of the mean. There is, however, only one generally recognised measure of skewness, and that is Pearson's measure (ref. 9)—

$$\text{skewness} = \frac{\text{mean} - \text{mode}}{\text{standard deviation}} \qquad . \qquad (12)$$

This is evidently zero for a symmetrical distribution, in which mode and mean coincide. No upper limit to the ratio is apparent from the formula, but, as a fact, the value does not exceed unity for frequency-distributions resembling generally the ideal distributions of fig. 9. As the mode is a difficult form of average to determine by elementary methods, it may be noted that the numerator of the above fraction may, in the case of frequency-distributions of the forms referred to, be replaced approximately by 3(mean − median), (*cf.* Chap. VII. § 20). The measure (12) is much more sensitive than (11) for moderate degrees of asymmetry.

27. *The Method of Percentiles.*—We may conclude this chapter by describing briefly a method that has been largely used in the past in lieu of the methods dealt with in Chapters VI. and VII., and the preceding paragraphs of this chapter, for summarising such statistics as we have been considering. If the values of the variable (variates, as they are sometimes termed) be ranged in order of magnitude, and a value P of the variable be determined such that a percentage p of the total frequency lies below it and $100 - p$ above, then P is termed a percentile. If a series of percentiles be determined for short intervals, *e.g.* 5 per cent. or 10 per cent., they suffice by themselves to show the general form of the distribution. This is Sir Francis Galton's method of percentiles. The deciles, or values of the variable which divide the total frequency into ten equal parts, form a natural and convenient series of percentiles to use. The fifth decile, or value of the variable which has 50 per cent. of the observed values

above it and 50 per cent. below, is the median : the two quartiles
lie between the second and third and the seventh and eighth
deciles respectively.

28. The deciles, like the median and quartiles, may be
determined either by arithmetical or by graphical interpolation,
excluding the cases in which, like the former constants, they
become indeterminate (*cf.* § 24). It is hardly necessary to give
an illustration of the former process, as the method is precisely
the same as for median and quartiles (Chap. VII. § 15, and above,
§ 22). Fig. 26 shows, of course on a very much reduced scale, the

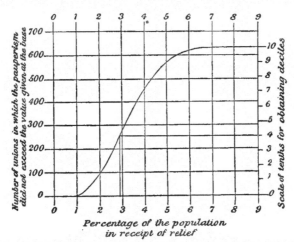

FIG. 26.—Curve showing the number of Districts of England and Wales in
which the Pauperism on 1st January 1891 did not exceed any given percentage of the population (same data as Fig. 10, p. 92): graphical
determination of Deciles.

curve used for obtaining the deciles by the graphical method in
the case of the distribution of pauperism (Example ii. above).
The figures of the original table are added up step by step from
the top, so as to give the total frequency not exceeding the upper
limit of each class-interval, and ordinates are then erected to a
horizontal base to represent on some scale these *integrated
frequencies*: a smooth curve is then drawn through the tops of
the ordinates so obtained. This curve, as will be seen from the
figure, rises slowly at first when the frequencies are small, then
more rapidly as they increase, and finally turns over again and
becomes quite flat as the frequencies tail off to zero. The deciles

may be readily obtained from such a curve by dividing the terminal ordinate into ten equal parts, and projecting the points so obtained horizontally across to the curve and then vertically down to the base. The construction is indicated on the figure for the fourth decile, the value of which is approximately 2·88 per cent.

29. The curve of fig. 26 may be drawn in a different way by taking a horizontal base divided into ten or a hundred equal parts (grades, as Sir Francis Galton has termed them), and erecting at each point so obtained a vertical proportional to the corresponding percentile. This gives the curve of fig. 27, which was obtained by merely redrafting fig. 26. The curve is of so-called

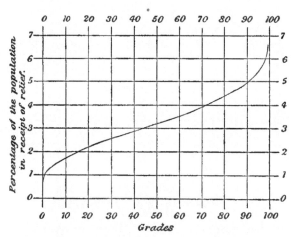

Fig. 27.—The curve of Fig. 26 redrawn so as to give the Pauperism corresponding to each grade : Galton's "Ogive."

ogive form. The ogive curve for the distribution of statures (Example iii.) is shown for comparison in fig. 28. It will be noticed that the ogive curve does not bring out the asymmetry of the distribution of pauperism nearly so clearly as the frequency-polygon, fig. 10, p. 92.

30. The method of percentiles has some advantages as a method of representation, as the meaning of the various percentiles is so simple and readily understood. An extension of the method to the treatment of non-measurable characters has also become of some importance. For example, the capacity of the different boys in a class as regards some school subject cannot be directly measured, but it may not be very difficult for the master to

arrange them in order of merit as regards this character: if the
boys are then "numbered up" in order, the number of each boy,
or his rank, serves as some sort of index to his capacity (*cf.* the
remarks in § 12. It should be noted that rank in this sense is
not quite the same as grade; if a boy is tenth, say, from the
bottom in a class of a hundred his grade is 9·5, but the method
is in principle the same with that of grades or percentiles).
The method of ranks, grades, or percentiles in such a case may
be a very serviceable auxiliary, though, of course, it is better if
possible to obtain a numerical measure. But if, in the case of a
measurable character, the percentiles are used not merely as

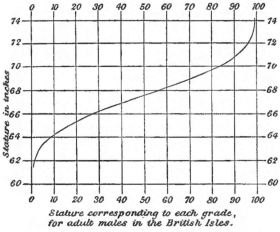

FIG. 28.—Ogive Curve for Stature, same data as Fig. 6, p. 89.

constants illustrative of certain aspects of the frequency-distribution, but entirely to replace the table giving the frequency-
distribution, serious inconvenience may be caused, as the
application of other methods to the data is barred. Given the
table showing the frequency-distribution, the reader can calculate
not only the percentiles, but any form of average or measure of
dispersion that has yet been proposed, to a sufficiently high
degree of approximation. But given only the percentiles, or at
least so few of them as the nine deciles, he cannot pass back to
the frequency-distribution, and thence to other constants, with any
degree of accuracy. In all cases of published work, therefore,
the figures of the frequency-distribution should be given; they
are absolutely fundamental.

REFERENCES.

General.

(1) FECHNER, G. T., "Ueber den Ausgangswerth der kleinsten Abweichungssumme, dessen Bestimmung, Verwendung und Verallgemeinerung," *Abh. d. kgl. sächs. Ges. d. Wissenschaften*, vol. xviii. (also numbered vol. xi. of the *Abh. d. math.-phys. Classe*) ; Leipzig, 1878, p. 1.

Standard Deviation.

(2) PEARSON, KARL, "Contributions to the Mathematical Theory of Evolution (i. On the Dissection of Asymmetrical Frequency-curves)," *Phil. Trans. Roy. Soc.*, Series A, vol. clxxxv., 1894, p. 71. (Introduction of the term "standard deviation," p. 80.)

Mean Deviation.

(3) LAPLACE, PIERRE SIMON, Marquis de, *Théorie analytique des probabilités* : 2me supplément, 1818. (Proof that the mean deviation is a minimum when taken about the median.)

(4) TRACHTENBERG, M. I., "A Note on a Property of the Median," *Jour. Roy. Stat. Soc.*, vol. lxxviii., 1915, p. 454. (A very simple proof of the same property.)

Method of Percentiles, including Quartiles, etc.

(5) GALTON, FRANCIS, "Statistics by Intercomparison, with Remarks on the Law of Frequency of Error," *Phil. Mag.*, vol. xlix. (4th Series), 1875, pp. 33–46.

(6) GALTON, FRANCIS, *Natural Inheritance* ; Macmillan, 1889. (The method of percentiles is used throughout, with the quartile deviation as the measure of dispersion.)

Relative Dispersion.

(7) PEARSON, KARL, "Regression, Heredity, and Panmixia," *Phil. Trans. Roy. Soc.*, Series A, vol. clxxxvii., 1896, p. 253. (Introduction of "coefficient of variation," pp. 276–7.)

(8) VERSCHAEFFELT, E., "Ueber graduelle Variabilität von pflanzlichen Eigenschaften," *Ber. deutsch. bot. Ges.*, Bd. xii., 1894, pp. 350–55.

Skewness.

(9) PEARSON, KARL, "Skew Variation in Homogeneous Material," *Phil. Trans. Roy. Soc.*, Series A, vol. clxxxvi., 1895, p. 343. (Introduction of term, p. 370.)

Calculation of Mean, Standard-deviation, or of the General Moments of a Grouped Distribution.

We have given a direct method that seems the simplest and best for the elementary student. A process of successive summation that has some advantages can, however, be used instead. The student will find a convenient description with illustrations in—

(10) ELDERTON, W. PALIN, *Frequency-curves and Correlation* ; C. & E. Layton, London, 1906.

EXERCISES.

1. Verify the following from the data of Table VI., Chap. VI., continuing the work from the stage reached for Qu. 1, Chap. VII.

| | Stature in Inches for Adult Males born in— | | | |
	England.	Scotland.	Wales.	Ireland.
Standard deviation . .	2·56	2·50	2·35	2·17
Mean deviation . . .	2·05	1·95	1·82	1·69
Quartile deviation . .	1·78	1·56	1·46	1·35
Mean deviation / standard deviation	0·80	0·78	0·78	0·78
Quartile deviation/standard deviation	0·69	0·62	0·62	0·62
Lower quartile . . .	65·55	66·92	65·06	66·39
Upper ,, . . .	69·10	70·04	67·98	69·10

2. (Continuing from Qu. 2, Chap. VII.) Find the standard deviation, mean deviation, quartiles and quartile deviation (or semi-interquartile range) for the distribution of weights of adult males in the United Kingdom given in the last column of Table IX., Chap. VI.

Compare the ratios of the mean and quartile deviations to the standard deviation with the ratios stated in §§ 19 and 23 to be usual.

Find the value of the skewness (equation 12), using the approximate value of the mode.

3. Using, or extending if necessary, your diagram for Question 4, Chap. VII., find the quartile values for houses assessed to inhabited house duty in 1885-6, from the data of Table IV., Chap. VI.

Find also the 9th decile (the value exceeded by 10 per cent. of the houses only).

4. Verify equation (9) by direct calculation of the standard deviation of the numbers 1 to 10.

5. (Data from Sauerbeck, *Jour. Roy. Stat. Soc.*, March 1909.) The following are the index-numbers (percentages) of prices of 45 commodities in 1908 on their average prices in the years 1867-77 :—40, 43, 43, 46, 46, 46, 54, 56, 59, 62, 64, 64, 66, 66, 67, 67, 68, 68, 69, 69, 69, 71, 75, 75, 76, 76, 78, 80, 82, 82, 82, 82, 82, 83, 84, 86, 88, 90, 90, 91, 91, 92, 95, 102, 127. Find the mean and standard deviation (1) without further grouping ; (2) grouping the numbers by fives (40-, 45-, 50-, etc.); (3) grouping by tens (40-, 50-, 60-, etc.).

6. (Continuing from Qu. 8, Chap. VII.) Supposing the frequencies of values 0, 1, 2, 3, . . . of a variable to be given by the terms of the binomial series

$$q^n, \; n.q^{n-1}.p, \; \frac{n(n-1)}{1 \cdot 2}q^{n-2}.p^2, \; \ldots .$$

where $p + q = 1$, find the standard deviation.

7. (*Cf.* the remarks at the end of § 17.) The sum of the deviations (without regard to sign) about the centre of the class-interval containing the mean

(or median), in a grouped frequency-distribution, is found to be S. Find the correction to be applied to this sum, in order to reduce it to the mean (or median) as origin, on the assumption that the observations are evenly distributed over each class-interval. Take the number of observations below the interval containing the mean (or median) to be n_1, in that interval n_2, and above it n_3 ; and the distance of the mean (or median) from the arbitrary origin to be d.

Show that the values of the mean deviation (from the mean and from the median respectively) for Example ii., found by the use of this formula, do not differ from the values found by the simpler method of §§ 16 and 17 in the second place of decimals.

8. (W. Scheibner, "Ueber Mittelwerthe," *Berichte der kgl. sächsischen Gesellschaft d. Wissenschaften*, 1873, p. 564, cited by Fechner, ref. 2 of Chap. VII. : the second form of the relation is given by G Duncker (*Die Methode der Variationsstatistik* ; Leipzig, 1899) as an empirical one.) Show that if deviations are small compared with the mean, so that $(x/M)^2$ may be neglected in comparison with x/M, we have approximately the relation

$$G = M\left(1 - \tfrac{1}{2}\frac{\sigma^2}{M^2}\right),$$

where G is the geometric mean, M the arithmetic mean, and σ the standard deviation : and consequently to the same degree of approximation $M^2 - G^2 = \sigma^2$.

9. (Scheibner, *loc. cit.*, Qu. 8.) Similarly, show that if deviations are small compared with the mean, we have approximately

$$H = M\left(1 - \frac{\sigma^2}{M^2}\right),$$

H being the harmonic mean.

CHAPTER IX.

CORRELATION.

1. In chapters VI.-VIII. we considered the frequency-distribution of a single variable, and the more important constants that may be calculated to describe certain characters of such distributions. We have now to proceed to the case of two variables, and the consideration of the relations between them.

2. If the corresponding values of two variables be noted together, the methods of classification employed in the preceding chapters may be applied to both, and a table of double entry or contingency-table (Chap. V.) be formed, exhibiting the frequencies of pairs of values lying within given class-intervals. Six such tables are given below as illustrations for the following variables :—Table I., two measurements on a shell (*Pecten*). Table II., ages of husbands and wives in England and Wales in 1901. Table III., statures of fathers and their sons (British). Table IV., fertility of mothers and their daughters (British peerage). Table V., the rate of discount and the ratio of reserves to deposits in American banks. Table VI., the proportion of male to total births, and the total numbers of births, in the registration districts of England and Wales.

Each row in such a table gives the frequency-distribution of the first variable for cases in which the second variable lies within the limits stated on the left of the row. Similarly, every column gives the frequency-distribution of the second variable for cases in which the value of the first variable lies within the limits stated at the head of the column. As "columns" and "rows" are distinguished only by the accidental circumstance

157

TABLE I.—*Correlation between* (1) *Antero-posterior and* (2) *Dorso-ventral Diameter in Lower Valve of Pecten opercularis.* Condensed from a Table given by C. B. Davenport, *Proc. Amer. Ac.*, xxxix. 149 (1903).] Measurements in millimetres.

(1) Antero-posterior diameter, mm.

A.-P. \ D.-V.	37–39	40–42	43–45	46–48	49–51	52–54	55–57	58–60	61–63	64–66	67–69	70–72	73–75	76–78	Total
37–39	4	—	—	—	—	—	—	—	—	—	—	—	—	—	4
40–42	1	12	6	—	—	—	—	—	—	—	—	—	—	—	19
43–45	—	1	35	12	—	—	—	—	—	—	—	—	—	—	48
46–48	—	—	1	35	22	1	—	—	—	—	—	—	—	—	59
49–51	—	—	—	2	22	17	3	—	—	—	—	—	—	—	44
52–54	—	—	—	—	—	29	68	8	—	—	—	—	—	—	105
55–57	—	—	—	—	—	—	32	90	25	—	—	—	—	—	147
58–60	—	—	—	—	—	—	—	14	59	7	—	—	—	—	80
61–63	—	—	—	—	—	—	—	—	4	13	3	1	—	—	21
64–66	—	—	—	—	—	—	—	—	—	—	5	1	—	—	6
67–69	—	—	—	—	—	—	—	—	—	—	—	1	—	1	2
70–72	—	—	—	—	—	—	—	—	—	—	—	—	—	2	2
Total	5	13	42	49	44	47	103	112	88	20	8	3	—	3	537

(2) Dorso-ventral diameter, mm.

TABLE II.—*Correlation between* (1) *the Age of Wife,* (2) *the Age of Husband, for all Husbands and Wives in England and Wales who were residing together on the night of the Census,* 1901. (Census, 1901, Summary Tables, p. 182.) Table based on 5,317,520 pairs; condensed by omitting 000's.

(2) Ages of Husbands.	(1) Ages of Wives.															Total.
	15-	20-	25-	30-	35-	40-	45-	50-	55-	60-	65-	70-	75-	80-	85-	
15-	2	2														4
20-	16	173	46	4	1											240
25-	4	185	402	84	10	2	1									688
30-	1	41	265	411	84	12	2	1								817
35-		9	69	251	369	80	12	2	1							793
40-		3	17	71	219	309	66	12	2	1						700
45-		1	6	20	66	178	252	59	10	2	1					595
50-			2	8	19	57	146	195	44	10	2					483
55-			1	3	8	18	46	110	141	35	6	1				369
60-				1	3	8	16	39	81	101	23	4	1			277
65-				1	1	3	6	11	26	53	58	13	2	1		175
70-					1	1	2	5	8	18	31	31	6	1		104
75-						1	1	2	3	5	10	14	12	2	1	50
80-							1	1	1	1	2	4	5	3		18
85-											1	1	1	1		4
Total	23	414	808	854	781	669	550	437	317	226	134	68	27	8	1	5317

TABLE III.—Correlation between (1) Stature of Father and (2) Stature of Son: 1 or 2 Sons only of each Father. [From Karl Pearson and Alice Lee, Biometrika, vol. ii. (1903), p. 415.] Measurements in inches.

(1) Stature of Father.

(2) Stature of Son	74·5-75·5	73·5-74·5	72·5-73·5	71·5-72·5	70·5-71·5	69·5-70·5	68·5-69·5	67·5-68·5	66·5-67·5	65·5-66·5	64·5-65·5	63·5-64·5	62·5-63·5	61·5-62·5	60·5-61·5	59·5-60·5	58·5-59·5	Total.
59·5-60·5																		2
60·5-61·5													·5					1·5
61·5-62·5								·5			1	·5	·5	2·25	·25	·25		3·5
62·5-63·5								1·25	1	·25	·25	1	·25	3·75	·25	·25		20·5
63·5-64·5							1·5	1·25	·5	5	4	·25	3·25	2	1·5	1	1	38·5
64·5-65·5						·25	3·5	5·5	2·75	9·25	8	4·25	3	2·25	·5	·5	2	61·5
65·5-66·5					·25	·75	5·25	18	8	10·75	13·5	9·5	5·25	4·75	1	1·5		89·5
66·5-67·5			1		1·25	2·5	12·5	19·5	17·5	16·75	19·75	13·75	3·5	2	2			148
67·5-68·5			2·25	1	2·5	2·5	29·5	23·5	25·75	26·5	10·25	10	7·5		·5			173·5
68·5-69·5			2·25	·5	3·25	13·75	29	24	31·5	24·25	12·75	5	5·25		1			149·5
69·5-70·5		1·5	3·5	9·5	8·5	13·25	22·5	19·5	16	18·25	5·75	3·25	1					128
70·5-71·5		1	5	8·5	10	21·5	14·75	19	11·75	18·75	5	·25	1					108
71·5-72·5	1		2·75	8	14·5	19·5	10·75	7·75	10·75	8·75	·75							63
72·5-73·5	1	·5	3·25	8·5	10·75	20·75	8·5	7·5	7	1·25	1·5							42
73·5-74·5			3·25	6·25	10	11·25	2·25	6·25	2·5	·75								29
74·5-75·5	·5	·5	1·75	3·25	7·5	6	2	1		1·5								8·5
75·5-76·5	2		1	·75	6·5	2·5	·25	1·25										4
76·5-77·5		·5	1·5	1	2·5	1	·25	1·25										4
77·5-78·5			·75	·25	·5	1	1											3
78·5-79·5			·25	·25														·5
Total	5·5	4	28·5	49	78	116	141·5	154	137·5	142	95·5	61·5	33·5	17	8	3·5	3	1078

(2) Stature of Son.

TABLE IV.—Correlation between the Number of Children (1) of a Woman, (2) of one of her Daughters. One Daughter only taken from each Mother. Marriages lasted at least 15 years in each case. British Peerage Statistics. [From Karl Pearson, Alice Lee, and L. Bramley Moore, Phil. Trans., A, vol. cxcii, (1899), table iv.]

(1) Number of Mother's Children.

(2) \ (1)	1.	2.	3.	4.	5.	6.	7.	8.	9.	10.	11.	12.	13.	14.	15.	16.	Total.
0	5	9	11	18	21	15	8	9	6	3	2	3					110
1	12	5	14	15	10	13	9	8	5	3	2	2					98
2	9	9	10	15	18	15	9	8	2	4	2					1	97
3	5	10	16	11	9	14	13	10	4	8	2	3					105
4	5	5	19	17	21	15	18	10	14	2	1	5	1				133
5	7	6	7	17	23	9	12	13	14	8	3	2	2				123
6	4	5	8	11	15	12	15	14	7	5	3	3	1				103
7	5	4	3	8	4	13	9	8	5	10	2	1	1				73
8	1	2	4	12	9	9	8	5	12	3	4	1	2				73
9			4	3	3	4	7	5	3	2	2	1		1			34
10			1	2	1	3	4	6	8	2		1					24
11			2	1	3	1			3	2				1			8
12		2	1	2	2		1	1	1		1		1		1		13
13						1					1		2			1	6
Total	53	57	100	132	140	124	113	92	76	52	25	22	10	2	1	1	1000

(2) Number of her Daughter's Children.

11

TABLE V.—Correlation between (1) Call Discount Rates and (2) Percentage of Reserves on Deposits in New York Associated Banks (Weekly Returns). (From Statistical Studies in the New York Money Market, by J. P. Norton. Publications of the Department of the Social Sciences, Yale University; The Macmillan Co., 1902.) Note that, after the column headed 8 per cent., blank columns have been omitted to save space.

(2) Percentage Ratio of Reserves to Deposits	(1) Call Discount Rates																					Total.
	1	1·5	2	2·5	3	3·5	4	4·5	5	5·5	6	6·5	7	7·5	8	9	10	12	15	20	25	
21									1							1						2
22							1															1
23									1													1
24																					1	9
25																			1			42
26					2	1		1	4	4	2	1	2				2		1		2	85
27					14	6	8	6	16	6	11	4	7		3	1	2	1	1	1		124
28					20	12	13	12	19	9	11	3	4		6	2					1	115
29		1	10	9	16	11	15	17	7	1	9	2	3		1		1					109
30	3	5	30	23	8	3	7	8	1		2		2									58
31	1	9	48	17	4	4	6	1	2													86
32	8	12	12	9	5	2	4		1													53
33	15	10	6	8		1	2															32
34	15	14	10	1																		14
35	2	8	4				2															14
36	8	11	1																			10
37	7	5	1																			9
38	8	2	1																			11
39	9		1																			21
40	19	1																				15
41	7	2																				10
42	7	8																				10
43	8	3	1																			1
44	1	2																				1
45	2																					2
	121	93	125	70	69	40	52	45	52	20	35	10	18	—	10	4	7	1	3	1	4	780

(2) Percentage Ratio of Reserves to Deposits.

TABLE VI.—Showing the Number of Registration Districts in England and Wales exhibiting (1) a given Proportion of Male Births, (2) a given Total Number of Births during the Decade 1881–90. (The Data as to Total Births and Numbers of Male and Female Births from Decennial Supplement to Report of the Registrar-General. Table from H. D. Vigor and G. U. Yule, Jour. Roy. Stat. Soc., vol. lxix., 1906.)

(1) Proportion of Male Births per 1000 of all Births.

Total Births (000's)	Total	543–45	540–42	537–39	534–36	531–33	528–30	525–27	522–24	519–21	516–18	513–15	510–12	507–09	504–06	501–03	498–500	495–97	492–94	489–91	486–88	483–85	480–82	477–79	474–76	471–73	468–70	465–67
0– 4	149	1	1		2	1	1	3	5	9	12	14	21	12	19	18	9	8	4	2	2	1	2			1		1
4– 8	204				1				4	10	18	36	42	29	27	20	7	5	2	2		1						
8–12	86							1	1	4	7	16	18	17	16	6	1	2										
12–16	48								1	1	6	8	12	8	10	1												
16–20	28									1	1	4	9	6	5													
20–24	15									1	1	4	4	5	1													
24–28	15										1	1	3	6	3		1											
28–32	12											1	2	5	2													
32–36	7											1		3	3													
36–40	6											2		4														
40–44	8										1	1	4		2													
44–48	11											1	2	6	2													
48–52	11												3	6	2													
52–56	7												2	3	2													
56–60	3												2		1													
60–64	5												1	1	3													
64–68	3												2	1														
68–72	3													3														
72–76	4												1	1	2													
76–80	—																											
80–84	1													1														
84–88	2												1	1														
88–92	2												1	1														
92–96	—																											
96–100	2												2															
100–04	—																											
104–08	1													1														
148–52	1												1															
Total	632	1	1	—	3	1	1	4	11	26	47	88	129	126	98	46	18	16	6	4	2	2	2	—	—	1	—	1

(2) Total Number of Births in District (000's omitted) during Decade.

of the one set running vertically and the other horizontally, and
the difference has no statistical significance, the word array
has been suggested as a convenient term to denote either a row
or a column. If the values of X in one array are associated
with values of Y between the limits $Y_n - \delta$ and $Y_n + \delta$, Y_n may be
termed the type of the array. (Pearson, ref. 6.) The special
kind of contingency tables with which we are now concerned
are called correlation tables, to distinguish them from tables
based on unmeasured qualities and so forth.

3. Nothing need be added to what was said in Chapter VI. as
regards the choice of magnitude and position of class-intervals.
When these have been fixed, the table is readily compiled by
taking a large sheet ruled with rows and columns properly
headed in the same way as the final table and entering a dot,
stroke, or small cross in the corresponding compartment for each
pair of recorded observations. If facility of checking be of
great importance, each pair of recorded values may be entered
on a separate card and these dealt into little packs on a board
ruled in squares, or into a divided tray; each pack can then be
run through to see that no card has been mis-sorted. The
difficulty as to the intermediate observations—values of the
variables corresponding to divisions between class-intervals—will
be met in the same way as before if the value of one variable
alone be intermediate, the unit of frequency being divided
between two adjacent compartments. If both values of the pair
be intermediates, the observation must be divided between *four*
adjacent compartments, and thus quarters as well as halves may
occur in the table, as, *e.g.*, in Table III. In this case the statures
of fathers and sons were measured to the nearest quarter-
inch and subsequently grouped by 1-inch intervals: a pair in
which the recorded stature of the father is 60·5 in. and that of
the son 62·5 in. is accordingly entered as 0·25 to each of the
four compartments under the columns 59·5–60·5, 60·5–61·5, and
the rows 61·5–62·5, 62·5–63·5. Workers will generally form
their own methods for entering such fractional frequencies
during the process of compiling, but one convenient method is
to use a small × to denote a unit and a dot for a quarter; the
four dots should be placed in the position of the four points
of the × and joined when complete. It is best to choose the
limits of class-intervals, where possible, in such a way as to avoid
fractional frequencies.

4. The distribution of frequency for two variables may be
represented by a surface or solid in the same way as the frequency-
distribution of a single variable may be represented by a plane
figure. We may imagine the surface to be obtained by erecting

at the centre of every compartment of the correlation-table a
vertical of length proportionate to the frequency in that compartment, and joining up the tops of the verticals. If the
compartments were made smaller and smaller while the class-
frequencies remained finite, the irregular figure so obtained would
approximate more and more closely towards a continuous curved
surface—a frequency-surface—corresponding to the frequency-
curves for single variables of Chapter VI. The volume of the
frequency-solid over any area drawn on its base gives the
frequency of pairs of values falling within that area, just as the
area of the frequency-curve over any interval of the base-line gives
the frequency of observations within that interval. Models of
actual distributions may be constructed by drawing the frequency-
distributions for all arrays of the one variable, to the same scale,
on sheets of cardboard, and erecting the cards vertically on a
base-board at equal distances apart, or by marking out a base-
board in squares corresponding to the compartments of the
correlation-table, and erecting on each square a rod of wood of
height proportionate to the frequency. Such solid representations
of frequency-distributions for two variables are sometimes termed
stereograms.

5. It is impossible, however, to group the majority of
frequency-surfaces, in the same way as the frequency-curves,
under a few simple types : the forms are too varied. The simplest
ideal type is one in which every section of the surface is a symmetrical curve—the first type of Chap. VI. (fig. 5, p. 89). Like
the symmetrical distribution for the single variable, this is a very
rare form of distribution in economic statistics, but approximate
illustrations may be drawn from anthropometry. Fig. 29 shows
the ideal form of the surface, somewhat truncated, and fig.
30 the distribution of Table III., which approximates to the same
type,—the difference in steepness is, of course, merely a matter of
scale. The maximum frequency occurs in the centre of the
whole distribution, and the surface is symmetrical round the
vertical through the maximum, equal frequencies occurring at
equal distances from the mode on opposite sides. The next
simplest type of surface corresponds to the second type of
frequency-curve—the moderately asymmetrical. Most, if not all,
of the distributions of arrays are asymmetrical, and like the distribution of fig. 9, p. 92 : the surface is consequently asymmetrical,
and the maximum does not lie in the centre of the distribution.
This form is fairly common, and illustrations might be drawn
from a variety of sources—economics, meteorology, anthropometry,
etc. The data of Table II. will serve as an example. The total
distributions and the distributions of the majority of the arrays

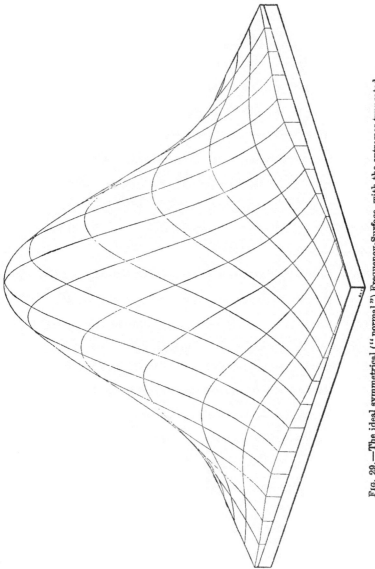

Fig. 29.—The ideal symmetrical ("normal") Frequency-Surface, with the extremes truncated.

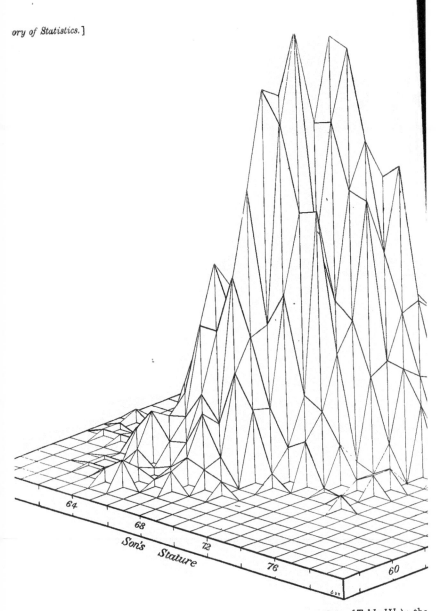

Fig. 30.—Frequency Surface for Stature of Father and Stature of Son (data of Table III.) : the or "normal" form.

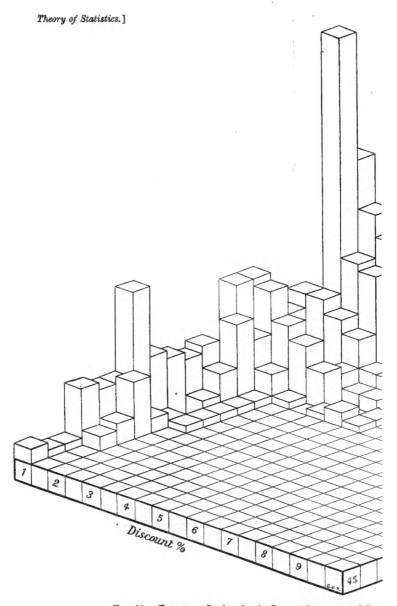

Fig. 31.—Frequency Surface for the Rate of Discount and Rat:

are asymmetrical, the skewness being positive for the rows at the top of the table (the mode being lower than the mean), and negative for the rows at the foot, the more central rows being nearly symmetrical. The maximum frequency lies towards the upper end of the table in the compartment under the row and column headed "30 – ". The frequency falls off very rapidly towards the lower ages, and slowly in the direction of old age. Outside these two forms, it seems impossible to delimit empirically any simple types. Tables V. and VI. are given simply as illustrations of two very divergent forms. Fig. 31 gives a graphical representation of the former by the method corresponding to the histogram of Chapter VI., the frequency in each compartment being represented by a square pillar. The distribution of frequency is very characteristic, and quite different from that of any of the Tables I., II., III., or IV.

6. It is clear that such tables may be treated by any of the methods discussed in Chapter V., which are applicable to all contingency-tables, however formed. The distribution may be investigated in detail by such methods as those of § 4, or tested for isotropy (§ 11), or the coefficient of contingency can be calculated (§§ 5–8). In applying any of these methods, however, it is desirable to use a coarser classification than is suited to the methods to be presently discussed, and it is not necessary to retain the constancy of the class-interval. The classification should, on the contrary, be arranged simply with a view to avoiding many scattered units or very small frequencies. A few examples should be worked as exercises by the student (Question 3).

7. But the coefficient of contingency merely tells us whether, and if so, how closely, the two variables are related, and much more information than this can be obtained from the correlation-table, seeing that the measures of Chapters VII. and VIII. can be applied to the arrays as well as to the total distributions. If the two variables are independent, the distributions of all parallel arrays are similar (Chap. V. § 13); hence their averages and dispersions, e.g. means and standard deviations, must be the same. In general they are not the same, and the relation between the mean or standard deviation of the array and its type requires investigation. Of the two constants, the mean is, in general, the more important, and our attention will for the present be confined to it. The majority of the questions of practical statistics relate solely to averages : the most important and fundamental question is whether, on an average, high values of the one variable show any tendency to be associated with high (or with low) values of the other. If possible, we also desire to know how great a divergence of the one variable from its average value is associated

with a unit divergence of the other, and to obtain some idea as to the closeness with which this relation is usually fulfilled.

8. Suppose a diagram (fig. 32) to be drawn representing the values of means of arrays. Let OX, OY be the scales of the two variables, *i.e.* the scales at the head and side of the table, 01, 12, etc., being successive class-intervals. Let M_1 be the mean value of X, and M_2 the mean value of Y. If the two variables be absolutely independent, the distributions of frequency in all parallel arrays are similar (Chap. V. § 13), and the means of arrays must lie on the vertical and horizontal lines M_1M, M_2M, the

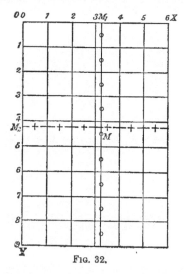

FIG. 32.

small circles denoting means of rows and the small crosses means of columns. (In any actual case, of course, the means would not lie so regularly, but, if the independence were almost complete, would only fluctuate slightly to the one side and the other of the two lines.)

The cases with which the experimentalist, *e.g.* the chemist or physicist, has to deal, where the observations are all crowded closely round a single line, lie at the opposite extreme from independence. The entries fall into a few compartments only of each array, and the means of rows and of columns lie approximately on one and the same curve, like the line RR of fig. 33.

The ordinary cases of statistics are intermediate between these two extremes, the lines of means being neither at right angles as in fig. 32, nor coincident as in fig. 33, but standing at an acute angle with one another as RR (means of rows) and CC (means of columns) in figs. 36–8. The *complete* problem of the statistician, like that of the physicist, is to find formulæ or equations which will suffice to describe approximately these curves.

9. In the general case this may be a difficult problem, but, in the first place, it often suffices, as already pointed out, to know merely whether on an average high values of the one variable show any tendency to be associated with high or with low values of the other, a purpose which will be served very fairly by fitting a

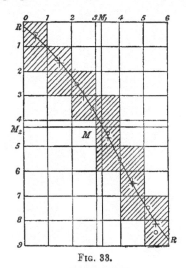

FIG. 33.

straight line; and further, in a large number of cases, it is found either (1) that the means of arrays lie very approximately round straight lines, or (2) that they lie so irregularly (possibly owing only to paucity of observations) that the real nature of the curve is not clearly indicated, and a straight line will do almost as well as any more elaborate curve. (*Cf.* figs. 36–38.) In such cases —and they are relatively more frequent than might be supposed —the fitting of straight lines to the means of arrays determines all the most important characters of the distribution. We might fit such lines by a simple graphical method, plotting the points representing means of arrays on a diagram like those of figures 36–38, and "fitting" lines to them, say, by means of a stretched black thread shifted about till it appeared to run as near as

might be to all the points. But such a method is hardly satisfactory, more especially if the points are somewhat scattered; it
leaves too much room for guesswork, and different observers obtain
very different results. Some method is clearly required which
will enable the observer to determine equations to the two lines
for a given distribution, however irregularly the means may lie,
as simply and definitely as he can calculate the means and
standard deviations.

10. Consider the simplest case in which the means of rows lie

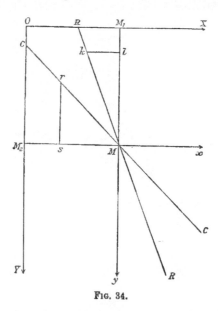

FIG. 34.

exactly on a straight line RR (fig. 34). Let M_2 be the mean
value of Y, and let RR cut M_2x, the horizontal through M_2, in M.
Then it may be shown that the vertical through M must cut OX
in M_1, the mean of X. For, let the slope of RR to the vertical,
i.e. the tangent of the angle M_1MR or ratio of kl to lM, be b_1,
and let deviations from My, Mx be denoted by x and y. Then for
any one row of type y in which the number of observations is n,
$\Sigma(x) = n.b_1y$, and therefore for the whole table, since $\Sigma(ny) = 0$.
$\Sigma(x) = b_1\Sigma(ny) = 0$. M_1 must therefore be the mean of X, and
M may accordingly be termed the mean of the whole distribution.
Knowing that RR passes through M, it remains only to determine

b_1. This may conveniently be done in terms of the mean product p of all pairs of associated deviations x and y, i.e.—

$$p = \frac{1}{N} \Sigma(xy) . \tag{1}$$

For any one row we have

$$\Sigma(xy) = y\Sigma(x) = n.b_1 y^2.$$

Therefore for the whole table

$$\Sigma(xy) = b_1 \Sigma(ny^2) = Nb_1.\sigma_y^2,$$

or

$$b_1 = \frac{p}{\sigma_y^2} . \tag{2}$$

Similarly, if CC be the line on which lie the means of columns and b_2 its slope to the horizontal, rs/sM,

$$b_2 = \frac{p}{\sigma_x^2} . \tag{3}$$

These two equations (2) and (3) are usually written in a slightly different form. Let

$$r = \frac{p}{\sigma_x \sigma_y} . \tag{4}$$

Then

$$b_1 = r\frac{\sigma_x}{\sigma_y} \qquad b_2 = r\frac{\sigma_y}{\sigma_x} \tag{5}$$

Or we may write the equations to RR and CC—

$$x = r\frac{\sigma_x}{\sigma_y}.y \qquad y = r\frac{\sigma_y}{\sigma_x}.x \tag{6}$$

These equations may, of course, be expressed, if desired, in terms of the absolute values of the variables X and Y instead of the deviations x and y.

11. The meaning of the above expressions when the means of rows and columns do not lie exactly on straight lines is very readily obtained. If the values of x and $b_1.y$ be noted for all pairs of associated deviations, we have for the sum of the squares of the differences, giving b_1 its value from (5),

$$\Sigma(x - b_1.y)^2 = N.\sigma_x^2.(1 - r^2) \tag{7}$$

If b_1 be given any other value, say $(r + \delta)\frac{\sigma_x}{\sigma_y}$, then

$$\Sigma(x - b_1.y)^2 = N\sigma_x^2(1 - r^2 + \delta^2).$$

This is necessarily greater than the value (7); hence $\Sigma(x - b_1 y)^2$ *has the lowest possible value when b_1 is put equal to $r\sigma_x/\sigma_y$.* Further, for any one row in which the number of observations is n, the deviation of the mean of the row from RR is d (fig. 35), and the standard deviation is s_{ax}, $\Sigma(x - b_1 y)^2 = ns_{ax}^2 + n.d^2$. Therefore for the whole table,

$$\Sigma(x - b_1.y)^2 = \Sigma(ns_{ax}^2) + \Sigma(nd^2).$$

But the first of the two sums on the right is unaffected by the

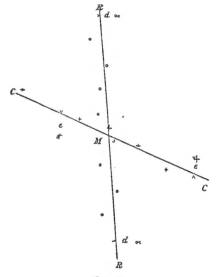

Fig. 35.

slope or position of RR, hence, the left-hand side being a minimum, the second sum on the right must be a minimum also. That is to say, *when b_1 is put equal to $r\,\sigma_x/\sigma_y$, the sum of the squares of the distances of the row-means from RR, each multiplied by the corresponding frequency, is the lowest possible.*

Similar theorems hold good, of course, with respect to the line CC. If b_2 be given the value $r\,\dfrac{\sigma_y}{\sigma_x}$, $\Sigma(x - b_2.y)^2$ is a minimum, and also $\Sigma(n.e^2)$ (fig. 35). Hence we may regard the equations (6) as being, either (a) equations for estimating each individual x from its associated y (and y from its associated x) in such a way as to make the sum of the squares of the errors of estimate the least possible ; or (*b*) equations for estimating the *mean* of the *x*'s associated with a given type of *y* (and the *mean* of the *y*'s associated with a given type of *x*) in such a way as to make the sum of the squares of the errors of estimate the least possible, when every mean is counted once for each observation on which it is based.

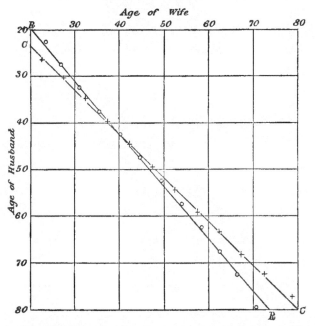

Fig. 36.—Correlation between Age of Husband and Age of Wife in England and Wales (Table II.) : means of rows shown by circles and means of columns by crosses : $r = +0.91$.

The lines represented by the two equations are thus, in a certain natural sense, "lines of best fit" to the two actual lines of means.

12. The constant r is of very great importance. It is evidently a pure number, and its magnitude is unaffected by the scales in which x and y are measured, for these scales will affect the numerator and denominator of (4) to the same extent. If the two variables are independent, r is zero, for b_1 and b_2 are zero (*cf.* § 8). The sign is the sign of the mean product p, and accordingly r is positive if large values of x

are associated with large values of y, and conversely (as in Tables I.–IV.), negative if small values of x are associated with large values of y and conversely (as in Table V.). The numerical value cannot exceed ± 1, for the sum of the series of squares in equation (7) is then zero and the sum of a series of squares cannot be negative. If $r = \pm 1$, it follows that all the observed pairs of deviations are subject to the relation $x/y = \sigma_x/\sigma_y$: this

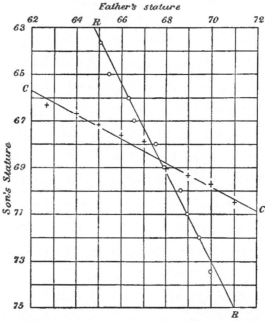

FIG. 37.—Correlation between Stature of Father and Stature of Son (Table III.): means of rows shown by circles and means of columns by crosses: $r = +0.51$.

would be the case if the circles and crosses in such a diagram as fig. 33 all lay on one and the same straight line. From these properties r is termed the **coefficient of correlation**, and the expression (4), $r = p/\sigma_x\sigma_y = \Sigma(xy)/N.\sigma_x\sigma_y$, should be remembered.

It should be noted that, while r is zero if the variables are independent, the converse is not necessarily true: the fact that r is zero only implies that the means of rows and columns lie *scattered round* two straight lines which do not exhibit

any definite trend, to right or to left, upward or downward.
Two variables for which r is zero are, however, conveniently
spoken of as *uncorrelated*. Table VI. and fig. 39 will serve as an
illustration of a case in which the variables are almost uncorrelated but by no means independent, r being very small (-0.014),
but the coefficient of contingency C (for grouping of qu. 3) 0.47.

Figs. 36, 37, 38 are drawn from the data of Tables II., III., and
IV., for which r has the values $+0.91$, $+0.51$, and $+0.21$ respectively, the correlation being positive in each case. The student

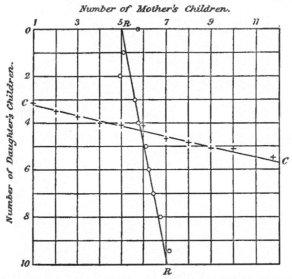

FIG. 38.—Correlation between number of a Mother's Children and number of
her Daughter's Children (Table IV.): means of rows shown by circles
and means of columns by crosses: $r = +0.21$.

should study such tables and diagrams closely, and endeavour to
accustom himself to estimating the value of r from the general
appearance of the table.

13. The two quantities

$$b_1 = r\frac{\sigma_x}{\sigma_y} \qquad b_2 = r\frac{\sigma_y}{\sigma_x}$$

are termed the coefficients of regression, or simply the regressions,
b_1 being the regression of x on y, or deviation in x corresponding
on the average to a unit change in the type of y, and b_2 being

similarly the regression of y on x. Whilst the coefficient of correlation is always a pure number, the regressions are only pure numbers if the two variables have the same dimensions, as in Tables I.–IV. : their magnitudes depend on the ratio of σ_x/σ_y, and consequently on the units in which x and y are measured. They are both necessarily of the same sign (the sign of r). Since r is

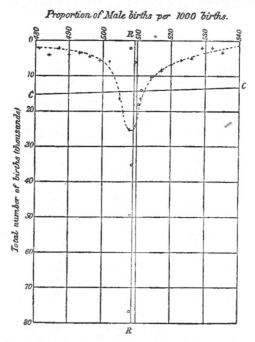

Proportion of Male births per 1000 births.

Fig. 39.—Correlation between Population of a Registration District and Proportion of Male Births per thousand of all births (England and Wales, 1881–90, Table VI.): means of rows shown by circles and means of columns by crosses : $r = -0\cdot014$.

not greater than unity, one at least of the regressions must be not greater than unity, but the other may be considerably greater if the ratio σ_x/σ_y or σ_y/σ_x be great. The name *regression* arose from the term being first introduced in the case of inheritance of stature (Galton, refs. 2, 3). In this case the two standard deviations are very nearly equal, so that both b_1 and b_2 are less than unity, say (using the more recent data of Table III.) $0\cdot50$ and $0\cdot52$.

Hence the sons of fathers of deviation x from the mean of all fathers have an average deviation of only $0{\cdot}52x$ from the mean of all sons; *i.e.* they step back or "regress" towards the general mean, and $0{\cdot}52$ may be termed the "ratio of regression." In general, however, the idea of a "stepping back" or "regression" towards a more or less stationary mean is quite inapplicable—obviously so where the variables are different in kind, as in Tables V. and VI.—and the term "coefficient of regression" should be regarded simply as a convenient name for the coefficients b_1 and b_2. RR and CC are generally termed the "lines of regression," and equations (6) the "regression equations." The expressions "characteristic lines," "characteristic equations" (Yule, ref. 8) would perhaps be better. Where the actual means of arrays appear to be given, to a satisfactory degree of approximation, by straight lines, we may say that the *regression is linear.* It is not safe, however, to assume that such linearity extends beyond the limits of observation.

14. The two standard deviations

$$s_x = \sigma_x \sqrt{1 - r^2} \qquad\qquad s_y = \sigma_y \sqrt{1 - r^2}$$

are of considerable importance. It follows from (7) that s_x is the standard deviation of $(x - b_1.y)$, and similarly s_y is the standard deviation of $(y - b_2.x)$. Hence we may regard s_x and s_y as the standard errors (root mean square errors) made in estimating x from y and y from x by the respective characteristic relations

$$x = b_1.y \qquad\qquad y = b_2.x.$$

s_x may also be regarded as a kind of average standard deviation of a row about RR, and s_y as an average standard deviation of a column about CC. In an ideal case, where the regression is truly linear and the standard deviations of all parallel arrays are equal, a case to which the distribution of Table III. is a rough approximation, s_x is the standard deviation of the x-array and s_y the standard deviation of the y-array (*cf.* Chap. X. § 19 (3)). Hence s_x and s_y are sometimes termed the "standard deviations of arrays."

15. Proceeding now to the arithmetical work, the only new expression that has to be calculated in order to determine r, b_1, b_2, s_x, and s_y is the product sum $\Sigma(xy)$ or the mean product p. As in the cases of means and standard deviations, the form of the arithmetic is slightly different according as the observations are few and ungrouped, or sufficient to justify the formation of a correlation-table. In the first case, as in Example i. below, the work is quite straightforward.

Example i., Table VII.—The variables are (1) X—the estimated

12

TABLE VII. THEORY OF CORRELATION: *Example i.*

1.	2.	3.	4.	5.	6.	7.	8.	9.
	X.	*Y.*	*x.*	*y.*			Products *xy.*	
Union.	Estimated Average Earnings of Agricultural Labourers. Shillings and Pence per Week.	Percentage of Population in receipt of Poor-law Relief.	Deviation of *x* from Mean (Pence).	Deviation of *y* from Mean.	x^2.	y^2.	Positive.	Negative.
	s. d.							
1. Glendale . .	20 9	2·40	+58	-1·27	3364	1·6129	—	73·66
2. Wigton . .	20 3	2·29	+52	-1·38	2704	1·9044	—	71·76
3. Garstang . .	19 8	1·39	+45	-2·28	2025	6·1984	—	102·60
4. Belper . .	18 6	1·92	+31	-1·75	961	3·0625	—	54·25
5. Nantwich .	17 8	2·98	+21	-0·69	441	0·4761	—	14·49
6. Atcham . .	17 6	1·17	+19	-2·50	361	6·2500	....	47·50
7. Driffield . .	17 1	3·79	+14	+0·12	196	0·0144	1·68	—
8. Uttoxeter .	17 0	3·01	+13	-0·66	169	0·4356	—	8·58
9. Wetherby .	17 0	2·39	+13	-1·28	169	1·6384	—	16·64
10. Easingwold .	16 11	2·78	+12	-0·89	144	0·7921	—	10·68
11. Southwell .	16 6	3·09	+ 7	-0·68	49	0·3364	—	4·06
12. Hollingbourn .	16 4	2·78	+ 6	-0·89	25	0·7921	—	4·45
13. Melton Mowbray	16 3	2·61	+ 4	-1·06	16	1·1236	—	4·24
14. Truro . .	16 3	4·33	+ 4	+0·66	16	0·4356	2·64	—
15. Godstone .	16 0	3·02	+ 1	-0·65	1	0·4225	—	0·65
16. Louth . .	16 0	4·20	+ 1	+0·53	1	0·2809	0·63	—
17. Brixworth .	16 9	1·29	- 2	-2·38	4	5·6644	4·76	—
18. Crediton .	15 8	5·16	3	+1·49	9	2·2201	—	4·47
19. Holbeach .	15 6	4·75	5	+1·08	25	1·1664	—	5·40
20. Maldon . .	15 6	4·64	5	+0·97	25	0·9409	—	4·85
21. Monmouth .	15 4	4·26	7	+0·69	49	0·3481	—	4·13
22. St Neots .	15 3	1·66	8	-2·01	64	4·0461	16·08	—
23. Swaffham .	15 0	5·37	-11	+1·76	121	2·8900	—	18·70
24. Thakeham .	15 0	3·38	-11	-0·29	121	0·0841	3·19	—
25. Thame . .	15 0	5·84	-11	+2·17	121	4·7089	—	23·87
26. Thingoe . .	15 0	4·63	-11	+0·96	121	0·9216	—	10·56
27. Basingstoke .	15 0	3·93	-11	+0·26	121	0·0676	—	2·86
28. Cirencester .	15 0·	4·54	-11	+0·87	121	0·7569	—	9·57
29. North Witchford	14 10	3·42	-13	-0·25	169	0·0625	3·25	—
30. Pewsey . .	14 9	5·88	-14	+2·21	196	4·8841	—	30·94
31. Bromyard .	14 0	4·36	-14	+0·69	196	0·4761	—	9·66
32. Wantage . .	14 9	3·85	-14	+0·18	196	0·0324	—	2·52
33. Stratford on Avon	14 7	3·02	-16	+0·26	256	0·0625	—	4·00
34. Dorchester .	14 6	4·48	-17	+0·81	289	0·6561	—	13·77
35. Woburn . .	14 6	5·67	-17	+2·00	289	4·0000	—	34·00
36. Buntingford .	14 4	4·91	-19	+1·24	361	1·5376	—	23·56
37. Pershore . .	13 6	4·34	-29	+0·67	841	0·4489	—	19·43
38. Langport . .	12 6	6·19	-41	+1·52	1681	2·3104	—	t 2·32
	Mean 15 11	Mean 3·67	—	—	16,018	63·0556	32·13	698·17
					σ_x 20·5d.	σ_y 1·29%		32·13
						$\Sigma(xy)= - 666\cdot04$		

average weekly earnings of agricultural labourers in 38 English Poor-law unions of an agricultural type (the data of Example i., Chap. VIII. p. 137). (2) Y—the percentage of the population in receipt of Poor-law relief on the 1st January 1891 in each of the same unions (B return). The means of each of the variables are calculated in the ordinary way, and then the deviations x and y from the mean are written down (columns 4 and 5): care must be taken to give each deviation the correct sign. These deviations are then squared (columns 6 and 7) and the standard deviations found as before (Chap. VIII. p. 136). Finally, every x is multiplied by the associated y and the product entered in column 8 or column 9 according to its sign. These columns are then added up separately and the algebraic sum of the totals gives $\Sigma(xy) = -666\cdot04$: therefore the mean product $p = \Sigma(xy)/N = -17\cdot53$, and

$$r = -\frac{17\cdot53}{20\cdot5 \times 1\cdot29} = -\cdot66.$$

There is therefore a well-marked relation exhibited by these data between the earnings of agricultural labourers in a district and the percentage of the population in receipt of Poor-law relief. A penny is rather a small unit in which to measure deviations in the average earnings, so for the regressions we may alter the unit of x to a shilling, making $\sigma_x = 1\cdot71$, and

$$b_1 = r\frac{\sigma_x}{\sigma_y} = -0\cdot87, \qquad b_2 = r\frac{\sigma_y}{\sigma_x} = -0\cdot50.$$

The regression equations are therefore, in terms of these units,

$$x = -0\cdot87y \qquad\qquad y = -0\cdot50x.$$

For practical purposes it is more convenient to express the equations in terms of the absolute values of the variables rather than the deviations: therefore, replacing x by $(X - 15\cdot94)$ and y by $(Y - 3\cdot67)$ and simplifying, we have

$$X = 19\cdot13 - 0\cdot87Y \qquad . \qquad . \qquad . \qquad (a)$$
$$Y = 11\cdot64 - 0\cdot50X \qquad . \qquad (b)$$

the units being 1s. for the earnings and 1 per cent. for the pauperism. The standard errors made in using these equations to estimate earnings from pauperism and pauperism from earnings respectively are

$$\sigma_x \sqrt{1 - r^2} = 15\cdot4\text{d.} = 1\cdot28\text{s.}$$
$$\sigma_y \sqrt{1 - r^2} = 0\cdot97 \text{ per cent.}$$

The equation (b) tells us therefore that a rise of 2s. in earnings in passing from one district to another means *on the average* a fall of 1 in the percentage in receipt of relief. A natural conclusion would be that this means a direct effect of the higher earnings in diminishing the necessity for relief, but such a conclusion cannot be accepted offhand. Equation (a) indicates, for instance, that every rise of a unit in the percentage relieved corresponds to a fall of 0·87 shillings, or 10½d. in earnings : this might mean that the giving of relief tends to depress wages. Which is the correct interpretation of the facts? The above

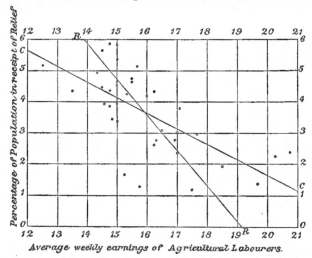

FIG. 40.—Correlation between Pauperism and Average Earnings of Agricultural Labourers for certain districts of England (data of Table VII.) : *RR*, *CC*, lines of regression : $r = -0.66$.

regression equations alone cannot tell us this, and it is in the discussion of such questions that most of the difficulties of statistical arguments arise.

As a check on the whole of the arithmetical work, and to test whether the correlation coefficient is unduly affected by a few outlying observations, or, perhaps, by the regression not being linear, it is always as well to draw a diagram representing the results obtained. Take scales along two axes at right angles (fig. 40) representing the variables, and insert a dot (better, for clearness, a small circle or a cross) at the point determined by each observed pair of *x* and *y*. Complete the diagram by inserting the two lines

RR and CC given by the regression equations (a) and (b). In doing this it is as well to determine a point at each end of both lines, and then to check the work by seeing that they meet in the mean of the whole distribution. Thus RR is determined from (a) by the points $Y=0$, $X=19\cdot13$ and $Y=6$, $X=13\cdot91$: CC is determined from (b) by the points $X=12$, $Y=5\cdot64$ and $X=21$, $Y=1\cdot14$. Marking in these points, and drawing the lines, they will be found to meet in the mean, $X=15\cdot94$, $Y=3\cdot67$. The diagram gives a very clear idea of the distribution; clearly the regression is as nearly linear as may be with so very scattered a distribution, and there are no very exceptional observations. The most exceptional districts are Brixworth and St Neots with rather low earnings but very low pauperism, and Glendale and Wigton with the highest earnings but a pauperism well above the lowest—over 2 per cent.

16. When a classified correlation-table is to be dealt with, the procedure is of precisely the same kind as was used in the calculation of a standard deviation, the same artifices being used to shorten the work. That is to say, (1) the product-sum is calculated in the first instance with respect to an arbitrary origin, and is afterwards reduced to the value it would have with respect to the mean ; (2) the arbitrary origin is taken at the centre of a class-interval ; (3) the class-interval is treated as the unit of measurement throughout the arithmetic.

Let deviations from the arbitrary origin be denoted by $\xi \eta$, and let $\bar{\xi} \bar{\eta}$ be the co-ordinates of the mean. Then

$$\xi = x + \bar{\xi} \qquad \eta = y + \bar{\eta}.$$
$$\therefore \quad \xi \eta = xy + \bar{\xi}y + \bar{\eta}x + \bar{\xi}\bar{\eta}.$$

Therefore, summing, since the second and third sums on the right vanish, being the sums of deviations from the mean,

$$\Sigma(\xi\eta) = \Sigma(xy) + N\bar{\xi}\bar{\eta},$$

or bringing $\Sigma(xy)$ to the left,

$$\Sigma(xy) = \Sigma(\xi\eta) - N\bar{\xi}\bar{\eta}.$$

That is, in terms of mean-products, using p' to denote the mean-product for the arbitrary origin,

$$p = p' - \bar{\xi}\bar{\eta}.$$

In any case where the origin from which deviations have been measured is not the mean, this correction must be used. It will sometimes give a sensible correction even for work in the form of

Example i., and in that case, of course, the standard deviations will also require reduction to the mean.

As the arithmetical process of calculating the correlation co-efficient from a grouped table is of great importance, we give two illustrations, the first economic, the second biological.

Example ii., Table VIII.—The two variables are (1) X, the percentage of males over 65 years of age in receipt of Poor-law relief in 235 unions of a mainly rural character in England and Wales ; (2) Y, the ratio of the numbers of persons given relief " out-doors " (in their own homes) to one " indoors " (in the workhouse). The figures refer to a one-day count (1st August 1890, No. 36, 1890), and the table is one of a series that were drawn up with the view to discussing the influence of administrative methods on pauperism. (*Economic Journal*, vol. vi., 1896, p. 613.)

The arbitrary origin for X was taken at the centre of the fourth column, or at 17·5 per cent. ; for Y at the centre of the fourth row, or 3·5. The following are the values found for the constants of the single distributions :—

$$\bar{\xi} = -0.1532 \text{ intervals} = -0.77 \text{ per cent., whence } M_x = 16.73 \text{ per cent.}$$

$$\sigma_x = 1.29 \text{ intervals} = 6.45 \text{ per cent.}$$

$$\bar{\eta} = +0.36 \text{ intervals or units, whence } M_y = 3.86.$$

$$\sigma_y = 2.98 \text{ units.}$$

To calculate $\Sigma(\xi\eta)$, the value of $\xi\eta$ is first written in every compartment of the table against the corresponding frequency, treating the class-interval as the unit: these are the figures in heavy type in Table VIII. In making these entries the sign of the product may be neglected, but it must be remembered that this sign will be positive in the upper left-hand and lower right-hand quadrants, negative in the two others. The frequencies are then collected as shown in columns 2 and 3 of Table VIIIA., being grouped according to the value and sign of $\xi\eta$. Thus for $\xi\eta = 1$, the total frequency in the positive quadrants is $13 + 8.5 = 21.5$, in the negative $14 + 6 = 20$: for $\xi\eta = 2$, $10 + 4.5 + 1 + 4.5 = 20$ in the positive quadrants, $5 + 2 + 1 + 3.5 = 11.5$ in the negative, and so on. When columns 2 and 3 are completed, they should first of all be checked to see that no frequency has been dropped, which may be readily done by adding together the totals of these two columns together with the frequency in row 4 and column 4 of Table VIII. (the row and column for which $\xi\eta = 0$), being careful not to count twice the frequency in the compartment common to the two ; this grand total must clearly be equal to the total number of observations N, or 235 in the present case. The algebraic sum of the frequencies in each line of columns 2 and 3 is

TABLE VIII. THEORY OF CORRELATION : *Example* ii.—*Old-age Pauperism and Proportion of Out-relief.* (The Frequencies are the figures printed in ordinary type. The numbers in heavy type are the Deviation-Products ($\xi\eta$).)

Number relieved Outdoors to One Indoors.	Percentage of Males over 65 in receipt of Relief.								Total.
	0–5.	5–10.	10–15.	15–20.	20–25.	25–30.	30–35.	35–40.	
0– 1	0·5 **9**	6·0 **6**	9·0 **3**	1·0 **0**	—	—	—	1·0 **12**	17·5 —
1– 2	3·5 **6**	13·0 **4**	10·0 **2**	14·0 **0**	5·0 **2**	—	—	—	45·5 —
2– 3	1·0 **3**	4·5 **2**	13·0 **1**	13·5 **0**	14·0 **1**	2·0 **2**	—	—	48·0 —
3– 4	1·0 **0**	4·5 **0**	7·5 **0**	14·0 **0**	14·0 **0**	3·0 **0**	—	—	44·0 —
4– 5	—	1·0 **2**	6·0 **1**	11·5 **0**	8·5 **1**	1·0 **2**	—	—	28·0 —
5– 6	—	—	3·5 **2**	3·0 **0**	4·5 **2**	2·0 **4**	—	—	13·0 —
6– 7	—	1·0 **6**	2·0 **3**	1·0 **0**	2·0 **3**	4·0 **6**	1·0 **9**	—	11·0 —
7– 8	—	0·5 **8**	1·0 **4**	1·0 **0**	3·0 **4**	—	—	—	5·5 —
8– 9	—	0·5 **10**	1·0 **5**	1·0 **0**	1·0 **5**	4·0 **10**	—	—	7·5 —
9–10	—	1·0 **12**	—	2·0 **0**	4·0 **6**	—	—	—	7·0 —
10–11	—	—	—	—	—	·—	—	—	—
11–12	—	—	—	—	2·0 **8**	—	—	—	2·0 —
12–13	—	—	1·0 **9**	—	—	—	—	—	1·0 —
13–14	—	1·0 **20**	—	—	—	—	—	—	1·0 —
14–15	—	—	—	—	—	—	—	—	—
15–16	—	—	—	1·0 **0**	—	1·0 **24**	—	—	2·0 —
16–17	—	—	—	—	—	—	—	—	—
17–18	—	—	—	—	—	1·0 **28**	—	—	1·0 —
18–19	—	—	—	—	1·0 **15**	—	—	—	1·0 —
Totals	6·0	33·0	54·0	63·0	59·0	18·0	1·0	1·0	285·0

Percentage in receipt of Relief . . Mean 16·73 per cent. σ_x 6·45 per cent.
Out-relief Ratio . . . Mean 3·86. σ_y 2·98.

TABLE VIIIA. CALCULATION OF THE PRODUCT SUM $\Sigma(\xi\eta)$.

1.	2.	3.	4.	5.	6.
	Frequencies.		Total.	Products.	
$\xi\eta$.	+ Quadrants.	− Quadrants.		Positive.	Negative.
1	21·5	20	+ 1·5	1·5	—
2	20	11·5	+ 8·5	17	—
3	12	2	+10	30	—
4	18	1	+17	68	—
5	1	1	—	—	—
6	17·5	1	+16·5	99	—
8	2	0·5	+ 1·5	12	—
9	1·5	1	+ 0·5	4·5	—
10	4	0·5	+ 3·5	35	—
12	—	2	− 2	—	24
15	1	—	+ 1	15	—
20	—	1	− 1	—	20
24	1	—	+ 1	24	—
28	1	—	+ 1	28	—
Totals	100·5 41·5 93	41·5	—	+334 − 44	− 44
	235			+ 290	

then entered in column 4, treating the frequencies in column 3 as if
they were themselves negative, and finally the figures of column 4
are multiplied by the values of $\xi\eta$ and the products entered in
column 5 or 6 according to sign. The algebraic sum of the totals
of columns 5 and 6 = + 290 = $\Sigma(\xi\eta)$. Whence $p' = \Sigma(\xi\eta)/N = 1\cdot234$.
To find the value of p we have, remembering that we are working
with class-intervals as the unit,

$$\bar{\xi}\bar{\eta} = -(0\cdot153 \times 0\cdot36) = -0\cdot055$$
$$p = p' - \bar{\xi}\bar{\eta} = 1\cdot234 + 0\cdot055 = +1\cdot289$$
$$r = + \frac{1\cdot289}{1\cdot29 \times 2\cdot98} = +0\cdot34.$$

The regression of pauperism on out-relief ratio is, reverting to
1 per cent. as the unit of pauperism instead of the class-interval,

$+0\cdot34 \times 6\cdot45/2\cdot98 = 0\cdot74$, and the regression equation accordingly $x = 0\cdot74y$, or

$$X = 13\cdot9 + 0\cdot74\,Y,$$

the standard error made in using the equation for estimating X from Y being $\sigma_x \sqrt{1 - r^2} = 6\cdot07$.

This is the equation of greatest practical interest, telling us that, as we pass from one district to another, a rise of 1 in the ratio of the numbers relieved in their own homes to the numbers relieved in the workhouse corresponds on an average to a rise of $0\cdot74$ in the percentage in receipt of relief. The result is such as to create a presumption in favour of the view that the giving of out-relief tends to increase the numbers relieved, and this can be taken as a working hypothesis for further investigation.

The student should work out the second regression equation, and check both by calculating the means of the principal rows and columns, and drawing a diagram like figs. 36, 37, and 38.

Example iii., Table IX.—(Unpublished data; measurements by G. U. Yule.) The two variables are (1) X, the length of a mother-frond of duckweed (*Lemna minor*); (2) Y, the length of the daughter-frond. The mother-frond was measured when the daughter-frond separated from it, and the daughter-frond when its first daughter-frond separated. Measures were taken from camera drawings made with the Zeiss-Abbé camera under a low power, the actual magnification being 24 : 1. The units of length in the tabulated measurements are millimetres on the drawings.

The arbitrary origin for both X and Y was taken at 105 mm. The following are the values found for the constants of the single distributions:—

$\bar{\xi} = -1\cdot058$ intervals $= -6\cdot3$ mm.	$M_1 = 98\cdot7$ mm. on drawing, $= 4\cdot11$ mm. actual.
$\sigma_x = 2\cdot828$ intervals $= 17\cdot0$ mm. on drawing $=$	$0\cdot707$ mm. actual.
$\bar{\eta} = -0\cdot203$,, $= -1\cdot2$ mm.	$M_2 = 103\cdot8$ mm. on drawing. $= 4\cdot32$ mm. actual.
$\sigma_y = 3\cdot084$,, $= 18\cdot5$ mm. on drawing $=$	$0\cdot771$ mm. actual.

The values of $\xi\eta$ are entered in every compartment of the table as before, and the frequencies then collected, according to the magnitude and sign of $\xi\eta$, in columns 2 and 3 of Table IXA. The entries in these two columns are next checked by adding to the totals the frequency in the row and column for which $\xi\eta$ is zero, and seeing that it gives the total number of observations (266). The numbers in column 4 are given by deducting the entries in column 3 from those in column 2. The totals so obtained are multiplied by $\xi\eta$ (column 1) and the products entered

TABLE IXA.

1.	2.	3.	4.	5.	6.
	Frequencies.		Total.	Products.	
$\xi\eta$.	+ Quadrants.	– Quadrants.		+	–
1	—	8·5	– 8·5	—	8·5
2	17	13·5	+ 3·5	7	—
3	10·5	9	+ 1·5	4·5	—
4	13·5	6·5	+ 7	28	—
5	2	0·5	+ 1·5	7·5	—
6	13·5	5	+ 8·5	51	—
8	13	1	+12	96	—
9	9	4	+ 5	45	—
10	6·5	1	+ 5·5	55	—
12	17·5	—	+17·5	210	—
14	1	—	+ 1	14	—
15	6	—	+ 6	90	—
16	7	—	+ 7	112	—
18	2	—	+ 2	36	—
20	8	—	+ 8	160	—
21	2	—	+ 2	42	—
24	6	—	+ 6	144	—
25	1	—	+ 1	25	—
28	1	—	+ 1	28	—
30	3	—	+ 3	90	—
36	1	—	+ 1	36	—
40	1	—	+ 1	40	—
42	2	—	+ 2	84	—
60	1	—	+ 1	60	—
63	1	—	+ 1	63	—
Totals	145·5 49 71·5	49	—	+1528 – 8·5	– 8·5
	266			1519·5	

in column 5 or 6 according to sign. The algebraic sum of the totals of these two columns gives $\Sigma(\xi\eta) = + 1519\cdot5$. Dividing by 266, $p' = 5\cdot712$. But $\bar{\xi}\bar{\eta} = + 1\cdot058 \times 0\cdot203 = + 0\cdot215$; therefore $p = 5\cdot712 - 0\cdot215 = 5\cdot497$.

$$r = + \frac{5\cdot497}{2\cdot828 \times 3\cdot084} = + 0\cdot63.$$

TABLE IX. THEORY OF CORRELATION : *Illustration* iii.—*Correlation between* (1) *daughter-frond, in Lemma minor.* [Unpublished data ; G. U. Yule.] (The frequ... type. The numbers in heavy type are the deviation-products ($\xi\eta$)).

(2) Length of daughter-frond.	(1) Length of mother-frond (mm. of camera drawing enlarg...												
	60-66.	66-72.	72-78.	78-84.	84-90.	90-96.	96-102.	102-108.	108-114.	114-120.	120-126.	126-132.	132-138.
60-66	—	2 / **42**	—	—	—	—	—	—	—	—	—	—	—
66-72	—	—	—	1 / **24**	2 / **18**	—	—	—	—	—	—	—	—
72-78	—	⌐	1 / **25**	3 / **20**	1 / **15**	—	2 / **5**	2 / **0**	0·5 / **5**	—	—	—	—
78-84	—	4 / **24**	2 / **20**	5 / **16**	6 / **12**	6 / **8**	—	3 / **0**	1·6 / **4**	—	—	—	—
84-90	2 / **21**	—	3 / **15**	4·5 / **12**	2 / **9**	2 / **6**	3 / **3**	5 / **0**	2 / **3**	2 / **6**	2 / **9**	—	—
90-96	1 / **14**	1 / **12**	3·6 / **10**	5 / **8**	6·5 / **6**	4·6 / **4**	4 / **2**	4 / **0**	3 / **2**	—	1 / **6**	—	—
96-102	—	—	—	8 / **4**	4·6 / **3**	7 / **2**	—	1 / **0**	3 / **1**	1 / **2**	—	—	—
102-108	—	—	1 / **0**	8 / **0**	7·5 / **0**	7 / **0**	3·5 / **0**	9 / **0**	3 / **0**	—	—	—	—
108-114	—	—	—	—	4 / **3**	5 / **2**	5·5 / **1**	6 / **0**	—	2 / **2**	—	—	—
114-120	—	—	—	—	1 / **6**	5 / **4**	4·6 / **2**	5·5 / **0**	4 / **2**	—	1 / **6**	—	1 / **10**
120-126	—	—	—	—	2 / **9**	1 / **6**	3 / **3**	2 / **0**	3 / **3**	3 / **8**	7 / **9**	2 / **12**	—
126-132	—	—	—	—	—	1 / **8**	—	3 / **0**	1 / **4**	3 / **8**	2 / **12**	2 / **16**	3 / **20**
132-138	—	—	—	—	—	1 / **10**	—	1 / **0**	—	2 / **10**	2 / **15**	—	—
138-144	—	—	—	—	—	—	—	—	1 / **6**	2 / **12**	—	—	1 / **30**
144-150	—	—	—	—	—	—	—	—	—	—	—	1 / **28**	—
150-156	—	—	—	—	—	—	—	—	—	—	1 / **24**	—	—
156-162	—	—	—	—	—	—	—	—	—	—	—	—	—
162-168	—	—	—	—	—	—	—	—	—	—	—	1 / **40**	—
Total	3	7	10·6	34·5	36·5	38·6	25·6	41·5	22	15	16	8	5

The regression of daughter-frond on mother-frond is 0·69 (a value which will not be altered by altering the units of measurement for both mother- and daughter-fronds, as such an alteration will affect both standard deviations equally). Hence the regression equation giving the average actual length (in millimetres) of daughter-fronds for mother-fronds of actual length X is

$$Y = 1·48 + 0·69X.$$

We again leave it to the student to work out the second regression equation giving the average length of mother-fronds for daughter-fronds of length Y, and to check the whole work by a diagram showing the lines of regression and the means of arrays for the central portion of the table.

17. The student should be careful to remember the following points in working :—

(1) To give p' and $\bar{\xi}\eta$ their correct signs in finding the true mean deviation-product p.

(2) To express σ_x and σ_y in terms of the class-interval as a unit, in the value of $r = p/\sigma_x \sigma_y$, for these are the units in terms of which p has been calculated.

(3) To use the proper units for the standard deviations (not class-intervals in general) in calculating the coefficients of regression : in forming the regression equation in terms of the absolute values of the variables, for example, as above, the work will be wrong unless means and standard deviations are expressed in the same units.

Further, it must always be remembered that correlation coefficients, like all other statistical measures, are subject to fluctuations of sampling (*cf.* Chap. III. §§ 7, 8). If we write on cards a series of pairs of *strictly* independent values of x and y and then work out the correlation coefficient for samples of, say, 40 or 50 cards taken at random, we are very unlikely ever to find $r = 0$ absolutely, but will find a series of positive and negative values centring round 0. No great stress can therefore be laid on small, or even on *moderately* large, values of r as indicating a true correlation if the numbers of observations be small. For instance, if $N = 36$, a value of $r = \pm 0·5$ *may* be merely a chance result (though a very infrequent one); if $N = 100$, $r = \pm 0·3$ may similarly be a mere fluctuation of sampling, though again an infrequent one. If $N = 900$, a value of $r = \pm 0·1$ might occur as a fluctuation of sampling of the same degree of infrequency. The student must therefore be careful in interpreting his coefficients. (See Chap. XVII. § 15.)

Finally, it should be borne in mind that any coefficient, *e.g.* the coefficient of correlation or the coefficient of· contingency, gives only a part of the information afforded by the original data or the correlation table. The correlation table itself, or the original data if no correlation table has been compiled, should always be given, unless considerations of space or of expense absolutely preclude the adoption of such a course.

REFERENCES.

The theory of correlation was first developed on definite assumptions as to the form of the distribution of frequency, the so-called "normal distribution" (Chap. XVI.) being assumed. In (1) Bravais introduced the product-sum, but not a single symbol for a coefficient of correlation. Sir Francis Galton, in (2), (3), and (4), developed the practical method, determining his coefficient (Galton's function, as it was termed at first) graphically. Edgeworth developed the theoretical side further in (5), and Pearson introduced the product-sum formula in (6)—both memoirs being written on the assumption of a "normal" distribution of frequency (*cf.* Chap. XVI.). The method used in the preceding chapter is based on (7) and (8).

(1) BRAVAIS, A., "Analyse mathématique sur les probabilités des erreurs de situation d'un point," *Acad. des Sciences : Mémoires présentés par divers savants*, II$_e$ série, t. ix., 1846, p. 255.
(2) GALTON, FRANCIS, "Regression towards Mediocrity in Hereditary Stature," *Jour. Anthrop. Inst.*, vol. xv., 1886, p. 246.
(3) GALTON, FRANCIS, "Family Likeness in Stature," *Proc. Roy. Soc.*, vol. xl., 1886, p. 42.
(4) GALTON, FRANCIS, "Correlations and their Measurement," *Proc. Roy. Soc.*, vol. xlv., 1888, p. 135.
(5) EDGEWORTH, F. Y., "On Correlated Averages," *Phil. Mag.*, 5th Series, vol. xxxiv., 1892, p. 190.
(6) PEARSON, KARL, "Regression, Heredity, and Panmixia," *Phil. Trans. Roy. Soc.*, Series A, vol. clxxxvii., 1896, p. 253.
(7) YULE, G. U., "On the significance of Bravais' Formulæ for Regression, etc., in the case of Skew Correlation," *Proc. Roy. Soc.*, vol. lx., 1897, p. 477.
(8) YULE, G. U., "On the Theory of Correlation," *Jour. Roy. Stat. Soc.*, vol. lx., 1897, p. 812.
(9) DARBISHIRE, A. D., "Some Tables for illustrating Statistical Correlation," *Mem. and Proc. of the Manchester Lit. and Phil. Soc.*, vol. li., 1907. (Tables and diagrams illustrating the meaning of values of the correlation coefficient from 0 to 1 by steps of a twelfth.)
Reference may also be made here to—
(10) EDGEWORTH, F. Y., "On a New Method of reducing Observations relating to several Quantities," *Phil. Mag.*, 5th Series, vol. xxiv., 1887, p. 222, and vol. xxv., 1888, p. 184. (A method of treating correlated variables differing entirely from that described in the preceding chapter, and based on the use of the median : the method involves the use of trial and error to some extent. For some illustrations see F. Y. Edgeworth and A. L. Bowley, *Jour. Roy. Stat. Soc.*, vol. lxv., 1902, p. 341 *et seq.*)
References to memoirs on the theory of non-linear regression are given at the end of Chapter X.

EXERCISES.

1. Find the correlation-coefficient and the equations of regression for the following values of X and Y.

X.	Y.
1	2
2	5
3	3
4	8
5	7

[As a matter of practice it is never worth calculating a correlation-coefficient for so few observations: the figures are given solely as a short example on which the student can test his knowledge of the work.]

2. The following figures show, for the districts of Example i., the ratios of the numbers of paupers in receipt of outdoor relief to the numbers in receipt of relief in the workhouse. Find the correlations between the out-relief ratio and (1) the estimated earnings of agricultural labourers; (2) the percentage of the population in receipt of relief.

1	6·40	14	7·50	27	2·97
2	4·04	15	4·44	28	5·38
3	7·90	16	8·34	29	3·24
4	3·31	17	0·69	30	7·61
5	7·85	18	9·89	31	5·87
6	0·45	19	4·00	32	5·50
7	10·00	20	6·02	33	3·58
8	4·43	21	8·27	34	6·93
9	4·78	22	1·58	35	6·02
10	4·73	23	16·04	36	4·92
11	6·66	24	1·96	37	4·64
12	1·22	25	9·28	38	10·56
13	4·27	26	8·72		

3. Verify the following data for the under-mentioned tables of the preceding chapter. Calculate the means of rows and columns and draw diagrams showing the lines of regression, as figs. 36-39, for one or two cases at least.

	I.	II.	III.	IV.	VI.
Mean of X . .	55·3 mm.	40·6 years	67·70 ins.	5·90	509·2
,, Y . .	53·1 ,,	42·8 ,,	68·66 ,,	4·33	14,500
Standard devia-tion of X . .	6·86 ,,	12·7 ,,	2·72 ,,	2·83	7·46
Standard devia-tion of Y . .	5·77 ,,	13·1 ,,	2·75 ,,	2·97	18,100
Coefficient of corre-lation . .	+0·97	+0·91	+0·51	+0·21	−0·014
Coefficient of con-tingency (for the grouping stated below) . .	0·90	0·81	0·51	0·31	0·47

In calculating the coefficient of contingency (coefficient of mean square contingency) use the following groupings, so as to avoid small scattered frequencies at the extremities of the tables and also excessive arithmetic :—

I. Group together (1) two top rows, (2) three bottom rows, (3) two first columns, (4) four last columns, leaving centre of table as it stands.

II. Regroup by ten-year intervals (15-, 25-, 35-, etc.) for both husband and wife, making the last group "65 and over."

III. Regroup by 2-inch intervals, 58·5-60·5, etc., for father, 59·5-61·5, etc., for son. If a 3-inch grouping be used (58·5-61·5, etc., for both father and son), the coefficient of mean square contingency is 0·465. [Both results cited from Pearson, ref. 1 of Chap. V.]

IV. For cols., group 1+2, 3+4, . . . , 11+12, 13 and upwards. Rows, 0, 1+2, 3+4, . . . , 9+10, 11 and upwards.

VI. For cols., group all up to 494·5 and all over 521·5, leaving central cols. Rows singly up 20 : then 20-28, 28-44, 44-56, 56 upwards.

CHAPTER X.

CORRELATION: ILLUSTRATIONS AND PRACTICAL METHODS.

1. THE student—especially the student of economic statistics, to whom this chapter is principally addressed—should be careful to note that the coefficient of correlation, like an average or a measure of dispersion, only exhibits in a summary and comprehensible form one particular aspect of the facts on which it is based, and the real difficulties arise in the interpretation of the coefficient when obtained. The value of the coefficient may be consistent with some given hypothesis, but it may be equally consistent with others; and not only are care and judgment essential for the discussion of such possible hypotheses, but also a thorough knowledge of the facts in all other possible aspects. Further, care should be exercised from the commencement in the selection of the variables between which the correlation shall be determined. The variables should be defined in such a way as to render the correlations as readily interpretable as possible, and, if several are to be dealt with, they should afford the answers to specific and definite questions. Unfortunately, the field of choice is frequently very much limited, by deficiencies in the available data and so forth, and consequently practical possibilities as well as ideal requirements have to be taken into account. No general rules can be laid down, but the following are given as illustrations of the sort of points that have to be considered.

2. **Illustration i.**—It is required to throw some light on the variations of pauperism in the unions (unions of parishes) of England. (*Cf.* Yule, ref. 2.)

One table (Table VIII.) bearing on a part of this question, viz. the influence of the giving of out-relief on the proportion of the aged in receipt of relief, was given in Chap. IX. (p. 183). The question was treated by correlating the percentage of the aged relieved in different districts with the ratio of numbers relieved outdoors to the numbers in the workhouse. Is such a method the best possible?

On the whole, it would seem better to correlate *changes* in pauperism with *changes* in various possible factors. If we say that a high rate of pauperism in some district is due to lax administration, we presumably mean that as administration became lax, pauperism rose, or that if administration were more strict, pauperism would decrease; if we say that the high pauperism is due to the depressed condition of industry, we mean that when industry recovers, pauperism will fall. When we say, in fact, that any one variable is a factor of pauperism, we mean that *changes* in that variable are accompanied by *changes* in the percentage of the population in receipt of relief, either in the same or the reverse direction. It will be better, therefore, to deal with changes in pauperism and possible factors. The next question is what factors to choose.

3. The possible factors may be grouped under three heads :—

(*a*) *Administration.*—Changes in the method or strictness of administration of the law.

(*b*) *Environment.*—Changes in economic conditions (wages, prices, employment), social conditions (residential or industrial character of the district, density of population, nationality of population), or moral conditions (as illustrated, *e.g.*, by the statistics of crime).

(*c*) *Age Distribution.*—the percentage of the population between given age-limits in receipt of relief increases very rapidly with old age, the actual figures given by one of the only two then existing returns of the age of paupers being—2 per cent. under age 16, 1 per cent. over 16 but under 65, 20 per cent. over 65. (Return 36, 1890.)

It is practically impossible to deal with more than three factors, one from each of the above groups, or four variables altogether, including the pauperism itself. What shall we take, then, as representative variables, and how shall we best measure "pauperism"?

4. *Pauperism.*—The returns give (*a*) cost, (*b*) numbers relieved. It seems better to deal with (*b*) (as in the illustration of Table

VIII., Chap. IX.), as numbers are more important than cost from the standpoint of the moral effect of relief on the population. The returns, however, generally include both lunatics and vagrants in the totals of persons relieved ; and as the administrative methods of dealing with these two classes differ entirely from the methods applicable to ordinary pauperism, it seems better to alter the official total by excluding them. Returns are available giving the numbers in receipt of relief on 1st January and 1st July; there does not seem to be any special reason for taking the one return rather than the other, but the return for 1st January was actually used. The percentage of the population in receipt of relief on 1st January 1871, 1881, and 1891 (the three census years), less lunatics and vagrants, was therefore tabulated for each union. (The investigation was carried out in 1898.)

5. *Administration.*—The most important point here, and one that lends itself readily to statistical treatment, is the relative proportion of indoor and outdoor relief (relief in the workhouse and relief in the applicant's home). The first question is, again, shall we measure this proportion by cost or by numbers? The latter seems, as before, the simpler and more important ratio for the present purpose, though some writers have preferred the statement in terms of expenditure (*e.g.* Mr Charles Booth, *Aged Poor—Condition,* 1894). If we decide on the statement in terms of numbers, we still have the choice of expressing the proportion (1) as the ratio of numbers given out-relief to numbers in the workhouse, or (2) as the percentage of numbers given out-relief on the total number relieved. The former method was chosen, partly on the simple ground that it had already been used in an earlier investigation, partly on the ground that the use of the ratio separates the higher proportions of out-relief more clearly from each other, and these differences seem to have significance. Thus a union with a ratio of 15 outdoor paupers to one indoor seems to be materially different from one with a ratio of, say, 10 to 1 ; but if we take, instead of the ratios, the percentages of outdoor to total paupers, the figures are 94 per cent. and 91 per cent. respectively, which are so close that they will probably fall into the same array. The ratio of numbers in receipt of outdoor relief to the numbers in the workhouse, in every union, was therefore tabulated for 1st January in the census years 1871, 1881, 1891.

6. *Environment.*—This is the most difficult factor of all to deal with. In Mr Booth's work the factors tabulated were (1) persons per acre ; (2) percentage of population living two or more to a room, *i.e.* "overcrowding"; (3) rateable value per head (*Aged Poor—Condition*). The data relating to overcrowding were first collected

13

at the census of 1891, and are not available for earlier years.
Some trial was made of rateable value per head, but with not
very satisfactory results. For any given year, and for a group of
unions of somewhat similar character, e.g. rural, the rateable value
per head appears to be highly (negatively) correlated with the
pauperism, but changes in the two are not very highly correlated :
probably the movements of assessments are sluggish and irregular,
especially in the case of falling assessments in rural unions, and
do not correspond at all accurately with the real changes in the
value of agricultural land. After some consideration, it was
decided to use a very simple index to the changing fortunes of a
district, viz. the movement of the population itself. If the
population of a district is increasing at a rate above the average,
this is *primâ facie* evidence that its industries are prospering ; if
the population is decreasing, or not increasing as fast as the
average, this strongly suggests that the industries are suffering
from a temporary lack of prosperity or permanent decay. The
population of every union was therefore tabulated for the censuses
of 1871, 1881, 1891.

7. *Age Distribution.*—As already stated, the figures that are
known clearly indicate a very rapid rise of the percentage relieved
after 65 years of age. The percentage of the population over 65
years of age was therefore worked out for every union and tabulated from the same three censuses. This is not, of course,
at all a complete index to the composition of the population as
affecting the rate of pauperism, which is sensibly dependent on
the proportion of the two sexes, and the numbers of children as
well. As the percentage in receipt of relief was, however, 20 per
cent. for those over 65, and only 1-2 per cent. for those under that
age, it is evidently a most important index. (A more complete
method might have been used by correcting the observed rate of
pauperism to the basis of a standard population with given numbers of each age and sex. (*Cf.* below, Chap. XI. pp. 223-25.)

8. The changes in each of the four quantities that had been
tabulated for every union were then measured by working out the
ratios for the intercensal decades 1871–81 and 1881–91, taking
the value in the earlier year as 100 in each case. The percentage
ratios so obtained were taken as the four variables. Further, as
the conditions are and were very different for rural and for urban
unions, it seemed very desirable to separate the unions into groups
according to their character. But this cannot be done with any
exactness : the majority of unions are of a mixed character, consisting, say, of a small town with a considerable extent of the
surrounding country. It might seem best to base the classification
on returns of occupations, *e.g.* the proportions of the population

engaged in agriculture, but the statistics of occupations are not given in the census for individual unions. Finally, it was decided to use a classification by density of population, the grouping used being—Rural, 0·3 person per acre or less : Mixed, more than 0·3 but not more than 1 person per acre : Urban, more than 1 person per acre. The metropolitan unions were also treated by themselves. The limit 0·3 for rural unions was suggested by the density of those agricultural unions the conditions in which were investigated by the Labour Commission (the unions of Table VII., Chap. IX.) : the average density of these was 0·25, and 34 of the 38 were under 0·3. The lower limit of density for urban unions—1 per acre—was suggested by a grouping of Mr Booth's (group xiv.) : of course 1 person per acre is not a density associated with an urban district in the ordinary sense of the term, but a country district cannot reach this density unless it include a small town or portion of a town, *i.e.* unless a large proportion of its inhabitants live under urban conditions.

The method by which the relations between four variables are discussed is fully described in Chapter XII. : at the present stage it can only be stated that the discussion is based on the correlations between all the possible (6) pairs that can be formed from the four variables.

9. **Illustration ii.**—The subject of investigation is the inheritance of fertility in man. (*Cf.* Pearson and others, ref. 3.) One table, from the memoir cited, was given as an example in the last chapter (Table IV.).

Fertility in man (*i.e.* the number of children born to a given pair) is very largely influenced by the age of husband and wife at marriage (especially the latter), and by the duration of marriage. It is desired to find whether it is also influenced by the heritable constitution of the parents, *i.e.* whether, allowance being made for the effect of such disturbing causes as age and duration of marriage, fertility is itself a heritable character.

The effect of duration of marriage may be largely eliminated by excluding all marriages which have not lasted, say, 15 years at least. This will rather heavily reduce the number of records available, but will leave a sufficient number for discussion. It would be desirable to eliminate the effect of late marriages in the same way by excluding all cases in which, say, husband was over 30 years of age or wife over 25 (or even less) at the time of marriage. But, unfortunately, this is impossible ; the age of the wife—the most important factor—is only exceptionally given in peerages, family histories, and similar works, from which the data must be compiled. All marriages must therefore be included, whatever the age of the parents at marriage, and the effect of the varying age at marriage must be estimated afterwards.

10. But the correlation between (1) number of children of a woman and (2) number of children of her daughter will be further affected according as we include in the record all her available daughters or only one. Suppose, *e.g.*, the number of children in the first generation is 5 (say the mother and her brothers and sisters), and that she has three daughters with 0, 2, and 4 children respectively: are we to enter all three pairs (5, 0), (5, 2), (5, 4) in the correlation-table, or only one pair? If the latter, which pair? For theoretical simplicity the second process is distinctly the best (though it still further limits the available data). If it be adopted, some regular rule will have to be made for the selection of the daughter whose fertility shall be entered in the table, so as to avoid bias: the first daughter married for whom data are given, and who fulfils the conditions as to duration of marriage, may, for instance, be taken in every case. (For a much more detailed discussion of the problem, and the allied problems regarding the inheritance of fertility in the horse, the student is referred to the original.)

11. **Illustration iii.**—The subject for investigation is the relation between the bulk of a crop (wheat and other cereals, turnips and other root crops, hay, etc.), and the weather. (*Cf.* Hooker, ref. 7.)

Produce-statistics for the more important crops of Great Britain have been issued by the Board of Agriculture since 1885: the figures are based on estimates of the yield furnished by official local estimators all over the country. Estimates are published for separate counties and for groups of counties (divisions). But the climatic conditions vary so much over the United Kingdom that it is better to deal with a smaller area, more homogeneous from the meteorological standpoint. On the other hand, the area should not be too small; it should be large enough to present a representative variety of soil. The group of eastern counties, consisting of Lincoln, Hunts, Cambridge, Norfolk, Suffolk, Essex, Bedford, and Hertford, was selected as fulfilling these conditions. The group includes the county with the largest acreage of each of the ten crops investigated, with the single exception of permanent grass.

12. The produce of a crop is dependent on the weather of a long preceding period, and it is naturally desired to find the influence of the weather at all successive stages during this period, and to determine, for each crop, which period of the year is of most critical importance as regards weather. It must be remembered, however, that the times of both sowing and

harvest are themselves very largely dependent on the weather, and consequently, on an average of many years, the limits of the critical period will not be very well defined. If, therefore, we correlate the produce of the crop (X) with the characteristics of the weather (Y) during successive intervals of the year, it will be as well not to make these intervals too short. It was accordingly decided to take successive groups of 8 weeks, overlapping each other by 4 weeks, i.e. weeks 1–8, 5–12, etc. Correlation coefficients were thus obtained at 4-weeks intervals, but based on 8 weeks' weather.

13. It remains to be decided what characteristics of the weather are to be taken into account. The rainfall is clearly one factor of great importance, temperature is another, and these two will afford quite enough labour for a first investigation. The weekly rainfalls were averaged for eight stations within the area, and the average taken as the first characteristic of the weather. Temperatures were taken from the records of the same stations. The average temperatures, however, do not give quite the sort of information that is required : at temperatures below a certain limit (about 42° Fahr.) there is very little growth, and the growth increases in rapidity as the temperature rises above this point (within limits). It was therefore decided to utilise the figures for "accumulated temperatures above 42° Fahr.," i.e. the total number of day-degrees above 42° during each of the 8-weekly periods, as the second characteristic of the weather; these "accumulated temperatures," moreover, show much larger variations than mean temperatures.

The student should refer to the original for the full discussion as to data. The method of treating the correlations between three variables, based on the three possible correlations between them, is described in Chapter XII.

14. Problems of a somewhat special kind arise when dealing with the relations between simultaneous values of two variables which have been observed during a considerable period of time, for the more rapid movements will often exhibit a fairly close consilience, while the slower changes show no similarity. The two following examples will serve as illustrations of two methods which are generally applicable to such cases.

Illustration iv.—Fig. 41 exhibits the movements of (1) the infantile mortality (deaths of infants under 1 year of age per 1000 births in the same year) ; (2) the general mortality (deaths at all ages per 1000 living) in England and Wales during the period 1838–1904. A very cursory inspection of the figure shows that when the infantile mortality rose from one year to the next the general mortality also rose, as a rule ; and similarly, when the infantile mortality fell, the general mortality also fell. There were, in fact, only five or six exceptions to this rule during the whole period under review. The correlation between the annual values of the two mortalities would nevertheless not be very high, as the general mortality has been falling more or less steadily since 1875 or thereabouts, while the infantile mortality attained almost a record value in 1899. During a long period of time the correlation between annual values may, indeed, very well vanish, for the two mortalities are affected by causes which are to a large extent different in the two cases. To exhibit, therefore, the closeness of the relation between infantile and general mortality, for such causes as show marked changes between one year and the next, it will be best to proceed by correlating the annual *changes*, and not the annual values. The work would be arranged in the following form (only sufficient years being given to exhibit the principle of the process), and the correlation worked out between the figures of cols. 3 and 5.

1.	2.	3.	4.	5.
Year.	Infantile Mortality per 1000 Births.	Increase or Decrease from Year before.	General Mortality per 1000 living.	Increase or Decrease from Year before.
1838	159	—	22·4	—
1839	151	−8	21·8	−0·6
1840	154	+3	22·9	+1·1
1841	145	−9	21·6	−1·3
1842	152	+7	21·7	+0·1
1843	150	−2	21·2	−0·5

For the period to which the diagram refers, viz. 1838–1904, the following constants were found by this method :—

Infantile mortality, mean annual change – 0·21
standard deviation   9·63
General mortality, mean annual change – 0·09
standard deviation   1·14
Coefficient of correlation + 0·77.

This is a much higher correlation than would arise from the mere fact that the deaths of infants form part of the general mortality, and consequently there must be a high correlation between the annual changes in the mortality of those who are over and under 1 year of age. (*Cf.* Exercises 7 and 8, Chap. XI.)

This method, which appears to have been first used by Miss Cave and by Mr Hooker independently in the papers cited in refs. 4 and 6, has recently been generalised by "Student" and the theory fully developed by O. Anderson (*cf.* refs. 13, 14, 15). By taking the first differences the influence of the slower changes of the two variables with time may not be wholly eliminated, but this elimination may be more completely effected by pro-

ceeding to the second differences, *i.e.* by working out the successive
differences of the differences in col. 3 and in col. 5 before corre-

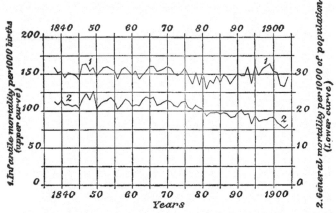

Fig. 41.—Infantile and General Mortality in England and Wales, 1838-1904.

lating. It may even be desirable to proceed to third, fourth or
higher differences before correlating.

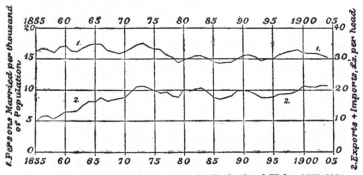

Fig. 42.—Marriage-rate and Foreign Trade, England and Wales, 1855-1904.

15. **Illustration v.**—The two curves of fig. 42 show (1) the
marriage-rate (persons married per 1000 of the population) for
England and Wales ; (2) the values of exports and imports per
head of the population of the United Kingdom for every year
from 1855 to 1904. Inspection of the diagram suggests a similar
relation to that of the last example, the one variable showing a

rise from one year to the next when the other rises, and a fall
when the other falls. The movement of both variables is, however, of a much more regular kind than that of mortality,
resembling a series of "waves" superposed on a steady general
trend, and it is the "waves" in the two variables—the short-period
movements, not the slower trends—which are so clearly related.

16. It is not difficult, moreover, to separate the short-period
oscillations, more or less approximately, from the slower movement.
Suppose the marriage-rate for each year replaced by the average
of an odd number of years of which it is the centre, the number
being as near as may be the same as the period of the "waves"—
e.g. nine years. If these short-period averages were plotted on
the diagram instead of the rates of the individual years, we should
evidently obtain a smoother curve which would clearly exhibit
the trend and be practically free from the conspicuous waves.
The excess or defect of each annual rate above or below the
trend, if plotted separately, would therefore give the "waves"
apart from the slower changes. The figures for foreign trade
may be treated in the same way as the marriage-rate, and we
can accordingly work out the correlation between the waves or
rapid fluctuations, undisturbed by the movements of longer period,
however great they may be. The arithmetic may be carried out
in the form of the following table, and the correlation worked out
in the ordinary way between the figures of columns 4 and 7.

1.	2.	3.	4.	5.	6.	7.
Year.	Marriage-rate (England and Wales).	Nine Years' Average.	Differ-ence.	Exports+Im-ports, £'s per head (U.K.).	Nine Years' Average.	Differ-ence.
1855	16·2	—	—	9·36	—	—
1856	16·7	—	—	11·14	—	—
1857	16·5	—	—	11·85	—	—
1858	16·0	—	—	10·73	—	—
1859	17·0	16·5	+0·5	11·72	12·15	-0·43
1860	17·1	16·6	+0·5	13·03	12·94	+0·09
1861	16·3	16·7	-0·4	13·01	13·52	-0·51
1862	16·1	16·8	-0·7	13·40	14·17	-0·77
1863	16·8	16·9	-0·1	15·13	14·81	+0·32
1864	17·2	—	—	16·43	—	—
1865	17·5	—	—	16·37	—	—
1866	17·5	—	—	17·72	—	—
1867	16·5	—	—	16·47	—	—

17. Fig. 43 is drawn from the figures of columns 4 and 7, and
shows very well how closely the oscillations of the marriage-rate
are related to those of trade. For the period 1861–95 the
correlation between the two oscillations (Hooker, ref. 5) is 0·86.
The method may obviously be extended by correlating the devia-

tion of the marriage-rate in any one year with the deviation of the exports and imports of the year before, or two years before, instead of the same year; if a sufficient number of years be taken, an estimate may be made, by interpolation, of the time-difference that would make the correlation a maximum if it were possible to obtain the figures for exports and imports for periods other than calendar years. Thus Mr Hooker finds (ref. 5) that on an average of the years 1861–95 the correlation would be a maximum between the marriage-rate and the foreign trade of about one-third of a year earlier. The method is an extremely useful one, and is obviously applicable to any similar case. The

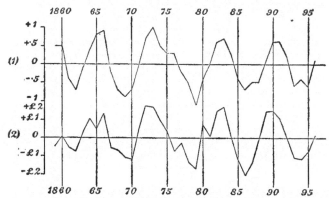

FIG. 43.—Fluctuations in (1) Marriage-rate and (2) Foreign Trade (Exports + Imports per head) in England and Wales: the Curves show Deviations from 9-year means. Data of R. H. Hooker, *Jour. Roy. Stat. Soc.*, 1901.

student should refer to the paper by Mr Hooker, cited. Reference may also be made to ref. 10, in which several diagrams are given similar to fig. 43, and the nature of the relationship between the marriage-rate and such factors as trade, unemployment, etc., is discussed, it being suggested that the relation is even more complex than appears from the above. The same method of separating the short-period oscillations was used at an earlier date by Poynting in ref. 16, to which the student is referred for a discussion of the method.

18. It was briefly mentioned in § 9 of the last chapter that the treatment of cases when the regression was non-linear was, in general, somewhat difficult. Such cases lie strictly outside the scope of the present volume, but it may be pointed out that if a relation between X and Y be suggested, either by

theory or by previous experience, it may be possible to throw that relation into the form

$$Y = A + B.\phi(X),$$

where A and B are the only unknown constants to be determined. If a correlation-table be then drawn up between Y and $\phi(X)$ instead of Y and X, the regression will be approximately linear. Thus in Table V. of the last chapter, if X be the rate of discount and Y the percentage of reserves on deposits, a diagram of the curves of regression, or curves on which the means of arrays lie, suggests that the relation between X and Y is approximately of the form

$$X(Y - B) = A,$$

A and B being constants ; that is,

$$XY = A + BX.$$

Or, if we make XY a new variable, say Z,

$$Z = A + BX.$$

Hence, if we draw up a new correlation-table between X and Z the regression will probably be much more closely linear.

If the relation between the variables be of the form

$$Y = AB^X$$

we have

$$\log Y = \log A + X. \log B,$$

and hence the relation between $\log Y$ and X is linear. Similarly, if the relation be of the form

$$X^n Y = A$$

we have

$$\log Y = \log A - n. \log X,$$

and so the relation between $\log Y$ and $\log X$ is linear. By means of such artifices for obtaining correlation-tables in which the regression is linear, it may be possible to do a good deal in difficult cases whilst using elementary methods only. The advanced student should refer to ref. 17 for a different method of treatment.

19. The only strict method of calculating the correlation coefficient is that described in Chapter IX. from the formula $r = \dfrac{\Sigma(xy)}{N.\sigma_1\sigma_2}$. Approximations to this value may, however, be

found in various ways, for the most part dependent either (1) on the formulæ for the two regressions $r\dfrac{\sigma_x}{\sigma_y}$ and $r\dfrac{\sigma_y}{\sigma_x}$, or (2) on the formulæ for the standard deviations of the arrays $\sigma_x \sqrt{1 - r^2}$ and $\sigma_y \sqrt{1 - r^2}$. Such approximate methods are not recommended for ordinary use, as they will lead to different results in different hands, but a few may be given here, as being occasionally useful for estimating the value of the correlation in cases where the data are not given in such a shape as to permit of the proper calculation of the coefficient.

(1) The means of rows and columns are plotted on a diagram, and lines fitted to the points by eye, say by shifting about a stretched black thread until it seems to run as near as may be to all the points. If b_1, b_2 be the slopes of these two lines to the vertical and the horizontal respectively,

$$r = \sqrt{b_1 . b_2}.$$

Hence the value of r may be estimated from any such diagram as figs. 36–40 in Chapter IX., in the absence of the original table. Further, if a correlation-table be not grouped by equal intervals, it may be difficult to calculate the product sum, but it may still be possible to plot approximately a diagram of the two lines of regression, and so determine roughly the value of r. Similarly, if only the means of two rows and two columns, or of one row and one column in addition to the means of the two variables, are known, it will still be possible to estimate the slopes of RR and CC, and hence the correlation coefficient.

(2) The means of one set of arrays only, say the rows, are calculated, and also the two standard-deviations σ_x and σ_y. The means are then plotted on a diagram, using the standard-deviation of each variable as the unit of measurement, and a line fitted by eye. The slope of this line to the vertical is r. If the standard deviations be not used as the units of measurement in plotting, the slope of the line to the vertical is $r\,\sigma_x/\sigma_y$, and hence r will be obtained by dividing the slope by the ratio of the standard-deviations.

This method, or some variation of it, is often useful as a makeshift when the data are too incomplete to permit of the proper calculation of the correlation, only one line of regression and the ratio of the dispersions of the two variables being required : the ratio of the quartile deviations, or other simple measures of dispersion, will serve quite well for rough purposes in lieu of the ratio of standard-deviations. As a special case, we may note that if the two dispersions are approximately the same, the slope of RR to the vertical is r.

Plotting the medians of arrays on a diagram with the quartile deviations as units, and measuring the slope of the line, was the method of determining the correlation coefficient ("Galton's function") used by Sir Francis Galton, to whom the introduction of such a coefficient is due. (Refs. 2–4 of Chap. IX. p. 188.)

(3) If s_x be the standard-deviation of errors of estimate like $x - b_1.y$, we have from Chap. IX. § 11—

$$s_x{}^2 = \sigma_x{}^2(1 - r^2),$$

and hence

$$r = \sqrt{1 - \frac{s_x{}^2}{\sigma_x{}^2}}.$$

But if the dispersions of arrays do not differ largely, and the regression is nearly linear, the value of s_x may be estimated from the average of the standard-deviations of a few rows, and r determined—or rather estimated—accordingly. Thus in Table III., Chap. IX., the standard-deviations of the ten columns headed 62·5–63·5, 63·5–64·5, etc., are—

2·56		2·26
2·11		2·26
2·55		2·45
2·24		2·33
2·23		
2·60	Mean	2·359

The standard-deviation of the stature of all sons is 2·75 : hence approximately

$$r = \sqrt{1 - \left(\frac{2 \cdot 359}{2 \cdot 75}\right)^2}$$

$$= 0 \cdot 514.$$

This is the same as the value found by the product-sum method to the second decimal place. It would be better to take an average by counting the square of each standard-deviation once for each observation in the column (or "weighting" it with the number of observations in the column), but in the present case this would only lead to a very slightly different result, viz. $\sigma = 2 \cdot 362$, $r = 0 \cdot 512$.

20. *The Correlation Ratio.*—The method clearly would not give an approximation to the correlation coefficient, however, in the case of such tables as V. and VI. of Chap. IX., in which the means of successive arrays do not lie closely round straight lines.

In such cases it would always tend to give a value for r markedly higher than that given by the product-sum method. The product-sum method gives in fact a value based on the standard-deviation round the line of regression ; the method used above gives a value dependent on the standard-deviation round a line which sweeps through all the means of arrays, and the second standard-deviation is necessarily less than the first. We reach, therefore, a generalised coefficient which measures the approach towards a curvilinear line of regression of any form.

Let s_{ax} denote the standard-deviation of any array of X's, and let n, as before, be the number of observations in this array (Chap. IX., § 11), and further let

$$\sigma_{ax}^2 = \Sigma(n \cdot s_{ax}^2)/N \quad . \qquad . \qquad . \qquad . \quad (1)$$

Then σ_{ax} is an average of the standard-deviations of the arrays obtained as suggested at the end of the last section. Now let

$$\sigma_{ax}^2 = \sigma_x^2(1 - \eta_{xy}^2) \quad . \qquad . \qquad . \qquad . \quad (2)$$

or

$$\eta_{xy}^2 = 1 - \frac{\sigma_{ax}^2}{\sigma_x^2} \qquad . \qquad . \qquad . \quad (3)$$

Then η_{xy} is termed by Professor Pearson a **correlation-ratio** (ref. 18). As there are clearly two correlation-ratios for any one table, it should be distinguished as the correlation-ratio of X on Y : it measures the approach of values of X associated with given values of Y to a single-valued relationship of any form. The calculation would be exceedingly laborious if we had actually to evaluate σ_{ax}, but this may be avoided and the work greatly simplified by the following consideration. If M_x denote the mean of all X's, m_x the mean of an array, then we have by the general relation given in § 11 of Chap. VIII. (p. 142)

$$N\sigma_x^2 = \Sigma n(s_{ax}^2 + [M_x - m_x]^2).$$

Or, using σ_{mx} to denote the standard-deviation of m_x,

$$\sigma_x^2 = \sigma_{ax}^2 + \sigma_{mx}^2 \quad . \qquad . \qquad . \qquad . \quad (4)$$

Hence, substituting in (3)

$$\eta_{xy} = \frac{\sigma_{mx}}{\sigma_x} . \qquad . \qquad . \qquad . \quad (5)$$

The correlation-ratio of X on Y is therefore determined when we have found, in addition to the standard-deviation of X, the standard-deviation of the means of its arrays.

21. The correlation-ratio of X on Y cannot be less than the correlation-coefficient for X and Y, and $\eta_{xy}^2 - r^2$ is a measure of the divergence of the regression of X on Y from linearity. For

if d denote, as in Chap. IX., the deviation of the mean of an array of X's from the line of regression, we have by the relation of Chap. IX., § 11, p. 172

$$\sigma_x^2(1 - r^2) = \sigma_{ax}^2 + \sigma_d^2. \qquad . \qquad . \qquad . \qquad (6)$$

Substituting for σ_a from (2), that is,

$$\sigma_d^2 = \sigma_x^2(\eta_{xy}^2 - r^2) \qquad . \qquad . \qquad . \qquad . \qquad (7)$$

But σ_d is necessarily positive, and therefore η_{xy} is not less than r. The magnitude of σ_d and therefore of $\eta^2 - r^2$ measures the divergence of the actual line through the means of arrays from the line of regression.

It should be noted that, owing to the fluctuations of sampling, r and η are almost certain to differ slightly, even though the regression may be truly linear. The observed value of $\eta^2 - r^2$ must be compared with the values that may arise owing to fluctuations of sampling alone, before a definite significance can be ascribed to it (cf. Pearson, ref. 19, Blakeman, ref. 22, and the formulæ cited therefrom on p. 352 below).

22. The following table illustrates the form of the arithmetic for the calculation of the correlation-ratio of son's stature on father's stature (Table III. of Chap. IX., p. 160). In the first column is given the type of the array (stature of father); in the second, the mean stature of sons for that array; in the third, the difference of the mean of the array from the mean stature of all sons. In the fourth column these differences are squared, and in the sixth they are multiplied by the frequency of the array, two decimal places only having been retained as sufficient for the present purpose. The sum-total of the last column divided by the number of observations (1078) gives $\sigma_{my}^2 = 2 \cdot 058$, or $\sigma_{my} = 1 \cdot 43$. As the standard-deviation of the sons' stature is $2 \cdot 75$ in. (cf. Chap. IX., question 3), $\eta_{yx} = 0 \cdot 52$. Before taking the differences for the third column of such a table, it is as well to check the means of the arrays by recalculating from them the mean of the whole distribution, i.e. multiplying each array-mean by its frequency, summing, and dividing by the number of observations. The form of the arithmetic may be varied, if desired, by working from zero as origin, instead of taking differences from the true mean. The square of the mean must then be subtracted from $\Sigma(f \cdot m_y^2)/N$ to give σ_{my}^2.

If the second correlation-ratio for this table be worked out in the same way, the value will be found to be the same to the second place of decimals: the two correlation-ratios for this table are, therefore, very nearly identical, and only slightly greater than the correlation-coefficient ($0 \cdot 51$). Both regressions, it follows from the last section, are very nearly linear, a result confirmed by the diagram of the regression lines (fig. 37, p. 174). On the other hand, it is evident from fig. 39, p. 176, that we should expect the two correlation-ratios for Table VI. of the same chapter to differ considerably from each other and from the correlation. The values found are $\eta_{xy} = 0.14$, $\eta_{yx} = 0.38$ ($r = -0.014$): η_{xy} is comparatively low as proportions of male births differ little in the successive arrays, but η_{yx} is higher since the line of regression of Y on X is sharply curved. For Table VIII., p. 183, the two ratios are $\eta_{xy} = 0.46$, $\eta_{yx} = 0.39$ ($r = 0.34$). The confirmation of these values is left to the student.

The student should notice that the correlation-ratio only affords a satisfactory test when the number of observations is sufficiently large for a grouped correlation table to be formed. In the case of a short series of observations such as that given in Table VII., p. 178, the method is inapplicable.

CALCULATION OF THE CORRELATION-RATIO : *Example.—Son's Stature on Father's Stature: Data of Table III., Chap. IX., p.* 160.

1.	2.	3.	4.	5.	6.
Type of Array (Father's Stature).	Mean of Array (Son's Stature).	Difference from Mean of all Sons (68·66).	Square of Difference.	Frequency.	Frequency × (difference)².
59	64·67	− 3·99	15·9201	3	47·76
60	65·64	− 3·02	9·1204	3·5	31·92
61	66·34	− 2·32	5·3824	8	43·06
62	65·56	− 3·10	9·6100	17	163·37
63	66·68	− 1·98	3·9204	33·5	131·33
64	66·74	− 1·92	3·6864	61·5	226·71
65	67·19	− 1·47	2·1609	95·5	206·37
66	67·61	− 1·05	1·1025	142	156·56
67	67·95	− 0·71	0·5041	137·5	69·31
68	69·07	+ 0·41	0·1681	154	25·89
69	69·39	+ 0·73	0·5329	141·5	75·41
70	69·74	+ 1·08	1·1664	116	135·30
71	70·50	+ 1·84	3·3856	78	264·08
72	70·87	+ 2·21	4·8841	49	239·32
73	72·00	+ 3·34	11·1556	28·5	317·93
74	71·50	+ 2·84	8·0656	4	32·26
75	71·73	+ 3·07	9·4249	5·5	51·84
Total	...	...	...	1078	2218·42

$$\sigma_{my}^2 = 2218 \cdot 42/1078 = 2 \cdot 058 \qquad \sigma_{my} = 1 \cdot 43$$
$$\eta_{yx} = 1 \cdot 43/2 \cdot 75 = 0 \cdot 52.$$

REFERENCES.

Illustrative Applications, principally to Economic Statistics, and Practical Methods.

(1) YULE, G. U., " On the Correlation of total Pauperism with Proportion of Out-relief," *Economic Jour.*, vol. v., 1895, p. 603, and vol. vi., 1896, p. 613.

(2) YULE, G. U., "An Investigation into the Causes of Changes in Pauperism in England chiefly during the last two Intercensal Decades," *Jour. Roy. Stat. Soc.*, vol. lxii., 1899, p. 249. (*Cf.* Illustration i.)

(3) PEARSON, KARL, ALICE LEE, and L. BRAMLEY MOORE, "Genetic (reproductive) Selection : Inheritance of Fertility in Man and of Fecundity in Thoroughbred Racehorses," *Phil. Trans. Roy. Soc.*, Series A, vol. cxcii., 1899, p. 257. (*Cf.* Illustration ii.)

(4) CAVE-BROWNE-CAVE, F. E., "On the Influence of the Time-factor on the Correlation between the Barometric Heights at Stations more than 1000 miles apart," *Proc. Roy. Soc.*, vol. lxxiv., 1904, pp. 403-413. (The difference-method of Illustration iv. used.)

(5) HOOKER, R. H., "On the Correlation of the Marriage-rate with Trade," *Jour. Roy. Stat. Soc.*, vol. lxiv., 1901, p. 485. (The method of Illustration v.)

(6) HOOKER, R. H., "On the Correlation of Successive Observations : illustrated by Corn-prices," *ibid.*, vol. lxviii., 1905, p. 696. (The method of Illustration iv.)

(7) HOOKER, R. H., "The Correlation of the Weather and the Crops," *ibid.*, vol. lxx., 1907, p. 1. (*Cf.* Illustration iii.)

(8) NORTON, J. P., *Statistical Studies in the New York Money Market*; Macmillan Co., New York, 1902. (Applications to financial statistics : an instantaneous average method, analogous to that of illustration v., is employed, but the instantaneous average is obtained by an interpolated logarithmic curve.)

(9) MARCH, L., "Comparaison numérique de courbes statistiques," *Jour. de la société de statistique de Paris*, 1905, pp. 255 and 306. (Uses the methods of Illustrations iv. and v., but obtaining the instantaneous average in the latter case by graphical interpolation.)

(10) YULE, G. U., "On the Changes in the Marriage and Birth Rates in England and Wales during the past Half Century, with an Inquiry as to their probable Causes," *Jour. Roy. Stat. Soc.*, vol. lxix., 1906, p. 88.

(11) HERON, D., *On the Relation of Fertility in Man to Social Status,* "Drapers' Co. Research Memoirs : Studies in National Deterioration," I. ; Dulau & Co., London, 1906.

(12) JACOB, S. M., "On the Correlations of Areas of Matured Crops and the Rainfall," *Mem. Asiatic Soc. Bengal*, vol. ii., 1910, p. 847.

(13) " STUDENT," "The Elimination of Spurious Correlation due to Position in Time or Space," *Biometrika*, vol. x., 1914, pp. 179-180. (The extension of the difference-method by the use of successive differences.)

(14) ANDERSON, O., "Nochmals über 'The Elimination of Spurious Correlation due to Position in Time or Space,'" *Biometrika*, vol. x., 1914, pp. 269-279. (Detailed theory of the same extended method.)

(15) CAVE, BEATRICE M., and KARL PEARSON, "Numerical Illustrations of the Variate-difference Correlation Method," *Biometrika*, vol. x., 1914, pp. 340-355.

(16) POYNTING, J. H., "A Comparison of the Fluctuations in the Price of Wheat, and in the Cotton and Silk Imports into Great Britain," *Jour.*

Roy. Stat. Soc., vol. xlvii., 1884, p. 34. (This paper was written before the invention of the correlation coefficient, but is cited because the method of Illustration v. is used to separate the periodic from the secular movement: see especially § ix. on the process of averaging employed.)

Theory of Correlation in the case of Non-linear Regression, and Curve or Line fitting generally.

(17) PEARSON, KARL, "On the Systematic Fitting of Curves to Observations and Measurements," *Biometriko*, vol. i. p. 265, and vol. ii. p. 1, 1902. (The second part is useful for the fitting of curves in cases of non-linear regression.)

(18) PEARSON, KARL, *On the General Theory of Skew Correlation and Non-linear Regression*, "Drapers' Co. Research Memoirs: Biometric Series," II. ; Dulau & Co., London, 1905. (The "correlation ratio.")

(19) PEARSON, KARL, "On a Correction to be made to the Correlation Ratio," *Biometrika*, vol. viii., 1911, p. 254.

(20) PEARSON, KARL, "On Lines and Planes of Closest Fit to Systems of Points in Space," *Phil. Mag.*, 6th Series, vol. ii., 1901, p. 559.

(21) PEARSON, KARL, "On a General Theory of the Method of False Position," *Phil. Mag.*, June 1903. (A method of curve fitting by the use of trial solutions.)

(22) BLAKEMAN, J., "On Tests for Linearity of Regression in Frequency-distributions," *Biometrika*, vol. iv., 1905, p. 332.

(23) SNOW, E. C., "On Restricted Lines and Planes of Closest Fit to Systems of Points in any number of Dimensions," *Phil. Mag.*, 6th Series, vol. xxi., 1911, p. 367.

(24) SLUTSKY, E., "On the Criterion of Goodness of Fit of the Regression Lines and the best Method of Fitting them to the Data," *Jour. Roy. Stat. Soc.*, vol. lxxvii., 1913, pp. 78–84.

Abbreviated Methods of Calculation.

See also references to Chapter XVI.

(25) HARRIS, J. ARTHUR, "A Short Method of Calculating the Coefficient of Correlation in the case of Integral Variates," *Biometrika*, vol. vii., 1909, p. 214. (Not an approximation, but a true short method.)

(26) HARRIS, J. ARTHUR, "On the Calculation of Intra-class and Inter-class Coefficients of Correlation from Class-moments when the Number of possible Combinations is large," *Biometrika*, vol. ix., 1914, pp. 446–472.

14

CHAPTER XI.

MISCELLANEOUS THEOREMS INVOLVING THE USE OF THE CORRELATION-COEFFICIENT.

1. It has already been pointed out that a statistical measure, if it is to be widely useful, should lend itself readily to algebraical treatment. The arithmetic mean and the standard-deviation derive their importance largely from the fact that they fulfil this requirement better than any other averages or measures of dispersion ; and the following illustrations, while giving a number of results that are of value in one branch or another of statistical work, suffice to show that the correlation-coefficient can be treated with the same facility. This might indeed be expected, seeing that the coefficient is derived, like the mean and standard-deviation, by a straightforward process of summation.

2. *To find the Standard-deviation of the sum or difference Z of corresponding values of two variables X_1 and X_2.*

Let z, x_1, x_2 denote deviations of the several variables from their arithmetic means. Then if

$$Z = X_1 \pm X_2,$$

evidently

$$z = x_1 \pm x_2.$$

Squaring both sides of the equation and summing,

$$\Sigma(z^2) = \Sigma(x_1^2) + \Sigma(x_2^2) \pm 2\Sigma(x_1 x_2).$$

That is, if r be the correlation between x_1 and x_2, and σ, σ_1, σ_2 the respective standard-deviations,

$$\sigma^2 = \sigma_1^2 + \sigma_2^2 \pm 2r.\sigma_1\sigma_2 \qquad . \qquad . \qquad . \quad (1)$$

If x_1 and x_2 are uncorrelated, we have the important special case

$$\sigma^2 = \sigma_1^2 + \sigma_2^2 \qquad . \qquad . \qquad . \qquad . \quad (2)$$

The student should notice that in this case the standard-deviation of the sum of corresponding values of the two variables is the same as the standard-deviation of their difference.

The same process will evidently give the standard-deviation of a linear function of any number of variables. For the sum of a series of variables $X_1, X_2 \ldots X_n$ we must have

$$\sigma^2 = \sigma_1^2 + \sigma_2^2 + \ldots + \sigma_n^2 + 2r_{12}.\sigma_1\sigma_2 + 2r_{13}.\sigma_1\sigma_3$$
$$+ \ldots + 2r_{23}.\sigma_2\sigma_3 + \ldots$$

r_{12} being the correlation beween X_1 and X_2, r_{23} the correlation between X_2 and X_3, and so on.

3. *Influence of Errors of Observation on the Standard-deviation.* —The results of § 2 may be applied to the theory of errors of observation. Let us suppose that, if *any* value of X be observed a large number of times, the arithmetic mean of the observations is approximately the true value, the arithmetic mean error being zero. Then, the arithmetic mean error being zero for all values of X, the error, say δ, is uncorrelated with X. In this case if x_1 be an observed deviation from the arithmetic mean, x the true deviation, we have from the preceding

$$\sigma_{x_1}^2 = \sigma_x^2 + \sigma_\delta^2 \qquad . \qquad . \qquad . \quad (3)$$

The effect of errors of observation is, consequently, to increase the standard-deviation above its true value. The student should notice that the assumption made does not imply the *complete independence* of X and δ: he is quite at liberty to suppose that errors fluctuate more, for example, with large than with small values of X, as might very probably happen. In that case the contingency-coefficient between X and δ would not be zero, although the correlation-coefficient might still vanish as supposed.

4. *Influence of Grouping on the Standard-deviation.*—The consequence of grouping observations to form the frequency distribution is to introduce errors that are, in effect, errors of

measurement. Instead of assigning to any observation its true value X, we assign to it the value X_1 corresponding to the centre of the class-interval, thereby making an error δ, where

$$X_1 = X + \delta.$$

To deduce from this equation a formula showing the nature of the influence of grouping on the standard-deviation we must know the correlation between the error δ and X or X_1. If the original distribution were a histogram, X_1 and δ would be uncorrelated, the mean value of δ being zero for every value of X_1: further, the standard-deviation of δ would be $c^2/12$, where c is the class-interval (Chap. VIII. § 12, eqn. (10)). Hence, if σ_1 be the standard-deviation of the grouped values X_1 and σ the standard-deviation of the true values X,

$$\sigma^2 = \sigma_1{}^2 + \frac{c^2}{12}.$$

But the true frequency distribution is rarely or never a histogram, and trial on any frequency distribution approximating to the symmetrical or slightly asymmetrical forms of fig. 5, p. 89, or fig. 9 (a), p. 92, shows that grouping tends to increase rather than reduce the standard-deviation. If we assume, as in § 3, that the correlation between δ and X, instead of δ and X_1, is appreciably zero and that the standard-deviation of δ may be taken as $c^2/12$, as before (the values of δ being to a first approximation uniformly distributed over the class-interval when all the intervals are considered together), then we have

$$\sigma^2 = \sigma_1{}^2 - \frac{c^2}{12} \qquad . \qquad . \qquad . \qquad . \qquad (4)$$

This is a formula of correction for grouping (Sheppard's correction, refs. 1 to 4) that is very frequently used, and that trial (ref. 1) shows to give very good results for a curve approximating closely to the form of fig. 5, p. 89. The strict proof of the formula lies outside the scope of an elementary work: it is based on two assumptions: (1) that the distribution of frequency is continuous, (2) that the frequency tapers off gradually to zero in both directions. The formula would not give accurate results in the case of such a distribution as that of fig. 9 (b), p. 92, or fig. 14, p. 97, neither is it applicable at all to the more divergent forms such as those of figs. 15, et seq.

5. If certain observations be repeated so that we have in every case two measures x_1 and x_2 of the same deviation x, it is possible to obtain the true standard-deviation σ_x if the further assumption is legitimate that the errors δ_1 and δ_2 are uncorrelated with each other. On this assumption

$$\Sigma(x_1 x_2) = \Sigma(x + \delta_1)(x + \delta_2)$$
$$= \Sigma(x^2),$$

and accordingly

$$\sigma_x^2 = \frac{\Sigma(x_1 x_2)}{N} \qquad . \qquad . \qquad . \qquad (5)$$

(This formula is part of Spearman's formula for the correction of the correlation-coefficient, *cf.* § 7.)

6. *Influence of Errors of Observation on the Correlation-coefficient.* —Let x_1, y_1 be the observed deviations from the arithmetic means, x, y the true deviations, and δ, ϵ the errors of observation. Of the four quantities x, y, δ, ϵ we will suppose x and y alone to be correlated. On this assumption

$$\Sigma(x_1 y_1) = \Sigma(xy) \qquad . \qquad . \qquad . \qquad (6)$$

It follows at once that

$$\frac{r_{xy}}{r_{x_1 y_1}} = \frac{\sigma_{x_1} \cdot \sigma_{y_1}}{\sigma_x \cdot \sigma_y},$$

and consequently the observed correlation is less than the true correlation. This difference, it should be noticed, no mere increase in the number of observations can in any way lessen.

7. *Spearman's Theorems.*—If, however, the observations of both x and y be repeated, as assumed in § 5, so that we have two measures x_1 and x_2, y_1 and y_2 of every value of x and y, the true value of the correlation can be obtained by the use of equations (5) and (6), on assumptions similar to those made above. For we have

$$r_{xy}^2 = \frac{\Sigma(x_1 y_1)\Sigma(x_2 y_2)}{\Sigma(x_1 x_2)\Sigma(y_1 y_2)} = \frac{\Sigma(x_1 y_2)\Sigma(x_2 y_1)}{\Sigma(x_1 x_2)\Sigma(y_1 y_2)}$$

$$= \frac{r_{x_1 y_1} \cdot r_{x_2 y_2}}{r_{x_1 x_2} \cdot r_{y_1 y_2}} = \frac{r_{x_1 y_2} \cdot r_{x_2 y_1}}{r_{x_1 x_2} \cdot r_{y_1 y_2}} \qquad . \qquad . \qquad (7)$$

Or, if we use all the four possible correlations between observed values of x and observed values of y,

$$r_{xy}^4 = \frac{r_{x_1 y_1} \cdot r_{x_2 y_2} \cdot r_{x_1 y_2} \cdot r_{x_2 y_1}}{\left(r_{x_1 x_2} \cdot r_{y_1 y_2}\right)^2} \qquad . \qquad . \qquad (8)$$

Equation (8) is the original form in which Spearman gave his correction formula (refs. 6, 7). It will be seen to imply the assumption that, of the six quantities x, y, δ_1, δ_2, ϵ_1, ϵ_2, x and y alone are correlated. The correction given by the second part of equation (7), also suggested by Spearman, seems, on the whole, to be safer, for it eliminates the assumption that the errors in x and in y, in the same series of observations, are uncorrelated. An insufficient though partial test of the correctness of the assumptions may be made by correlating $x_1 - x_2$ with $y_1 - y_2$: this correlation should vanish. Evidently, however, it may vanish from symmetry without thereby implying that all the correlations of the errors are zero.

8. *Mean and Standard-deviation of an Index.*—(Ref. 11.) The means and standard-deviations of non-linear functions of two or more variables can in general only be expressed in terms of the means and standard-deviations of the original variables to a first approximation, on the assumption that deviations are small compared with the mean values of the variables. Thus let it be required *to find the mean and standard-deviation of a ratio or index* $Z = X_1/X_2$, in terms of the constants for X_1 and X_2. Let I be the mean of Z, M_1 and M_2 the means of X_1 and X_2. Then

$$I = \frac{1}{N}\Sigma\left(\frac{X_1}{X_2}\right) = \frac{1}{N}\frac{M_1}{M_2}\Sigma\left(1 + \frac{x_1}{M_1}\right)\left(1 + \frac{x_2}{M_2}\right)^{-1}.$$

Expand the second bracket by the binomial theorem, assuming that x_2/M_2 is so small that powers higher than the second can be neglected. Then to this approximation

$$I = \frac{1}{N}\frac{M_1}{M_2}\left[N - \frac{1}{M_1 M_2}\Sigma(x_1 x_2) + \frac{1}{M_2^2}\Sigma(x_2^2)\right].$$

That is, if r be the correlation between x_1 and x_2, and if $v_1 = \sigma_1/M_1$, $v_2 = \sigma_2/M_2$,

$$I = \frac{M_1}{M_2}(1 - rv_1 v_2 + v_2^2) \qquad . \qquad . \qquad . \quad (9)$$

If s be the standard-deviation of Z we have

$$s^2 + I^2 = \frac{1}{N}\Sigma\left(\frac{X_1}{X_2}\right)^2$$

$$= \frac{1}{N}\frac{M_1^2}{M_2^2}\Sigma\left(1 + \frac{x_1}{M_1}\right)^2\left(1 + \frac{x_2}{M_2}\right)^{-2}.$$

Expanding the second bracket again by the binomial theorem, and neglecting terms of all orders above the second,

$$s^2 + I^2 = \frac{1}{N}\frac{M_1^2}{M_2^2}\Sigma\left(1 + \frac{x_1}{M_1}\right)^2\left(1 - 2\frac{x_2}{M_2} + 3\frac{x_2^2}{M_2^2}\right)$$

$$= \frac{M_1^2}{M_2^2}(1 + v_1^2 - 4rv_1 v_2 + 3v_2^2)$$

or from (9)

$$s^2 = \frac{M_1^2}{M_2^2}(v_1^2 - 2rv_1v_2 + v_2^2) \qquad . \qquad (10)$$

9. *Correlation between Indices.*—(Ref. 11.) The following problem affords a further illustration of the use of the same method.
Required to find approximately the correlation between two ratios
$Z_1 = X_1/X_3$, $Z_2 = X_2/X_3$, X_1 X_2 *and* X_3 *being uncorrelated.*
Let the means of the two ratios or indices be I_1 I_2 and the
standard-deviations s_1 s_2; these are given approximately by (9)
and (10) of the last section. The required correlation ρ will be
given by

$$N.\rho s_1 s_2 = \Sigma\left(\frac{X_1}{X_3} - I_1\right)\left(\frac{X_2}{X_3} - I_2\right)$$

$$= \Sigma\left(\frac{X_1 X_2}{X_3^2}\right) - N.I_1 I_2$$

$$= N.\frac{M_1 M_2}{M_3^2}\Sigma\left(1 + \frac{x_1}{M_1}\right)\left(1 + \frac{x_2}{M_2}\right)\left(1 + \frac{x_3}{M_3}\right)^{-2} - NI_1 I_2.$$

Neglecting terms of higher order than the second as before and
remembering that all correlations are zero, we have

$$\rho s_1 s_2 = \frac{M_1 M_2}{M_3^2}(1 + 3v_3^2) - I_1 I_2$$

$$= \frac{M_1 M_2}{M_3^2}v_3^2,$$

where, in the last step, a term of the order v_3^4 has again been
neglected. Substituting from (10) for s_1 and s_2, we have finally—

$$\rho = \frac{v_3^2}{\sqrt{(v_1^2 + v_3^2)(v_2^2 + v_3^2)}} \qquad . \qquad . \qquad (11)$$

This value of ρ is obviously positive, being equal to 0·5 if
$v_1 = v_2 = v_3$; and hence even if X_1 and X_2 are independent, the indices formed by taking their ratios to a common denominator X_3 will
be correlated. The value of ρ is termed by Professor Pearson the
"spurious correlation." Thus if measurements be taken, say, on
three bones of the human skeleton, and the measurements grouped
in threes absolutely at random, there will, nevertheless, be a
positive correlation, probably approaching 0·5, between the indices
formed by the ratios of two of the measurements to the third.   To
give another illustration, if two individuals both observe the same
series of magnitudes quite independently, there may be little, if

any, correlation between their absolute errors. But if the errors be expressed as percentages of the magnitude observed, there may be considerable correlation. It does not follow of necessity that the correlations between indices or ratios are misleading. If the indices are uncorrelated, there will be a similar "spurious" correlation between the absolute measurements $Z_1.X_3 = X_1$ and $Z_2.X_3 = X_2$, and the answer to the question whether the correlation between indices or that between absolute measures is misleading depends on the further question whether the indices or the absolute measures are the quantities directly determined by the causes under investigation (cf. ref. 13).

The case considered, where X_1 X_2 X_3 are uncorrelated, is only a special one ; for the general discussion cf. ref. 11. For an interesting study of actual illustrations cf. ref. 14.

10. *The Correlation-coefficient for a two- × two-fold Table.*—The correlation-coefficient is in general only calculated for a table with a considerable number of rows and columns, such as those given in Chapter IX. In some cases, however, a theoretical value is obtainable for the coefficient, which holds good even for the limiting case when there are only two values possible for each variable (e.g. 0 and 1) and consequently two rows and two columns (cf. one illustration in § 11, and for others the references given in questions 11 and 12). It is therefore of some interest to obtain an expression for the coefficient in this case in terms of the class-frequencies.

Using the notation of Chapters I.-IV. the table may be written in the form

Values of Second Variable.	Values of First Variable.		
	X_1	X'_1	Total
X_2	(AB)	(αB)	(B)
X'_2	$(A\beta)$	$(\alpha\beta)$	(β)
Total	(A)	(α)	N

Taking the centre of the table as arbitrary origin and the class-interval, as usual, as the unit, the co-ordinates of the mean are

$$\bar{\xi} = \frac{1}{2N}\{(\alpha) - (A)\}$$

$$\bar{\eta} = \frac{1}{2N}\{(\beta) - (B)\}.$$

The standard-deviations σ_1, σ_2 are given by

$$\sigma_1^2 = 0.25 - \bar{\xi}^2 = (A)(a)/N^2$$
$$\sigma_2^2 = 0.25 - \bar{\eta}^2 = (B)(\beta)/N^2.$$

Finally,

$$\Sigma(xy) = \tfrac{1}{4}\{(AB) + (a\beta) - (A\beta) - (aB)\} - N\bar{\xi}\bar{\eta}.$$

Writing

$$(AB) - (A)(B)/N = \delta$$

(as in Chap. III. §§ 11–12) and replacing $\bar{\xi}$, $\bar{\eta}$ by their values, this reduces to

$$\Sigma(xy) = \delta.$$

Whence

$$r = \frac{N.\delta}{\sqrt{(A)(a)(B)(\beta)}}. \qquad \qquad (12)$$

This value of r can be used as a coefficient of association, but, unlike the association-coefficient of Chap. III. § 13, which is unity if either $(AB) = (A)$ or $(AB) = (B)$, r only becomes unity if $(AB) = (A) = (B)$. This is the only case in which both frequencies (aB) and $(A\beta)$ can vanish so that (AB) and $(a\beta)$ correspond to the frequencies of two points $X_1 Y_1$, $X_2 Y_2$ on a line. Obviously this alone renders the numerical values of the two coefficients quite incomparable with each other. But further, while the association coefficient is the same for all tables derived from one another by multiplying rows or columns by arbitrary coefficients, the correlation coefficient (12) is greatest when $(A) = (a)$ and $(B) = (\beta)$, i.e. when the table is symmetrical, and its value is lowered when the symmetrical table is rendered asymmetrical by increasing or reducing the number of A's or B's. For moderate degrees of association, the association coefficient gives much the larger values. The two coefficients possess, in fact, essentially different properties, and are *different* measures of association in the same sense that the geometric and arithmetic means are different forms of average, or the interquartile range and the standard-deviation different measures of dispersion.

The student is again referred to ref. 3 of Chap. III. for a general discussion of various measures of association, including these and others, that have been proposed.

11. *The Correlation-coefficient for all possible pairs of N values of a Variable.*—In certain cases a correlation-table is formed by combining N observations in pairs in all possible ways. If, for example, a table is being formed to illustrate, say, the correlation between brothers for *stature*, and there are three brothers in

one family with statures 5 ft. 9, 5 ft. 10, and 5 ft. 11, these are regarded as giving the six pairs

5 ft. 9 with 5 ft. 10	5 ft. 10 with 5 ft. 9
,, ,, 5 ft. 11	5 ft. 11 ,, ,,
5 ft. 10 ,, ,,	,, ,, 5 ft. 10

which may be entered into the table. The entire table will be formed from the aggregate of such subsidiary tables, each due to one family. Let it be required to find the correlation-coefficient, however, for a single subsidiary table, due to a family with N members, the numbers of pairs being therefore $N(N-1)$.

As each observed value of the variable occurs $N-1$ times, *i.e.* once in combination with every other value, the means and standard-deviations of the totals of the correlation-table are the same as for the original N observations, say M and σ. If $x_1\ x_2\ x_3\ \ldots$ be the observed deviations, the product sum may be written

$$x_1x_2 + x_1x_3 + x_1x_4 + \ldots$$
$$+ x_2x_1 + x_2x_3 + x_2x_4 + \ldots$$
$$+ x_3x_1 + x_3x_2 + x_3x_4 + \ldots$$
$$+ \quad . \qquad . \qquad . \qquad .$$
$$= x_1\{\Sigma(x) - x_1\} + x_2\{\Sigma(x) - x_2\} + x_3\{\Sigma(x) - x_3\} + \ldots$$
$$= -x_1^2 - x_2^2 - x_3^2 - \ldots = -N\sigma^2,$$

whence, there being $N(N-1)$ pairs,

$$r = -\frac{N\sigma^2}{N(N-1)\sigma^2} = -\frac{1}{N-1} \quad . \qquad . \qquad . \quad (13)$$

For $N = 2, 3, 4 \ldots$ this gives the successive values of $r = -1$, $-\frac{1}{2}, -\frac{1}{3} \ldots$ It is clear that the first value is right, for two values x_1, x_2 only determine the two points $(x_1,\ x_2)$ and $(x_2,\ x_1)$, and the slope of the line joining them is negative.

The student should notice that a corresponding negative association will arise between the first and second member of the pair if all possible pairs are formed in a mixture of A's and a's. Looking at the association, in fact, from the standpoint of § 10, the equation (13) still holds, even if the variables can only assume two values, *e.g.* 0 and 1. This result is utilised in § 14 of Chapter XIV.

12. *Correlation due to Heterogeneity of Material.*—The following theorem offers some analogy with the theorem of Chap. IV. § 6 for attributes.—*If X and Y are uncorrelated in each of two records, they will nevertheless exhibit some correlation when the*

two records are mingled, unless the mean value of X in the second record is identical with that in the first record, or the mean value of Y in the second record is identical with that in the first record, or both.

This follows almost at once, for if M_1, M_2 are the mean values of X in the two records K_1, K_2, the mean values of Y, N_1, N_2 the numbers of observations, and M, K the means when the two records are mingled, the product-sum of deviations about M, K is

$$N_1(M_1 - M)(K_1 - K) + N_2(M_2 - M)(K_2 - K).$$

Evidently the first term can only be zero if $M = M_1$ or $K = K_1$. But the first condition gives

$$\frac{N_1 M_1 + N_2 M_2}{N_1 + N_2} = M_1,$$

that is,

$$M_1 = M_2.$$

Similarly, the second condition gives $K_1 = K_2$. Both the first and second terms can, therefore, only vanish if $M_1 = M_2$ or $K_1 = K_2$. Correlation may accordingly be created by the mingling of two records in which X and Y vary round different means. (For a more general form of the theorem *cf.* ref. 20.)

13. *Reduction of Correlation due to mingling of uncorrelated with correlated pairs.*—Suppose that n_1 observations of x and y give a correlation-coefficient

$$r_1 = \frac{\Sigma(xy)}{n_1 \sigma_x \sigma_y}.$$

Now let n_2 pairs be added to the material, the means and standard-deviations of x and y being the same as in the first series of observations, but the correlation zero. The value of $\Sigma(xy)$ will then be unaltered, and we will have

$$r_2 = \frac{\Sigma(xy)}{(n_1 + n_2)\sigma_x \sigma_y}.$$

Whence

$$\frac{r_2}{r_1} = \frac{n_1}{n_1 + n_2} \qquad . \qquad . \qquad . \qquad (14)$$

Suppose, for example, that a number of bones of the human skeleton have been disinterred during some excavations, and a correlation r_2 is observed between pairs of bones presumed to come from the same skeleton, this correlation being rather lower than might have been expected, and subject to some uncertainty owing to doubts as to the allocation of certain bones. If r_1 is the value that would be expected from other records, the difference might be accounted for on the hypothesis

that, in a proportion $(r_1 - r_2)/r_1$ of all the pairs, the bones do
not really belong to the same skeleton, and have been virtually
paired at random. (For a more general form of the theorem *cf.*
again ref. 20.)

14. *The Weighted Mean.*—The arithmetic mean M of a series
of values of a variable X was defined as the quotient of the sum
of those values by their number N, or

$$M = \Sigma(X)/N.$$

If, on the other hand, we multiply each several observed
value of X by some numerical coefficient or *weight* W, the
quotient of the sum of such products by the sum of the weights
is defined as a *weighted mean* of X, and may be denoted by M'
so that

$$M' = \Sigma(W.X)/\Sigma(W).$$

The distinction between "weighted" and "unweighted" means
is, it should be noted, very often formal rather than essential,
for the "weights" may be regarded as actual, estimated, or
virtual frequencies. The weighted mean then becomes simply
an arithmetic mean, in which some new quantity is regarded
as the unit. Thus if we are given the means M_1, M_2, M_3 . . . .
M_r of r series of observations, but do not know the number
of observations in every series, we may form a general average
by taking the arithmetic mean of all the means, viz. $\Sigma(M)/r$,
treating the series as the unit. But if we know the number
of observations in every series it will be better to form the
weighted mean $\Sigma(NM)/\Sigma(N)$, weighting each mean in proportion
to the number of observations in the series on which it is based.
The second form of average would be quite correctly spoken
of as a weighted mean of the means of the several series : at
the same time it is simply the arithmetic mean of all the
series pooled together, *i.e.* the arithmetic mean obtained by
treating the observation and not the series as the unit.
(Chap. VII. § 13.)

15. To give an arithmetical illustration, if a commodity is sold
at different prices in different markets, it will be better to form
an average price, not by taking the arithmetic mean of the several
market prices, treating the market as the unit, but by weighting
each price in proportion to the quantity sold at that price, if
known, *i.e.* treating the unit of quantity as the unit of frequency.
Thus if wheat has been sold in market A at an average price of
29s. 1d. per quarter, in market B at an average price of 27s. 7d.,
and in market C at an average price of 28s. 4d., we may, if no
statement is made as to the quantities sold at these prices (as very

often happens in the case of statements as to market prices), take the arithmetic mean (28s. 4d.) as the general average. But if we know that 23,930 qrs. were sold at A, only 26 qrs. at B, and 3933 qrs. at C, it will be better to take the *weighted mean*

$$\frac{(29s.\ 1d. \times 23{,}930) + (27s.\ 7d. \times 26) + (28s.\ 4d. \times 3933)}{27889} = 29s.$$

to the nearest penny. This is appreciably higher than the arithmetic mean price, which is lowered by the undue importance attached to the small markets B and C.

In the case of index-numbers for exhibiting the changes in average prices from year to year (*cf.* Chap. VII. § 25), it may make a sensible difference whether we take the simple arithmetic mean of the index-numbers for different commodities in any one year as representing the price-level in that year, or *weight* the index-numbers for the several commodities according to their importance from some point of view ; and much has been written as to the weights to be chosen. If, for example, our standpoint be that of some average consumer, we may take as the *weight* for each commodity the sum which he spends on that commodity in an average year, so that the frequency of each commodity is taken as the number of shillings or pounds spent thereon instead of simply as unity.

Rates or ratios like the birth-, death-, or marriage-rates of a country may be regarded as weighted means. For, treating the rate for simplicity as a fraction, and not as a rate per 1000 of the population,

$$\text{Birth-rate of whole country} = \frac{\text{total births}}{\text{total population}}$$

$$= \frac{\Sigma(\text{birth-rate in each district} \times \text{population in that district})}{\Sigma(\text{population of each district})}$$

i.e. the rate for the whole country is the mean of the rates in the different districts, weighting each in proportion to its population. We use the weighted and unweighted means of such rates as illustrations in § 17 below.

16. It is evident that any weighted mean will in general differ from the unweighted mean of the same quantities, and it is required to find an expression for this difference. If r be the correlation between weights and variables, σ_w and σ_x the standard-deviations, and $\bar{w}$ the mean weight, we have at once

$$\Sigma(W.X) = N(M.\bar{w} + r\sigma_w\sigma_x),$$

whence $$M' = M + r\sigma_x \frac{\sigma_w}{\bar{w}}. \qquad (15)$$

That is to say, if the weights and variables are positively correlated, the weighted mean is the greater; if negatively, the less. In some cases r is very small, and then weighting makes little difference, but in others the difference is large and important, r having a sensible value and $\sigma_x \sigma_w / \bar{w}$ a large value.

17. The difference between weighted and unweighted means of death-rates, birth-rates or other rates on the population in different districts is, for instance, nearly always of importance. Thus we have the following figures for rates of pauperism (*Jour. Stat. Soc.*, vol. lix. (1896), p. 349).

| January 1. | Percentages of the Population in receipt of Relief. | |
	Arithmetic Mean of Rates in different Districts.	England and Wales as a whole.
1850	6·51	5·80
1860	5·20	4·26
1870	5·45	4·77
1881	3·68	3·12
1891	3·29	2·69

In this case the weighted mean is markedly the less, and the correlation between the population of a district and its pauperism must therefore be negative, the larger (on the whole urban) districts having the lower percentage in receipt of relief. On the other hand, for the decade 1881–90 the average birth-rate for England and Wales was 32·34 per thousand, the arithmetic mean of the rates for the different districts 30·34 only. The weighted mean was therefore the greater, the birth-rate being higher in the more populous (urban) districts, in which there is a greater proportion of young married persons.

For the year 1891 the average population of a Poor-law district was found to be roughly 45,900 and the standard-deviation σ_w 56,400 (populations ranging from under 2000 to over half a million). The standard-deviation σ_x of the percentages of the population in receipt of relief was 1·24. We have therefore, for the correlation between pauperism and population,

$$r = -\frac{3·29 - 2·69}{1·24} \times \frac{459}{564}$$

$$= -0·39.$$

For the birth-rate, on the other hand, assuming that $\sigma_w/\bar{w}$ is approximately the same for the decade 1881–90 as in 1891, we have, σ_z being 4·08,

$$r = \frac{32 \cdot 34 - 30 \cdot 34}{4 \cdot 08} \times \frac{459}{564}$$

$$= + \cdot 40.$$

The closeness of the numerical values of r in the two cases is, of course, accidental.

18. The principle of weighting finds one very important application in the treatment of such rates as death-rates, which are largely affected by the age and sex-composition of the population. Neglecting, for simplicity, the question of sex, suppose the numbers of deaths are noted in a certain district for, say, the age-groups 0–, 10–, 20–, etc., in which the fractions of the whole population are p_0, p_1, p_2, etc., where $\Sigma(p) = 1$. Let the death-rates for the corresponding age-groups be d_0, d_1, d_2, etc. Then the ordinary or *crude* death-rate for the district is

$$D = \Sigma(d.p) \quad . \quad . \quad . \quad . \quad (16)$$

For some other district taken as a basis of comparison, perhaps the country as a whole, the death-rates and fractions of the population in the several age-groups may be δ_1 δ_2 δ_3 . . . , π_1 π_2 π_3 . . . , and the crude death-rate

$$\Delta = \Sigma(\delta.\pi) \quad . \quad . \quad . \quad . \quad (17)$$

Now D and Δ may differ either because the d's and δ's differ or because the p's and π's differ, or both. It may happen that really both districts are about equally healthy, and the death-rates approximately the same for all age-classes, but, owing to a difference of *weighting*, the first average may be markedly higher than the second, or *vice versâ*. If the first district be a rural district and the second urban, for instance, there will be a larger proportion of the old in the former, and it may possibly have a higher crude death-rate that the second, in spite of lower death-rates in every class. The comparison of crude death-rates is therefore liable to lead to erroneous conclusions. The difficulty may be got over by averaging the age-class death-rates in the district not with the weights p_1 p_2 p_2 . . . . given by its own population, but with the weights, π_1 π_2 π_3 . . . . given by the population of the standard district. The *corrected death-rate* for the district will then be

$$D' = \Sigma(d.\pi) \quad . \quad . \quad . \quad (18)$$

and D' and Δ will be comparable as regards age-distribution. There is obviously no difficulty in taking sex into account as well as age if necessary. The death-rates must be noted for each sex separately in every age-class and averaged with a system of weights based on the standard population. The method is also of importance for comparing death-rates in different classes of the population, e.g. those engaged in given occupations, as well as in different districts, and is used for both these purposes in the *Decennial Supplements* to the Reports of the Registrar General for England and Wales (ref. 16).

19. Difficulty may arise in practical cases from the fact that the death-rates $d_1\ d_2\ d_3\ \ldots$ are not known for the districts or classes which it is desired to compare with the standard population, but only the crude rates D and the fractional populations of the age-classes $p_1\ p_2\ p_3\ \ldots$ The difficulty may be partially obviated (*cf.* Chap. IV. § 9, pp. 51-3) by forming what may be termed a *potential* or *standard* death-rate Δ' for the class or district, Δ' being given by

$$\Delta' = \Sigma(\delta.p) \qquad . \qquad . \qquad . \qquad . \quad (19)$$

i.e. the rates of the standard population averaged with the weights of the district population. It is the crude death-rate that there would be in the district if the rate in every age-class were the same as in the standard population. An approximate corrected death-rate for the district or class is then given by

$$D'' = D \times \frac{\Delta}{\Delta'} \qquad . \qquad . \qquad . \qquad . \quad (20)$$

D'' is not necessarily, nor generally, the same as D'. It can only be the same if

$$\frac{\Sigma(d.\pi)}{\Sigma(d.p)} = \frac{\Sigma(\delta.\pi)}{\Sigma(\delta.p)},$$

This will hold good if, *e.g.*, the death-rates in the standard population and the district stand to one another in the same ratio in all age-classes, *i.e.* $\delta_1/d_1 = \delta_2/d_2 = \delta_3/d_3 = $ etc. This method of correction is used in the Annual Summaries of the Registrar General for England and Wales.

Both methods of correction—that of § 18 and that of the present section—are of great and growing importance. They are obviously applicable to other rates besides death-rates, *e.g.* birth-rates (*cf.* refs. 17, 18). Further, they may readily be extended into quite different fields. Thus it has been suggested (ref. 19) that *corrected average heights* or *corrected average weights* of the children in different schools might be obtained on the basis of a standard school population of given age and sex composition, or indeed of given composition as regards hair and eye-colour as well.

20. In §§ 14–17 we have dealt only with the theory of the weighted arithmetic mean, but it should be noted that any form of average can be weighted. Thus a weighted median can be formed by finding the value of the variable such that the sum of the weights of lesser values is equal to the sum of the weights of greater values. A weighted mode could be formed by finding the value of the variable for which the sum of the weights was greatest, allowing for the smoothing of casual fluctuations. Similarly, a weighted geometric mean could be calculated by weighting the logarithms of every value of the variable before taking the arithmetic mean, *i.e.*

$$\log G_w = \frac{\Sigma(W. \log X)}{\Sigma(W)}.$$

REFERENCES.

Effect of Grouping Observations.

(1) SHEPPARD, W. F., " On the Calculation of the Average Square, Cube, etc., of a large number of Magnitudes," *Jour. Roy. Stat. Soc.*, vol. lx., 1897, p. 698.

(2) SHEPPARD, W. F., "On the Calculation of the most probable Values of Frequency Constants for Data arranged according to Equidistant Divisions of a Scale," *Proc. Lond. Math. Soc.*, vol. xxix. p. 353. (The result given in eqn. (4) for the correction of the standard-deviation is Sheppard's result.)

(3) SHEPPARD, W. F., "The Calculation of Moments of a Frequency-distribution," *Biometrika*, v., 1907, p. 450.

(4) PEARSON, KARL, and others [editorial], "On an Elementary Proof of Sheppard's Formulæ for correcting Raw Moments, and on other allied points," *Biometrika*, vol. iii., 1904, p. 308.

(5) PEARSON, KARL, "On the Influence of 'Broad Categories' on Correlation," *Biometrika*, vol. ix., 1913, pp. 116–139.

Effect of Errors of Observation on the Correlation-coefficient.

(6) SPEARMAN, C., " The Proof and Measurement of Association between Two Things," *Amer. Jour. of Psychology*, vol. xv., 1904, p. 88. (Formula (8).)

(7) SPEARMAN, C., "Demonstration of Formulæ for True Measurement of Correlation," *Amer. Jour. of Psychology*, vol. xviii., 1907, p. 161. (Proof of formula (8), but on different lines to that given in the text, which was communicated to Spearman in 1908, and published by Brown and by Spearman in (8) and (10).)

(8) SPEARMAN, C., "Correlation calculated from Faulty Data," *British Jour. of Psychology*, vol. iii., 1910, p. 271.

(9) JACOB, S. M., "On the Correlations of Areas of Matured Crops and the Rainfall," *Mem. Asiatic Soc. Bengal*, vol. ii., 1910, p. 847. (§ 7 contains remarks on the effects of errors on the correlations and regressions, with especial reference to this problem.)

(10) BROWN, W., "Some Experimental Results in Correlation," *Proceedings of the Sixth International Congress of Psychology, Geneva*, August 1909.

Correlations between Indices, etc.

(11) PEARSON, KARL, "On a Form of Spurious Correlation which may arise when Indices are used in the Measurement of Organs," *Proc. Roy. Soc.*, vol. lx., 1897, p. 489. (§§ 8, 9.)

(12) GALTON, FRANCIS, "Note to the Memoir by Prof. Karl Pearson on Spurious Correlation," *ibid.*, p. 498.

(13) YULE, G. U., "On the Interpretation of Correlations between Indices or Ratios," *Jour. Roy. Stat. Soc.*, vol. lxxiii., 1910, p. 644.

(14) BROWN, J. W., M. GREENWOOD, and FRANCES WOOD, "A Study of Index-Correlations," *Jour. Roy. Stat. Soc.*, vol. lxxvii., 1914, pp.317-46.

The Weighted Mean.

(15) PEARSON, KARL, "Note on Reproductive Selection," *Proc. Roy. Soc.*, vol. lix., 1896, p. 301. (Eqn. (15).)

Correction of Death-rates, etc.

(16) TATHAM, JOHN, *Supplement to the Fifty-fifth Annual Report of the Registrar-General for England and Wales: Introductory Letters to Pt. I. and Pt. II.* Also *Supplement to Sixty-fifth Report: Introductory Letter to Pt. II.* (Cd. 7769, 1895 ; 8503, 1897 ; 2619, 1908).

(17) NEWSHOLME, A., and T. H. C. STEVENSON, "The Decline of Human Fertility in the United Kingdom and other Countries, as shown by Corrected Birth-rates," *Jour. Roy. Stat. Soc.*, vol. lxix., 1906, p. 34.

(18) YULE, G. U., "On the Changes in the Marriage and Birth Rates in England and Wales during the past Half Century," etc., *ibid.*, p. 88.

(19) HERON, DAVID, "The Influence of Defective Physique and Unfavourable Home Environment on the Intelligence of School Children," *Eugenics Laboratory Memoirs*, viii. ; Dulau & Co., London, 1910.

Miscellaneous.

(20) PEARSON, KARL, ALICE LEE, and L. BRAMLEY-MOORE, "Genetic (reproductive) Selection: Inheritance of Fertility in Man and of Fecundity in Thoroughbred Racehorses," *Phil. Trans. Roy. Soc.*, Series A, vol. cxcii., 1899, p. 257.

(A number of theorems of general application are given in the introductory part of this memoir, some of which have been utilised in §§ 12-13 of the preceding chapter.)

EXERCISES.

1. Find the values obtained for the standard-deviations in Examples ii. (p. 139) and iii. (p. 141) of Chapter VIII. on applying Sheppard's correction for grouping.

2. Show that if a range of six times the standard-deviation covers at least 18 class-intervals (*cf.* Chap. VI. § 5), Sheppard's correction will make a difference of less than 0·5 per cent. in the rough value of the standard-deviation.

3. (Data from the decennial supplements to the Annual Reports of the Registrar-General for England and Wales.) The following particulars are

found for 36 small registration districts in which the number of births in a decade ranged between 1500 and 2500 :—

Decade.	Proportion of Male Births per 1000 of all Births.	
	Mean.	Standard-deviation.
1881–1890 . .	508·1	12·80
1891–1900 . .	508·4	10·37
Both decades	508·25	11·65

It is believed, however, that a great part of the observed standard-deviation is due to mere "fluctuations of sampling" of no real significance.

Given that the correlation between the proportions of male births in a district in the two decades is + 0·36, estimate (1) the true standard-deviation freed from such fluctuations of sampling ; (2) the standard-deviation of fluctuations of sampling, i.e. of the errors produced by such fluctuations in the observed proportions of male births.

4. (Data from Pearson, ref. 11.) The coefficients of variation for breadth, height, and length of certain skulls are 3·89, 3·50, and 3·24 per cent. respectively. Find the "spurious correlation" between the breadth/length and height/length indices, absolute measures being combined at random so that they are uncorrelated.

5. (Data from Boas, communicated to Pearson : cf. Fawcett and Pearson, Proc. Roy. Soc., vol. lxii. p. 413.) From short series of measurements on American Indians the mean coefficient of correlation found between father and son, and father and daughter, for cephalic index, is 0·14 ; between mother and son, and mother and daughter 0·33. Assuming these coefficients should be the same if it were not for the looseness of family relations, find the proportion of children not due to the reputed father.

6. Find the correlation between $X_1 + X_2$ and $X_2 + X_3$; X_1, X_2 and X_3 being uncorrelated.

7. Find the correlation between X_1 and $aX_1 + bX_2$, X_1 and X_2 being uncorrelated.

8. (Referring to illustration iv., § 14, Chap. X.) Use the answer to question 7 to estimate, very roughly, the correlation that would be found between annual movements in infantile and general mortality if the mortality of those under and over 1 year of age were uncorrelated. Note that—

general mortality per }
    1000 of population } = infantile mortality per 1000 births × $\dfrac{\text{births}}{\text{population}}$

+ deaths over one year per 1000 of population.

and treat the ratio of births to population as if it were constant at a rough average value, say 0·033. The standard-deviation of annual movements in infantile mortality is (loc. cit.) 9·6, and that of annual movements in mortality other than infantile may be taken as sensibly the same as that of general mortality, or say 1 unit.

9. If the relation

$$a.x_1 + b.x_2 + c.x_3 = 0$$

holds for all values of x_1, x_2 and x_3 (which are, in our usual notation, deviations from their respective arithmetic means), find the correlations between x_1, x_2 and x_3 in terms of their standard-deviations and the values of a, b and c.

10. What is the effect on a weighted mean of errors in the weights or the quantities weighted, such errors being uncorrelated with each other, with the weights, or with the variables—(1) if the arithmetic mean values of the errors are zero ; (2) if the arithmetic mean values of the errors are not zero ?

11. *Cf.* (Pearson, "On a Generalised Theory of Alternative Inheritance," *Phil. Trans.*, vol. cciii., A, 1904, p. 53). If we consider the correlation between number of recessive couplets in parent and in offspring, in a Mendelian population breeding at random (such as would ultimately result from an initial cross between a pure dominant and a pure recessive), the correlation is found to be 1/3 for a total number of couplets n. If $n=1$, the only possible numbers of recessive couplets are 0 and 1, and the correlation table between parent and offspring reduces to the form

Offspring.	Parent.		
	0	1	Total
0	5	1	6
1	1	1	2
Total	6	2	8

Verify the correlation, and work out the association coefficient Q.

12. (*Cf.* the above, and also Snow, *Proc. Roy. Soc.*, vol. lxxxiii., B, 1910, Table III., p. 42.) For a similar population the correlation between brothers, assuming a practically infinite size of family, is 5/12. The table is

Second Brother.	First Brother.		
	0	1	Total.
0	41	7	48
1	7	9	16
Total	48	16	64

Verify the correlation, and work out the association coefficient Q.

13. Referring to the notation of § 10, show that we have the following expressions for the regressions in a fourfold table :—

$$r\frac{\sigma_1}{\sigma_2}=\frac{N.\delta}{(B)(\beta)}=\frac{(AB)}{(B)}-\frac{(A\beta)}{(\beta)}$$

$$r\frac{\sigma_2}{\sigma_1}=\frac{N\delta}{(A)(a)}=\frac{(AB)}{(A)}-\frac{(aB)}{(a)}.$$

Verify on the tables of questions 11 and 12.

CHAPTER XII.

PARTIAL CORRELATION.

1. In Chapters IX.–XI. the theory of the correlation-coefficient for a single pair of variables has been developed and its applications illustrated. But in the case of statistics of attributes we found it necessary to proceed from the theory of simple association for a single pair of attributes to the theory of association for several attributes, in order to be able to deal with the complex causation characteristic of statistics ; and similarly the student will find it impossible to advance very far in the discussion of many problems in correlation without some knowledge of the theory of *multiple correlation*, or correlation between several variables. In such a problem as that of illustration i., Chap. X., for instance, it might be found that changes in pauperism were highly correlated (positively) with changes in the out-relief ratio, and also with changes in the proportion of old ; and the question might arise how far the first correlation was due merely to a tendency to give out-relief more freely to the old than the young, *i.e.* to a correlation between changes in out-relief and changes in proportion of old. The question could not at the present stage be answered by working out the correlation-coefficient between the last pair of variables, for we have as yet no guide as to how far a correlation between

the variables 1 and 2 can be accounted for by correlations between 1 and 3 and 2 and 3. Again, in the case of illustration iii., Chap. X., a marked positive correlation might be observed between, say, the bulk of a crop and the rainfall during a certain period, and practically no correlation between the crop and the accumulated temperature during the same period ; and the question might arise whether the last result might not be due merely to a negative correlation between rain and accumulated temperature, the crop being favourably affected by an increase of accumulated temperature *if other things were equal*, but failing as a rule to obtain this benefit owing to the concomitant deficiency of rain. In the problem of inheritance in a population, the corresponding problem is of great importance, as already indicated in Chapter IV. It is essential for the discussion of possible hypotheses to know whether an observed correlation between, say, grandson and grandparent can or cannot be accounted for solely by observed correlations between grandson and parent, parent and grandparent.

2. Problems of this type, in which it is necessary to consider simultaneously the relations between at least three variables, and possibly more, may be treated by a simple and natural extension of the method used in the case of two variables. The latter case was discussed by forming linear equations between the two variables, assigning such values to the constants as to make the sum of the squares of the errors of estimate as low as possible : the more complicated case may be discussed by forming linear equations between any one of the n variables involved, taking each in turn, and the $n-1$ others, again assigning such values to the constants as to make the sum of the squares of the errors of estimate a minimum. If the variables are $X_1 X_2 X_3 \ldots X_n$, the equation will be of the form

$$X_1 = a + b_2.X_2 + b_3.X_3 + \ldots + b_n.X_n.$$

If in such a generalised **regression** or **characteristic equation** we find a sensible positive value for any one coefficient such as b_2, we know that there must be a positive correlation between X_1 and X_2 that cannot be accounted for by mere correlations of X_1 and X_2 with X_3, X_4, or X_n, for the effects of changes in these variables are allowed for in the remaining terms on the right. The magnitude of b_2 gives, in fact, the mean change in X_1 associated with a unit change in X_2 when all the remaining variables are kept constant. The correlation between X_1 and X_2 indicated by b_2 may be termed a **partial correlation**, as corresponding with the *partial association* of Chapter IV., and it is required to deduce from the values of the coefficients b, which may be termed **partial regressions, partial coefficients of corre-**

lation giving the correlation between X_1 and X_2 or other pair of variables *when the remaining variables* X_3 .... X_n *are kept constant*, or when changes in these variables are corrected or allowed for, so far as this may be done with a linear equation. For examples of such generalised regression-equations the student may turn to the illustrations worked out below (pp. 239-247).

3. With this explanatory introduction, we may now proceed to the algebraic theory of such generalised regression-equations and of multiple correlation in general. It will first, however, be as well to revert briefly to the case of two variables. In Chapter IX., to obtain the greatest possible simplicity of treatment, the value of the coefficient $r = p/\sigma_1\sigma_2$ was deduced on the special assumption that the means of all arrays were strictly collinear, and the meaning of the coefficient in the more general case was subsequently investigated. Such a process is not conveniently applicable when a number of variables are to be taken into account, and the problem has to be faced directly : i.e. *required, to determine the coefficients and constant term, if any, in a regression-equation, so as to make the sum of the squares of the errors of estimate a minimum.* We will take this problem first for the case of two variables, introducing a notation that can be conveniently adapted to more. Let us take the arithmetic means of the variables as origins of measurement, and let x_1, x_2 denote deviations of the two variables from their respective means. Then it is required to determine a_1 and b_{12} in the regression-equation

$$x_1 = a_1 + b_{12}.x_2 \qquad . \qquad . \qquad . \qquad . \qquad (a)$$

so as to make $\Sigma(x_1 - \overline{a_1 + b_{12}.x_2})^2$, for all associated pairs of deviations x_1 and x_2, the least possible. Put more briefly, if we write

$$N.s_{1.2}^2 = \Sigma(x_1 - \overline{a_1. + b_{12}.x_2})^2 \qquad . \qquad . \qquad (b)$$

so that $s_{1.2}$ is the root-mean-square value of the errors of estimate in using regression-equation (a) (*cf.* Chap. IX. § 14), it is required to make $s_{1.2}$ a minimum. Suppose any value whatever to be assigned to b_{12}, and a series of values of a_1 to be tried, $s_{1.2}$ being calculated for each. Evidently $s_{1.2}$ would be very large for values of a_1 that erred greatly either in excess or defect of the best value (for the given value of b_{12}), and would continuously decrease as this best value was approached ; the value of $s_{1.2}$ could never become negative, though possibly, but exceptionally, zero. If therefore the values of $s_{1.2}$ were plotted to the values of a_1 on a diagram, a curve would be obtained more or less like that of fig. 44. The best value of a_1, for which $s_{1.2}$ attained its minimum value, say $\sigma_{1.2}$, could be approximately estimated from such a diagram ; but it can be calculated with much more exactness from the condition that *if a'_1 a''_1 be two values close above and below the best, the corresponding values of $s_{1.2}$ are equal.* Let a_1 and $(a_1 + \delta)$ be two such values.   Then if

$$\Sigma(x_1 - \overline{a_1 + b_{12}.x_2})^2 = \Sigma(x_1 - \overline{a_1 + \delta + b_{12}.x_2})^2$$

when δ is very small, the value of a_1 is the best for the assigned value of b_{12}.   But, evidently, the equation gives, neglecting the term in δ^2,

$$\Sigma(x_1 - \overline{a_1 + b_{12}.x_2}) = 0,$$

that is,

$$a_1 = 0$$

whatever the value of b_{12}.   This is the direct proof of the

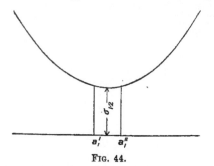

Fig. 44.

result that no constant term need be introduced on the right of a regression-equation when written in terms of deviations from the arithmetic mean, or that the two lines of regression must pass through the mean (Chap. IX. § 10).   We may therefore omit any constant term.   If, now, b_{12} is to be assigned the best value, we must have, by similar reasoning, for slightly differing values, b_{12}, $b_{12} + \delta$,

$$\Sigma(x_1 - b_{12}.x_2)^2 = \Sigma(x_1 - [b_{12} + \delta]x_2)^2.$$

That is, again neglecting terms in δ^2,

$$\Sigma x_2(x_1 - b_{12}.x_2) = 0 \qquad . \qquad . \qquad . \quad (c)$$

or, breaking up the sum,

$$b_{12} = \frac{\Sigma(x_1 x_2)}{\Sigma(x_2{}^2)} = r_{12}\frac{\sigma_1}{\sigma_2},$$

which is the value found by the previous indirect method of Chapter IX. From the fact that b_{12} is determined so as to make the value of $\Sigma(x_1 - b_{12}x_2)^2$ the least possible, the method of determination is sometimes called the *method of least squares.* Evidently all the remaining results of Chapter IX. follow from this, and notably we have for $\sigma_{1.2}$, the minimum value of $s_{1.2}$, the standard-deviation of errors of estimate

$$\sigma_{1.2}{}^2 = \sigma_1{}^2(1 - r_{12}{}^2) \qquad . \qquad . \qquad . \qquad . \qquad (d)$$

4. Now apply the same method to the regression-equation for n variables. Writing the equation in terms of deviations, it follows from reasoning precisely similar to that given above that no constant term need be entered on the right-hand side. For the **partial regression-coefficients** (the coefficients of the x's on the right) a special notation will be used in order that the exact position of each coefficient may be rendered quite definite. The first subscript affixed to the letter b (which will always be used to denote a regression) will be the subscript of the x on the left (the dependent variable), and the second will be the subscript of the x to which it is attached; these may be called the **primary subscripts**. After the primary subscripts, and separated from them by a point, are placed the subscripts of all the remaining variables on the right-hand side as **secondary subscripts**. The regression-equation will therefore be written in the form

$$x_1 = b_{12.34} \ldots {}_n \cdot x_2 + b_{13.24} \ldots {}_n \cdot x_3 + \ldots + b_{1n.23} \ldots {}_{(n-1)} \cdot x_n \qquad . \quad (1)$$

The order in which the secondary subscripts are written is, it should be noted, quite indifferent, but the order of the primary subscripts is material; *e.g.* $b_{12.3} \ldots {}_n$ and $b_{21.3} \ldots {}_n$ denote quite distinct coefficients, x_1 being the dependent variable in the first case and x_2 in the second. A coefficient with p secondary subscripts may be termed a regression of the pth order. The regressions b_{12}, b_{21}, b_{13}, b_{31}, etc., in the case of two variables may be regarded as of order zero, and may be termed **total** as distinct from **partial** regressions.

5. In the case of two variables, the correlation-coefficient r_{12} may be regarded as defined by the equation

$$r_{12} = (b_{12} \cdot b_{21})^{\frac{1}{2}}.$$

We shall generalise this equation in the form

$$r_{12.34} \ldots {}_n = (b_{12.34} \ldots {}_n \cdot b_{21.34} \ldots {}_n)^{\frac{1}{2}} \qquad . \qquad . \quad (2)$$

This is at present a pure definition of a new symbol, and it remains to be shown that $r_{12.34} \ldots {}_n$ may really be regarded as, and possesses all the properties of, a correlation-coefficient; the name may, however, be applied to it, pending the proof. A correlation-coefficient with p secondary subscripts will be termed a correlation of order p. Evidently, in the case of a correlation-coefficient, the order in which both primary and secondary subscripts is written is indifferent, for the right-hand side of equation (2) is unaltered by writing 2 for 1 and 1 for 2. The correlations r_{12}, r_{13}, etc., may be regarded as of order zero, and spoken of as *total*, as distinct from partial, correlations.

6. If the regressions $b_{12.34 \ldots n}$, $b_{13.24 \ldots n}$, etc., be assigned the "best" values, as determined by the method of least squares, the difference between the actual value of x_1 and the value assigned by the right-hand side of the regression-equation (1), that is, the error of estimate, will be denoted by $x_{1.23 \ldots n}$; *i.e.* as a definition we have

$$x_{1.23 \ldots n} = x_1 - b_{12.34 \ldots n} . x_2 - b_{13.24 \ldots n} . x_3 - \ldots - b_{1n.23 \ldots (n-1)} . x_n \quad . \quad (3)$$

where x_1 x_2 . . . . x_n are assigned any one set of observed values. Such an error (or *residual*, as it is sometimes called) denoted by a symbol with p secondary suffixes, will be termed a *deviation* of the pth order. Finally, we will define a generalised standard-deviation $\sigma_{1.23 \ldots n}$ by the equation

$$N.\sigma_{1.23 \ldots n}^2 = \Sigma(x_{1.23 \ldots n}^2) \quad . \quad . \quad . \quad (4)$$

N being, as usual, the number of observations. A standard-deviation denoted by a symbol with p secondary suffixes will be termed a standard-deviation of the pth order, the standard-deviations σ_1 σ_2, etc., being regarded as of order zero, the standard-deviations $\sigma_{1.2}$ $\sigma_{2.1}$ etc., (*cf.* eqn. (*d*) of § 3) of the first order, and so on.

7. From the reasoning of § 3 it follows that the "least-square" values of the partial regressions $b_{12.34 \ldots n}$, etc., will be given by equations of the form

$$\Sigma(x_1 - \overline{b_{12.34 \ldots n} . x_2 + \ldots . + b_{1n.23 \ldots (n-1) . x_n}})^2$$
$$= \Sigma(x_1 - (\overline{b_{12.34 \ldots n} + \delta)x_2 + \ldots . + b_{1n.23 \ldots (n-1) . x_n}})^2$$

δ being very small. That is, neglecting the term in δ^2,

$$\Sigma x_2(x_1 - \overline{b_{12.34 \ldots n} . x_2 + \ldots . + b_{1n.23 \ldots (n-1) . x_n}}) = 0,$$

or, more briefly, in terms of the notation of equation (3),

$$\Sigma(x_2 . x_{1.23 \ldots n}) = 0 \quad . \quad . \quad . \quad (5)$$

There are a large number of these equations, $(n-1)$ for determining the coefficients $b_{12.34 \ldots n}$, etc., $(n-1)$ again for determining the coefficients $b_{21.34} \ldots \text{...}_n$, etc., and so on: they are sometimes termed the **normal equations**. If the student will follow the process by which (5) was obtained, he will see that when the condition is expressed that $b_{12.34} \ldots \text{...}_n$ shall possess the "least-square" value, x_2 enters into the product-sum with $x_{1.23} \ldots \text{...}_n$; when the same condition is expressed for $b_{13.24} \ldots \text{...}_n$, x_3 enters into the product-sum, and so on. Taking each regression in turn, in fact, every x the suffix of which is included in the secondary suffixes of $x_{1.23} \ldots \text{...}_n$ enters into the product-sum. The normal equations of the form (5) are therefore equivalent to the theorem—

The product-sum of any deviation of order zero with any deviation of higher order is zero, provided the subscript of the former occur among the secondary subscripts of the latter.

8. But it follows from this that

$$\Sigma(x_{1.34} \ldots _n . x_{2.34} \ldots _n) = \Sigma x_{1.34} \ldots _n(x_2 - b_{23.4} \ldots _n . x_3 - \ldots - b_{2n.34} \ldots _{(n-1)} . x_n)$$
$$= \Sigma(x_{1.34} \ldots _n . x_2).$$

Similarly,

$$\Sigma(x_{1.34} \ldots _n . x_{2.34} \ldots _n) = \Sigma(x_1 . x_{2.34} \ldots _n).$$

Similarly again,

$$\Sigma(x_{1.34} \ldots _n . x_{2.34} \ldots _{(n-1)}) = \Sigma(x_{1.34} \ldots _n . x_2),$$

and so on. Therefore, quite generally,

$$\left.\begin{aligned}
\Sigma(x_{1.34} \ldots _n . x_{2.34} \ldots _n) &= \Sigma(x_{1.34} \ldots _{(n-1)} . x_{2.34} \ldots _n) \\
&= \ . \qquad . \qquad . \qquad . \\
&= \Sigma(x_1 . x_{2.34} \ldots _n) \\
&= \Sigma(x_{1.34} \ldots _n . x_{2.34} \ldots _{(n-1)}) \\
&= \ . \qquad . \qquad . \qquad . \\
&= \Sigma(x_{1.34} \ldots _n . x_2)
\end{aligned}\right\} \quad . \quad (6)$$

Comparing all the equal product-sums that may be obtained in this way, we see that *the product-sum of any two deviations is unaltered by omitting any or all of the secondary subscripts of either which are common to the two, and, conversely, the product-sum of any deviation of order p with a deviation of order p + q, the p subscripts being the same in each case, is unaltered by adding to the secondary subscripts of the former any or all of the q additional subscripts of the latter.*

It follows therefore from (5) that *any product-sum is zero if all the subscripts of the one deviation occur among the secondary subscripts of the other.* As the simplest case, we may note that x_1 is uncorrelated with $x_{2.1}$, and x_2 uncorrelated with $x_{1.2}$.

The theorems of this and of the preceding paragraph are of fundamental importance, and should be carefully remembered.

9. We have now from §§ 7 and 8—

$$0 = \Sigma(x_{2.34 \ldots n} \cdot x_{1.234 \ldots n})$$
$$= \Sigma x_{2.34 \ldots n} (x_1 - b_{12.34 \ldots n} \cdot x_2 - \text{terms in } x_3 \text{ to } x_n)$$
$$= \Sigma(x_1 \cdot x_{2.34 \ldots n}) - b_{12.34 \ldots n} \Sigma(x_2 \cdot x_{2.34 \ldots n})$$
$$= \Sigma(x_{1.34 \ldots n} \cdot x_{2.34 \ldots n}) - b_{12.34 \ldots n} \Sigma(x^2_{2.34 \ldots n}).$$

That is

$$b_{12.34 \ldots n} = \frac{\Sigma(x_{1.34 \ldots n} \cdot x_{2.34 \ldots n})}{\Sigma(x^2_{2.34 \ldots n})} \qquad . \qquad (7)$$

But this is the value that would have been obtained by taking a regression-equation of the form

$$x_{1.34 \ldots n} = b_{12.34 \ldots n} \cdot x_{2.34 \ldots n}$$

and determining $b_{12.34 \ldots n}$ by the method of least-squares, *i.e.* $b_{12.34 \ldots n}$ is the regression of $x_{1.34 \ldots n}$ on $x_{2.34 \ldots n}$. It follows at once from (2) that $r_{12.34 \ldots n}$ is the correlation between $x_{1.34 \ldots n}$ and $x_{2.34 \ldots n}$, and from (4) that we may write

$$b_{12.34 \ldots n} = r_{12.34 \ldots n} \frac{\sigma_{1.34 \ldots n}}{\sigma_{2.34 \ldots n}} \qquad . \qquad (8)$$

an equation identical with the familiar relation $b_{12} = r_{12} \cdot \sigma_1 / \sigma_2$, with the secondary suffixes $34 \ldots n$ added throughout.

To illustrate the meaning of the equation by the simplest case, if we had three variables only, x_1, x_2, and x_3, the value of $b_{12.3}$ or $r_{12.3}$ could be determined (1) by finding the correlations r_{13} and r_{23} and the corresponding regressions b_{13} and b_{23}; (2) working out the residuals $x_1 - b_{13} \cdot x_3$ and $x_2 - b_{23} \cdot x_3$ for all associated deviations; (3) working out the correlation between the residuals associated with the same values of x_3. The method would not, however, be a practical one, as the arithmetic would be extremely lengthy, much more lengthy than the method given below for expressing a correlation of order p in terms of correlations of order $p - 1$.

10. Any standard-deviation of order p may be expressed in terms of a standard-deviation of order $p - 1$ and a correlation of order $p - 1$. For,

$$\Sigma(x^2_{1.23 \ldots n}) = \Sigma(x_{1.23 \ldots (n-1)} \cdot x_{1.23 \ldots n})$$
$$= \Sigma(x_{1.23 \ldots (n-1)})(x_1 - b_{1n.23 \ldots (n-1)} x_n - \text{terms in } x_2 \text{ to } x_{n-1})$$
$$= \Sigma(x^2_{1.23 \ldots (n-1)}) - b_{1n.23 \ldots (n-1)} \Sigma(x_{1.23 \ldots (n-1)} \cdot x_{n.23 \ldots (n-1)})$$

or, dividing through by the number of observations,

$$\sigma^2_{1.23 \ldots n} = \sigma^2_{1.23 \ldots (n-1)}(1 - b_{1n.23 \ldots (n-1)} \cdot b_{n1.23 \ldots (n-1)})$$
$$= \sigma^2_{1.23 \ldots (n-1)}(1 - r^2_{1n.23 \ldots (n-1)}) \qquad . \qquad . \qquad (9)$$

This is again the relation of the familiar form—

$$\sigma_{1.n}^2 = \sigma_1^2(1 - r_{1n}^2)$$

with the secondary suffixes 23 .... $(n-1)$ added throughout. It is clear from (9) that $r_{1n.23}$ .... $_{(n-1)}$, like any correlation of order zero, cannot be numerically greater than unity. It also follows at once that if we have been estimating x_1 from x_2, x_3 .... x_{n-1}, x_n will not increase the accuracy of estimate unless $r_{1n.23}$ .... $_{(n-1)}$ (not r_{1n}) differ from zero. This condition is somewhat interesting, as it leads to rather unexpected results. For example, if $r_{12} = +0.8$, $r_{13} = +0.4$, $r_{23} = +0.5$, it will not be possible to estimate x_1 with any greater accuracy from x_2 and x_3 than from x_2 alone, for the value of $r_{13.2}$ is zero (see below, § 13).

11. It should be noted that, in equation (9), any other subscript can be eliminated in the same way as subscript n from the suffix of $\sigma_{1.23}$ .... $_m$ so that a standard-deviation of order p can be expressed in p ways in terms of standard-deviations of the next lower order. This is useful as affording an independent check on arithmetic. Further, $\sigma_{1.23}$ .... $_{(n-1)}$ can be expressed in the same way in terms of $\sigma_{1.23}$ .... $_{(n-2)}$, and so on, so that we must have

$$\sigma_{1.23\dots n}^2 = \sigma_1^2(1 - r_{12}^2)(1 - r_{13.2}^2)(1 - r_{14.23}^2) \dots (1 - r_{1n.23\dots(n-1)}^2) . \quad (10)$$

This is an extremely convenient expression for arithmetical use; the arithmetic can again be subjected to an absolute check by eliminating the subscripts in a different, say the inverse, order. Apart from the algebraic proof, it is obvious that the values must be identical; for if we are estimating one variable from n others, it is clearly indifferent in what order the latter are taken into account.

12. Any regression of order p may be expressed in terms of regressions of order $p - 1$. For we have

$$\Sigma(x_{1.34\dots n} . x_{2.34\dots n}) = \Sigma(x_{1.34\dots(n-1)} . x_{2.34\dots n})$$
$$= \Sigma x_{1.34\dots(n-1)}(x_2 - b_{2n.34\dots(n-1)} . x_n - \text{terms in } x_3 \text{ to } x_{n-1})$$
$$= \Sigma(x_{1.34\dots(n-1)} . x_{2.34\dots(n-1)}) - b_{2n.34\dots(n-1)}\Sigma(x_{1.34\dots(n-1)} . x_{n.34\dots(n-1)}).$$

Replacing $b_{2n.34\dots(n-1)}$ by $b_{n2.34\dots(n-1)} . \sigma_{2.34\dots(n-1)}^2 / \sigma_{n.34\dots(n-1)}^2$, we have

$$b_{12.34\dots n} . \sigma_{2.34\dots n}^2 = b_{12.34\dots(n-1)} . \sigma_{2.34\dots(n-1)}^2 - b_{1n.34\dots(n-1)} . b_{n2.34\dots(n-1)} . \sigma_{2.34\dots(n-1)}^2,$$

or, from (9),

$$b_{12.34\dots n} = \frac{b_{12.34\dots(n-1)} - b_{1n.34\dots(n-1)} . b_{n2.34\dots(n-1)}}{1 - b_{2n.34\dots(n-1)} . b_{n2.34\dots(n-1)}} \quad (11)$$

The student should note that this is an expression of the form

$$b_{12.n} = \frac{b_{12} - b_{1n} . b_{n2}}{1 - b_{2n} . b_{n2}}$$

with the subscripts $34 \ldots (n-1)$ added throughout. The coefficient $b_{12.34 \ldots n}$ may therefore be regarded as determined from a regression-equation of the form

$$x_{1.34 \ldots (n-1)} = b_{12.34 \ldots n} \cdot x_{2.34 \ldots (n-1)} + b_{1n.23 \ldots (n-1)} \cdot x_{n.34 \ldots (n-1)},$$

i.e. it is the partial regression of $x_{1.34 \ldots (n-1)}$ on $x_{2.34 \ldots (n-1)},$ $x_{n.34 \ldots (n-1)}$ being given. As any other secondary suffix might have been eliminated in lieu of n, we might also regard it as the partial regression of $x_{1.45 \ldots n}$ on $x_{2.45 \ldots n}, x_{3.45 \ldots n}$ being given, and so on.

13. From equation (11) we may readily obtain a corresponding equation for correlations. For (11) may be written

$$b_{12.34} {}_{n} = \frac{r_{12.34 \ldots (n-1)} - r_{1n.34 \ldots (n-1)} \cdot r_{2n.34 \ldots (n-1)}}{1 - r^2_{2n.34 \ldots (n-1)}} \cdot \frac{\sigma_{1.34 \ldots (n-1)}}{\sigma_{2.34 \ldots (n-1)}}$$

Hence, writing down the corresponding expression for $b_{21.34 \ldots n}$ and taking the square root

$$r_{12.34 \ldots n} = \frac{r_{12.34 \ldots (n-1)} - r_{1n.34 \ldots (n-1)} \cdot r_{2n.34 \ldots (n-1)}}{\left(1 - r^2_{1n.34 \ldots (n-1)}\right)^{\frac{1}{2}} \left(1 - r^2_{2n.34 \ldots (n-1)}\right)^{\frac{1}{2}}} \quad . \quad (12)$$

This is, similarly, the expression for three variables

$$r_{12.n} = \frac{r_{12} - r_{1n} \cdot r_{2n}}{\left(1 - r^2_{1n}\right)^{\frac{1}{2}} \left(1 - r^2_{2n}\right)^{\frac{1}{2}}}$$

with the secondary subscripts added throughout, and $r_{12.34 \ldots n}$ can be assigned interpretations corresponding to those of $b_{12.34 \ldots n}$ above. Evidently equation (12) permits of an absolute check or the arithmetic in the calculation of all partial coefficients of an order higher than the first, for any one of the secondary suffixes of $r_{12.34 \ldots n}$ can be eliminated so as to obtain another equation of the same form as (12), and the value obtained for $r_{12.34 \ldots n}$ by inserting the values of the coefficients of lower order in the expression on the right must be the same in each case.

14. The equations now obtained provide all that is necessary for the arithmetical solution of problems in multiple correlation. The best mode of procedure on the whole, having calculated all the correlations and standard-deviations of order zero, is (1) to calculate the correlations of higher order by successive applications of equation (12); (2) to calculate any required standard-deviations by equation (10); (3) to calculate any required regressions by equation (8): the use of equation (11) for calculating the regressions of successive orders directly from each other is comparatively clumsy. We will give two illustrations, the first for

three and the second for four variables. The introduction of more variables does not involve any difference in the form of the arithmetic, but rapidly increases the amount.

Example i.—The first illustration we shall take will be a continuation of example i. of Chapter IX., in which the correlation was worked out between (1) the average earnings of agricultural labourers and (2) the percentage of the population in receipt of Poor-law relief in a group of 38 rural districts. In Question 2 of the same chapter are given (3) the ratios of the numbers in receipt of outdoor relief to the numbers relieved in the workhouse, in the same districts. Required to work out the partial correlations, regressions, etc., for these three variables.

Using as our notation X_1 = average earnings, X_2 = percentage of population in receipt of relief, X_3 = out-relief ratio, the first constants determined are—

$$M_1 = 15\cdot9 \text{ shillings} \qquad \sigma_1 = 1\cdot71 \text{ shillings} \qquad r_{12} = -0\cdot66$$
$$M_2 = 3\cdot67 \text{ per cent.} \qquad \sigma_2 = 1\cdot29 \text{ per cent.} \qquad r_{13} = -0\cdot13$$
$$M_3 = 5\cdot79 \qquad\qquad \sigma_3 = 3\cdot09 \qquad\qquad r_{23} = +0\cdot60$$

To obtain the partial correlations, equation (12) is used direct in its simplest form—

$$r_{12\cdot3} = \frac{r_{12} - r_{13} \cdot r_{23}}{(1 - r_{13}^2)^{\frac{1}{2}} (1 - r_{23}^2)^{\frac{1}{2}}}.$$

The work is best done systematically and the results collected in tabular form, especially if logarithms are used, as many of the logarithms occur repeatedly. First it will be noted that the logarithms of $(1 - r^2)^{\frac{1}{2}}$ occur in all the denominators; these had, accordingly, better be worked out at once and tabulated (col. 2 of the table below). In col. 3 the product term of the numerator of

1.	2.	3.	4.	5.	6.	7.	8.	9.
						Correlation of First Order.		
r.	$\log \sqrt{1-r^2}$.	Product Term.	Numerator.	log Num.	log Denom.	log.	Value.	$\log \sqrt{1-r^2}$.
$r_{12} = -0\cdot66$	$\bar{1}\cdot87580$	$-0\cdot0780$	$-0\cdot5820$	$\bar{1}\cdot76492$	$\bar{1}\cdot89038$	$\bar{1}\cdot86554$	$r_{12\cdot3} -0\cdot73$	$\bar{1}\cdot83216$
$r_{13} = -0\cdot13$	$\bar{1}\cdot99629$	$-0\cdot3960$	$+0\cdot2660$	$\bar{1}\cdot42488$	$\bar{1}\cdot77889$	$\bar{1}\cdot64599$	$r_{13\cdot2} +0\cdot44$	$\bar{1}\cdot95267$
$r_{23} = +0\cdot60$	$\bar{1}\cdot90309$	$+0\cdot0858$	$+0\cdot5142$	$\bar{1}\cdot71113$	$\bar{1}\cdot87209$	$\bar{1}\cdot83904$	$r_{23\cdot1} +0\cdot69$	$\bar{1}\cdot85946$

each partial coefficient is entered, *i.e.* the product of the two other coefficients on the remaining lines in col. 1 ; subtracting this from the coefficient on the same line in col. 1 we have the numerator (col. 4) and can enter its logarithm. The logarithm of the denominator (col. 6) is obtained at once by adding the two logarithms of $(1 - r^2)^{\frac{1}{2}}$ on the remaining lines of the table, and subtracting the logarithms of the denominators from those of the numerators we have the logarithms of the correlations of the first-order. It is also as well to calculate at once, for reference in the calculation of standard-deviations of the second-order, the values of $\log \sqrt{1 - r^2}$ for the first-order coefficients (col. 9).

Having obtained the correlations we can now proceed to the regressions. If we wish to find all the regression-equations, we shall have six regressions to calculate from equations of the form

$$b_{12.3} = r_{12.3} \cdot \sigma_{1.3}/\sigma_{2.3}.$$

These will involve all the six standard-deviations of the first order $\sigma_{1.2}$, $\sigma_{1.3}$, $\sigma_{2.1}$, $\sigma_{2.3}$, etc. But the standard-deviations of the first-order are not in themselves of much interest, and the standard-deviations of the second-order are so, as being the standard-errors or root-mean-square errors of estimate made in using the regression-equations of the second-order. We may save needless arithmetic, therefore, by replacing the standard-deviations of the first-order by those of the second, omitting the former entirely, and transforming the above equation for $b_{12.3}$ to the form

$$b_{12.3} = r_{12.3} \cdot \sigma_{1.23}/\sigma_{2.13}.$$

This transformation is a useful one and should be noted by the student. The values of each σ may be calculated twice independently by the formulæ of the form

$$\sigma_{1.23} = \sigma_1(1 - r_{12}^2)^{\frac{1}{2}} (1 - r_{13.2}^2)^{\frac{1}{2}}$$
$$= \sigma_1(1 - r_{13}^2)^{\frac{1}{2}} (1 - r_{12.3}^2)^{\frac{1}{2}}$$

so as to check the arithmetic; the work is rapidly done if the values of $\log \sqrt{1 - r^2}$ have been tabulated. The values found are

$$\log \sigma_{1.23} = 0.06146 \qquad \sigma_{1.23} = 1.15$$
$$\log \sigma_{2.13} = \bar{1}.84584 \qquad \sigma_{2.13} = 0.70$$
$$\log \sigma_{3.12} = 0.34571 \qquad \sigma_{3.12} = 2.22$$

From these and the logarithms of the r's we have

$$\log b_{12.3} = 0.08116, \; b_{12.3} = -1.21 : \log b_{13.2} = \bar{1}.36174, \; b_{13.2} = +0.23$$
$$\log b_{21.3} = \bar{1}.64993, \; b_{21.3} = -0.45 : \log b_{23.1} = \bar{1}.33917, \; b_{23.1} = +0.22$$
$$\log b_{31.2} = \bar{1}.93024, \; b_{31.2} = +0.85 : \log b_{32.1} = 0.33891, \; b_{32.1} = +2.18$$

That is, the regression-equations are

(1) $x_1 = -1.21 \, x_2 + 0.23 \, x_3$
(2) $x_2 = -0.45 \, x_1 + 0.22 \, x_3$
(3) $x_3 = +0.85 \, x_1 + 2.18 \, x_2$

or, transferring the origins to zero,

(1) *Earnings* $X_1 = +19 \cdot 0 - 1 \cdot 21 \, X_2 + 0 \cdot 23 \, X_3$
(2) *Pauperism* $X_2 = +9 \cdot 55 - 0 \cdot 45 \, X_1 + 0 \cdot 22 \, X_3$
(3) *Out-relief ratio* $X_3 = -15 \cdot 7 + 0 \cdot 85 \, X_1 + 2 \cdot 18 \, X_2$

The units are throughout one shilling for the earnings X_1, 1 per cent. for the pauperism X_2, and 1 for the out-relief ratio X_3.

The first and second regression-equations are those of most practical importance. The argument has been advanced that the giving of out-relief tends to lower earnings, and the total coefficient ($r_{13} = -0 \cdot 13$) between earnings (X_1) and out-relief (X_3), though very small (*cf.* Chap. IX. § 17), does not seem inconsistent with such a hypothesis. The partial correlation coefficient ($r_{13.2} = +0 \cdot 44$) and the regression-equation (1), however, indicate that in unions with a *given* percentage of the population in receipt of relief (X_2) the earnings are highest where the proportion of out-relief is highest; and this is, in so far, against the hypothesis of a tendency to lower wages. It remains possible, of course, that out-relief may adversely affect the *possibility of earning*, *e.g.* by limiting the employment of the old. As regards pauperism, the argument might be advanced that the observed correlation ($r_{23} = +0 \cdot 60$) between pauperism and out-relief was in part due to the negative correlation ($r_{13} = -0 \cdot 13$) between earnings and out-relief. Such a hypothesis would have little to support it in view of the smallness and doubtful significance of r_{13}, and is definitely contradicted by the positive partial correlation $r_{23.1} = +0 \cdot 69$, and the second regression-equation. The third regression-equation shows that the proportion of out-relief is on the whole highest where earnings are highest and pauperism greatest. It should be noticed, however, that a negative ratio is clearly impossible, and consequently the relation cannot be strictly linear; but the third equation gives *possible* (positive) average ratios for all the combinations of pauperism and earnings that actually occur.

Example ii.—(Four variables.) As an illustration of the form of the work in the case of four variables, we will take a portion of the data from another investigation into the causation of pauperism, viz. that described in the first illustration of Chapter X., to which the student should refer for details. The variables are the ratios of the values in 1891 to the values in 1881 (taken as 100) of—

1. The percentage of the population in receipt of relief,
2. The ratio of the numbers given outdoor relief to the numbers relieved in the workhouse,
3. The percentage of the population over 65 years of age,

16

4. The population itself,
in the metropolitan group of 32 unions, and the fundamental
constants (means, standard-deviations and correlations) are as
follows:—

TABLE I.

1. Means.		2. Standard-deviations.		3. Correlation-coefficient.		4. $\log \sqrt{1 - r^2}$.
1	104·7	1	29·2	12	+0·52	$\overline{1}$·93154
2	90·6	2	41·7	13	+0·41	$\overline{1}$·96003
3	107·7	3	5·5	14	−0·14	$\overline{1}$·99570
4	111·3	4	23·8	23	+0·49	$\overline{1}$·94038
—	—	—	—	24	+0·23	$\overline{1}$·98820
—	—	—	—	34	+0·25	$\overline{1}$·98598

It is seen that the average changes are not great; the percentages of the population in receipt of relief have increased on
an average by 4·7 per cent., the out-relief ratio has dropped by
9·4 per cent., and the percentage of old has increased by 7·7
per cent., at the same time as the population of the unions has
risen on the average by 11·3 per cent. At the same time the
standard-deviations of the first, second, and fourth variables are
very large. As a matter of fact, while in one union the
pauperism decreased by nearly 50 per cent. and in others by
20 per cent., in some there were increases of 60, 80, and 90
per cent.; similarly, in the case of the out-relief, in several unions
the ratio was decreased by 40 to 60 per cent., a consistent
anti-out-relief policy having been enforced; in others the ratio
was doubled, and more than doubled. As regards population,
the more central districts show decreases ranging up to 20 and
25 per cent., the circumferential districts increases of 45 to 80
per cent. The correlations of order zero are not large, the
changes in the rate of pauperism exhibiting the highest correlation
with changes in the out-relief ratio, slightly less with changes
in the proportion of old, and very little with changes in
population.

The correlations of the second order are obtained in two steps.
In the first place, the six coefficients of order zero are grouped in
four sets of three, corresponding to the four sets of three variables
formed by omitting each one of the four variables in turn (Table
II. col. 1). Each of these sets of three coefficients is then
treated in the same manner as in the last example, and so the

TABLE II.

1. Correlation-coefficient (Zero Order).		2. Product Term of Numerator.	3. Numerator.	4. Correlation-coefficient (First Order).		5. $\log \sqrt{1-r^2}$.
12	+0·52	+0·2009	+0·3191	12·3	+0·4013	Ī·96187
13	+0·41	+0·2548	+0·1552	13·2	+0·2084	Ī·99035
23	+0·49	+0·2132	+0·2768	23·1	+0·3553	Ī·97070
12	+0·52	−0·0322	+0·5522	12·4	+0·5731	Ī·91355
14	−0·14	+0·1196	−0·2596	14·2	−0·3123	Ī·97772
24	+0·23	−0·0728	+0·3028	24·1	+0·3580	Ī·97022
13	+0·41	−0·0350	+0·4450	13·4	+0·4642	Ī·94731
14	−0·14	+0·1025	−0·2425	14·3	−0·2746	Ī·98297
34	+0·25	−0·0574	+0·3074	34·1	+0·3404	Ī·97326
23	+0·49	+0·0575	+0·4325	23·4	+0·4590	Ī·94863
24	+0·23	+0·1225	+0·1075	24·3	+0·1274	Ī·99645
34	+0·25	+0·1127	+0·1373	34·2	+0·1618	Ī·99424

TABLE III.

1. Correlation-coefficient (First Order).		2. Product Term of Numerator.	3. Numerator.	4. Correlation-coefficient (Second Order).		5. $\log \sqrt{1-r^2}$.
12·4	+0·5731	+0·2131	+0·3600	12·34	+0·457	Ī·94901
13·4	+0·4642	+0·2631	+0·2011	13·24	+0·276	Ī·98277
23·4	+0·4590	+0·2660	+0·1930	23·14	+0·266	Ī·98408
12·3	+0·4013	−0·0350	+0·4363	12·34	+0·457	—
14·3	−0·2746	+0·0511	−0·3257	14·23	−0·359	Ī·97013
24·3	+0·1274	−0·1102	+0·2376	24·13	+0·270	Ī·98359
13·2	+0·2084	−0·0505	+0·2589	13·24	+0·276	—
14·2	−0·3123	+0·0337	−0·3460	14·23	−0·359	—
34·2	+0·1618	−0·0651	+0·2269	34·12	+0·244	Ī·98664
23·1	+0·3553	+0·1219	+0·2334	23·14	+0·266	—
24·1	+0·3580	+0·1209	+0·2371	24·13	+0·270	—
34·1	+0·3404	+0·1272	+0·2132	34·12	+0·244	—

correlations of the first order (Table II. col. 4) are obtained. The first-order coefficients are then regrouped in sets of three, with the same secondary suffix (Table III. col. 1), and these are treated precisely in the same way as the coefficients of order zero. In this way, it will be seen, the value of each coefficient of the second order is arrived at in two ways independently, and so the arithmetic is checked : $r_{12.34}$ occurs in the first and fourth lines, for instance, $r_{13.24}$ in the second and seventh, and so on. Of course slight differences may occur in the last digit if a sufficient number of digits is not retained, and for this reason the intermediate work should be carried to a greater degree of accuracy than is necessary in the final result; thus four places of decimals were retained throughout in the intermediate work of this example, and three in the final result. If he carries out an independent calculation, the student may differ slightly from the logarithms given in this and the following work, if more or fewer figures are retained.

Having obtained the correlations, the regressions can be calculated from the third-order standard-deviations by equations of the form (as in the last example),

$$b_{12.34} = r_{12.34} \frac{\sigma_{1.234}}{\sigma_{2.134}},$$

so the standard-deviations of lower orders need not be evaluated. Using equations of the form

$$\sigma_{1.234} = \sigma_1(1 - r_{12}^2)^{\frac{1}{2}}(1 - r_{13.2}^2)^{\frac{1}{2}}(1 - r_{14.23}^2)^{\frac{1}{2}}$$
$$= \sigma_1(1 - r_{14}^2)^{\frac{1}{2}}(1 - r_{13.4}^2)^{\frac{1}{2}}(1 - r_{12.34}^2)^{\frac{1}{2}}$$

we find

$$
\begin{aligned}
&\log \sigma_{1.234} = 1\cdot 35740 &\qquad &\sigma_{1.234} = 22\cdot 8 \\
&\log \sigma_{2.134} = 1\cdot 50597 &\qquad &\sigma_{2.134} = 32\cdot 1 \\
&\log \sigma_{3.124} = 0\cdot 65773 &\qquad &\sigma_{3.124} = 4\cdot 55 \\
&\log \sigma_{4.123} = 1\cdot 32914 &\qquad &\sigma_{4.123} = 21\cdot 3
\end{aligned}
$$

All the twelve regressions of the second order can be readily calculated, given these standard deviations and the correlations, but we may confine ourselves to the equation giving the changes in pauperism (X_1) in terms of other variables as the most important. It will be found to be

$$x_1 = 0\cdot 325x_2 + 1\cdot 383x_3 - 0\cdot 383x_4,$$

or, transferring the origins and expressing the equation in terms of percentage-ratios,

$$X_1 = -31\cdot 1 + 0\cdot 325X_2 + 1\cdot 383X_3 - 0\cdot 383X_4,$$

XII.—PARTIAL CORRELATION.

or, again, in terms of percentage-changes (ratio – 100) : —
Percentage change in pauperism

   = + 1·4 per cent.
    + 0·325 times the change in out-relief ratio. .
    + 1·383   „   „   proportion of old.
    – 0·383   „   „   population.

These results render the interpretation of the total coefficients, which might be equally consistent with several hypotheses, more clear and definite. The questions would arise, for instance, whether the correlation of changes in pauperism with changes in out-relief might not be due to correlation of the latter with the other factors introduced, and whether the negative correlation with changes in population might not be due solely to the correlation of the latter with changes in the proportion of old. As a matter of fact, the partial correlations of changes in pauperism with changes in out-relief and in proportion of old are slightly less than the total correlations, but the partial correlation with changes in population is numerically greater, the figures being

$$r_{12} = + 0·52 \qquad r_{12·34} = + 0·46$$
$$r_{13} = + 0·41 \qquad r_{13·24} = + 0·28$$
$$r_{14} = - 0·14 \qquad r_{14·23} = - 0·36$$

So far, then, as we have taken the factors of the case into account, there appears to be a true correlation between changes in pauperism and changes in out-relief, proportion of old, and population—the latter serving, of course, as some index to changes in general prosperity. The relative influences of the three factors are indicated by the regression-equation above. [For the full discussion of the case cf. *Jour. Roy. Stat. Soc.*, vol. lxii., 1899.]

15. The correlation between pauperism and labourers' earnings exhibited by the figures of Example i. was illustrated by a diagram (fig. 40, p. 180), in which scales of "pauperism" and "earnings" were taken along two axes at right angles, and every observed pair of values was entered by marking the corresponding point with a small circle : the diagram was completed by drawing in the lines of regression. In precisely the same way the correlation between three variables may be represented by a model showing the distribution of points in space ; for any set of observed values X_1, X_2, X_3 may be regarded as determining a point in space, just as any pair of values X_1 and X_2 may be regarded as determining a point in a plane. Fig. 45 is drawn from such a model, constructed from the data of Example i. Four pieces of wood are fixed together

like the bottom and three sides of a box. Supposing the open
side to face the observer, a scale of pauperism is drawn vertically
upwards along the left-hand angle at the back of the "box," the

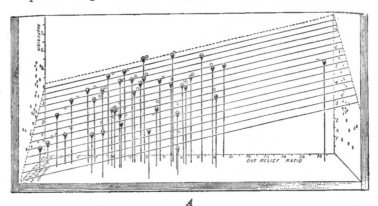

A

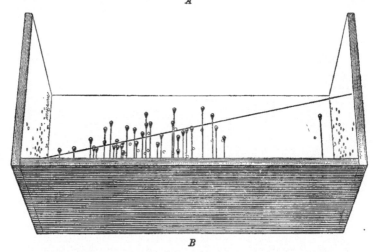

B

FIG. 45.—Model illustrating the Correlation between three Variables: (1)
Pauperism (percentage of the population in receipt of Poor-law relief);
(2) Out-relief ratio (numbers given relief in their homes to one in the
workhouse); (3) Average Weekly Earnings of agricultural labourers,
(data pp. 178 and 189). A, front view; B, view of model tilted till the
plane of regression for pauperism on the two remaining variables is seen
as a straight line.

scale starting from zero, as very small values of pauperism occur : a scale of out-relief ratio is taken along the angle between the back and bottom of the box, starting from zero at the left : finally, the scale of earnings is drawn out towards the observer along the angle between the left-hand side and the bottom, but as earnings lower than 12s. do not occur, the scale may start from 12s. at the corner. Suitable scales are : pauperism, 1 in. = 1 per cent. ; out-relief ratio, 1 in. = 1 unit ; earnings, 1 in. = 1s. ; and the inside measures of the model may then be 17 in. × 10 in. × 8 in. high, the dimensions of the model constructed. Given these three scales, any set of observed values determine a point within the "box." The *earnings* and *out-relief ratio* for some one union are noted first, and the corresponding point marked on the baseboard ; a steel wire is then inserted vertically in the base at this point and cut off at the height corresponding, on the scale chosen, to the pauperism in the same union, being finally capped with a small ball or knob to mark the "point" clearly. The model shows very well the general tendency of the pauperism to be the higher the lower the wages and the higher the out-relief, for the highest points lie towards the back and right-hand side of the model. If some representation of all three equations of regression were to be inserted in the model, the result would be rather confusing ; so the most important equation, viz. the second, giving the average rate of pauperism in terms of the other variables, may be chosen. This equation represents a plane : the lines in which it cuts the right- and left-hand sides of the "box" should be marked, holes drilled at equal intervals on these lines on the opposite sides of the box (the holes facing each other), and threads stretched through these holes, thus outlining the plane as shown in the figure. In the actual model the correlation-diagrams (like fig. 40) corresponding to the three pairs of variables were drawn on the back sides and base : they represent, of course, the elevations and plan of the points.

The student possessing some skill in handicraft would find it worth while to make such a model for some case of interest to himself, and to study on it thoroughly the nature of the plane of regression, and the relations of the partial and total correlations.

16. If we write

$$\sigma^2_{1.23\ldots n} = \sigma^2_1(1 - R^2_{1(23\ldots n)}) \quad . \quad . \quad (13)$$

it may be shown that $R_{1(23\ldots n)}$ is the correlation between x_1 and the expression on the right-hand side of the regression-equation, say $e_{1.23\ldots n}$, where

$$e_{1.23\ldots n} = b_{12.34\ldots n} \cdot x_2 + b_{13.24\ldots n} \cdot x_3 + \ldots + b_{1n.23\ldots(n-1)} \cdot x_n \quad . \quad (14)$$

For we have

$$\Sigma(x_1 \cdot e_{1.23} \ldots {}_n) = \Sigma x_1(x_1 - x_{1.23} \ldots {}_n) = N(\sigma_1^2 - \sigma_{1.23}^2 \ldots {}_n)$$

and also

$$\Sigma(e_{1.23}^2 \ldots {}_n) = \Sigma(x_1 - x_{1.23} \ldots {}_n)^2 = N(\sigma_1^2 - \sigma_{1.23}^2 \ldots {}_n)$$

whence the correlation between x_1 and $e_{1.23} \ldots {}_n$ is

$$\frac{(\sigma_1^2 - \sigma_{1.23}^2 \ldots {}_n)^{\frac{1}{2}}}{\sigma_1},$$

i.e. the value of $R_{1(23} \ldots {}_n)$ given by (13). The value of R is accordingly a useful datum as indicating how closely x_1 can be expressed in terms of a linear function of $x_2, x_3 \ldots x_n$, and the values of the regressions may be regarded as determined by the condition that R shall be a maximum. Its value is essentially positive as the product-sum $\Sigma(x_1 . e_{1.23} \ldots {}_n)$ is positive. R may be termed a coefficient of $(n-1)$-fold (or double, triple, etc.) correlation; for n variables there are n such correlations, but in the limiting case of two variables the two are identical. The value may be readily calculated, either from $\sigma_{1.23} \ldots {}_n$ and σ_1 or directly from the equation

$$1 - R_{1(23 \ldots n)}^2 = (1 - r_{12}^2)(1 - r_{13.2}^2)(1 - r_{14.23}^2) \ldots (1 - r_{1n.23 \ldots (n-1)}^2). \quad (15)$$

It is obvious from this equation that since every bracket on the right is not greater than unity,

$$1 - R_{1(23} \ldots {}_n)^2 \not> 1 - r_{12}^2.$$

Hence $R_{1(23} \ldots {}_n)$ cannot be numerically less than r_{12}. For the same reason, rewriting (15) in every possible form, $R_{1(23 \ldots n)}$ cannot be numerically less than $r_{12}, r_{13}, \ldots r_{1n}$, *i.e.* any one of the possible constituent coefficients of order zero. Further, for similar reasons, $R_{1(23} \ldots {}_n)$ cannot be numerically less than any possible constituent coefficient of any higher order. That is to say, $R_{1(23} \ldots {}_n)$ is not numerically less than the greatest of all the possible constituent coefficients, and is usually, though not always, markedly greater. Thus in Example i., $R_{2(13)}$ (the coefficient of double correlation between pauperism on the one hand, out-relief and labourers' earnings on the other) is 0·839, and the numerically greatest of the possible constituent coefficients is $r_{12.3} = -0·73$. Again, in Example ii., $R_{1(234)}$ is 0·626, and the numerically greatest of the possible constituent coefficients is $r_{12.4} = +0·573$.

The student should notice that R is necessarily positive. Further, even if all the variables $X_1, X_2, \ldots X_n$ were strictly uncorrelated in the original universe as a whole, we should expect $r_{12}, r_{13.2}, r_{14.23}$, etc., to exhibit values (whether positive or negative) differing from zero in a limited sample. Hence, R will not tend, on an average of such samples, to be zero, but will fluctuate round some mean value. This mean value will be the greater the smaller the number of observations in the sample, and also the greater the number of variables. When only a small number of observations are available it is, accordingly, little use to deal with a large number of variables. As a limiting case, it is evident that if we deal with n variables and possess only n observations, all the partial correlations of the highest possible order will be unity.

17. It is obvious that as equations (11) and (12) enable us to express regressions and correlations of higher orders in terms of those of lower orders, we must similarly be able to express the coefficients of lower in terms of those of higher orders. Such expressions are sometimes useful for theoretical work. Using the same method of expansion as in previous cases, we have

$$0 = \Sigma(x_{1.23\ \ldots\ n} \cdot x_{2.34\ \ldots\ (n-1)})$$
$$= \Sigma(x_1 \cdot x_{2.34\ \ldots\ (n-1)}) - b_{12.34\ \ldots\ n}\,\Sigma(x_2 \cdot x_{2.34\ \ldots\ (n-1)})$$
$$- b_{1n.23\ \ldots\ (n-1)}\,\Sigma(x_n \cdot x_{2.34\ \ldots\ (n-1)})$$

That is,

$$b_{12.34\ \ldots\ (n-1)} = b_{12.34\ \ldots\ n} + b_{1n.23\ \ldots\ (n-1)} \cdot b_{n2.34\ \ldots\ (n-1)}.$$

In this equation the coefficient on the left and the last on the right are of order $n-3$, the other two of order $n-2$. We therefore wish to eliminate the last coefficient on the right. Interchanging the suffixes 1 for n and n for 1, we have

$$b_{n2.34\ \ldots\ (n-1)} = b_{n2.13\ \ldots\ (n-1)} + b_{n1.23\ \ldots\ n-1} \cdot b_{12.34\ \ldots\ (n-1)}.$$

Substituting this value for $b_{n2.34\ \ldots\ (n-1)}$ in the first equation we have

$$b_{12.34\ \ldots\ (n-1)} = \frac{b_{12.34\ \ldots\ n} + b_{1n.23\ \ldots\ (n-1)} \cdot b_{n2.13\ \ldots\ (n-1)}}{1 - b_{1n.23\ \ldots\ (n-1)} \cdot b_{n1.23\ \ldots\ (n-1)}}. \quad (16)$$

This is the required equation for the regressions; it is the equation

$$b_{12} = \frac{b_{12.n} + b_{1n.2} \cdot b_{n2.1}}{1 - b_{1n.2} \cdot b_{n1.2}}$$

with secondary suffixes $34 \ldots (n-1)$ added throughout. The corresponding equation for the correlations is obtained at once by writing down equation (16) for $b_{21.34\ \ldots\ (n-1)}$ and taking the square root of the product (*cf.* § 13); this gives

$$r_{12.34\ \ldots\ (n-1)} = \frac{r_{12.34\ \ldots\ n} + r_{1n.23\ \ldots\ (n-1)} \cdot r_{2n.13\ \ldots\ (n-1)}}{(1 - r^2_{1n.23\ \ldots\ (n-1)})^{\frac{1}{2}}(1 - r^2_{2n.13\ \ldots\ (n-1)})^{\frac{1}{2}}}. \quad (17)$$

which is similarly the equation

$$r_{12} = \frac{r_{12.n} + r_{1n.2} \cdot r_{2n.1}}{(1 - r_{1n.2}^2)^{\frac{1}{2}}(1 - r_{2n.1}^2)^{\frac{1}{2}}}$$

with the secondary suffixes 34 .... $(n-1)$ added throughout.

18. Equations (12) and (17) imply that certain limiting inequalities must hold between the correlation-coefficients in the expression on the right in each case in order that real values (values between ± 1) may be obtained for the correlation-coefficient on the left. These inequalities correspond precisely with those "conditions of consistence" between class-frequencies with which we dealt in Chapter II., but we propose to treat them only briefly here. Writing (12) in its simplest form for $r_{12.3}$, we must have $r_{12.3}^2 < 1$ or

$$\frac{(r_{12} - r_{13} \cdot r_{23})^2}{(1 - r_{13}^2)(1 - r_{23}^2)} < 1.$$

that is,

$$r_{12}^2 + r_{13}^2 + r_{23}^2 - 2r_{12}r_{13}r_{23} < 1 \quad . \quad . \quad . \quad (18)$$

if the three r's are consistent with each other. If we take r_{12}, r_{13} as known, this gives as limits for r_{23}

$$r_{12}r_{13} \pm \sqrt{1 - r_{12}^2 - r_{13}^2 + r_{12}^2 r_{13}^2}.$$

Similarly writing (17) in its simplest form for r_{12} in terms of $r_{12.3}$, $r_{13.2}$ and $r_{23.1}$, we must have

$$r_{12.3}^2 + r_{13.2}^2 + r_{23.1}^2 + 2r_{12.3}r_{13.2}r_{23.1} < 1 \quad . \quad . \quad (19)$$

and therefore, if $r_{12.3}$ and $r_{13.2}$ are given, $r_{23.1}$ must lie between the limits

$$-r_{12.3}r_{13.2} \pm \sqrt{1 - r_{12.3}^2 - r_{13.2}^2 + r_{12.3}^2 r_{13.2}^2}.$$

The following table gives the limits of the third coefficient in a few special cases, for the three coefficients of zero order and of the first order respectively :—

Value of		Limits of	
r_{12} or $r_{12.3}$	r_{13} or $r_{13.2}$	r_{23}.	$r_{23.1}$.
0	0	± 1	± 1
± 1	± 1	$+1$	-1
± 1	∓ 1	-1	$+1$
$\pm \sqrt{0.5}$	$\pm \sqrt{0.5}$	$0, +1$	$0, -1$
$\pm \sqrt{0.5}$	$\mp \sqrt{0.5}$	$0, -1$	$0, +1$

The student should notice that the set of three coefficients of order zero and value unity are only consistent if either one only, or all three, are positive, *i.e.* $+1$, $+1$, $+1$, or -1, -1, $+1$; but not -1, -1, -1. On the other hand, the set of three coefficients of the first order and value unity are only consistent if one only, or all three, are negative : the only consistent sets are $+1$, $+1$, -1 and -1, -1, -1. The values of the two given r's need to be very high if even the sign of the third can be inferred; if the two are equal, they must be at least equal to $\sqrt{0.5}$ or $\cdot707$ . . . . Finally, it may be noted that no two values for the known coefficients ever permit an inference of the value zero for the third; the fact that 1 and 2, 1 and 3 are uncorrelated, pair and pair, permits no inference of any kind as to the correlation between 2 and 3, which may lie anywhere between $+1$ and -1.

19. We do not think it necessary to add to this chapter a detailed discussion of the nature of fallacies on which the theory of multiple correlation throws much light. The general nature of such fallacies is the same as for the case of attributes, and was discussed fully in Chap. IV. §§ 1-8. It suffices to point out the principal sources of fallacy which are suggested at once by the form of the partial correlation

$$r_{12.3} = \frac{r_{12} - r_{13} \cdot r_{23}}{\sqrt{(1 - r_{13}^2)(1 - r_{23}^2)}} \qquad . \quad . \quad . \quad (a)$$

and from the form of the corresponding expression for r_{12} in terms of the partial coefficients

$$r_{12} = \frac{r_{12.3} + r_{13.2} \cdot r_{23.1}}{\sqrt{(1 - r_{13.2}^2)(1 - r_{23.1}^2)}} \qquad . \quad . \quad . \quad (b)$$

From the form of the numerator of (a) it is evident (1) that even if r_{12} be zero, $r_{12.3}$ will not be zero unless either r_{13} or r_{23}, or both, are zero. If r_{13} and r_{23} are of the same sign the partial correlation will be negative; if of opposite sign, positive. Thus the quantity of a crop might appear to be unaffected, say, by the amount of rainfall during some period preceding harvest : this might be due merely to a correlation between rain and low temperature, the partial correlation between crop and rainfall being positive and important. We may thus easily misinterpret a coefficient of correlation which is zero. (2) $r_{12.3}$ may be, indeed often is, of opposite sign to r_{12}, and this may lead to still more serious errors of interpretation.

From the form of the numerator of (b), on the other hand, we see that, conversely, r_{12} will not be zero even though $r_{12.3}$ is zero, unless either $r_{13.2}$ or $r_{23.1}$ is zero. This corresponds to the theorem of Chap. IV. § 6, and indicates a source of fallacies similar to those there discussed.

20. We have seen (§ 9) that $r_{12.3}$ is the correlation between $x_{1.3}$ and $x_{2.3}$, and that we might determine the value of this partial correlation by drawing up the actual correlation table for the two residuals in question. Suppose, however, that instead of drawing up a single table we drew up a series of tables for values of $x_{1.3}$ and $x_{2.3}$ associated with values of x_3 lying within successive class-intervals of its range. In general the value of $r_{12.3}$ would not be the same (or approximately the same) for all such tables, but would exhibit some systematic change as the value of x_3 increased. Hence $r_{12.3}$ should be regarded, in general, as of the nature of an average correlation: the cases in which it measures the correlation between $x_{1.3}$ and $x_{2.3}$ for *every* value of x_3 (*cf.* Chap. XVI.) are probably exceptional. The process for determining partial associations (*cf.* Chap. IV.) is, it will be remembered, thorough and complete, as we always obtain the actual tables exhibiting the association between, say, A and B in the universe of C's and the universe of γ's : that these two associations may differ materially, is illustrated by Example i. of Chap. IV. (pp. 45–6). It might sometimes serve as a useful check on partial-correlation work to reclassify the observations by the fundamental methods of that chapter. For the general case an extension of the method of the "correlation-ratio" (Chap. X., § 20) might be useful, though exceedingly laborious. It is actually employed in the paper cited in ref. 7 and the theory more fully developed in ref. 8.

REFERENCES.

The preceding chapter is written from the standpoint of refs. 3 and 4, and with the notation and method of ref. 5. The theory of correlation for several variables was developed by Edgeworth and Pearson (refs. 1 and 2) from the standpoint of the "normal" distribution of frequency (*cf.* Chap. XVI.).

Theory.

(1) EDGEWORTH, F. Y., "On Correlated Averages," *Phil. Mag.*, 5th Series, vol. xxxiv., 1892, p. 194.
(2) PEARSON, KARL, "Regression, Heredity, and Panmixia," *Phil. Trans. Roy. Soc.*, Series A, vol. clxxxvii., 1896, p. 253.
(3) YULE, G. U., "On the Significance of Bravais' Formulæ for Regression, etc., in the case of Skew Correlation," *Proc. Roy. Soc.*, vol. lx., 1897, p. 477.
(4) YULE, G. U., "On the Theory of Correlation," *Jour. Roy. Stat. Soc.*, vol. lx., 1897, p. 812.
(5) YULE, G. U., "On the Theory of Correlation for any number of Variables treated by a New System of Notation," *Proc. Roy. Soc.*, Series A, vol. lxxix., 1907, p. 182.
(6) HOOKER, R. H., and G. U. YULE, "Note on Estimating the Relative Influence of Two Variables upon a Third," *Jour. Roy. Stat. Soc.*, vol. lxix., 1906, p. 197.
(7) BROWN, J. W., M. GREENWOOD, and FRANCES WOOD, "A Study of Index-Correlations," *Jour. Roy. Stat. Soc.*, vol. lxxvii., 1914, pp. 317-46. (The partial or "solid" correlation-ratio is used.)
(8) ISSERLIS, L., "On the Partial Correlation-Ratio, Pt. I. Theoretical," *Biometrika*, vol. x., 1914, pp. 391-411.

Illustrative Applications of Economic Interest.

(9) YULE, G. U., " An Investigation into the Causes of Changes in Pauperism in England, etc.," *Jour. Roy. Stat. Soc.*, vol. lxii., 1899, p. 249.

(10) HOOKER, R. H., "The Correlation of the Weather and the Crops," *Jour. Roy. Stat. Soc.*, vol. lxx., 1907, p. 1.

(11) SNOW, E. C.. "The Application of the Method of Multiple Correlation to the Estimation of Post-censal Populations," *Jour. Roy. Stat. Soc.*, vol. lxxiv., 1911, p. 575.

EXERCISES.

1. (Ref. 10.) The following means, standard-deviations, and correlations are found for

X_1 = seed-hay crops in cwts. per acre,
X_2 = spring rainfall in inches,
X_3 = accumulated temperature above 42° F. in spring,

in a certain district of England during 20 years.

$$M_1 = 28 \cdot 02 \qquad \sigma_1 = 4 \cdot 42 \qquad r_{12} = +0 \cdot 80$$
$$M_2 = 4 \cdot 91 \qquad \sigma_2 = 1 \cdot 10 \qquad r_{13} = -0 \cdot 40$$
$$M_3 = 594 \qquad \sigma_3 = 85 \qquad r_{23} = -0 \cdot 56$$

Find the partial correlations and the regression-equation for hay-crop on spring rainfall and accumulated temperature.

2. (The following figures must be taken as an illustration only : the data on which they were based do not refer to uniform times or areas.)

X_1 = deaths of infants under 1 year per 1000 births in same year (infantile mortality).

X_2 = proportion per thousand of married women occupied for gain.

X_3 = death-rate of persons over 5 years of age per 10,000.

X_4 = proportion per thousand of population living 2 or more to a room (overcrowding).

Taking the figures below for 30 urban areas in England and Wales, find the partial correlations and the regression-equation for infantile mortality on the other factors.

$$M_1 = 164 \qquad \sigma_1 = 20 \cdot 0 \qquad r_{12} = +0 \cdot 49 \qquad r_{23} = +0 \cdot 15$$
$$M_2 = 158 \qquad \sigma_2 = 74 \cdot 9 \qquad r_{13} = +0 \cdot 78 \qquad r_{24} = -0 \cdot 37$$
$$M_3 = 143 \qquad \sigma_3 = 22 \cdot 4 \qquad r_{14} = +0 \cdot 20 \qquad r_{34} = +0 \cdot 23$$
$$M_4 = 205 \qquad \sigma_4 = 130 \cdot 0$$

3. If all the correlations of order zero are equal, say = r, what are the values of the partial correlations of successive orders ?

Under the same condition, what is the limiting value of r if all the equal correlations are negative and n variables have been observed ?

4. What is the correlation between $x_{1.2}$ and $x_{2.1}$?

5. Write down from inspection the values of the partial correlations for the three variables

$$X_1, \ X_2, \text{ and } X_3 = a \cdot X_1 + b \cdot X_2.$$

Check the answer to Qu. 7, Chap. XI., by working out the partial correlations.

6. If the relation

$$a \cdot x_1 + b \cdot x_2 + c \cdot x_3 = 0$$

holds for all sets of values of x_1, x_2, and x_3, what must the partial correlations be ?

Check the answer to Qu. 9, Chap. XI., by working out the partial correlations.

PART III.—THEORY OF SAMPLING.

CHAPTER XIII.

SIMPLE SAMPLING OF ATTRIBUTES.

1. On several occasions in the preceding chapters it has been pointed out that small differences between statistical measures like percentages, averages, measures of dispersion and so forth cannot in general be assumed to indicate the action of definite and assignable causes. Small differences may easily arise from indefinite and highly complex causation such as determines the fluctuating proportions of heads and tails in tossing a coin, of black balls in drawing samples from a bag containing a mixture of black and white balls, or of cards bearing measurements within some given class-interval in drawing cards, say, from an anthropometric record. In 100 throws of a coin, for example, we may have noted 56 heads and only 44 tails, but we cannot conclude that the coin is biassed: on repeating our throws we may get only 48 heads and 52 tails. Similarly, if on measuring the statures of 1000 men in each of two nations we find that the mean stature is slightly greater for

254

nation A than for nation B, we cannot necessarily conclude that the real mean stature is greater in the case of nation A : possibly if the observations were repeated on different samples of 1000 men the ratio might be reversed.

2. The theory of such fluctuations may be termed the **theory of sampling**, and there are two chief sections of the theory corresponding to the theory of attributes and the theory of variables respectively. In tossing a coin we only classify the results of the tosses as heads or tails ; in drawing balls from a mixture of black and white balls, we only classify the balls drawn as black or as white. These cases correspond to the theory of attributes, and the general case may be represented as the drawing of a sample from a universe containing both A's and a's, the number or proportion of A's in successive samples being observed. If, on the other hand, we put in a bag a number of cards bearing different values of some variable X and draw sample batches of cards, we can form averages and measures of dispersion for the successive batches, and these averages and measures of dispersion will vary slightly from one batch to another. If associated measures of two variables X and Y are recorded on each card, we can also form correlation-coefficients for the different batches, and these will vary in a similar manner. These cases correspond to the theory of variables, and it is the function of the theory of sampling for such cases to inform us as to the fluctuations to be expected in the averages, measures of dispersion, correlation-coefficients, etc., in successive samples. In the present and the three following chapters the theory of sampling is dealt with for the case of attributes alone. The theory is of great importance and interest, not only from its applications to the checking and control of statistical results, but also from the theoretical forms of frequency-distribution to which it leads. Finally, in Chapter XVII. one or two of the more important cases of the theory of sampling for variables are briefly treated, the greater part of the theory, owing to its difficulty, lying somewhat outside the limits of this work.

3. The theory of sampling attains its greatest simplicity if every observation contributed to the sample may be regarded as independent of every other. This condition of independence holds good, *e.g.*, for the tossing of a coin or the throwing of a die : the result of any one throw or toss does not affect, and is unaffected by, the results of the preceding and following tosses. It does not hold good, on the other hand, for the drawing of balls from a bag : if a ball be drawn from a bag containing 3 black and 3 white balls, the remainder may be either 2 black and 3 white, or 2 white and 3 black, according as the first ball was black or white. The result of drawing a second ball is therefore

dependent on the result of drawing the first. The disturbance can only be eliminated by drawing from a bag containing a number of balls that is infinitely large compared with the total number drawn, or by returning each ball to the bag before drawing the next. In this chapter our attention will be confined to the case of independent sampling, as in coin-tossing or dice-throwing—the simplest cases of an artificial kind suitable for theoretical study and experimental verification. For brevity, we may refer to such cases of sampling as simple sampling : the implied conditions are discussed more fully in § 8 below.

4. If we may regard an ideal coin as a uniform, homogeneous circular disc, there is nothing which can make it tend to fall more often on the one side than on the other; we may expect, therefore, that in any long series of throws the coin will fall with either face uppermost an approximately equal number of times, or with, say, heads uppermost approximately half the times. Similarly, if we may regard the ideal die as a perfect homogeneous cube, it will tend, in any long series of throws, to fall with each of its six faces uppermost an approximately equal number of times, or with any given face uppermost one-sixth of the whole number of times. These results are sometimes expressed by saying that the chance of throwing heads (or tails) with a coin is $1/2$, and the chance of throwing six (or any other face) with a die is $1/6$. To avoid speaking of such particular instances as coins or dice, we shall in future, using terms which have become conventional, refer to an *event* the chance of *success* of which is p and the chance of *failure* q. Obviously $p + q = 1$.

5. Suppose we take N samples with n events in each. What will be the values towards which the mean and standard-deviation of the number of successes in a sample will tend ? The mean is given at once, for there are $N.n$ events, of which approximately pNn will be successes, and the mean number of successes in a sample will therefore tend towards pn. As regards the standard-deviation, consider first the single event ($n = 1$). The single event may give either no successes or one success, and will tend to give the former qN, the latter pN, times in N trials. Take this frequency-distribution and work out the standard-deviation of the number of successes for the single event, as in the case of an arithmetical example :—

Frequency f.	Successes ξ.	$f\xi$.	$f\xi^2$.
qN	0	—	—
pN	1	pN	pN
N	—	pN	pN

We have therefore $M = p$, and

$$\sigma_1^2 = p - p^2 = pq.$$

But the number of successes in a group of n such events is the sum of successes for the single events of which it is composed, and, all the events being independent, we have therefore, by the usual rule for the standard-deviation of the sum of independent variables (Chap. XI. § 2, equation (2)), σ_n being the standard-deviation of the number of successes in n events,

$$\sigma_n^2 = npq \quad . \qquad . \qquad . \qquad . \qquad (1)$$

This is an equation of fundamental importance in the theory of sampling. The student should particularly bear in mind that the standard-deviation of the number of successes, due to fluctuations of simple sampling alone, in a group of n events varies, not directly as n, but as the square root of n.

6. In lieu of recording the absolute number of successes in each sample of n events, we might have recorded the proportion of such successes, i.e. $1/n$th of the number in each sample. As this would amount to merely dividing all the figures of the original record by n, the mean proportion of successes—or rather the value towards which the mean tends to approach—must be p, and the standard-deviation of the proportion of successes s_n be given by

$$s_n^2 = \sigma_n^2 / n^2 = pq/n \quad . \qquad . \qquad . \qquad . \qquad (2)$$

The standard-deviation of the proportion of successes in samples of such independent events varies therefore inversely as the square root of the number on which the proportion is calculated. Now if we regard the observed proportion in any one sample as a more or less unreliable determination of the true proportion in a very large sample from the same material, the standard-deviation of sampling may fairly be taken as a measure of the *unreliability* of the determination—the greater the standard-deviation, the greater the fluctuations of the observed proportion, although the true proportion is the same throughout. The reciprocal of the standard-deviation $(1/s)$, on the other hand, may be regarded as a measure of *reliability*, or, as it is sometimes termed, *precision*, and consequently *the reliability or precision of an observed proportion varies as the square root of the number of observations on which it is based*. This is again a very important rule with many practical applications, but the limitations of the case to which it applies, and the exact conditions from which it has been deduced, should be borne in mind. We return to this point again below (§ 8 and Chap. XIV.).

7. Experiments in coin tossing, dice throwing, and so forth have been carried out by various persons in order to obtain ex-

perimental verification of these results. The following will serve
as illustrations, but the student is strongly recommended to
carry out a few series of such experiments personally, in order to
acquire confidence in the use of the theory. It may be as well
to remark that if ordinary commercial dice are to be used for the
trials, care should be taken to see that they are fairly true cubes,
and the marks not cut very deeply. Cheap dice are generally
very much out of truth, and if the marks are deeply cut the
balance of the die may be sensibly affected. A convenient mode
of throwing a number of dice, suggested, we believe, by the late
Professor Weldon, is to roll them down an inclined gutter of
corrugated paper, so that they roll across the corrugations.

(1) (W. F. R. Weldon, cited by Professor F. Y. Edgeworth,
Encycl. Brit., 11th edn., vol. xxii. p. 394. Totals of the columns
in the table there given.)

Twelve dice were thrown 4096 times ; a throw of 4, 5, or 6 points
reckoned a success, therefore $p = q = 0\cdot5$. Theoretical mean $M = 6$;
theoretical value of the standard-deviation $\sigma_{12} = \sqrt{0\cdot5 \times 0\cdot5 \times 12} =$
$1\cdot732$.

The following was the frequency-distribution observed :—

Successes.	Frequency.	Successes.	Frequency.
0	—	7	847
1	7	8	536
2	60	9	257
3	198	10	71
4	430	11	11
5·	731	12	—
6	948	Total	4096

Mean $M = 6\cdot139$, standard-deviation $\sigma = 1\cdot712$. The proportion of
successes is $6\cdot139/12 = 0\cdot512$ instead of $0\cdot5$.

(2) (W. F. R. Weldon, *loc. cit.*, p. 400. Totals of columns of
the table given.)

Twelve dice were thrown 4096 times ; only a throw of 6 was
counted a success, so $p = 1/6$, $q = 5/6$. Theoretical mean $M = 2$,
standard-deviation $\sigma = \sqrt{1/6 \times 5/6 \times 12} = 1\cdot291$.

The following was the observed frequency-distribution :—

Successes.	Frequency.	Successes.	Frequency.
0	447	5	115
1	1145	6	24·
2	1181	7	7
3	796	8	1
4	380	Total	4096

Mean $M = 2\cdot000$, standard-deviation $\sigma = 1\cdot296$. Actual proportion of successes $2\cdot00/12 = 0\cdot1667$, agreeing with the theoretical value to the fourth place of decimals. Of course such very close agreement is accidental, and not to be always expected.

(3) (G. U. Yule.) The following may be taken as an illustration based on a smaller number of observations. Three dice were thrown 648 times, and the numbers of 5's or 6's noted at each throw. $p = 1/3$, $q = 2/3$. Theoretical mean 1. Standard-deviation, $0\cdot816$.

Frequency-distribution observed :—

Successes.	Frequency.
0	179
1	298
2	141
3	30
Total	648

$M = 1\cdot034$, $\sigma = 0\cdot823$. Actual proportion of successes $0\cdot345$.

For other illustrations, some of which are cited in the questions at the end of this chapter, the student may be referred to the list of references on p. 273. The student should notice that in all the distributions given a range of six times the standard-deviation includes either all, or the great bulk of, the observations, as in most frequency-distributions of the same general form. We shall make use of this rule below, § 13.

8. In deducing the formulæ (1) and (2) for the standard-deviations of *simple* sampling in the cases with which we have been dealing, only one condition has been explicitly laid down as necessary, viz. the independence of the several drawings, tossings, or other events composing the sample. But in point of fact this is not the only nor the most fundamental condition which has been explicitly or implicitly assumed, and it is necessary to realise all the conditions in order to grasp the limitations under which alone the formulæ arrived at will hold. Supposing, for example, that we observe among groups of 1000 persons, at different times or in different localities, various percentages of individuals possessing certain characteristics—dark hair, or blindness, or insanity, and so forth. Under what conditions should we expect the observed percentages to obey the law of sampling that we have found, and show a standard-deviation given by equation (2)?

(a) In the first place we have tacitly assumed throughout the preceding work that our dice or our coins were the same set or identically similar throughout the experiment, so that the chance of throwing "heads" with the coins or, say, "six" with the dice was the same throughout: we did not commence an experiment with dice loaded in one way and later on take a fresh set of dice loaded in another way. Consequently if formula (2) is to hold good in our practical case of sampling there must not be a difference in any essential respect—*i.e.* in any character that can affect the proportion observed—between the localities from which the observations are drawn, nor, if the observations have been made at different epochs, must any essential change have taken place during the period over which the observations are spread. Where the causation of the character observed is more or less unknown, it may, of course, be difficult or impossible to say what differences or changes are to be regarded as essential, but, where we have more knowledge, the condition laid down enables us to exclude certain cases at once from the possible applications of formula (1) or (2). Thus it is obvious that the theory of simple sampling cannot apply to the variations of the death-rate in localities with populations of different age and sex compositions, nor to death-rates in a mixture of healthy and unhealthy districts, nor to death-rates in successive years during a period of continuously improving sanitation. In all such cases variations due to definite causes are superposed on the fluctuations of sampling.

(*b*) In the second place, we have also tacitly assumed not only that we were using the same set of coins or dice throughout, so that the chances p and q were the same at every trial, but also that all the coins and dice in the set used were identically similar, so that the chances p and q were the same for every coin or die. Consequently, if our formulæ are to apply in the practical case of sampling, the conditions that regulate the appearance of the character observed must not only be the same for every sample, but also for every individual in every sample. This is again a very marked limitation. To revert to the case of death-rates, formulæ (1) and (2) would not apply to the numbers of persons dying in a series of samples of 1000 persons, even if these samples were all of the same age and sex composition, and living under the same sanitary conditions, unless, further, each sample only contained persons of one sex and one age. For if each sample included persons of both sexes and different ages, the condition would be broken, the chance of death during a given period not being the same for the two sexes, nor for the young and the old. The groups would not be homogeneous in the sense required by the conditions from which our formulæ have been deduced. Similarly, if we were observing hair-colours, our formulæ would not apply if the samples were compounded by always taking one person from district A, another from district B, and so on, these districts not being similar as regards the distribution of hair-colour.

The above conditions were only tacitly assumed in our previous work, and consequently it has been necessary to emphasise them specially. The third condition was explicitly stated : (c) The individual "events," or appearances of the character observed, must be completely independent of one another, like the throws of a die, or sensibly so, like the drawings of balls from a bag containing a number of balls that is very large compared with the number drawn. Reverting to the illustration of a death-rate, our formulæ would not apply even if the sample populations were composed of persons of one age and one sex, if we were dealing, for example, with deaths from an infectious or contagious disease. For if one person in a certain sample has contracted the disease in question, he has increased the possibility of others doing so, and hence of dying from the disease. The same thing holds good for certain classes of deaths from accident, e.g. railway accidents due to derailment, and explosions in mines : if such an accident is fatal to one person it is probably fatal to others also, and consequently the annual returns show large and more or less erratic variations.

When we speak of simple sampling in the following pages, the term is intended to imply the fulfilment of all the conditions (a), (b), and (c), all the samples and all the individual contributions to each sample being taken under precisely the same conditions, and the individual "events" or appearances of the character being quite independent. It may be as well expressly to note that we need not make any assumption as to the conditions that determine p unless we have to estimate $\sqrt{npq}$ a priori. If we draw a sample and observe in it the actual proportion of, say, A's : draw another sample under precisely the same conditions, and observe the proportion of A's in the two samples together : add to these a third sample, and so on, we will find that p approaches —not continuously, but with some fluctuations—closer and closer to some limiting value. It is this limiting value which is to be used in our formulæ—the value of p that would be observed in a very large sample. The standard-deviation of the number of sixes thrown with n dice, on this understanding, may be $\sqrt{npq}$, even if the dice be out of truth or loaded so that p is no longer $1/6$. Similarly, the standard-deviation of the number of black balls in samples of n drawn from an infinitely large mixture of black and white balls in equal proportions may be $\sqrt{npq}$ even if p is, say, 1/3, and not 1/2 owing to the black balls, for some reason, tending to slip through our fingers. (*Cf.* Chap. XIV. § 4.)

9. It is evident that these conditions very much limit the field of practical cases of an economic or sociological character to which formulæ (1) and (2) can apply without considerable modification. The formulæ appear, however, to hold to a high degree of approximation in certain biological cases, notably in the proportions of offspring of different types obtained on crossing hybrids, and, with some limitations, to the proportions of the two sexes at birth. It is possible, accordingly, that in these cases all the necessary conditions are fulfilled, but this is not a necessary inference from the mere applicability of the formulæ (*cf.* Chap. XIV. § 15). In the case of the sex-ratio at birth, it seems doubtful whether the rule applies to the frequency of the sexes in individual families of given numbers (ref. 9), but it does apply fairly closely to the sex-ratios of births in different localities, and still more closely to the ratios in one locality during successive periods. That is to say, if we note the number of males in a series of groups of n births each, the standard-deviation of that number is approximately $\sqrt{npq}$, where p is the chance of a male birth; or, otherwise, $\sqrt{pq/n}$ is the standard-deviation of the proportion of male births. We are not able to assign an *a priori* value to the chance p as in the case of dice-throwing, but it is quite sufficiently accurate for practical purposes to use the proportion of male births actually observed if that proportion be based on a moderately large number of observations.

10. In Table VI. of Chap. IX. (p. 163) was given a correlation-table between the total numbers of births in the registration districts of England and Wales during the decade 1881–90 and the proportion of male births. The table below gives some similar figures, based on the same data, for a few isolated groups of districts containing not less than 30 to 40 districts each. In both tables the drop in dispersion as we pass from the small to the large districts is extremely striking. The actual standard-deviations, and the standard-deviations of simple sampling corresponding to the mid-numbers of births, are given at the foot of the table, and it will be seen that the two agree, on the whole, with surprising closeness, considering the small numbers of observations. The actual standard-deviation is, however, the larger of the two in every case but one. The corresponding standard-deviations for Table VI. of Chap. IX. are given in Qu. 7 at the end of this chapter, and show the same general agreement with the standard-deviations of simple sampling; the actual standard-deviations are, however, again, as a rule, slightly in excess of the theoretical values.

TABLE *showing Frequencies of Registration Districts in England and Wales with Different Ratios of Male to Total Births during the Decade 1881–90, for Groups of Districts with the Numbers of Births in the Decade lying between Certain Limits.* [Data based on *Decennial Supplement to Fifty-fifth Annual Report of the Registrar-General for England and Wales.*]

Male Births per Thousand Total Births.	Number of Births in Decade.						
	1500 to 2500.	3500 to 4000.	4500 to 5000.	10,000 to 15,000.	15,000 to 20,000.	30,000 to 50,000.	50,000 to 90,000.
466–67	1	—	—	—	—	—	—
482– 3	1	—	—	—	—	—	—
492– 3	1	—	1	—	—	—	—
494– 5	1	—	1	—	—	—	—
496– 7	2	3	—	—	—	—	—
498– 9	—	1	—	—	—	1	—
500– 1	2	4	2	1	—	—	—
502– 3	3	3	3	3	—	—	—
504– 5	3	1	3	10	4	4	6
506– 7	5	5	3	6	6	6	10
508– 9	—	3	3	9	4	16	12
510– 1	4	3	9	15	5	8	5
512– 3	1	5	2	8	9	4	2
514– 5	2	2	3	10	2	3	—
516– 7	—	3	3	5	2	1	—
518– 9	4	—	3	4	—	—	—
520– 1	1	—	1	—	1	—	—
522– 3	2	1	3	1	—	—	—
524– 5	1	2	—	—	—	—	—
526– 7	1	1	—	1	—	—	—
528– 9	—	—	—	—	—	—	—
530– 1	—	1	—	—	—	—	—
532– 3	—	—	—	—	—	—	—
534– 5	—	—	—	—	—	—	—
536– 7	1	—	—	—	—	—	—
Total	36	38	40	73	33	43	35
Mean	508·2	509·5	510·2	510·6	510·3	509·0	507·8
Standard deviation s	12·8	8·53	7·12	4·98	3·87	3·22	2·20
Theo. st. deviation corresponding to mean births s_0	11·2	8·16	7·25	4·47	3·78	2·50	1·89
$\sqrt{s^2 - s_0^2}$ *	6·2	2·5	—	2·2	0·8	2·0	1·1

* The meaning of this expression is explained in § 10 of Chap. XIV.

The student should note that in both cases the standard-deviations given are standard-deviations of the proportion of male births *per 1000 of all births*, that is, 1000 times the values given by equation (2). These values are given by simply substituting the proportions per 1000 for p and q in the formula. Thus for the first column of Table I. the proportion of males is 508 per 1000 births, the mid-number of births 2000, and therefore—

$$s_0 = \left(\frac{508 \times 492}{2000}\right)^{\frac{1}{2}} = 11 \cdot 2.$$

11. In the above illustration the difficulty due to the wide variation in the number of births n in different districts has been surmounted by grouping these districts in limited class intervals, and assuming that it would be sufficiently accurate for practical purposes to treat all the districts in one class as if the sex-ratios had been based on the mid-numbers of births. Given a sufficiently large number of observations, such a process does well enough, though it is not very good. But if the number of observations does not exceed, perhaps, 50 or 60 altogether, grouping is obviously out of the question, and some other procedure must be adopted.

Suppose, then, that a series of samples have been taken from the same material, f_1 samples containing n_1 individuals or observations each, f_2 containing n_2, f_3 containing n_3, and so on: What would be the standard-deviation of the observed proportions in these samples? Evidently the square of the standard-deviation in the first group would be pq/n_1, in the second pq/n_2, and so on: therefore, as the means tend to the same values in all the groups, we must have for the whole series—

$$N.S^2 = pq\left(\frac{f_1}{n_1} + \frac{f_2}{n_2} + \frac{f_3}{n_3} + \ \ . \ \ . \ \ . \right).$$

But if H be the harmonic mean of $n_1 \ n_2 \ n_3 \ . \ . \ . \ .$

$$\frac{N}{H} = \frac{f_1}{n_1} + \frac{f_2}{n_2} + \frac{f_3}{n_3} + \ . \ . \ . \ .$$

and accordingly

$$S^2 = \frac{pq}{H} \ . \qquad . \qquad . \qquad . \qquad . \quad (3)$$

That is to say, where the number of observations varies from one sample to another, the harmonic mean number of observations in a sample must be substituted for n in equation (2).

Thus the following percentages (taken to the nearest unit) of albinos were obtained in 121 litters from hybrids of Japanese waltzing mice by albinos, crossed *inter se* (A. D. Darbishire, *Biometrika*, iii. p. 30):—

Percentage.	Frequency.	Percentage.	Frequency.
0	40	40	3
14	4	43	2
17	9	50	16
20	9	57	1
22	1	60	3
25	10	67	4
29	3	80	1
33	13	100	2

The distribution is very irregular owing to the small numbers in the litters, and the standard-deviation is 23·09 per cent. The numbers of litters of different sizes were given in § 27 of Chap. VII. p. 128, and the harmonic mean size of litter was found to be 3·53. The expected proportion of albinos is 25 per cent., and hence the standard-deviation of sampling is

$$\left(\frac{25 \times 75}{3\cdot53}\right)^{\frac{1}{2}} = 23\cdot05,$$

in very close agreement with the actual value. The proportion of albinos amongst all the offspring together was 24·7 per cent.

12. If one of the two proportions p and q become very small, equation (1) may be put into an approximate form that is very useful. Suppose p to be the proportion that becomes very small, so that we may neglect p^2 compared with p : then

$$pq = p - p^2 = p \text{ approximately,}$$

and consequently we have approximately

$$\sigma_n = \sqrt{n.p} = \sqrt{M} \qquad . \qquad . \qquad . \qquad (4)$$

That is to say, *if the proportion of successes be small, the standard-deviation of the number of successes is the square root of the mean number of successes.* Hence we can find the standard-deviation of sampling even though p be unknown, provided only we know that it is small.

Thus (ref. 15) in 10 Prussian army corps in 20 years (1875–1894) there were 122 men killed by the kick of a horse, or, on an average, there were 0·61 deaths from that cause in each army corps annually. From equation (4) we accordingly have for the standard-deviation of simple sampling.

$$\sigma = (0\cdot61)^{\frac{1}{2}} = 0\cdot78.$$

The frequency-distribution of the number of deaths per army
corps per annum was

Deaths.	Frequency.
0	109
1	65
2	22
3	3
4	1

whence

$$\sigma^2 = 0.6079$$
$$\sigma = 0.78$$

—an almost exact agreement with the standard-deviation of simple
sampling.

13. We may now turn from these verifications of the theoretical
results for various special cases, to the use of the formulæ for
checking and controlling the interpretation of statistical results.
If we observe, in a statistical sample, a certain proportion of
objects or individuals possessing some given character—say A's—
this proportion differing more or less from the proportion which
for some reason we expected, the question always arises whether
the difference may be due to the fluctuations of simple sampling
only, or may be indicative of definite differences between the
conditions in the universe from which the sample has been drawn
and the assumed conditions on which we based our expectation.
Similarly, if we observe a different proportion in one sample from
that which we have observed in another, the question again arises
whether this difference may be due to fluctuations of simple
sampling alone, or whether it indicates a difference between the
conditions subsisting in the universes from which the two samples
were drawn : in the latter case the difference is often said to be
significant.   These questions can be answered, though only more
or less roughly at present, by comparing the observed difference
with the standard-deviation of simple sampling.   We know
roughly that the great bulk at least of the fluctuations of sampling lie within a range of ± three times the standard-deviation ;
and if an observed difference from a theoretical result greatly
exceeds these limits it cannot be ascribed to a fluctuation of
"simple sampling" as defined in § 8 : it may therefore be significant.   The "standard-deviation of simple sampling" being the
basis of all such work, it is convenient to refer to it by a shorter
name.   The observed proportions of A's in given samples being
regarded as differing by larger or smaller errors from the true
proportion in a very large sample from the same material, the

"standard-deviation of simple sampling" may be regarded as a measure of the magnitude of such errors, and may be called accordingly the standard error.

Three principal cases of comparison may be distinguished.

Case I.—It is desired to know whether the deviation of a certain observed number or proportion from an expected theoretical value is possibly due to errors of sampling.

In this case the observed difference is to be compared with the standard error of the theoretical number or proportion, for the number of observations contained in the sample.

Example i.—In the first illustration of § 7, 25,145 throws of a 4, 5, or 6 were made in lieu of the 24,576 expected (out of 49,152 throws altogether). The excess is 569 throws. Is this excess possibly due to mere fluctuations of sampling?

The standard error is

$$\sigma = \sqrt{\tfrac{1}{2} \times \tfrac{1}{2} \times 49152}$$
$$= 110\cdot9.$$

The deviation observed is 5·1 times the standard error, and, practically speaking, could not occur as a fluctuation of simple sampling. It may perhaps indicate a slight bias in the dice.

The problem might, of course, have been attacked equally well from the standpoint of the *proportion* in lieu of the absolute number of 4's, 5's, or 6's thrown. This proportion is 0·5116 instead of the theoretical 0·5000, difference in excess 0·0116. The standard error of the proportion is

$$s = \sqrt{\tfrac{1}{2} \times \tfrac{1}{2} \times \frac{1}{49152}} = 0\cdot00226,$$

and the difference observed bears the same ratio to the standard error as before, as of course it must.

Example ii.—(Data from the *Second Report of the Evolution Committee of the Royal Society*, 1905, p. 72.)

Certain crosses of *Pisum sativum* gave 5321 yellow and 1804 green seeds. The expectation is 25 per cent. of green seeds, or 1781. Can the divergence from the exact theoretical result have arisen owing to errors of sampling only?

The numerical difference from the expected result is 23. The standard error is

$$\sigma = \sqrt{0\cdot25 \times 0\cdot75 \times 7125} = 36\cdot8.$$

Hence the divergence from theory is only some 3/5 of the standard error, and may very well have arisen owing simply to fluctuations of sampling.

Working from the observed *proportion* of green seeds, viz. $0·2532$ instead of the theoretical $0·25$, we have

$$s = \sqrt{0·25 \times 0·75/7125} = 0·0051,$$

and similarly the divergence from theory is only some 3/5 of the standard error, as before.

It should be noted that this method must not be used as a test of association by comparing the difference of (AB) from $(A)(B)/N$ with a standard error calculated from the latter value as a "theoretical number," for it is not a theoretical number given *a priori* as in the above illustrations, and (A) and (B) are themselves liable to errors of sampling. If we formed an association-table between the results of tossing two coins N times, $\sigma = \sqrt{N.\frac{1}{4}.\frac{3}{4}}$ would be the standard error for the divergence of (AB) from the *a priori* value $n/4$, not the standard error for differences of (AB) from $(A)(B)/N$, (A) and (B) being the numbers of heads thrown in the case of the first and the second coin respectively.

Case II.—Two samples from distinct materials or different universes give proportions of A's p_1 and p_2, the numbers of observations in the samples being n_1 and n_3 respectively. (a) Can the difference between the two proportions have arisen merely as a fluctuation of simple sampling, the two universes being really similar as regards the proportion of A's therein? (b) If the difference indicated were a real one, might it vanish, owing to fluctuations of sampling, in other samples taken in precisely the same way? This case corresponds to the testing of an association which is indicated by a comparison of the proportion of A's amongst B's and β's

(a) We have no theoretical expectation in this case as to the proportion of A's in the universe from which either sample has been taken.

Let us find, however, whether the observed difference between p_1 and p_2 may not have arisen solely as a fluctuation of simple sampling, the proportion of A's being really the same in both cases, and given, let us say, by the (weighted) mean proportion in our two samples together, *i.e.* by

$$p_0 = \frac{n_1 p_1 + n_2 p_2}{n_1 + n_2}$$

(the best guide that we have).

Let ϵ_1 ϵ_2 be the standard errors in the two samples, then

$$\epsilon_1^2 = p_0 q_0/n_1, \quad \epsilon_3^2 = p_0 q_0/n_2.$$

If the samples are simple samples in the sense of the previous work, then the mean difference between p_1 and p_2 will be zero, and the standard error of the difference ϵ_{12}, the samples being independent, will be given by

$$\epsilon_{12}^2 = p_0 q_0 \left(\frac{1}{n_1} + \frac{1}{n_2} \right) \quad . \quad . \quad . \quad . \quad (5)$$

If the observed difference is less than some three times ϵ_{12} it may have arisen as a fluctuation of simple sampling only.

(b) If, on the other hand, the proportions of A's are not the same in the material from which the two samples are drawn, but p_1 and p_2 are the true values of the proportions, the standard errors of sampling in the two cases are

$$\epsilon_1^2 = p_1 q_1 / n_1 \qquad \epsilon_2^2 = p_2 q_2 / n_2$$

and consequently

$$\epsilon_{12}^2 = \frac{p_1 q_1}{n_1} + \frac{p_2 q_2}{n_2} \quad . \quad . \quad . \quad . \quad (6)$$

If the difference between p_1 and p_2 does not exceed some three times this value of ϵ_{12}, it may be obliterated by an error of simple sampling on taking fresh samples in the same way from the same material.

Further, the student should note that the value of ϵ_{12} given by equation (6) is frequently employed, in lieu of that given by equation (5), for testing the significance of an observed difference. The justification of this usage we indicate briefly later (Chap. XIV, § 3). Here it is sufficient to state that, if n be large, equation (6) gives approximately the standard-deviation of the true values of the difference for a given observed value, and hence, if the observed difference is greater or less than some three times the value of ϵ_{12} given by (6), it is hardly possible that the true value of the difference can be zero. The difference between the values of ϵ_{12} given by (5) and (6) is indeed, as a rule, of more theoretical than practical importance, for they do not differ largely unless p_1 and p_2 differ largely, and in that case either formula will place the difference outside the range of fluctuations of sampling.

Example iii.—The following data were given in Qu. 3 of Chap. III. for plants of *Lobelia fulgens* obtained by cross- and self-fertilisation respectively :—

Parentage Cross-fertilised. Height—		Parentage Self-fertilised. Height—	
Above Average.	Below Average.	Above Average.	Below Average.
17	**17**	**12**	**22**

The figures indicate an association between tallness and cross-fertilisation of parentage. Is this association significant of some real difference, or may it have arisen solely as an "error of

sampling"? The proportion of plants above average height in the
two classes (cross- and self-fertilised) together is 29/68. The
standard-deviation of the differences due to simple sampling
between the proportions of "tall" plants in two samples of 34
observations each is therefore

$$\epsilon_{12} = \left(\frac{29}{68} \times \frac{39}{68} \times \frac{2}{34} \right)^{\frac{1}{2}} = 0.120,$$

or 12·0 per cent. The actual proportions observed are 50 per
cent. and 35 per cent.—difference 15 per cent. As this difference
is only slightly in excess of the standard error of the difference,
for samples of 34 observations drawn from identical material, no
definite significance could be attached to it—if it stood alone.

The student will notice, however, that all the other cases cited
from Darwin in the question referred to show an association of
the same sign, but rather more marked. Hence the difference
observed may be a real one, or perhaps the real difference may be
greater and may be partially masked by a fluctuation of sampling.
If 50 per cent. and 35 per cent. were the true proportions in the
two classes, the standard error of the percentage difference would
be, by equation (6),

$$\epsilon_{12} = \left(\frac{50 \times 50}{34} + \frac{35 \times 65}{34} \right)^{\frac{1}{2}} = 11.9 \text{ per cent.},$$

and consequently the actual difference might not infrequently be
completely masked by fluctuations of sampling, so long as experiments were only conducted on the same small scale.

Example iv.—(Data from J. Gray, Memoir on the Pigmentation
Survey of Scotland, *Jour. of the Royal Anthropological Institute*,
vol. xxxvii., 1907.) The following are extracted from the tables
relating to hair-colour of girls at Edinburgh and Glasgow :—

	Of Medium Hair-colour.	Total observed.	Per cent. Medium.
Edinburgh . .	4,008	9,743	41·1
Glasgow . .	17,529	39,764	44·1

Can the difference observed in the percentage of girls of medium
hair-colour have arisen solely through fluctuations of sampling?

In the two towns together the percentage of girls with medium
hair-colour is 43·5 per cent. If this were the true percentage,
the standard error of sampling for the difference between percentages observed in samples of the above sizes would be—

$$\epsilon_{12} = (43.5 \times 56.5)^{\frac{1}{2}} \times \left(\frac{1}{9743} + \frac{1}{39,764} \right)^{\frac{1}{2}}$$
$$= 0.56 \text{ per cent.}$$

The actual difference is $3 \cdot 0$ per cent., or over 5 times this, and could not have arisen through the chances of simple sampling.

If we assume that the difference is a real one and calculate the standard error by equation (6), we arrive at the same value, viz. $0 \cdot 56$ per cent. With such large samples the difference could not, accordingly, be obliterated by the fluctuations of simple sampling alone.

Case III.—Two samples are drawn from distinct material or different universes, as in the last case, giving proportions of A's p_1 and p_2, but in lieu of comparing the proportion p_1 with p_2 it is compared with the proportion of A's in the two samples together, viz. p_0, where, as before,

$$p_0 = \frac{n_1 p_1 + n_2 p_2}{n_1 + n_2}$$

Required to find whether the difference between p_1 and p_0 can have arisen as a fluctuation of simple sampling, p_0 being the true proportion of A's in both samples.

This case corresponds to the testing of an association which is indicated by a comparison of the proportion of A's amongst the B's with the proportion of A's in the universe. The general treatment is similar to that of Case II., but the work is complicated owing to the fact that errors in p_1 and p_0 are not independent.

If ϵ_{01} be the standard error of the difference between p_1 and p_0, we have at once

$$\epsilon_{01}^2 = \epsilon_0^2 + \epsilon_1^2 - 2r_{01} \cdot \epsilon_0 \epsilon_1$$

$$= p_0 q_0 \left\{ \frac{1}{n_1 + n_2} + \frac{1}{n_1} - 2r_{01} \frac{1}{\sqrt{n_1} \sqrt{n_1 + n_2}} \right\}$$

r_{01} being the correlation between errors of simple sampling in p_1 and p_0. But, from the above equation relating p_0 to p_1 and p_2, writing it in terms of deviations in p_0 p_1 and p_2, multiplying by the deviation in p_1 and summing, we have, since errors in p_1 and p_2 are uncorrelated,

$$r_{01} = \frac{n_1}{n_1 + n_2} \frac{\epsilon_1}{\epsilon_0} = \sqrt{\frac{n_1}{n_1 + n_2}}.$$

Therefore finally

$$\epsilon_{01}^2 = \frac{p_0 q_0}{n_1 + n_2} \cdot \frac{n_2}{n_1} \qquad \cdot \quad \cdot \qquad (7)$$

Unless the difference between p_0 and p_1 exceed, say, some three times this value of ϵ_{01}, it may have arisen solely by the chances of simple sampling.

It will be observed that if n_1 be very small compared with n_2, ϵ_{01} approaches, as it should, the standard error for a sample of n_1 observations.

We omit, in this case, the allied problem whether, if the difference between p_1 and p_0 indicated by the samples were real, it might be wiped out in other samples of the same size by fluctuations of simple sampling alone. The solution is a little complex as we no longer have $\epsilon_0^2 = p_0 q_0 / (n_1 + n_2)$.

Example v.—Taking the data of Example iii., suppose that we compare the proportion of tall plants amongst the offspring resulting from cross-fertilisations (viz. 50 per cent.) with the proportion amongst all offspring (viz. 29/68, or 42·6 per cent.). As, in this case, both the subsamples have the same number of observations, $n_1 = n_2 = 34$, and

$$\epsilon_{01} = \left(\frac{29}{68} \times \frac{39}{68} \times \frac{1}{68}\right)^{\frac{1}{2}} = 0.060$$

or 6 per cent. As in the working of Example iii., the observed difference is only 1·25 times the standard error of the difference, and consequently it may have arisen as a mere fluctuation of sampling.

Example vi.—Taking now the figures of Example iv., suppose that we had compared the proportion of girls of medium hair-colour in Edinburgh with the proportion in Glasgow and Edinburgh together. The former is 41·1 per cent., the latter 43·5 per cent., difference 2·4 per cent. The standard error of the difference between the percentages observed in the sub-sample of 9743 observations and the entire sample of 49,507 observations is therefore

$$\epsilon_{01} = (43.5 \times 56.5)^{\frac{1}{2}} \left(\frac{39,764}{49,507 \times 9743}\right)^{\frac{1}{2}} = 0.45 \text{ per cent.}$$

The actual difference is over five times this (the ratio must, of course, be the same as in Example iv.), and could not have occurred as a mere error of sampling.

REFERENCES.

The theory of sampling, for the cases dealt with in this chapter, is generally treated by first determining the frequency-distribution of the number of successes in a sample. This frequency-distribution is not considered till Chapter XV., and the student will be unable to follow much of the literature until he has read that chapter.

Experimental results of dice throwing, coin tossing, etc.

(1) QUETELET, A., *Lettres* . . . . *sur la théorie des probabilités* ; Bruxelles, 1846 (English translation by O. G. Downes; C. & E. Layton, London, 1849). See especially letter xiv. and the table on p. 374 of the French, p. 255 of the English, edition.

(2) WESTERGAARD, H., *Die Grundzüge der Theorie der Statistik*; Fischer, Jena, 1890.

(3) EDGEWORTH, F. Y., Article on the "Law of Error" in the Tenth Edition of the *Encyclopædia Britannica*, vol. xxviii., 1902, p. 280; or on "Probability," Eleventh Edition, vol. xxii. (especially Part II., pp. 390 *et seq.*).

(4) DARBISHIRE, A. D., "Some Tables for illustrating Statistical Correlation," *Mem. and Proc. of the Manchester Lit. and Phil. Soc.*, vol. li., 1907.

General : and applications to sex-ratio of births.

(5) POISSON, S. D., "Sur la proportion des naissances des filles et des garçons," *Mémoires de l'Acad. des Sciences*, vol. ix., 1829, p. 239. (Principally theoretical : the statistical illustrations very slight.)

(6) LEXIS, W., *Zur Theorie der Massenerscheinungen in der menschlichen Gesellschaft*; Freiburg, 1877.

(7) LEXIS, W., *Abhandlungen zur Theorie der Bevölkerungs und Moralstatistik*; Fischer, Jena, 1903. (Contains, with new matter, reprints of some of Professor Lexis' earlier papers in a form convenient for reference.)

(8) EDGEWORTH, F. Y., "Methods of Statistics," *Jour. Roy. Stat. Soc.*, jubilee volume, 1885, p. 181.

(9) VENN, JOHN, *The Logic of Chance*, 3rd edn. ; Macmillan, London, 1888. (*Cf.* the data regarding the distribution of sexes in families on p. 264, to which reference was made in § 9.)

(10) PEARSON, KARL, "Skew Variation in Homogeneous Material," *Phil. Trans. Roy. Soc.*, Series A, vol. clxxxvi., 1895, p. 343. (Sections 2 to 6 on the binomial distribution.)

(11) EDGEWORTH, F. Y., "Miscellaneous Applications of the Calculus of Probabilities," *Jour. Roy. Stat. Soc.*, vols. lx., lxi., 1897–8 (especially part ii., vol. lxi. p. 119).

(12) VIGOR, H. D., and G. U. YULE, "On the Sex-ratios of Births in the Registration Districts of England and Wales, 1881–90," *Jour. Roy. Stat. Soc.*, vol. lxix., 1906, p. 576. (Use of the harmonic mean as in § 11.)

As regards the sex-ratio, reference may also be made to papers in vols. v. and vi. of *Biometrika* by Heron, Weldon, and Woods.

(13) YULE, G. U., "Fluctuations of Sampling in Mendelian Ratios," *Proc. Camb. Phil. Soc.*, vol. xvii., 1914, p. 425.

The law of small chances (§ 12).

(14) POISSON, S. D., *Recherches sur la probabilité des jugements, etc.* ; Paris, 1837. (Pp. 205–7.)

(15) BORTKEWITSCH, L. VON, *Das Gesetz der kleinen Zahlen* ; Teubner, Leipzig, 1898.

(16) STUDENT, "On the Error of Counting with a Hæmacytometer," *Biometrika*, vol. v. p. 351, 1907.

(17) RUTHERFORD, E., and H. GEIGER, with a note by H. BATEMAN, "The probability variations in the distribution of α particles," *Phil. Mag.*, Series 6, vol. xx., 1910, p. 698. (The frequency of particles emitted during a small interval of time follows the law of small chances : the law deduced by Bateman in ignorance of previous work.)

(18) SOPER, H. E., "Tables of Poisson's Exponential Binomial Limit," *Biometrika*, vol. x., 1914, pp. 25–35.

(19) WHITTAKER, LUCY, "On Poisson's Law of Small Numbers," *Biometrika*, vol. x., 1914, pp. 36–71.

EXERCISES.

1. (Ref. 4: total of columns of all the 13 tables given.)

Compare the actual with the theoretical mean and standard-deviation for the following record of 6500 throws of 12 dice, 4, 5, or 6 being reckoned as a "success."

Successes.	Frequency.	Successes.	Frequency.
0	1	7	1351
1	14	8	844
2	103	9	391
3	302	10	117
4	711	11	21
5	1231	12	3
6	1411		
		Total	6500

2. (Ref. 1.)

Balls were drawn from a bag containing equal numbers of black and white balls, each ball being returned before drawing another. The records were then grouped by counting the number of black balls in consecutive 2's, 3's, 4's, 5's, etc. The following give the distributions so derived for grouping by 5's, 6's, and 7's. Compare actual with theoretical means and standard-deviations.

Successes.	(a) Grouping by Fives.	(b) Grouping by Sixes.	(c) Grouping by Sevens.
0	30	17	9
1	125	65	34
2	277	166	104
3	224	192	151
4	136	166	148
5	27	69	95
6	—	8	40
7	—	—	4
Total	819	683	585

3. (Ref. 2, p. 22.)

Ten thousand drawings of a ball from a bag containing equal numbers of black and white were made in the same manner as in the preceding example, and then grouped into 100 sets of 100. The following gives the resulting frequency of different numbers of white balls. Compare mean and standard-deviation with theory.

Number.	Frequency.	Number.	Frequency.	Number.	Frequency.
34	1	44	3	54	8
35	—	45	4	55	3
36	—	46	5	56	5
37	—	47	6	57	4
38	—	48	5	58	4
39	1	49	11	59	—
40	2	50	9	60	—
41	2	51	5	61	1
42	2	52	10	62	1
43	3	53	4	63	1

4. The proportion of successes in the data of Qu. 1 is 0·5097. Find the standard-deviation of the proportion with the given number of throws, and state whether you would regard the excess of successes as probably significant of bias in the dice.

5. In the 4096 drawings on which Qu. 2 is based 2030 balls were black and 2066 white. Is this divergence probably significant of bias?

6. If a frequency-distribution such as those of Questions 1, 2, and 3 be given, show how n and p, if unknown, may be approximately determined from the mean and standard-deviation of the distribution.

Find n and p in this way from the data of Qu. 1 and Qu. 3.

7. Verify the following results for Table VI. of Chapter IX. p. 163, and compare the results of the different grouping of the table on p. 263. In calculating the actual standard-deviation, use Sheppard's correction for grouping (p. 212).

Row or Rows.	Mean.	Actual Standard-deviation s.	Standard-deviation * of Sampling s_0.
1	508·2	11·60	11·18
2	509·5	6·79	6·45
3	510·0	5·28	5·00
4	511·1	5·03	4·22
5	510·2	3·67	3·73
6, 7	509·7	4·13	3·24
8, 9, 10, 11	508·7	3·10	2·69
12, 13, 14	508·4	2·55	2·25
15 and upwards.	508·2	2·13	1·85

8. In a case of mice-breeding (see reference given in § 11) the harmonic mean number in a litter was 4·735, and the expected proportion of albinos 50 per cent. Find the standard-deviation of simple sampling for the proportion of albinos in a litter, and state whether the actual standard-deviation (21·63 per cent.) probably indicates any *real* variation, or not.

9. (Data from Report i., Evolution Committee of the Royal Society, p. 17.) In breeding certain stocks 408 hairy and 126 glabrous plants were obtained. If the expectation is one-fourth glabrous, is the divergence significant, or might it have occurred as a fluctuation of sampling?

10. (Data of Example viii. and Qu. 5, Chap. III.) Is the association in either of the following cases likely to have arisen as a fluctuation of simple sampling?

(a) $(AB)=47$ $(A\beta)=12$ $(\alpha B)=21$ $(\alpha\beta)=3$
(b) $(AB)=309$ $(A\beta)=214$ $(\alpha B)=132$ $(\alpha\beta)=119$

11. The sex-ratio at birth is sometimes given by the ratio of male to female births, instead of the proportion of male to total births. If Z is the ratio, *i.e.* $Z=p/q$, show that the standard error of Z is approximately $(1+Z)\sqrt{\dfrac{Z}{n}}$, n being large, so that deviations are small compared with the mean. (The student may find it useful to refer to § 8, Chap. XI.)   .

* Based on the mid-value of the class-interval for single rows, or the harmonic mean of the mid-values for groups of rows.

CHAPTER XIV

SIMPLE SAMPLING CONTINUED: EFFECT OF
REMOVING THE LIMITATIONS OF SIMPLE SAMPLING.

1. Warning as to the assumption that three times the standard error gives the range for the majority of fluctuations of simple sampling of either sign —2. Warning as to the use of the observed for the true value of p in the formula for the standard error—3. The inverse standard error, or standard error of the true proportion for a given observed proportion: equivalence of the direct and inverse standard errors when n is large— 4-8. The importance of errors other than fluctuations of "simple sampling" in practice: unrepresentative or biassed samples—9-10. Effect of divergences from the conditions of simple sampling: (a) effect of variation in p and q for the several universes from which the samples are drawn—11-12. (b) Effect of variation in p and q from one sub-class to another within each universe—13-14. (c) Effect of a correlation between the results of the several events—15. Summary.

1. THERE are two warnings as regards the methods adopted in the examples in the concluding section of the last chapter which the student should note, as they may become of importance when the number of observations is small. In the first place, he should remember that, while we have taken three times the standard error as giving the limits within which the great majority of errors of sampling *of either sign* are contained, the limits are not, as a rule, strictly the same for positive and for negative errors. As is evident from the examples of actual distributions in § 7, Chap. XIII., the distribution of errors is not strictly symmetrical unless $p = q = 0.5$. No theoretical rule as to the limits can be given, but it appears from the examples referred to and from the calculated distributions in Chap. XV. § 3, that a range of three times the standard error includes the great majority of the deviations in the direction of the *longer* "tail" of the distribution, while the same range on the shorter side may extend beyond the limits of the distribution altogether. If, therefore, p be less than 0.5, our assumed range may be greater than is possible for negative errors, or if p be

greater than 0·5, greater than is possible for positive errors. The assumption is not, however, likely as a rule to lead to a serious mistake; as stated at the commencement of this paragraph, the point is of importance only when n is small, for when n is large the distribution tends to become sensibly symmetrical even for values of p differing considerably from 0·5. (*Cf.* Chap. XV. for the properties of the limiting form of distribution.)

2. In the second place, the student should note that, where we were unable to assign any *a priori* value to p, we have assumed that it is sufficiently accurate to replace p in the formula for the standard error by the proportion actually observed, say π. Where n is large so that the standard error of p becomes small relatively to the product pq the assumption is justifiable, and no serious error is possible. If, however, n be small, the use of the observed value π may lead to an under- or over-estimation of the standard error which cannot be neglected. To get some rough idea of the possible importance of such effects, the approximate standard error ϵ may first be calculated as usual from the observed proportion π, and then fresh values recalculated, replacing π by $\pi \pm 3\epsilon$. It should be remembered that the maximum value of the product pq is given by $p = q = 0·5$, and hence these values, if within the limits of fluctuations of sampling, will give one limiting value for the standard error. The procedure is by no means exact, but may serve to give a useful warning.

Thus in Example iii. of Chap. XIII. the observed proportion of tall plants is 29/68, or, say, 43 per cent. The standard error of this proportion is 6 per cent., and a true proportion of 50 per cent. is therefore well within the limits of fluctuations of sampling. The maximum value of the standard error is therefore

$$\left(\frac{50 \times 50}{68}\right)^{\frac{1}{2}} = 6·06 \text{ per cent.}$$

On the other hand, the standard error is unlikely to be lower than that based on a proportion of $43 - 18 = 25$ per cent.,

$$\left(\frac{25 \times 75}{68}\right)^{\frac{1}{2}} = 5·25 \text{ per cent.}$$

3. The two difficulties mentioned in §§ 1 and 2 arise when n, the number of cases in the sample, is small. The interpretation of the value of the standard error is also more limited in this case than when n is large. Suppose a large number of observations to be made, by means of samples of n observations each, on different masses of material, or in different universes, for each of which the true value of p is known. On these data we could

form a correlation-table between the true proportion p in a given universe and the observed proportion π in a sample of n observations drawn therefrom. What we have found from the work of the last chapter is that the standard-deviation of an array of π's associated with a certain true value p, in this table, is $(pq/n)^{\frac{1}{2}}$; but the question may be asked —What is the standard-deviation of the array at right angles to this, i.e. the array of p's associated with a certain observed proportion π? In other words, given an observed proportion π, what is the standard-deviation of the true proportions? This is the inverse of the problem with which we have been dealing, and it is a much more difficult problem. On general principles, however, we can see that if n be large, the two standard-deviations will tend, on the average of all values of p, to be nearly the same, while if n be small the standard-deviation of the array of π's will tend to be appreciably the greater of the two. For if $\pi = p + \delta$, δ is uncorrelated with p, and therefore if σ_p be the standard-deviation of p in all the universes from which samples are drawn, σ_π the standard-deviation of observed proportions in the samples, and σ_δ the standard-deviation of the differences,

$$\sigma_\pi^2 = \sigma_p^2 + \sigma_\delta^2.$$

But σ_δ^2 varies inversely as n. Hence if n become very large, σ_δ becomes very small, σ_π becomes sensibly equal to σ_p, and therefore the standard-deviations of the arrays, on an average, are also sensibly equal. If n be large, therefore, $[\pi(1 - \pi)/n]^{\frac{1}{2}}$ may be taken as giving, with sufficient exactness, the standard-deviation of the true proportion p for a given observed proportion π. But if n be small, σ_δ cannot be neglected in comparison with σ_p, σ_π is therefore appreciably greater than σ_p, and the standard-deviation of the array of π's is, on an average of all arrays, correspondingly greater than the standard deviation of the array of p's—the statement is not true for every pair of corresponding arrays, especially for extreme values of p near 0 and 1. Further, it should be noticed that, while the regression of π on p is unity—i.e. the mean of the array of π's is identical with p, the type of the array—the regression of p on π is less than unity. If we assume, therefore, that a tabulation of all possible chances, observed for every conceivable subject, would give a distribution of p ranging uniformly between 0 and 1, or indeed grouped symmetrically in any way round 0·5, any observed value π greater than 0·5 will probably correspond to a true value of p slightly lower than π, and conversely. We have already referred to the use of the inverse standard error in § 13 of Chap. XIII. (Case II., p. 269). If we determine, for example, the standard error of the difference between two observed proportions by equation (6) of that chapter, this may be taken, provided n be large, as approximately the standard-deviation of true differences for the given observed difference.

4. The use of standard errors must be exercised with care. It is very necessary to remember the limited assumptions on which the theory of *simple sampling* is based, and to bear in mind that it covers those fluctuations alone which exist when all the assumed conditions are fulfilled. The formulæ obtained for the standard errors of proportions and of their differences have no bearing except on the one question, whether an observed divergence of a certain proportion from a certain other proportion that might be observed in a more extended series of observations, or that has actually been observed in some other series, might or might not be due to fluctuations of simple sampling alone. Their use is thus quite restricted, for in many cases of practical sampling this is not the principal question at issue. The principal question in many such cases concerns quite a different point, viz. whether the observed proportion π in the sample may not diverge from the proportion p existing in the universe from which it was drawn, owing to the nature of the conditions under which the sample was taken, π tending to be definitely greater or definitely less than p. Such divergence between π and p might arise in two distinct ways, (1) owing to variations of classification in sorting the A's and a's, the characters not being well defined—a source of error which we need not further discuss, but one which may lead to serious results [*cf.* ref. 5 of Chap. V.]. (2) Owing to either A's or a's tending to escape the attentions of the sampler. To give an illustration from artificial chance, if on drawing samples from a bag containing a very large number of black and white balls the observed proportion of black balls was π, we could not necessarily infer that the proportion of black balls in the bag was approximately π, even though the standard error were small, and we knew that the proportions in successive samples were subject to the law of simple sampling. For the black balls might be, say, much more highly polished than the white ones, so as to tend to escape the fingers of the sampler, or they might be represented by a number of lively black insects sheltering amongst white stones : in neither case would the ratio of black balls to white, or of insects to stones, be represented in their proper proportions. Clearly, in any parallel case, inferences as to the material from which the sample is drawn are of a very doubtful and uncertain kind, and it is this uncertainty whether the chance of inclusion in the sample is the same for A's and a's, far more than the mere divergences between different samples drawn in

the same way, which renders many statistical results based on samples so dubious.

5. Thus in collecting returns as to family income and expenditure from working-class households, the families with lower incomes are almost certain to be under-represented; they largely "escape the sampler's fingers" from their simple lack of ability to keep the necessary accounts. It is almost impossible to say, however, to what extent they are under-represented, or to form any estimate as to the possible error when two such samples taken by different persons at different times, or in different places, are compared. Again, if estimates as to crop-production are formed on the basis of a limited number of voluntary returns, the estimates are likely to err in excess, as the persons who make the returns will probably include an undue proportion of the more intelligent farmers whose crops will tend to be above average. Whilst voluntary returns are in this way liable to lead to more or less unrepresentative samples, compulsory sampling does not evade the difficulty. Compulsion could not ensure equally accurate and trustworthy returns from illiterate and well-educated workmen, from intelligent and unintelligent farmers. The following of some definite rule in drawing the sample may also produce unrepresentative samples: if samples of fruit were taken solely from the top layers of baskets exposed for sale, the results might be unduly favourable; if from the bottom layer, unduly unfavourable.

6. In such cases we can see that any sample, taken in the way supposed, is likely to be definitely *biassed*, in the sense that it will not tend to include, even in the long run, equal proportions of the A's and a's in the original material. In other cases there may be no obvious reason for presuming such *bias*, but, on the other hand, no certainty that it does not exist. Thus if we noted the hair-colours of the children in, say, one school in ten in a large town, the question would arise whether this method would tend to give an unbiassed sample of all the children. No assured answer could be given: conjectures on the matter would be based in part on the way in which the schools were selected, *e.g.* the volunteering of teachers for the work might in itself introduce an element of bias. Again, if say 10,000 herrings were measured as landed at various North Sea ports, and the question were raised whether the sample was likely to be an unbiassed sample of North Sea herrings, no assured answer could be given. There may be no definite reason for expecting definite bias in either case, but it may exist, and no mere examination of the sample itself can give any information as to whether it exists or no.

7. Such an examination may be of service, however, as indicating one possible source of bias, viz. great heterogeneity in the original material. If, for example, in the first illustration, the hair-colours of the children differed largely in the different schools—much more largely than would be accounted for by fluctuations of simple sampling—it would be obvious that *one* school would tend to give an unrepresentative sample, and questionable therefore whether the five, ten or fifteen schools observed might not also have given an unrepresentative sample. Similarly, if the herrings in different catches varied largely, it would, again, be difficult to get a representative sample for a large area. But while the dissimilarity of subsamples would then be evidence as to the difficulty of obtaining a representative sample, the similarity of subsamples would, of course, be no evidence that the sample was representative, for some very different material which should have been represented might have been missed or overlooked.

8. The student must therefore be very careful to remember that even if some observed difference exceed the limits of fluctuation in simple sampling, it does not follow that it exceeds the limits of fluctuation due to what the practical man would regard—and quite rightly regard—as the chances of sampling. Further, he must remember that if the standard error be small, it by no means follows that the result is necessarily trustworthy : the smallness of the standard error only indicates that it is not *untrustworthy owing to the magnitude of fluctuations of simple sampling*. It may be quite untrustworthy for other reasons : owing to bias in taking the sample, for instance, or owing to definite errors in classifying the A's and a's. On the other hand, of course, it should also be borne in mind that an observed proportion is not necessarily incorrect, but merely to a greater or less extent untrustworthy if the standard error be large. Similarly, if an observed proportion π_1 in a sample drawn from one universe be greater than an observed proportion π_2 in a sample drawn from another universe, but $\pi_1 - \pi_2$ is considerably less than three times the standard error of the difference, it does not, of course, follow that the true proportion for the given universes, p_1 and p_2, are most probably equal. On the contrary, p_1 most likely exceeds p_2 ; the standard error only warns us that this conclusion is more or less uncertain, and that *possibly* p_2 may even exceed p_1.

9. Let us now consider the effect, on the standard-deviation of sampling, of divergences from the conditions of simple sampling which were laid down in § 8 of Chap. XIII.

First suppose the condition (*a*) to break down, so that there is some essential difference between the localities from which, or the conditions under which, samples are drawn, or that some essential change has taken place during the period of sampling. We may represent such circumstances in a case of artificial chance by supposing that for the first f_1 throws of n dice the chance of success for each die is p_1, for the next f_2 throws p_2, for the next f_3 throws p_3, and so on, the chance of success varying from time to time, just as the chance of death, even for individuals of the same age and sex, varies from district to district. Suppose, now, that the records of all these throws are pooled together. The mean number of successes per throw of the n dice is given by

$$M = \frac{n}{N}(f_1 p_1 + f_2 p_2 + f_3 p_3 + \quad \dots \quad) = n.p_0,$$

where $N = \Sigma(f)$ is the whole number of throws and p_0 is the mean value $\Sigma(fp)/N$ of the varying chance p. To find the standard-deviation of the number of successes at each throw consider that the first set of throws contributes to the sum of the squares of deviations an amount

$$f_1[n p_1 q_1 + n^2(p_1 - p_0)^2],$$

$n.p_1 q_1$ being the square of the standard-deviation for these throws, and $n(p_1 - p_0)$ the difference between the mean number of successes for the first set and the mean for all the sets together. Hence the standard-deviation σ of the whole distribution is given by the sum of all quantities like the above, or

$$N\sigma^2 = n\Sigma(fpq) + n^2 \, \Sigma f(p - p_0)^2.$$

Let σ_p be the standard-deviation of p, then the last sum is $N.n^2\sigma_p^2$, and substituting $1 - p$ for q, we have

$$\sigma^2 = np_0 - np_0^2 - n\sigma_p^2 + n^2\sigma_p^2$$
$$= np_0 q_0 + n(n - 1)\sigma_p^2 \quad . \quad \quad . \quad \quad . \quad (1)$$

This is the formula corresponding to equation (1) of Chap. XIII.: if we deal with the standard-deviation of the *proportion* of successes, instead of that of the absolute number, we have, dividing through by n^2, the formula corresponding to equation (2) of Chap. XIII., viz.—

$$s^2 = \frac{p_0 q_0}{n} + \frac{n - 1}{n}\sigma_p^2 \quad . \quad \quad . \quad \quad . \quad (2)$$

10. If n be large and s_0 be the standard-deviation calculated from the mean proportion of successes p_0, equation (2) is sensibly of the form

$$s^2 = s_0^2 + \sigma_p^2,$$

TABLE *showing Frequencies of Registration Districts in England and Wales
with Different Proportions of Deaths in Childbirth (including Deaths
from Puerperal Fever) per 1000 Births in the same Year, for the same
Groups of Districts as in the Table of Chap. XIII. § 10.* Data from same
source. Decade 1881-90.

Deaths in Childbirth per 1000 Births.	Number of Births in the Decade.						
	1500 to 2500.	3500 to 4000.	4500 to 5000.	10,000 to 15,000.	15,000 to 20,000.	30,000 to 50,000.	50,000 to 90,000.
1·5– 2·0	—	—	2	—	—	—	—
2·0– 2·5	1	—	1	1	—	—	—
2·5– 3·0	1	3	1	—	—	—	—
3·0– 3·5	1	5	2	4	—	1	2
3·5– 4·0	5	6	5	8	5	5	9
4·0– 4·5	6	5	8	23	4	9	6
4·5– 5·0	2	5	9	14	11	7	5
5·0– 5·5	7	3	6	14	6	8	7
5·5– 6·0	5	3	4	5	2	5	4
6·0– 6·5	1	5	1	—	4	1	1
6·5– 7·0	3	1	1	3	—	2	1
7·0– 7·5	1	1	—	—	—	4	—
7·5– 8·0	—	—	—	—	—	1	—
8·0– 8·5	—	—	—	—	—	—	—
8·5– 9·0	1	1	—	—	1	—	—
9·0– 9·5	—	—	—	—	—	—	—
9·5–10·0	1	—	—	1	—	—	—
10·0–10·5	—	—	—	—	—	—	—
10·5–11·0	1	—	—	—	—	—	—
Total	36	38	40	73	33	43	35
Mean	5·29	4·71	4·45	4·68	4·99	5·13	4·64
Standard-deviation	1·77	1·37	1·09	1·01	0·99	1·12	0·87
Theoretical standard-deviation corresponding to mean births	1·62	1·12	0·97	0·61	0·53	0·36	0·26
$\sqrt{s^2 - s_0^2}$	0·71	0·80	0·51	0·80	0·84	1·07	0·83

and hence, knowing s and s_0, we can find σ_p the standard-deviation
of the chance or proportion in the universes from which the
samples have been drawn.

The values of $\sqrt{s^2 - s_0^2}$ are tabulated at the foot of the table
showing the distribution of the proportion of male births in

certain registration districts of England, in § 10 of Chap. XIII.
p. 263. It will be seen that in the first group of small districts
there appears to be a significant standard-deviation of some 6
units in the proportion of male births per thousand, but in the
more urban districts this falls to 1 or 2 units ; in one case only
does s fall short of s_0. In the table on p. 283 are given some
different data relating to the deaths of women in childbirth in the
same groups of districts, and in this case the effect of definite
causes is relatively larger, as one might expect. The values of
$\sqrt{s^2 - s_0^2}$ suggest an almost uniform significant standard-deviation
$\sigma_p = 0\cdot 8$ in the deaths of women per thousand births, five out of
the eight values being very close to this average. The figures of
this case also bring out clearly one important consequence of (2),
viz. that if we make n large s becomes sensibly equal to σ_p, while
if we make n small s becomes more nearly equal to $p_0 q_0/n$. Hence
if we want to know the significant standard-deviation of the proportion p—the measure of its fluctuation owing to definite causes
—n should be made as large as possible ; if, on the other hand, we
want to obtain good illustrations of the theory of simple sampling
n should be made small. If n be very large the actual standard-
deviation may evidently become almost indefinitely large compared with the standard-deviation of sampling. Thus during the
20 years 1855–74 the death-rate in England and Wales fluctuated
round a mean value of $22\cdot 2$ per thousand with a standard-deviation of $0\cdot 86$. Taking the mean population as roughly 21 millions,
the standard-deviation of sampling is approximately

$$\sqrt{\frac{22 \times 978}{21 \times 10^6}} = 0\cdot 032.$$

This is only about one twenty-seventh of the actual value.

11. Now consider the effect of altering the second condition
of simple sampling, given in § 8 (b) of Chapter XIII., viz. the
condition that the chances p and q shall be the same for every
die or coin in the set, or the circumstances that regulate the
appearance of the character observed the same for every individual
or every sub-class in each of the universes from which samples
are drawn. Suppose that in the group of n dice thrown the
chances for m_1 dice are $p_1\ q_1$; for m_2 dice, $p_2\ q_2$, and so on,
the chances varying for different dice, but being constant
throughout the experiment. The case differs from the last, as
in that the chances were the same for every die, at any one
throw, but varied from one throw to another: now they are constant from throw to throw, but differ from one die to another as
they would in any ordinary set of badly made dice. Required to
find the effect of these differing chances.

For the mean number of successes we evidently have

$$M = m_1 p_1 + m_2 p_2 + m_3 p_3 + \ldots$$
$$= n.p_0$$

p_0 being the mean chance $\Sigma(mp)/n$. To find the standard-deviation of the number of successes at each throw, it should be noted that this may be regarded as made up of the number of successes in the m_1 dice for which the chances are $p_1 q_1$, together with the number of successes amongst the m_2 dice for which the chances are $p_2 q_2$, and so on: and these numbers of successes are all independent. Hence

$$\sigma^2 = m_1 p_1 q_1 + m_2 p_2 q_2 + m_3 p_3 q_3 + \ldots$$
$$= \Sigma(mpq),$$

Substituting $1 - p$ for q, as before, and using σ_p to denote the standard-deviation of p,

$$\sigma^2 = n.p_0 q_0 - n\sigma_p^2 \quad . \quad . \quad . \quad . \quad (3)$$

or if s be, as before, the standard-deviation of the *proportion* of successes,

$$s^2 = \frac{p_0 q_0}{n} - \frac{\sigma_p^2}{n} \quad . \quad . \quad . \quad (4)$$

12. The effect of the chances varying for the individual dice or other "events" is therefore to lower the standard-deviation, as calculated from the mean proportion p_0, and the effect may conceivably be considerable. To take a limiting case, if p be zero for half the events and unity for the remainder, $p_0 = q_0 = \frac{1}{2}$, and $\sigma_p = \frac{1}{2}$, so that s is zero. To take another illustration, still somewhat extreme, if the values of p are uniformly distributed over the whole range between 0 and 1, $p_0 = q_0 = \frac{1}{2}$ as before but $\sigma_p^2 = 1/12 = 0.0833$ (Chap. VIII. § 12, p. 143). Hence $s^2 = 0.1667/n$, $s = 0.408/\sqrt{n}$, instead of $0.5/\sqrt{n}$, the value of s if the chances are $\frac{1}{2}$ in every case. In most practical cases, however, the effect will be much less. Thus the standard-deviation of sampling for a death-rate of, say, 18 per thousand in a population of uniform age and one sex is $(18 \times 982)^{\frac{1}{2}}/\sqrt{n} = 133/\sqrt{n}$. In a population of the age composition of that of England and Wales, however, the death-rate is not, of course, uniform, but varies from a high value in infancy (say 150 per thousand), through very low values (2 to 4 per thousand) in childhood to continuously increasing values in old age ; the standard-deviation of the rate within such a population is roughly about 30 per thousand. But the effect of this

variation on the standard-deviation of simple sampling is quite small, for, as calculated from equation (4),

$$s^2 = \frac{1}{n}(18 \times 982 - 900)$$

$$s = 130/\sqrt{n}$$

as compared with $133/\sqrt{n}$.

13. We have finally to pass to the third condition (c) of § 8, Chap. XIII., and to discuss the effect of a certain amount of dependence between the several " events " in each sample. We shall suppose, however, that the two other conditions (a) and (b) are fulfilled, the chances p and q being the same for every event at every trial, and constant throughout the experiment. The problem is again most simply treated on the lines of § 5 of the last chapter. The standard-deviation for each event is $(pq)^{\frac{1}{2}}$ as before, but the events are no longer independent: instead, therefore, of the simple expression

$$\sigma^2 = n.pq,$$

we must have (cf. Chap. XI. § 2)

$$\sigma^2 = n.pq + 2pq(r_{12} + r_{13} + \cdots \quad r_{21} + \cdots),$$

where, r_{12}, r_{13}, etc. are the correlations between the results of the first and second, first and third events, and so on—correlations for variables (number of successes) which can only take the values 0 and 1, but may nevertheless, of course, be treated as ordinary variables (cf. Chap. XI. § 10). There are $n(n-1)/2$ correlation-coefficients, and if, therefore, r is the arithmetic mean of the correlations we may write

$$\sigma^2 = npq[1 + r(n-1)]. \qquad . \qquad . \qquad . \quad (5)$$

The standard-deviation of simple sampling will therefore be increased or diminished according as the average correlation between the results of the single events is positive or negative, and the effect may be considerable, as σ may be reduced to zero or increased to $n(pq)^{\frac{1}{2}}$. For the standard deviation of the proportion of successes in each sample we have the equation

$$s^2 = \frac{pq}{n}[1 + r(n-1)] \qquad . \qquad . \qquad . \quad (6)$$

It should be noted that, as the means and standard-deviations for our variables are all identical, r is the correlation-coefficient for a table formed by taking all possible pairs of results in the n events of each sample.

It should also be noted that the case when r is positive covers the departure from the rules of simple sampling discussed in §§ 9–10 : for if we draw successive samples from different records, this introduces the positive correlation at once, even although the results of the events *at each trial* are quite independent of one another. Similarly, the case discussed in §§ 11–12 is covered by the case when r is negative : for if the chances are not the same for every event at each trial, and the chance of success for some one event is above the average, the mean chance of success for the remainder must be below it. The cases (a), (b) and (c) are, however, best kept distinct, since a positive or negative correlation may arise for reasons quite different from those discussed in §§ 9–12.

14. As a simple illustration, consider the important case of sampling from a limited universe, *e.g.* of drawing n balls in succession from the whole number w in a bag containing pw white balls and qw black balls. On repeating such drawings a large number of times, we are evidently equally likely to get a white ball or a black ball for the first, second, or nth ball of the sample : the correlation-table formed from all possible pairs of every sample will therefore tend in the long run to give just the same form of distribution as the correlation-table formed from all possible pairs of the w balls in the bag. But from Chap. XI. § 11 we know that the correlation-coefficient for this table is $-1/(w-1)$, whence

$$\sigma^2 = n.pq\left(1 - \frac{n-1}{w-1}\right)$$

$$= n.pq\frac{w-n}{w-1}.$$

If $n = 1$, we have the obviously correct result that $\sigma = (pq)^{\frac{1}{2}}$, as in drawing from unlimited material : if, on the other hand, $n = w$, σ becomes zero as it should, and the formula is thus checked for simple cases. For drawing 2 balls out of 4, σ becomes 0·816 $(npq)^{\frac{1}{2}}$; for drawing 5 balls out of 10, 0·745 $(npq)^{\frac{1}{2}}$; in the case of drawing half the balls out of a very large number, it approximates to $(0·5.npq)^{\frac{1}{2}}$, or 0·707 $(npq)^{\frac{1}{2}}$.

In the case of contagious or infectious diseases, or of certain forms of accident that are apt, if fatal at all, to result in wholesale deaths, r is positive, and if n be large (as it usually is in such cases) a very small value of r may easily lead to a very great increase in the observed standard-deviation. It is difficult to give a really good example from actual statistics, as the conditions are hardly ever constant from one year to another, but the following will

serve to illustrate the point. During the twenty years 1887–1906
there were 2107 deaths from explosions of firedamp or coal-dust
in the coal-mines of the United Kingdom, or an average of 105
deaths per annum. From § 12 of Chap. XIII. it follows that this
should be the square of the standard-deviation of simple sampling,
or the standard-deviation itself approximately 10·3. But the
square of the actual standard-deviation is 7178, or its value 84·7,
the numbers of deaths ranging between 14 (in 1903) and 317
(in 1894). This large standard-deviation, to judge from the
figures, is partly, though not wholly, due to a general tendency to
decrease in the numbers of deaths from explosions in spite of a
large increase in the number of persons employed ; but even if we
ignore this, the magnitude of the standard-deviation can be
accounted for by a very small value of the correlation r, expressive
of the fact that if an explosion is sufficiently serious to be fatal to
one individual, it will probably be fatal to others also. For if σ_0
denote the standard-deviation of simple sampling, σ the standard-
deviation of sampling given by equation (5), we have

$$r = \frac{\sigma^2 - \sigma_0^2}{(n-1)\sigma_0^2}.$$

Whence, from the above data, taking the numbers of persons
employed underground at a rough average of 560,000,

$$r = \frac{7073}{560000 \times 105} = +0 \cdot 00012.$$

15. Summarising the preceding paragraphs, §§ 9–14, we see
that if the chances p and q differ for the various universes,
districts, years, materials, or whatever they may be from which
the samples are drawn, the standard-deviation observed will be
greater than the standard-deviation of simple sampling, as
calculated from the average values of the chances : if the average
chances are the same for each universe from which a sample is
drawn, but vary from individual to individual or from one sub-
class to another within the universe, the standard-deviation
observed will be less than the standard-deviation of simple
sampling as calculated from the mean values of the chances :
finally, if p and q are constant, but the events are no longer
independent, the observed standard-deviation will be greater or
less than the simplest theoretical value according as the correlation between the results of the single events is positive or
negative. These conclusions further emphasise the need for
caution in the use of standard errors. If we find that the

standard-deviation in some case of sampling exceeds the standard-deviation of simple sampling, two interpretations are possible : *either* that p and q are different in the various universes from which samples have been drawn (*i.e.* that the variations are more or less definitely significant in the sense of § 13, Chap. XIII.), *or* that the results of the events are positively correlated *inter se*. If the actual standard-deviation fall short of the standard-deviation of simple sampling two interpretations are again possible, *either* that the chances p and q vary for different individuals or sub-classes in each universe, while approximately constant from one universe to another, *or* that the results of the events are negatively correlated *inter se*. Even if the actual standard-deviation approaches closely to the standard-deviation of simple sampling, it is only a conjectural and not a necessary inference that all the conditions of " simple sampling " as defined in § 8 of the last chapter are fulfilled. Possibly, for example, there may be a positive correlation r between the results of the different events, masked by a variation of the chances p and q in sub-classes of each universe.

Sampling which fulfils the conditions laid down in § 8 . of Chap. XIII., simple sampling as we have called it, is generally spoken of as *random* sampling. We have thought it better to avoid this term, as the condition that the sampling shall be random—haphazard—is not the only condition tacitly assumed.

REFERENCES.

Cf. generally the references to Chap. XIII., to which may be added—

(1) PEARSON, KARL, "On certain Properties of the Hypergeometrical Series, and on the fitting of such Series to Observation Polygons in the Theory of Chance," *Philosophical Magazine*, 5th Series, vol. xlvii., 1899, p. 236. (An expansion of one section of ref. 10 of Chap. XIII., dealing with the first problem of our § 14, *i.e.* drawing samples from a bag containing a limited number of white and black balls, from the standpoint of the frequency-distribution of the number of white or black balls in the samples.)

(2) GREENWOOD, M., "On Errors of Random Sampling in certain Cases not suitable for the Application of a 'Normal Curve of Frequency,'" *Biometrika*, vol. ix., 1913, pp. 69-90. (If an event has succeeded p times in n trials, what are the chances of $0, 1, \ldots m$ successes in m subsequent trials ? Tables for small samples.)

EXERCISES.

1. Referring to Question 7 of Chap. XIII., work out the values of the significant standard-deviation σ_p (as in § 10) for each row or group of rows there given, but taking row 5 with rows 6 and 7.

2. For all the districts in England and Wales included in the same table (Table VI., Chap. IX.) the standard-deviation of the proportion of male births per 1000 of all births is 7·46 and the mean proportion of male births 509·2. The harmonic mean number of births in a district is 5070. Find the significant standard-deviation σ_p.

3. If for one half of n events the chance of success is p and the chance of failure q, whilst for the other half the chance of success is q and the chance of failure p, what is the standard-deviation of the number of successes, the events being all independent?

4. The following are the deaths from small-pox during the 20 years 1882–1901 in England and Wales:—

1882	1317	1892	431
83	957	93	1457
84	2234	94	820
85	2827	95	223
86	275	96	541
87	506	97	25
88	1026	98	253
89	23	99	174
90	16	1900	85
91	49	1901	356

The death-rate from small-pox being very small, the rule of § 12, Chap. XIII., may be applied to estimate the standard-deviation of simple sampling. Assuming that the excess of the actual standard-deviation over this can be entirely accounted for by a correlation between the results of exposure to risk of the individuals composing the population, estimate r. The mean population during the period may be taken in round numbers as 29 millions.

CHAPTER XV.

THE BINOMIAL DISTRIBUTION AND THE NORMAL CURVE.

1. In Chapters XIII. and XIV. the standard-deviation of the number of successes in n events was determined for the several more important cases, and the applications of the results indicated. For the simpler cases of artificial chance it is possible, however, to go much further, and determine not merely the standard-deviation but the entire frequency-distribution of the number of "successes." This we propose to do for the case of "simple sampling," in which all the events are completely independent, and the chances p and q the same for each event and constant throughout the trials. The case corresponds to the tossing of ideally perfect coins (homogeneous circular discs), or the throwing of ideally perfect dice (homogeneous cubes).

2. If we deal with one event only, we expect in N trials, Nq failures and Np successes. Suppose we now combine with the results of this first event the results of a second. The two events are quite independent, and therefore, according to the rule of

Number of Successes.		0	1	2	3	4
One event		$N.q$	$N.p$			
		$N.q^2$	$N.pq + N.pq$	$N.p^2$		
Two events		$N.q^2$	$2N.pq$	$N.p^2$		
		$N.q^3$	$N.pq^2 + 2N.pq^2$	$2N.p^2q + N.p^2q$	$N.p^3$	
Three events		$N.q^3$	$3N.pq^2$	$3N.p^2q$	$N.p^3$	
		$N.q^4$	$N.pq^3 + 3N.pq^3$	$3N.p^2q^2 + 3N.p^2q^2$	$3N.p^3q + N.p^3q$	$N.p^4$
Four events		$N.q^4$	$4N.pq^3$	$6N.p^2q^2$	$4N.p^3q$	$N.p^4$

independence, of the Nq failures of the first event $(Nq)q$ will be associated (on an average) with failures of the second event, and $(Nq)p$ with successes of the second event (*cf.* row 2 of the scheme on p. 292). Similarly of the Np successful first events, $(Np)q$ will be associated (on an average) with failures of the second event and $(Np)p$ with successes. In trials of two events we would therefore expect approximately Nq^2 cases of no success, $2Npq$ cases of one success and one failure, and Np^2 cases of two successes, as in row 3 of the scheme. The results of a third event may be combined with those of the first two in precisely the same way. Of the Nq^2 cases in which both the first two events failed, $(Nq^2)q$ will be associated (on an average) with failure of the third also, $(Nq^2)p$ with success of the third. Of the $2Npq$ cases of one success and one failure, $(2Npq)q$ will be associated with failure of the third event and $(2Npq)p$ with success, and similarly for the Np^2 cases in which both the first two events succeeded. The result is that in N trials of three events we should expect Nq^3 cases of no success, $3\,Npq^2$ cases of one success, $3\,Np^2q$ cases of two successes, and Np^3 cases of three successes, as in row 5 of the scheme. The scheme is continued for the results of a fourth event, and it is evident that all the results are included under a very simple rule: the frequencies of 0, 1, 2 . . . . successes are given

for *one* event by the binomial expansion of $N(q+p)$
for *two* events   ,,   ,, $N(q+p)^2$
for *three* events   ,,   ,, $N(q+p)^3$
for *four* events   ,,   ,, $N(q+p)^4$

and so on. Quite generally, in fact :—*the frequencies of* 0, 1, 2 . . . . *successes in N trials of n events are given by the successive terms in the binomial expansion of* $N(q+p)^n$, viz.—

$$N\left\{q^n + n.q^{n-1}p + \frac{n(n-1)}{1.2}.q^{n-2}p^2 + \frac{n(n-1)(n-2)}{1.2.3}q^{n-3}p^3 + \dots\right\}$$

This is the first theoretical expression that we have obtained for the form of a frequency-distribution.

3. The general form of the distributions given by such binomial series will have been evident from the experimental examples given in Chapter XIII., *i.e.* they are distributions of greater or less asymmetry, tailing off in either direction from the mode. The distribution is, however, of so much importance that it is worth while considering the form in greater detail. This form evidently depends (1) on the values of q and p, (2) on the value of the exponent n. If p and q are equal, evidently the distribution must be symmetrical, for

p and q may be interchanged without altering the value of any term, and consequently terms equidistant from either end of the series are equal. If p and q are unequal, on the other hand, the distribution is asymmetrical, and the more asymmetrical, for the same value of n, the greater the inequality of the chances. The following table shows the calculated distributions for $n = 20$ and values of p, proceeding by 0.1, from 0.1 to 0.5. When $p = 0.1$, cases of two successes are the

$A.$—*Terms of the Binomial Series* 10,000 $(q+p)^{20}$ *for Values of p from* 0·1 *to* 0·5. (*Figures given to the nearest unit.*)

Number of Successes.	$p = 0.1$ $q = 0.9$	$p = 0.2$ $q = 0.8$	$p = 0.3$ $q = 0.7$	$p = 0.4$ $q = 0.6$	$p = 0.5$ $q = 0.5$
0	1216	115	8	—	—
1	2702	576	68	5	—
2	2852	1369	278	31	2
3	1901	2054	716	123	11
4	898	2182	1304	350	46
5	319	1746	1789	746	148
6	89	1091	1916	1244	370
7	20	545	1643	1659	739
8	4	222	1144	1797	1201
9	1	74	654	1597	1602
10	—	20	308	1171	1762
11	—	5	120	710	1602
12	—	1	39	355	1201
13	—	—	10	146	739
14	—	—	2	49	370
15	—	—	—	13	148
16	—	—	—	3	46
17	—	—	—	—	11
18	—	—	—	—	2
19	—	—	—	—	—
20	—	—	—	—	—

most frequent, but cases of one success almost equally frequent : even nine successes may, however, occur about once in 10,000 trials. As p is increased, the position of the maximum frequency gradually advances, and the two tails of the distribution become more nearly equal, until $p = 0.5$, when the distribution is symmetrical. Of course, if the table were continued, the distribution for $p = 0.6$ would be similar to that for $q = 0.6$, but reversed end for end, and so on. Since the standard-deviation is $(npq)^{\frac{1}{2}}$ and the maximum value of pq is given by $p = q$, the symmetrical distribution has the greatest dispersion.

If $p = q$ the effect of increasing n is to raise the mean and increase the dispersion. If p is not equal to q, however, not only does an increase in n raise the mean and increase the dispersion, but it also lessens the asymmetry; the greater n, for the same value of p and q, the less the asymmetry. Thus if we compare the first distribution of the above table with that given by $n = 100$, we have the following :—

B.—*Terms of the Binomial Series* $10,000 (0.9 + 0.1)^{100}$. (*Figures given to the nearest unit.*)

Number of Successes.	Frequency.	Number of Successes.	Frequency.	Number of Successes.	Frequency.
0	—	8	1148	16	193
1	3	9	1304	17	106
2	16	10	1319	18	54
3	59	11	1199	19	26
4	159	12	988	20	12
5	339	13	748	21	5
6	596	14	513	22	2
7	889	15	327	23	1

The maximum frequencies now occur for 9 and 10 successes, and the two " tails " are much more nearly equal. If, on the other hand, n is reduced to 2, the distribution is—

Number of Successes.	Frequency.
0	8100
1	1800
2	100

and the maximum frequency is at one end of the range. Whatever the values of p and q, if n is only increased sufficiently, the distribution may be treated as sensibly symmetrical, the necessary condition being (we state this without proof) that $p - q$ shall be small compared with the standard-deviation $\sqrt{npq}$. It is left to the student to calculate as an exercise the theoretical distributions corresponding to the experimental results cited in Chapter XIII. (Question 1).

4. The property of the binomial series used in the scheme of § 2 for deducing the series with exponent n from that with exponent $n-1$ leads to two interesting methods—graphical and mechanical — for constructing approximate representations of

binomial distributions. It will have been noted that any one term—say the rth—in one series is obtained by taking q times the rth term together with p times the $(r-1)$th term of the preceding series. Now if AP, CR (figure 46) be two verticals, and a third, BQ, be erected between them, cutting PR in Q, so that $AB : BC :: q : p$, then

$$BQ = p.AP + q.CR.$$

(This follows at once on joining AR and considering the two segments into which BQ is divided.) Consider then some binomial, say for the case $p = \frac{1}{4}$, $q = \frac{3}{4}$. Draw a series of verticals (the heavy verticals of fig. 47) at any convenient distance apart

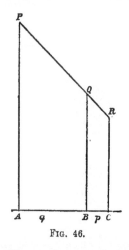

FIG. 46.

on a horizontal base line, and erect other verticals (the lighter verticals) dividing the distance between them in the ratio of $q : p$, viz. $3 : 1$. Next, choosing a vertical scale, draw the binomial polygon for the simplest case $n = 1$; in the diagram N has been taken $= 4096$, and the polygon is $abcd$, $ob = 3072$, $1c = 1024$. The polygons for higher values of n may now be constructed graphically. Mark the points where ab, bc, cd respectively cut the intermediate verticals and project them horizontally to the right on to the thick verticals. This gives the polygon $ab'c'd'e'$ for $n = 2$. For $ob' = q.ob$, $1c' = p.ob + q.1c$, and so on. Similarly, if the points where ab', $b'c'$, etc., cut the intermediate verticals are projected horizontally on to the thick verticals, we have the polygon $ab''c''d''e''f''$ for $n = 3$. The process may be continued indefinitely, though it will be found difficult to maintain any high degree of accuracy after the first few constructions.

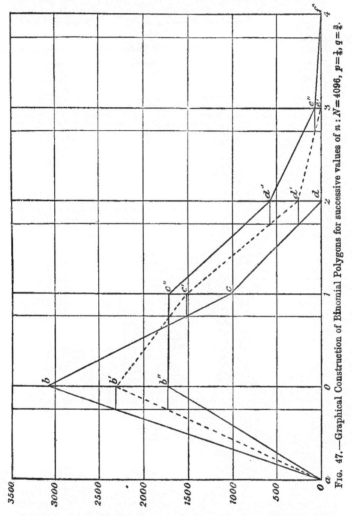

FIG. 47.—Graphical Construction of Binomial Polygons for successive values of $n : N = 4096, p = \frac{1}{4}, q = \frac{3}{4}$.

5. The mechanical method of constructing the representation of a binomial series is indicated diagrammatically by fig. 48. The

apparatus consists of a funnel opening into a space—say a $\frac{1}{4}$ inch in depth—between a sheet of glass and a back-board. This space is broken up by successive rows of wedges like 1, 2 3, 4 5 6, etc., which will divide up into streams any granular material such as shot or mustard seed which is poured through the funnel when the apparatus is held at a slope. At the foot these wedges are replaced by vertical strips, in the spaces between which the

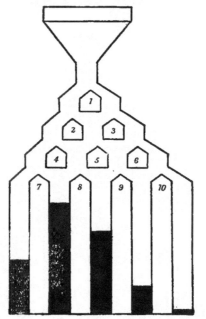

Fig. 48.—The Pearson-Galton Binomial Apparatus.

material can collect. Consider the stream of material that comes from the funnel and meets the wedge 1. This wedge is set so as to throw q parts of the stream to the left and p parts to the right (of the observer). The wedges 2 and 3 are set so as to divide the resultant streams in the same proportions. Thus wedge 2 throws q^2 parts of the original material to the left and qp to the right, wedge 3 throws pq parts of the original material to the left and p^2 to the right. The streams passing these wedges are therefore in the ratio of $q^2 : 2qp : p^2$. The next row of wedges is again set so as to divide these streams in the same proportions as before, and the four streams that result will bear the proportions $q^3 : 3q^2p : 3qp^2 : p^3$. The final set, at the heads of the vertical strips, will give the streams proportions $q^4 : 4q^3p : 6q^2p^2 : 4qp^3 : p^4$, and these streams will accumulate between the strips and give a representation of the binomial by a kind of histogram, as shown. Of course as many rows of wedges may be provided as may be desired.

This kind of apparatus was originally devised by Sir Francis Galton (ref. 1) in a form that gives roughly the symmetrical binomial, a stream of shot being allowed to fall through rows of nails, and the resultant streams being collected in partitioned spaces. The apparatus was generalised by Professor Pearson, who used rows of wedges fixed to movable slides, so that they could be adjusted to give any ratio of $q : p$. (Ref. 13.)

6. The values of the mean and standard-deviation of a binomial distribution may be found from the terms of the series directly, as well as by the method of Chap. XIII. (the calculation was in fact given as an exercise in Question 8, Chap. VII., and Question 6, Chap. VIII.). Arrange the terms under each other as in col. 1 below, and treat the problem as if it were an arithmetical example, taking the arbitrary origin at 0 successes: as N is a factor all through, it may be omitted for convenience.

(1) Frequency f.	(2) Dev. ξ.	(3) $f\xi$.	(4) $f\xi^2$.
q^n	0	—	—
$n.q^{n-1}p$	1	$n.q^{n-1}p$	$n.q^{n-1}p$
$\dfrac{n(n-1)}{1.2}q^{n-2}p^2$	2	$n(n-1)q^{n-2}p^2$	$2n(n-1)q^{n-2}p^2$
$\dfrac{n(n-1)(n-2)}{1.2.3}q^{n-3}p^3$	3	$\dfrac{n(n-1)(n-2)}{1.2}q^{n-3}p^3$	$\dfrac{3n(n-1)(n-2)}{1.2}q^{n-3}p^3$
.	.	.	.
.	.	.	.
.	.	.	.

The sum of col. 1 is of course unity, *i.e.* we are treating N as unity, and the mean is therefore given by the sum of the terms in col. (3). But this sum is

$$np \left\{ q^{n-1} + (n-1)q^{n-2}p + \frac{(n-1)(n-2)}{1.2}q^{n-3}p^2 + \ldots \right\}$$
$$= np(q+p)^{n-1} = np.$$

That is, the mean M is np, as by the method of Chap. XIII

The square of the standard-deviation is given by the sum of
the terms in col. (4) less the square of the mean, that is,

$$\sigma^2 = np\left\{ q^{n-1} + 2(n-1)q^{n-2}p + 3\frac{(n-1)(n-2)}{1.2}q^{n-3}p^2 + \ldots \right\} - n^2p^2.$$

But the series in the bracket is the binomial series $(q+p)^{n-1}$
with the successive terms multiplied by 1, 2, 3, . . . It therefore
gives the difference of the mean of the said binomial from -1,
and its sum is therefore $(n-1)p+1$. Therefore

$$\sigma^2 = np\{(n-1)p + 1\} - n^2p^2$$
$$= np - np^2 = npq.$$

7. The terms of the binomial series thus afford a means of
completely describing a certain class of frequency-distributions—
i.e. of giving not merely the mean and standard-deviation in
each case, but of describing the whole form of the distribution.
If N samples of n cards each be drawn from an indefinitely large
record of cards marked with A or a, the proportion of A-cards
in the record being p, then the successive terms of the series
$N(q+p)^n$ give the frequencies to be expected in the long run of
0, 1, 2, . . . A-cards in the sample, the actual frequencies only
deviating from these by errors which are themselves fluctuations
of sampling. The three constants N, p, n, therefore, determine
the average or smoothed form of the distribution to which actual
distributions will more or less closely approximate.

Considered, however, as a formula which may be generally
useful for describing frequency-distributions, the binomial series
suffers from a serious limitation, viz. that it only applies to a
strictly discontinuous distribution like that of the number of
A-cards drawn from a record containing A's and a's, or the number
of heads thrown in tossing a coin. The question arises whether
we can pass from this discontinuous formula to an equation
suitable for representing a continuous distribution of frequency.

8. Such an equation becomes, indeed, almost a necessity for
certain cases with which we have already dealt. Consider, for
example, the frequency-distribution of the number of male births
in batches of 10,000 births, the mean number being, say, 5100.
The distribution will be given by the terms of the series
$(0.49 + 0.51)^{10000}$ and the standard-deviation is, in round numbers,
50 births. The distribution will therefore extend to some 150
births or more on either side of the mean number, and in order
to obtain it we should have to calculate some 300 terms of a
binomial series with an exponent of 10,000! This would not
only be practically impossible without the use of certain methods
of approximation, but it would give the distribution in quite

unnecessary detail: as a matter of practice, we would not have compiled a frequency-distribution by single male births, but would certainly have grouped our observations, taking probably 10 births as the class-interval. We want, therefore, to replace the binomial series by some continuous curve, having approximately the same ordinates, the curve being such that the area between any two ordinates y_1 and y_2 will give the frequency of observations between the corresponding values of the variable x_1 and x_2.

9. It is possible to find such a continuous limit to the binomial series for any values of p and q, but in the present work we will confine ourselves to the simplest case in which $p = q = 0\cdot5$, and the binomial is symmetrical. The terms of the series are

$$N(\tfrac{1}{2})^n \left\{ 1 + n + \frac{n(n-1)}{1.2} + \frac{n(n-1)(n-2)}{1.2.3} + \ldots \right\}.$$

The frequency of m successes is

$$N(\tfrac{1}{2})^n \frac{\lfloor n}{\lfloor m \lfloor n-m}$$

and the frequency of $m+1$ successes is derived from this by multiplying it by $(n-m)/(m+1)$. The latter frequency is therefore greater than the former so long as

$$n - m > m + 1$$

or

$$m < \frac{n-1}{2}.$$

Suppose, for simplicity, that n is even, say equal to $2k$; then the frequency of k successes is the greatest, and its value is

$$y_0 = N(\tfrac{1}{2})^{2k} \frac{\lfloor 2k}{\lfloor k \lfloor k} \qquad \qquad . \qquad . \qquad . \qquad (1)$$

The polygon tails off symmetrically on either side of this greatest ordinate. Consider the frequency of $k + x$ successes; the value is

$$y_x = N(\tfrac{1}{2})^{2k} \frac{\lfloor 2k}{\lfloor k+x \lfloor k-x} \qquad \qquad . \qquad . \qquad . \qquad (2)$$

and therefore

$$\frac{y_x}{y_0} = \frac{(k)(k-1)(k-2) \ldots \ldots (k-x+1)}{(k+1)(k+2)(k+3) \ldots \ldots (k+x)}$$

$$= \frac{\left(1-\frac{1}{k}\right)\left(1-\frac{2}{k}\right)\left(1-\frac{3}{k}\right) \ldots \ldots \left(1-\frac{x-1}{k}\right)}{\left(1+\frac{1}{k}\right)\left(1+\frac{2}{k}\right)\left(1+\frac{3}{k}\right) \ldots \ldots \left(1+\frac{x-1}{k}\right)\left(1+\frac{x}{k}\right)} \qquad . \qquad (3)$$

Now let us approximate by assuming, as suggested in § 8, that k is very large, and indeed large compared with x, so that $(x/k)^2$ may be neglected compared with (x/k). This assumption does not involve any difficulty, for we need not consider values of x much greater than three times the standard-deviation or $3\sqrt{k/2}$, and the ratio of this to k is $3/\sqrt{2k}$, which is necessarily small if k be large. On this assumption we may apply the logarithmic series

$$\log_\epsilon(1 + \delta) = \delta - \frac{\delta^2}{2} + \frac{\delta^3}{3} - \frac{\delta^4}{4} + \ \cdots$$

to every bracket in the fraction (3), and neglect all terms beyond the first. To this degree of approximation,

$$\log\frac{y_x}{y_0} = -\frac{2}{k}(1 + 2 + 3 + \ \cdots + \overline{x-1}) - \frac{x}{k}$$

$$= -\frac{x(x-1)}{k} - \frac{x}{k}$$

$$= -\frac{x^2}{k}.$$

Therefore, finally,

$$y_x = y_0 e^{-\frac{x^2}{k}} = y_0 e^{-\frac{x^2}{2\sigma^2}} \quad . \qquad . \qquad . \qquad . \quad (4)$$

where, in the last expression, the constant k has been replaced by the standard-deviation σ, for $\sigma^2 = k/2$.

The curve represented by this equation is symmetrical about the point $x = 0$, which gives the greatest ordinate $y = y_0$. Mean, median, and mode therefore coincide, and the curve is, in fact, that drawn in fig. 5, p. 89, and taken as the ideal form of the symmetrical frequency-distribution in Chap. VI. The curve is generally known as the normal curve of errors or of frequency, or the law of error.

10. A normal curve is evidently defined completely by giving the values of y_0 and σ and assigning the origin of x. If we desire to make a normal curve fit some given distribution as near as may be, the last two data are given by the standard-deviation and the mean respectively; the value of y_0 will be given by the fact that the areas of the two distributions, or the numbers of observations which these areas represent, must be the same.

This condition does not, however, lead in any simple and elementary algebraic way to an expression for y_0, though such a value could be found arithmetically to any desired degree of approximation. For it is evident that (1) any alteration in

y_0 produces a proportionate alteration in the area of the curve, e.g. doubling y_0 doubles every ordinate y_x and therefore doubles the area: (2) any alteration in σ produces a proportionate alteration in the area, for the values of y_x are the same for the same values of x/σ, and therefore doubling σ doubles the distance of every ordinate from the mean, and consequently doubles the area. The area of the curve, or the number of observations represented, is therefore proportional to $y_0\sigma$, or we must have

$$N = a \times y_0\sigma$$

where a is a numerical constant. The value of a may be found approximately by taking y_0 and σ both equal to unity, calculating the values of the ordinates y_x for equidistant values of x, and taking the area, or number of observations N, as given by the sum of the ordinates multiplied by the interval.

11. The table below gives the values of y for values of x proceeding by fifths of a unit; the values are, of course, the same for positive and negative values of x. For the *whole* curve the sum of the ordinates will be found to be 12·53318, the interval being 0·2 units; the area is therefore, approximately, 2·50664,

Ordinates of the Curve $y = e^{-\frac{x^2}{2}}$. (*For references to more extended tables, see list on pp. 357-8.*)

x.	y.	Log y.	x.	y.	Log y.
0	1·00000	0	2·6	·03405	$\bar{2}$·53209
0·2	·98020	$\bar{1}$·99131	2·8	·01984	$\bar{2}$·29757
0·4	·92312	$\bar{1}$·96526	3·0	·01111	$\bar{2}$·04567
0·6	·83527	$\bar{1}$·92183	3·2	·00598	$\bar{3}$·77641
0·8	·72615	$\bar{1}$·86103	3·4	·00309	$\bar{3}$·48978
1·0	·60653	$\bar{1}$·78285	3·6	·00153	$\bar{3}$·18577
1·2	·48675	$\bar{1}$·68731	3·8	·00073	$\bar{4}$·86439
1·4	·37531	$\bar{1}$·57439	4·0	·00034	$\bar{4}$·52564
1·6	·27804	$\bar{1}$·44410	4·2	·00015	$\bar{4}$·16952
1·8	·19790	$\bar{1}$·29644	4·4	·00006	$\bar{5}$·79603
2·0	·13534	$\bar{1}$·13141	4·6	·00003	$\bar{5}$·40516
2·2	·08892	$\bar{2}$·94901	4·8	·00001	$\bar{6}$·99693
2·4	·05614	$\bar{2}$·74923	5·0	·00000	$\bar{6}$·57132

and this is the approximate value of a. The value is more than sufficiently accurate for practical purposes, for the exact value is $\sqrt{2\pi} = 2·506627 \ldots$. The proof of this value cannot be given here, but it may be deduced from an important approximate expression for the factorials of large numbers, due to James

Stirling (1730). If n be large, we have, to a high degree of approximation,

$$\lfloor n = \sqrt{2n\pi}\; \frac{n^n}{e^n}.$$

Applying Stirling's theorem to the factorials in equation (1) we have

$$y_0 = \frac{N}{\sqrt{\pi.k}} = \frac{N}{\sqrt{2\pi}.\sigma} \qquad . \quad . \quad . \quad (5)$$

The complete expression for the normal curve is therefore

$$y = \frac{N}{\sqrt{2\pi}.\sigma}\; e^{-\frac{x^2}{2\sigma^2}} \qquad . \quad . \quad . \quad (6)$$

The exponent may be written x^2/c^2 where $c = \sqrt{2}.\sigma$, and this is the origin of the use of $\sqrt{2} \times \sigma$ (the "modulus") as a measure of dispersion, of $1/\sqrt{2}.\sigma$ as a measure of "precision," and of $2\sigma^2$ as "the fluctuation" (cf. Chap. VIII. § 13).   The use of the factor 2 or $\sqrt{2}$ becomes meaningless if the distribution be not *normal*.

Another rule cited in Chap. VIII., viz. that the mean deviation is approximately 4/5 of the standard-deviation, is strictly true for the normal curve only. For this distribution the mean deviation $= \sigma\sqrt{2/\pi} = 0.79788\ldots \sigma$: the proof cannot be given within the limitations of the present work. The rule that a range of 6 times the standard-deviation includes the great majority of the observations and that the quartile deviation is about 2/3 of the standard-deviation were also suggested by the properties of this curve (see below §§ 16, 17).

12. In the proof of § 9 the assumption was made that k (the half of the exponent of the binomial) was very large compared with x (any deviation that had to be considered). In point of fact, however, the normal curve gives the terms of the symmetrical binomial surprisingly closely even for moderate values of n. Thus if $n = 64$, $k = 32$, and the standard-deviation is 4. Deviations x have therefore to be considered up to ± 12 or more, which is over 1/3 of k. As will be seen, however, from the annexed table, the ordinates of the normal curve agree with those of the binomial to the nearest unit (in 10,000 observations) up to $x = \pm 15$. The closeness of approximation is partly due to the fact that, in applying the logarithmic series to the fraction on the right of equation (3), the terms of the second order in expansions of corresponding brackets in numerator and denominator cancel each other: these terms, therefore, do not

accumulate, but only the terms of the third order. There is
only one second-order term that has been neglected, viz. that due
to the last bracket in the denominator. Even for much lower
values of n than that chosen for the illustration—*e.g.* 10 or 12
(*cf.* Qu. 4 at the end of this chapter)—the normal curve still
gives a very fair approximation.

TABLE *showing* (1) *Ordinates of the Binomial Series* $10,000 \ (\frac{1}{2}+\frac{1}{2})^{64}$ *and*

(2) *Corresponding Ordinates of the Normal Curve* $y = \dfrac{10,000}{4\sqrt{2\pi}} \, e^{-\frac{x^2}{32}}$.

Term.	Binomial Series.	Normal Curve.	Term.	Binomial Series.	Normal Curve.
32	993	997	24 and 40	136	135
31 and 33	963	967	23 ,, 41	80	79
30 ,, 34	878	880	22 ,, 42	44	44
29 ,, 35	753	753	21 ,, 43	23	23
28 ,, 36	606	605	20 ,, 44	11	11
27 ,, 37	459	457	19 ,, 45	5	5
26 ,, 38	326	324	18 ,, 46	2	2
25 ,, 39	217	216	17 ,, 47	1	1

13. But if the normal curve were limited in its application to
distributions which were certainly of binomial type, its use in
practice (apart from its theoretical applications to many cases of
the theory of sampling) would be very restricted. As suggested,
however, by the illustrations given in Chap. VI., a certain, though
not a large, number of distributions—more particularly among
those relating to measurements on man and other animals—are
approximately of normal form, even although such distributions
have not obviously originated in the same way as a binomial
distribution. Take, for example, the distribution of statures in
the United Kingdom (Chap. VI., Table VI.). The mean stature
is 67·46 inches, the standard-deviation 2·57 inches (the values are
worked out in the illustrations of Chaps. VII. and VIII.), and the
number of observations 8585. This gives $y_0 = 1333$, and all the
data necessary for plotting a normal curve of the same mean and
standard-deviation (the process of fitting is dealt with at greater
length in § 14 below). The two distributions are shown together
in fig. 49, the continuous curve being the normal curve, and the
small circles showing the observed frequencies. It is evident that
they agree very closely. Other body measurements, *e.g.* skull
measurements, etc., also follow the normal law ; it also applies to
certain characters in plants (*e.g.* number of seeds per capsule in

Nelumbium, Pearl, *American Naturalist,* Nov. 1906). The question arises, therefore, why, in such cases, the distribution should be approximately normal, a form of distribution which we have only shown to arise if the variable is the sum of a large number of elements, each of which can take the values 0 and 1 (or other two constant values), these values occurring independently, and with equal frequency.

In the first place, it should be stated that the conditions of the deduction given in § 9 were made a little unnecessarily restricted,

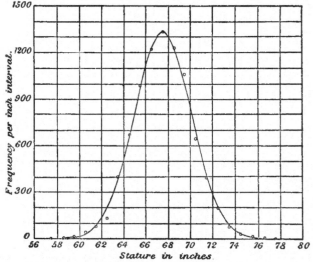

Fig. 49.—The Distribution of Stature for Adult Males in the British Isles (fig. 6, p. 89), fitted with a Normal Curve : to avoid confusing the figure, the frequency-polygon has not been drawn in, the tops of the ordinates being shown by small circles.

with a view to securing simplicity of algebra. The deduction may be generalised, whilst retaining the same type of proof, by assuming that p and q are unequal (provided $p - q$ be small compared with $\sqrt{npq}$, cf. § 3), that p and q are not quite the same for all the events, that all the events are not quite independent, or that n is not large, but that some sort of continuous variation is possible in the values of the elementary variables, these being no longer restricted to 0 and 1, or two other discrete values. (*Cf.* the deduction given by Pearson in ref. 13.) Proceeding further from this last idea, the deduction may be rendered more general still, without introducing the conception of the binomial at all, by founding the curve on more or less complex cases of the theory of sampling for variables instead of for attributes. If a variable is the sum (or, within limits, some slightly more complicated function) of a *large number* of other variables, then the distribution of the compound or resultant variable is normal, provided that the elementary variables are independent, or nearly so (*cf.* ref. 6). The forms of the frequency-distributions of the elementary variables affect the final distribution less and less as their number is increased : only if their number is moderate, and the distributions all exhibit a comparatively high degree of asymmetry of uniform sign, will the same sign of asymmetry be sensibly evident in the distribution of the compound variable. On this sort of hypothesis, the expectation of normality in the case of stature may be based on the fact that it is a highly compound character—depending on the sizes of the bones of the head, the vertebral column, and the legs, the thickness of the intervening cartilage, and the curvature of the spine—the elements of which it is composed being at least to some extent independent, *i.e.* by no means perfectly correlated with each other, and their frequency-distributions exhibiting no very high degree of asymmetry of one and the same sign. The comparative rarity of normal distributions in economic statistics is probably due in part to the fact that in most cases, while the entire causation is certainly complex, relatively few causes have a largely predominant influence (hence also the frequent occurrence of irregular distributions in this field of work), and in part also to a high degree of asymmetry in the distributions of the elements on which the compound variable depends. Errors of observation may in general be regarded as compounded of a number of elements, due to various causes, and it was in this connection that the normal curve was first deduced, and received its name of the curve of errors, or law of error.

14. If it be desired to compare some actual distribution with the normal distribution, the two distributions should be superposed on one diagram, as in fig. 49, though, of course, on a much larger scale. When the mean and standard-deviation of the actual distribution have been determined, y_0 is given by equation (5) ; the fit will probably be slightly closer if the standard-deviation is adjusted by Sheppard's correction (Chap. XI. § 4). The normal curve is then most readily drawn by plotting a scale showing fifths of the standard-deviation along the base line of the frequency diagram, taking the mean as origin, and marking over these points the ordinates given by the figures of the table on p. 303, multiplied in each case by y_0. The curve

can be drawn freehand, or by aid of a curve ruler, through the
tops of the ordinates so determined. The logarithms of y in the
table on p. 303 are given to facilitate the multiplication. The only
point in which the student is likely to find any difficulty is
in the use of the scales : he must be careful to remember
that the standard-deviation must be expressed *in terms of the
class-interval as a unit* in order to obtain for y_0 a number of
observations per interval comparable with the frequencies of his
table.

The process may be varied by keeping the normal curve
drawn to one scale, and redrawing the actual distribution
so as to make the area, mean, and standard-deviation the
same. Thus suppose a diagram of a normal curve was printed
once for all to a scale, say, of $y_0 = 5$ inches, $\sigma = 1$ inch, and
it were required to fit the distribution of stature to it.
Since the standard-deviation is 2·57 inches of stature, the
scale of stature is 1 inch = 2·57 inch of stature, or 0·389 inches
= 1 inch of stature ; this scale must be drawn on the base of the
normal-curve diagram, being so placed that the mean falls
at 67·46. As regards the scale of frequency-per-interval, this
is given by the fact that the whole area of the polygon showing
the actual distribution must be equal to the area of the
normal curve, that is 5 $\sqrt{2\pi} = 12.53$ square inches. If, therefore,
the scale required is n observations per interval to the inch,
we have, the number of observations being 8585,

$$\frac{8585}{n \times 2·57} = 12·53,$$

which gives $n = 266·6$.

Though the second method saves curve drawing, the first,
on the whole, involves the least arithmetic and the simplest
plotting.

15. Any plotting of a diagram, or the equivalent arithmetical
comparison of actual frequencies with those given by the
fitted normal distribution, affords, of course, in itself, only a
rough test, of a practical kind, of the normality of the given
distribution. The question whether all the observed differences
between actual and calculated frequencies, taken together,
may have arisen merely as fluctuations of sampling, so that the
actual distribution may be regarded as strictly normal, neglecting
such errors, is a question of a kind that cannot be answered in
an elementary work (*cf.* ref. 22). At present the student is in
a position to compare the divergences of actual from calculated
frequencies with fluctuations of sampling in the case of single
class-intervals, or single groups of class-intervals only. If the

expected theoretical frequency in a certain interval is f, the standard error of sampling is $\sqrt{f(N-f)}/N$; and if the divergence of the observed from the theoretical frequency exceed some three times this standard error, the divergence is unlikely to have occurred as a mere fluctuation of sampling.

It should be noted, however, that the ordinate of the normal curve at the middle of an interval does not give accurately the area of that interval, or the number of observations within it: it would only do so if the curve were sensibly straight. To deal strictly with problems as to fluctuations of sampling in the frequencies of single intervals or groups of intervals, we require, accordingly, some convenient means of obtaining the number of observations, in a given normal distribution, lying between any two values of the variable.

16. If an ordinate be erected at a distance x/σ from the mean, in a normal curve, it divides the whole area into two parts, the ratio of which is evidently, from the mode of construction of the curve, independent of the values of y_0 and of σ. The calculation of these fractions of area for given values of x/σ, though a long and tedious matter, can thus be done once for all, and a table giving the results is useful for the purpose suggested in § 15 and in many other ways. References to complete tables are cited at the end of this work (list of tables, pp. 357–8), the short table below being given only for illustrative purposes. The table shows the greater fraction of the area lying on one side of any given ordinate; e.g. 0·53983 of the whole area lies on one side of an ordinate at 0·1σ from the mean, and 0·46017 on the other side. It will be seen that an ordinate drawn at a distance from the mean equal to the standard-deviation cuts off some 16 per cent. of the whole area on one side; some 68 per cent. of the area will therefore be contained between ordinates at $\pm \sigma$. An ordinate at twice the standard-deviation cuts off only 2·3 per cent., and therefore some 95·4 per cent. of the whole area lies within a range of $\pm 2\sigma$. As three times the standard-deviation the fraction of area cut off is reduced to 135 parts in 100,000, leaving 99·7 per cent. within a range of $\pm 3\sigma$. This is the basis of our rough rule that a range of 6 times the standard-deviation will in general include the great bulk of the observations: the rule is founded on, and is only strictly true for, the normal distribution. For other forms of distribution it need not hold good, though experience suggests that it more often holds than not. The binomial distribution, especially if p and q be unequal, only becomes approximately normal when n is large, and this limitation must be remembered in applying the table given, or similar more complete tables, to cases in which the distribution is strictly binomial.

TABLE *showing the Greater Fraction of the Area of a Normal Curve to One Side of an Ordinate of Abscissa x/σ.* (*For references to more extended tables, see list on pp. 357–8.*)

x/σ.	Greater Fraction of Area.	x/σ.	Greater Fraction of Area.
0	·50000	2·1	·98214
0·1	·53983	2·2	·98610
0·2	·57926	2·3	·98928
0·3	·61791	2·4	·99180
0·4	·65542	2·5	·99379
0·5	·69146	2·6	·99534
0·6	·72575	2·7	·99653
0·7	·75804	2·8	·99744
0·8	·78814	2·9	·99813
0·9	·81594	3·0	·99865
1·0	·84134	3·1	·99903
1·1	·86433	3·2	·99931
1·2	·88493	3·3	·99952
1·3	·90320	3·4	·99966
1·4	·91924	3·5	·99977
1·5	·93319	3·6	·99984
1·6	94520	3·7	·99989
1·7	·95543	3·8	·99993
1·8	·96407	3·9	·99995
1·9	·97128	4·0	·99997
2·0	·97725	4·1	·99998

17. If we try to determine the quartile deviation in terms of the standard-deviation from the table, we see that it lies between 0·6 and 0·7σ. Interpolating, it is given approximately by

$$\left\{ 0·6 + 0·1\frac{2425}{3229} \right\} \sigma = 0·675\sigma.$$

More exact interpolation gives the value 0·67448975σ. This result, again, is the foundation of the rough rule that the semi-inter-quartile range is usually some 2/3 of the standard-deviation : it is strictly true for the normal curve only. It may be noted that the constant 0·67448975 . . . . can be determined by processes of interpolation only, and cannot be expressed exactly, like the mean deviation, in terms of any other known constant, such as π.

It has become customary to use 0·674 . . . . times the standard error rather than the standard error itself as a measure of the unreliability of observed statistical results, and the term **probable error** is given to this quantity. It should be noted that the word "probable" is hardly used in its usual sense in this connection: the probable error is merely a quantity such that we may expect greater and less errors of simple sampling with about equal frequency, provided always that the distribution of errors is normal. On the whole, the use of the "probable error" has little advantage compared with the standard, and consequently little stress is laid on it in the present work; but the term is in constant use, and the student must be familiar with it.

It is true that the "probable error" has a simpler and more direct significance than the standard error, but this advantage is lost as soon as we come to deal with multiples of the probable error. Further, the best modern tables of the ordinates and area of the normal curve are given in terms of the standard-deviation or standard error, not in terms of the probable error, and the multiplication of the former by 0·6745, to obtain the probable error, is not justified unless the distribution is normal. For very large samples the distribution is approximately normal, even though p and q are unequal; but this is not so for small samples, such as often occur in practice. In the case of small samples the use of the "probable error" is consequently of doubtful value, while the standard error retains its significance as a measure of dispersion. The "probable error," it may be mentioned, is often stated after an observed proportion with the ± sign before it; a percentage given as 20·5 ± 2·3 signifying "20·5 per cent., with a probable error of 2·3 per cent."

If an error or deviation in, say, a certain proportion p only just exceed the probable error, it is as likely as not to occur in simple sampling: if it exceed twice the probable error (in either direction), it is likely to occur as a deviation of simple sampling about 18 times in 100 trials—or the odds are about 4·6 to 1 against its occurring at any one trial. For a range of three times the probable error the odds are about 22 to 1, and for a range of four times the probable error 142 to 1. Until a deviation exceeds, then, 4 times the probable error, we cannot feel any *great* confidence that it is likely to be "significant." It is simpler to work with the standard error and take ± 3 times the standard error as the critical range: for this range the odds are about 370 to 1 against such a deviation occurring in simple sampling at any one trial.

18. The following are a few miscellaneous examples of the use of the normal curve and the table of areas.

Example i.—A hundred coins are thrown a number of times. How often approximately in 10,000 throws may (1) exactly 65 heads, (2) 65 heads or more, be expected?

The standard-deviation is $\sqrt{0\cdot5 \times 0\cdot5 \times 100} = 5$. Taking the distribution as normal, $y_0 = 797\cdot9$.

The mean number of heads being 50, $65 - 50 = 3\sigma$. The frequency of a deviation of 3σ is given at once by the table (p. 303) as $797\cdot9 \times \cdot0111 \ldots = 8\cdot86$, or nearly 9 throws in 10,000. A throw of 65 heads will therefore be expected about 9 times.

The frequency of throws of 65 heads *or more* is given by the area table (p. 310), but a little caution must now be used, owing to the discontinuity of the distribution. A throw of 65 heads is equivalent to a range of $64\cdot5$–$65\cdot5$ on the continuous scale of the normal curve, the division between 64 and 65 coming at $64\cdot5$. $64\cdot5 - 50 = + 2\cdot9\sigma$, and a deviation of $+ 2\cdot9.\sigma$ or more, will only occur, as given by the table, 187 times in 100,000 throws, or, say, 19 times in 10,000.

Example ii.—Taking the data of the stature-distribution of fig. 49 (mean $67\cdot46$, standard-deviation $2\cdot57$ in.), what proportion of all the individuals will be within a range of $\pm$ 1 inch of the mean?

1 inch $= 0\cdot389\sigma$. Simple interpolation in the table of p. 310 gives $0\cdot65129$ of the area below this deviation, or a more extended table the more accurate value $0\cdot65136$. Within a range of $\pm 0\cdot389\sigma$ the fraction of the whole area is therefore $0\cdot30272$, or the statures of about 303 per thousand of the given population will lie within a range of ± 1 inch from the mean.

Example iii.—In a case of crossing a Mendelian recessive by a heterozygote the expectation of recessive offspring is 50 per cent. (1) How often would 30 recessives or more be expected amongst 50 offspring owing simply to fluctuations of sampling? (2) How many offspring would have to be obtained in order to reduce the probable error to 1 per cent.?

The standard error of the percentage of recessives for 50 observations is $50 \sqrt{1/50} = 7\cdot07$. Thirty recessives in fifty is a deviation of 5 from the mean, or, if we take thirty as representing $29\cdot5$ or more, $4\cdot5$ from the mean ; that is, $0\cdot636.\sigma$. A positive deviation of this amount or more occurs about 262 times in 1000, so that 30 recessives or more would be expected in more than a quarter of the batches of 50 offspring. We have assumed normality for rather a small value of n, but the result is sufficiently accurate for practical purposes.

As regards the second part of the question we are to have

$$\cdot6745 \times 50 \sqrt{1/n} = 1,$$

n being the number of offspring. This gives $n = 1137$ to the nearest unit.

Example iv.—The diagram of fig. 49 shows that the number of statures recorded in the group "62 in. and less than 63" is markedly less than the theoretical value. Could such a difference occur owing to fluctuations of simple sampling; and if so, how often might it happen?

The actual frequency recorded is 169. To obtain the theoretical frequency we may either take it as given roughly by the ordinate in the centre of the interval, or, better, use the integral table. Remembering that statures were only recorded to the nearest $\frac{1}{8}$ in., the true limits of the interval are $61\frac{15}{16}$–$62\frac{15}{16}$, or 61·94–62·94, mid-value 62·44. This is a deviation from the mean (67·46) of 5·02. Calculating the ordinate of the normal curve directly we find the frequency 197·8. This is certainly, as is evident from the form of the curve, a little too small. The interval actually lies between deviations of 4·52 in. and 5·52 in., that is, 1·759σ and 2·148σ. The corresponding fractions of area are 0·96071 and 0·98418, difference, or fraction of area between the two ordinates, 0·02347. Multiplying this by the whole number of observations (8585) we have the theoretical frequency 201·5.

The difference of theoretical and observed frequencies is therefore 32·5. But the proportion of observations which should fall into the given class is 0·023, the proportion falling into other classes 0·977, and the standard error of the class frequency is accordingly $\sqrt{0·023 \times 0·977 \times 8585} = 14·0$. As the actual deviation is only 2·32 times this, it could certainly have occurred as a fluctuation of sampling.

The question how often it might have occurred can only be answered if we assume the distribution of fluctuations of sampling to be approximately normal. It is true that p and q are very unequal, but then n is very large (8585)—so large that the difference of the chances is fairly small compared with $\sqrt{npq}$ (about one-fifteenth). Hence we may take the distribution of errors as roughly normal to a first approximation, though a first approximation only. The tables give 0·990 of the area below a deviation of 2·32σ, so we would expect an equal or greater deficiency to occur about 10 times in 1000 trials, or once in a hundred.

REFERENCES.

The Binomial Machine.

(1) GALTON, FRANCIS, *Natural Inheritance;* Macmillan & Co. London, 1889, (Mechanical method of forming a binomial or normal distribution, chap. v., p. 63; for Pearson's generalised machine, see below, ref. 13.)

Frequency Curves.

For the early classical memoirs on the normal curve or law of error by Laplace, Gauss, and others, see Todhunter's *History* (Introduction: ref. 7). The literature of this subject is too extensive to enable us to do more than cite a few of the more recent memoirs, of which 6, 7, and 13 are of fundamental importance. The student will find other citations in 6, 8, and 14.

(2) CHARLIER, C. V. L., "Researches into the Theory of Probability" (*Communications from the Astronomical Observatory*, Lund); Lund, 1906.

(3) CUNNINGHAM, E., "The ω-Functions, a Class of Normal Functions occurring in Statistics," *Proc. Roy. Soc.*, Series A, vol. lxxxi., 1908, p. 310.

(4) EDGEWORTH, F. Y., "On the Representation of Statistics by Mathematical Formulæ," *Jour. Roy. Stat. Soc.*, vol. lxi., 1898 ; vol. lxii., 1899 ; and vol. lxiii., 1900.

(5) EDGEWORTH, F. Y., Article on the "Law of Error" in the *Encyclopædia Britannica*, 10th edn., vol. xxviii., 1902, p. 280.

(6) EDGEWORTH, F. Y., "The Law of Error," *Cambridge Phil. Trans.*, vol. xx., 1904, pp. 36–65, 113–141 (and an appendix, pp. i–xiv, not printed in the *Cambridge Phil. Trans.*).

(7) EDGEWORTH, F. Y., "The Generalised Law of Error, or Law of Great Numbers," *Jour. Roy. Stat. Soc.*, vol. lxix., 1906, p. 497.

(8) EDGEWORTH, F. Y., "On the Representation of Statistical Frequency by a Curve," *Jour. Roy. Stat. Soc.*, vol. lxx., 1907, p. 102.

(9) FECHNER, G. T., *Kollektivmasslehre* (herausgegeben von G. F. Lipps ; Engelmann, Leipzig, 1897.)

(10) KAPTEYN, J. C., *Skew Frequency Curves in Biology and Statistics* ; Noordhoff, Groningen ; Wm. Dawson & Sons, London, 1903.

(11) MACALISTER, DONALD, "The Law of the Geometric Mean," *Proc. Roy. Soc.*, vol. xxix., 1879, p. 367.

(12) NIXON, J. W., "An Experimental Test of the Normal Law of Error," *Jour. Roy. Stat. Soc.*, vol. lxxvi., 1913, pp. 702–706.

(13) PEARSON, KARL, "Skew Variation in Homogeneous Material," *Phil. Trans. Roy. Soc.*, Series A, vol. clxxxvi., 1895, p. 343.
  For the generalised binomial machine, see § 1. The memoir deals with curves derived from the general binomial, and from a somewhat analogous series derived from the case of sampling from limited material. Supplement to the memoir, *ibid.*, vol. cxcvii., 1901, p. 443. For a derivation of the same curves from a modified standpoint, ignoring the binomial and analogous distributions, *cf.* Chap. X., ref. 18.

(14) PEARSON, KARL, "Das Fehlergesetz und eeine Verallgemeinerungen durch Fechner und Pearson" : A Rejoinder, *Biometrika*, vol. iv., 1905, p. 169.

(15) PEROZZO, LUIGI, "Nuove Applicazioni del Calcolo delle Probabilità allo Studio dei Fenomeni Statistici e Distribuzione dei Matrimoni secondo l'Età degli Sposi," *Mem. della Classe di Scienze morali, etc., Reale Accad. dei Lincei*, vol. x., Series 3, 1882.

(16) SHEPPARD, W. F., "On the Application of the Theory of Error to Cases of Normal Distribution and Normal Correlation," *Phil. Trans. Roy. Soc.*, Series A, vol. cxcii., 1898, p. 101. (Includes a geometrical treatment of the normal curve.)

(17) YULE, G. U., "On the Distribution of Deaths with Age when the Causes of Death act cumulatively, and similar Frequency-distributions,"

Jour. Roy. Stat. Soc., vol. lxxiii., 1910, p. 26. (A binomial distribution with negative index, and the related curve, *i.e.* a special case of one of Pearson's curves, ref. 13.)

The Resolution of a Distribution compounded of two Normal Curves into its Components.

(18) PEARSON, KARL, " Contributions to the Mathematical Theory of Evolution (on the Dissection of Asymmetrical Frequency Curves)," *Phil. Trans. Roy. Soc.*, Series A, vol. clxxxv., 1894, p. 71.

(19) EDGEWORTH, F. Y., " On the Representation of Statistics by Mathematical Formulæ," part ii., *Jour. Roy. Stat. Soc.*, vol. lxii., 1899, p. 125.

(20) PEARSON, KARL, "On some Applications of the Theory of Chance to Racial Differentiation," *Phil. Mag.*, 6th Series, vol. i., 1901, p. 110.

(21) HELGUERO, FERNANDO DE, "Per la risoluzione delle curve dimorfiche," *Biometrika*, vol. iv., 1905, p. 230. Also memoir under the same title in the Transactions of the Reale Accademia dei Lincei, Rome, vol. vi., 1906. (The first is a short note, the second the full memoir.)

See also the memoir by Charlier, cited in (2), section vi. of that memoir dealing with the problem of dissection.

Testing the Fit of an Observed to a Theoretical or another Observed Distribution.

(22) PEARSON, KARL, "On the Criterion that a given System of Deviations from the Probable, in the Case of a Correlated System of Variables, is such that it can be reasonably supposed to have arisen from random sampling," *Phil. Mag.*, 5th Series, vol. l., 1900, p. 157.

(23) PEARSON, KARL, "On the Probability that Two Independent Distributions of Frequency are really Samples from the same Population," *Biometrika*, vol. viii., 1911, p. 250 ; also *Biometrika*, vol. x., 1914, pp. 85-143.

EXERCISES.

1. Calculate the theoretical distributions for the three experimental cases (1), (2), and (3) cited in § 7 of Chapter XIII.

2. Show that if np be a whole number, the mean of the binomial coincides with the greatest term.

3. Show that if two symmetrical binomial distributions of degree n (and of the same number of observations) are so superposed that the rth term of the one coincides with the $(r+1)$th term of the other, the distribution formed by adding superposed terms is a symmetrical binomial of degree $\overline{n+1}$.

[Note: it follows that if two normal distributions of the same area and standard-deviation are superposed so that the difference between the means is small compared with the standard-deviation, the compound curve is very nearly normal.]

4. Calculate the ordinates of the binomial 1024 $(0\cdot5 + 0\cdot5)^{10}$, and compare them with those of the normal curve.

5. Draw a diagram showing the distribution of statures of Cambridge students (Chap. VI., Table VII.), and a normal curve of the same area, mean, and standard-deviation superposed thereon.

6. Compare the values of the semi-interquartile range for the stature distributions of male adults in the United Kingdom and Cambridge students, (1) as found directly, (2) as calculated from the standard-deviation, on the assumption that the distribution is normal.

7. Taking the mean stature for the British Isles as 67·46 in. (the distribution of fig. 49), the mean for Cambridge students as 68·85 in., and the common standard-deviation as 2·56 in., what percentage of Cambridge students exceed the British mean in stature, assuming the distribution normal ?

8. As stated in Chap. XIII., Example ii., certain crosses of *Pisum sativum* based on 7125 seeds gave 25·32 per cent. of green seeds instead of the theoretical proportion 25 per cent., the standard error being 0·51 per cent. In what percentage of experiments based on the same number of seeds might an equal or greater percentage be expected to occur owing to fluctuations of sampling alone?

9. In what proportion of similar experiments based on (1) 100 seeds, (2) 1000 seeds, might (a) 30 per cent. or more, (b) 35 per cent. or more, of green seeds, be expected to occur, if ever ?

10. In similar experiments, what number of seeds must be obtained to make the " probable error " of the proportion 1 per cent. ?

11. If skulls are classified as *dolichocephalic* when the length-breadth index is under 75, *mesocephalic* when the same index lies between 75 and 80, and *brachycephalic* when the index is over 80, find approximately (assuming that the distribution is normal) the mean and standard-deviation of a series in which 58 per cent. are stated to be dolichocephalic, 38 per cent. mesocephalic, and 4 per cent. brachycephalic.

CHAPTER XVI.

NORMAL CORRELATION.

1. THE expression that we have obtained for the "normal" distribution of a single variable may readily be made to yield a corresponding expression for the distribution of frequency of pairs of values of two variables. This normal distribution for two variables, or "normal correlation surface," is of great historical importance, as the earlier work on correlation is, almost without exception, based on the assumption of such a distribution; though when it was recognised that the properties of the correlation-coefficient could be deduced, as in Chap. IX., without reference to the form of the distribution of frequency, a knowledge of this special type of frequency-surface ceased to be so essential. But the generalised normal law is of importance in the theory of sampling: it serves to describe very approximately certain actual distributions (*e.g.* of measurements on man); and if it can be assumed to hold good, some of the expressions in the theory of correlation, notably the standard-deviations of arrays (and, if more than two variables are involved, the partial correlation-coefficients), can be assigned more simple and definite meanings than in the general case. The student should, therefore, be familiar with the more fundamental properties of the distribution.

317

2. Consider first the case in which the two variables are completely independent. Let the distributions of frequency for the two variables x_1 and x_2, singly, be

$$\left. \begin{array}{c} y_1 = y_1' e^{-\frac{x_1^2}{2\sigma_1^2}} \\[2em] y_2 = y_2' e^{-\frac{x_2^2}{2\sigma_2^2}} \end{array} \right\} \qquad . \qquad . \qquad (1)$$

Then, assuming independence, the frequency-distribution of pairs of values must, by the rule of independence, be given by

$$y_{12} = y_{12}' e^{-\frac{1}{2}\left(\frac{x_1^2}{\sigma_1^2} + \frac{x_2^2}{\sigma_2^2}\right)} \qquad . \qquad . \qquad (2)$$

where

$$y_{12}' = \frac{y_1'.y_2'}{N} = \frac{N}{2\pi.\sigma_1\sigma_2} \qquad . \qquad (3)$$

Equation (2) gives a normal correlation surface for one special case, the correlation-coefficient being zero. If we put $x_2 = a$ constant, we see that every section of the surface by a vertical plane parallel to the x_1 axis, i.e. the distribution of any array of x_1's, is a normal distribution, with the same mean and standard-deviation as the total distribution of x_1's, and a similar statement holds for the array of x_2's; these properties must hold good, of course, as the two variables are assumed independent (cf. Chap. V. § 13). The contour lines of the surface, that is to say, lines drawn on the surface at a constant height, are a series of similar ellipses with major and minor axes parallel to the axes of x_1 and x_2 and proportional to σ_1 and σ_2, the equations to the contour lines being of the general form

$$\frac{x_1^2}{\sigma_1^2} + \frac{x_2^2}{\sigma_2^2} = C^2 \qquad . \qquad . \qquad . \qquad (4)$$

Pairs of values of x_1 and x_2 related by an equation of this form are, therefore, equally frequent.

3. To pass from this special case of independence to the general case of two correlated variables, remember (Chap. XII. § 8) that if

$$x_{1.2} = x_1 - b_{12}.x_2$$
$$x_{2.1} = x_2 - b_{21}.x_1$$

x_1 and $x_{2.1}$, as also x_2 and $x_{1.2}$ are uncorrelated. If they are not merely uncorrelated but completely independent, and if the distribution of each of the deviations singly be normal, we must have for the frequency-distribution of pairs of deviations of x_1 and $x_{2 \cdot 1}$

$$y_{12} = y'_{12} e^{-\frac{1}{2}\left(\frac{x_1^2}{\sigma_1^2} + \frac{x_{2 \cdot 1}^2}{\sigma_{2 \cdot 1}^2}\right)} \qquad \qquad . \qquad . \qquad (5)$$

But

$$\frac{x_1^2}{\sigma_1^2} + \frac{x_{2 \cdot 1}^2}{\sigma_{2 \cdot 1}^2} = \frac{x_1^2}{\sigma_1^2(1 - r_{12}^2)} + \frac{x_2^2}{\sigma_2^2(1 - r_{12}^2)} - 2r_{12}\frac{x_1 x_2}{\sigma_1 \sigma_2(1 - r_{12}^2)}$$

$$= \frac{x_1^2}{\sigma_{1 \cdot 2}^2} + \frac{x_2^2}{\sigma_{2 \cdot 1}^2} - 2r_{12}\frac{x_1 x_2}{\sigma_{1 \cdot 2} \cdot \sigma_{2 \cdot 1}}.$$

Evidently we would also have arrived at precisely the same expression if we had taken the distribution of frequency for x_2 and $x_{1 \cdot 2}$, and reduced the exponent

$$\frac{x_2^2}{\sigma_2^2} + \frac{x_{1 \cdot 2}^2}{\sigma_{1 \cdot 2}^2}.$$

We have, therefore, the general expression for the normal correlation surface for two variables

$$y_{12} = y'_{12} e^{-\frac{1}{2}\left(\frac{x_1^2}{\sigma_{1 \cdot 2}^2} + \frac{x_2^2}{\sigma_{2 \cdot 1}^2} - 2r_{12}\frac{x_1 x_2}{\sigma_{1 \cdot 2}\sigma_{2 \cdot 1}}\right)} \qquad . \qquad (6)$$

Further, since x_1 and $x_{2 \cdot 1}$, x_2 and $x_{1 \cdot 2}$, are independent, we must have

$$y'_{12} = \frac{N}{2\pi . \sigma_1 \sigma_{2 \cdot 1}} = \frac{N}{2\pi . \sigma_2 \sigma_{1 \cdot 2}} = \frac{N}{2\pi . \sigma_1 . \sigma_2 (1 - r_{12}^2)^{\frac{1}{2}}} \qquad . \qquad (7)$$

4. If we assign to x_2 some fixed value, say h_2, we have the distribution of the array of x_1's of type h_2,

$$y_{12} = y'_{12} \cdot e^{-\frac{1}{2}\left(\frac{x_1^2}{\sigma_{1 \cdot 2}^2} + \frac{h_2^2}{\sigma_{2 \cdot 1}^2} - 2r_{12}\frac{x_1 \cdot h_2}{\sigma_{1 \cdot 2}\sigma_{2 \cdot 1}}\right)}$$

$$= y'_{12} \cdot e^{-\frac{h_2^2}{2\sigma_2^2}} \cdot e^{-\frac{\left(x_1 - r_{12}\frac{\sigma_1}{\sigma_2}h_2\right)^2}{2\sigma_{1 \cdot 2}^2}}.$$

This is a normal distribution of standard-deviation $\sigma_{1 \cdot 2}$, with a mean deviating by $r_{12}\frac{\sigma_1}{\sigma_2} \cdot h_2$ from the mean of the whole distribution of x_1's. As h_2 represents any value whatever of x_2, we see (1) that the standard-deviations of all arrays of x_1 are the same, and equal to $\sigma_{1.2}$: (2) that the regression of x_1 on x_2 is strictly linear.   Similarly, of course, if we assign to x_1 any value h_1, we will find (1) that the standard-deviations of all arrays of x_2 are the same : (2) that the regression of x_2 on x_1 is strictly linear.

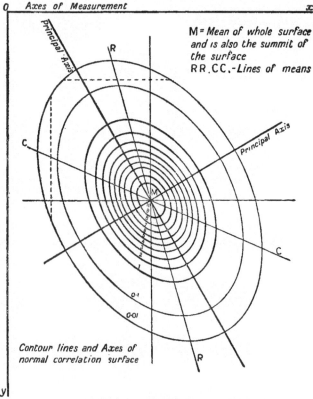

FIG. 50.—Principal Axes and Contour Lines of the normal
Correlation Surface.

5. The contour lines are, as in the case of independence, a series of concentric and similar ellipses ; the major and minor axes are, however, no longer parallel to the axes of x_1 and x_2, but make a certain angle with them.   Fig. 50 illustrates the calculated form of the contour lines for one case, RR and CC being the lines of regression.   As each line of regression cuts every

array of x_1 or of x_2 in its mean, and as the distribution of every array is symmetrical about its mean, RR must bisect every horizontal chord and CC every vertical chord, as illustrated by the two chords shown by dotted lines: it also follows that RR cuts all the ellipses in the points of contact of the horizontal tangents to the ellipses, and CC in the points of contact of the vertical tangents. The surface or solid itself, somewhat truncated, is shown in fig. 29, p. 166.

6. Since, as we see from fig. 50, a normal surface for two correlated variables may be regarded merely as a certain surface for which r is zero turned round through some angle, and since for every angle through which it is turned the distributions of all x_1 arrays and x_2 arrays are normal, it follows that every section of a normal surface by a vertical plane is a normal curve, *i.e.* the distributions of arrays taken at any angle across the surface are normal. It also follows that, since the total distributions of x_1 and x_2 must be normal for every angle though which the surface is turned, the distributions of totals given by slices or arrays taken at any angle across a normal surface must be normal distributions. But these would give the distributions of functions like $a.x_1 \pm b.x_2$, and consequently (1) the distribution of any linear function of two normally distributed variables x_1 and x_2 must also be normal; (2) the correlation between any two linear functions of two normally distributed variables must be normal correlation.

To find the angle θ through which the surface has been turned, from the position for which the correlation is zero to the position for which the coefficient has some assigned value r, we must use a little trigonometry. The major and minor axes of the ellipses are sometimes termed the principal axes. If ξ_1, ξ_2 be the co-ordinates referred to the principal axes (the ξ_1-axis being the x_1 axis in its new position) we have for the relation between ξ_1, ξ_2, x_1, x_2, the angle θ being taken as positive for a rotation of the x_1-axis which will make it, if continued through 90°, coincide in direction and sense with the x_2-axis,

$$\left. \begin{array}{l} \xi_1 = x_1. \cos \theta + x_2. \sin \theta \\ \xi_2 = x_2. \cos \theta - x_1. \sin \theta \end{array} \right\} \qquad . \qquad . \qquad (8)$$

But, since $\xi_1 \, \xi_2$ are uncorrelated, $\Sigma(\xi_1 \xi_2) = 0$. Hence, multiplying together equations (8) and summing,

$$0 = (\sigma_2^2 - \sigma_1^2) \sin 2\theta + 2r_{12}.\sigma_1\sigma_2 \cos 2\theta$$

$$\tan 2\theta = \frac{2r_{12}.\sigma_1\sigma_2}{\sigma_1^2 - \sigma_2^2} \qquad . \qquad . \qquad . \qquad (9)$$

It should be noticed that if we *define* the principal axes of any distribution for two variables as being a pair of axes at right angles for which the variables ξ_1, ξ_2 are uncorrelated, equation (9) gives the angle that they make with the axes of measurement whether the distribution be normal or no.

7. The two standard-deviations, say Σ_1 and Σ_2, about the principal axes are of some interest, for evidently from § 2 the major and minor axes of the contour-ellipses are proportional to these two standard-deviations. They may be most readily determined as follows. Squaring the two transformation equations (8), summing and adding, we have

$$\Sigma_1^2 + \Sigma_2^2 = \sigma_1^2 + \sigma_2^2 \quad . \qquad . \quad . \quad (10)$$

Referring the surface to the axes of measurement, we have for the central ordinate by equation (7)

$$y'_{12} = \frac{N}{2\pi\sigma_1\sigma_2(1 - r_{12}^2)^{\frac{1}{2}}}. \qquad \bullet$$

Referring it to the principal axes, by equation (3)

$$y'_{12} = \frac{N}{2\pi . \Sigma_1\Sigma_2}.$$

But these two values of the central ordinate must be equal, therefore

$$\Sigma_1\Sigma_2 = \sigma_1\sigma_2(1 - r_{12}^2)^{\frac{1}{2}} \qquad\qquad (11)$$

(10) and (11) are a pair of simultaneous equations from which Σ_1 and Σ_2 may be very simply obtained in any arithmetical case. Care must, however, be taken to give the correct signs to the square root in solving. $\Sigma_1 + \Sigma_2$ is necessarily positive, and $\Sigma_1 - \Sigma_2$ also if r is positive, the major axes of the ellipses lying along ξ_1 : but if r be negative, $\Sigma_1 - \Sigma_2$ is also negative. It should be noted that, while we have deduced (11) from a simple consideration depending on the normality of the distribution, it is really of general application (like equation 10), and may be obtained at somewhat greater length from the equations for transforming co-ordinates.

8. As stated in Chap. XV. § 13, the frequency-distribution for any variable may be expected to be approximately normal if that variable may be regarded as the sum (or, within limits, some slightly more complex function) of a large number of other variables, provided that these elementary component variables are independent, or nearly so. Similarly, the correlation between two variables may be expected to be approximately normal if

each of the two variables may be regarded as the sum, or some slightly more complex function, of a large number of elementary component variables, the intensity of correlation depending on the proportion of the components common to the two variables.

Stature is a highly compound character of this kind, and we have seen that, in one instance at least, the distribution of stature for a number of adults is given approximately by the normal curve. We can now utilise Table III., Chap. IX., p. 160, showing the correlation between stature of father and son, to test, as far as we can by elementary methods, whether the normal surface will fit the distribution of the same character in pairs of individuals : we leave it to the student to test, as far as he can do so by simple graphical methods, the approximate normality of the total distributions for this table. The first important property of the normal distribution is the linearity of the regression. This was well illustrated in fig. 37, p. 174, and the closeness of the regression to linearity was confirmed by the values of the correlation-ratios (p. 206), viz., 0·52 in each case as compared with a correlation of 0·51. Subject to some investigation as to the possibility of the deviations that do occur arising as fluctuations of simple sampling, when drawing samples from a record for which the regression is strictly linear, we may conclude that the regression is appreciably linear.

9. The second important property of the normal distribution for two variables is the constancy of the standard-deviation for all parallel arrays. We gave in Chap. X. p. 204 the standard-deviations of ten of the columns of the present table, from the column headed 62·5–63·5 onwards ; these were—

2·56	2·60
2·11	2·26
2·55	2·26
2·24	2·45
2·23	2·33

the mean being 2·36. The standard-deviations again only fluctuate irregularly round their mean value. The mean of the first five is 2·34, of the second five 2·38, a difference of only 0·04 : of the first group, two are greater and three are less than the mean, and the same is true of the second group. There does not seem to be any indication of a general tendency for the standard-deviation to increase or decrease as we pass from one end of the table to the other. We are not yet in a position to test how far the differences from the average standard-deviation might arise in sampling from a record in which the distribution was strictly normal, but, as a fact, a rough test suggests that they might have done so.

10. Next we note that the distributions of all arrays of a normal surface should themselves be normal. Owing, however, to the small numbers of observations in any array, the distributions of arrays are very irregular, and their normality cannot be tested in any very satisfactory way : we can only say that they do not exhibit any marked or regular asymmetry. But we can test the allied property of a normal correlation-table, viz. that the totals of arrays must give a normal distribution even if the arrays be taken diagonally across the surface, and not parallel to either axis of measurement (*cf.* § 6). From an ordinary correlation-table we cannot find the totals of such diagonal arrays exactly, but the totals of arrays at an angle of 45° will be given with sufficient accuracy for our present purpose by the totals of lines of diagonally adjacent compartments. Referring again to Table III., Chap. IX., and forming the totals of such diagonals (running up from left to right), we find, starting at the top left-hand corner of the table, the following distribution :—

0·25	78·75
2	81·25
3.25	67·5
6·25	59·25
8	42·25
9·75	30·75
17	29·25
34·5	19
41	10·75
46·25	7
60·5	4·25
67·5	3·5
85·75	1·75
87·25	1
78	0·25
94·25	———

Total   1078

The mean of this distribution is at 0·368 of an interval above the centre of the interval with frequency 78 : its standard-deviation is 4·755 intervals, or, remembering that the interval is $1/\sqrt{2}$ of an inch, 3·362 inches. (This value may be checked directly from the constants for the table given in Chap. IX., Question 3, p. 189, for we have from the first of the transformation equations (8),

$$\sigma_\xi^2 = \sigma_1^2 . \cos^2 \theta + \sigma_2^2 \sin^2 \theta + 2r_{12}\sigma_1\sigma_2 . \sin \theta \cos \theta,$$

and inserting $\sigma_1 = 2\cdot72$, $\sigma_2 = 2\cdot75$, $r_{12} = 0\cdot51$, $\sin \theta = \cos \theta = 1/\sqrt{2}$ find $\sigma_\xi = 3\cdot361$). Drawing a diagram and fitting a normal curve we have fig. 51 ; the distribution is rather irregular but the fit is fair ; certainly there is no marked asymmetry, and, so far as the graphical test goes, the distribution may be regarded as appreciably normal. One of the greatest divergences of the actual distribution from the normal curve occurs in the almost central interval with frequency 78 : the difference between the observed and calculated frequencies is here 12 units, but the standard error is 9·1, so that it may well have occurred as a fluctuation of simple sampling.

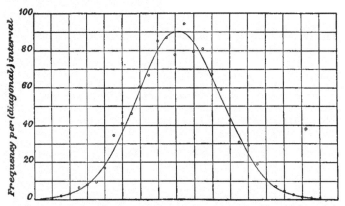

Fig. 51.—Distribution of Frequency obtained by addition of Table III., Chap. IX., along Diagonals running up from left to right, fitted with a Normal Curve.

11. So far, we have seen (1) that the regression is approximately linear ; (2) that, in the arrays which we have tested, the standard-deviations are approximately constant, or at least that their differences are only small, irregular and fluctuating ; (3) that the distribution of totals for one set of diagonal arrays is approximately normal. These results suggest, though they cannot completely prove, that the whole distribution of frequency may be regarded as approximately normal, within the limits of fluctuations of sampling. We may therefore apply a more searching test, viz. the form of the contour lines and the closeness of their fit to the contour-ellipses of the normal surface. We can see at once, however, that no very close fit can be expected. Since the frequencies in the compartments of the table are small, the standard error of any frequency is given approximately by its

square root (Chap. XIII. § 12), and this implies a standard error of about 5 units at the centre of the table, 3 units for a frequency of 9, or 2 units for a frequency of 4 : such fluctuations might cause wide divergences in the corresponding contour lines.

Using the suffix 1 to denote the constants relating to the distribution of stature for fathers, and 2 the same constants for the sons,

$$N = 1078 \qquad M_1 = 67{\cdot}70 \qquad M_2 = 68{\cdot}66 \qquad r_{12} = 0{\cdot}51$$
$$\sigma_1 = 2{\cdot}72 \qquad \sigma_2 = 2{\cdot}75$$

Hence we have from equation (7)

$$y'_{12} = 26{\cdot}7$$

and the complete expression for the fitted normal surface is

$$y = 26{\cdot}7 e^{-\frac{1}{2}\left(\frac{x_1^2}{5{\cdot}47} + \frac{x_2^2}{5{\cdot}60} - \frac{x_1 x_2}{5{\cdot}43}\right)}.$$

The equation to any contour ellipse will be given by equating the index of e to a constant, but it is very much easier to draw the ellipses if we refer them to their principal axes. To do this we must first determine θ, Σ_1 and Σ_2. From (9),

$$\tan 2\theta = -46{\cdot}49,$$

whence $2\theta = 91° \ 14'$, $\theta = 45° \ 37'$, the principal axes standing very nearly at an angle of 45° with the axes of measurement, owing to the two standard-deviations being very nearly equal. They should be set off on the diagram, not with a protractor, but by taking $\tan \theta$ from the tables (1·022) and calculating points on each axis on either side of the mean.

To obtain Σ_1 and Σ_2 we have from (10) and (11)

$$\Sigma_1^2 + \Sigma_2^2 = 14{\cdot}961$$
$$2\Sigma_1 \Sigma_2 = 12{\cdot}868$$

Adding and subtracting these equations from each other and taking the square root,

$$\Sigma_1 + \Sigma_2 = 5{\cdot}275$$
$$\Sigma_1 - \Sigma_2 = 1{\cdot}447$$

whence $\Sigma_1 = 3{\cdot}36$, $\Sigma_2 = 1{\cdot}91$; owing to the principal axes standing nearly at 45° the first value is sensibly the same as that found for σ_ξ in § 10. The equations to the contour ellipses, referred to the principal axes, may therefore be written in the form

$$\frac{\xi_1^2}{(3{\cdot}36)^2} + \frac{\xi_2^2}{(1{\cdot}91)^2} = c^2,$$

the major and minor axes being $3\cdot36 \times c$ and $1\cdot91 \times c$ respectively. To find c for any assigned value of the frequency y we have

$$y_{12} = y'_{12}e^{-\frac{1}{2}c^2}$$

$$c^2 = \frac{2(\log y'_{12} - \log y_{12})}{\log e}.$$

Supposing that we desire to draw the three contour-ellipses for $y = 5$, 10 and 20, we find $c = 1\cdot83$, $1\cdot40$ and $0\cdot76$, or the following

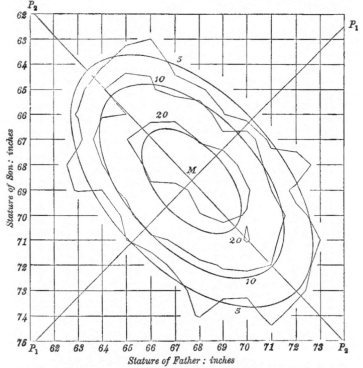

FIG. 52.—Contour Lines for the Frequencies 5, 10 and 20 of the distribution of Table III., Chap. IX., and corresponding Contour Ellipses of the fitted Normal Surface. $P_1 P_1$, $P_2 P_2$, principal axes : M, mean.

values for the major and minor axes of the ellipses :—semi-major axes, $6\cdot15$, $4\cdot70$, $2\cdot55$: semi-minor axes, $3\cdot50$, $2\cdot67$, $1\cdot45$. The ellipses drawn with these axes are shown in fig. 52, very much

reduced, of course, from the original drawing, one of the squares
shown representing a square inch on the original. The actual
contour lines for the same frequencies are shown by the irregular
polygons superposed on the ellipses, the points on these polygons
having been obtained by simple graphical interpolation between
the frequencies in each row and each column—diagonal interpolation between the frequencies in a row and the frequencies in a
column not being used. It will be seen that the fit of the two
lower contours is, on the whole, fair, especially considering the
high standard errors. In the case of the central contour, $y = 20$,
the fit looks very poor to the eye, but if the ellipse be compared
carefully with the table, the figures suggest that here again we
have only to deal with the effects of fluctuations of sampling.
For father's stature = 66 in., son's stature = 70 in., there is
a frequency of 18·75, and an increase in this much less than the
standard error would bring the actual contour outside the ellipse.
Again, for father's stature = 68 in., son's stature = 71 in., there
is a frequency of 19, and an increase of a single unit would give
a point on the actual contour below the ellipse. Taking the
results as a whole, the fit must be regarded as quite as good as
we could expect with such small frequencies. It is perhaps of
historical interest to note that Sir Francis Galton, working without a knowledge of the theory of normal correlation, suggested
that the contour lines of a similar table for the inheritance of
stature seemed to be closely represented by a series of concentric
and similar ellipses (ref. 2): the suggestion was confirmed when
he handed the problem, in abstract terms, to a mathematician,
Mr J. D. Hamilton Dickson (ref. 4), asking him to investigate
"the Surface of Frequency of Error that would result from
these data, and the various shapes and other particulars of its
sections that were made by horizontal planes" (ref. 3, p. 102).

12. The normal distribution of frequency for two variables is
an isotropic distribution, to which all the theorems of Chap. V.
§§ 11–12 apply. For if we isolate the four compartments of the
correlation-table common to the rows and columns centring
round values of the variables x_1, x_2, x_1', x_2', we have for the ratio
of the cross-products (frequency of $x_1 x_2$ multiplied by frequency
of x_1', x_2', divided by frequency of $x_1 x_2'$ multiplied by frequency of
$x_1' x_2$),

$$e^{\frac{r_{12}}{\sigma_{1.2}\sigma_{2.1}}(x_1' - x_1)(x_2' - x_2).}$$

Assuming that $x_1' - x_1$ has been taken of the same sign as $x_2' - x_2$,
the exponent is of the same sign as r_{12}. Hence the association for

this group of four frequencies is also of the same sign as r_{12}, the ratio of the cross-products being unity, or the association zero, if r_{12} is zero. In a normal distribution, the association is therefore of the same sign—the sign of r_{12}—for every tetrad of frequencies in the compartments common to two rows and two columns; that is to say, the distribution is isotropic. It follows that every grouping of a normal distribution is isotropic whether the class-intervals are equal or unequal, large or small, and the sign of the association for a normal distribution grouped down to 2- × 2-fold form must always be the same whatever the axes of division chosen.

These theorems are of importance in the applications of the theory of normal correlation to the treatment of qualitative characters which are subjected to a manifold classification. The contingency tables for such characters are sometimes regarded as groupings of a normal distribution of frequency, and the coefficient of correlation is determined on this hypothesis by a rather lengthy procedure (ref. 14). Before applying this procedure it is well, therefore, to see whether the distribution of frequency may be regarded as approximately isotropic, or reducible to isotropic form by some alteration in the order of rows and columns (Chap. V. §§ 9-10). If only reducible to isotropic form by some rearrangement, this rearrangement should be effected before grouping the table to 2- × 2-fold form for the calculation of the correlation coefficient by the process referred to. If the table is not reducible to isotropic form by any rearrangement, the process of calculating the coefficient of correlation on the assumption of normality is to be avoided. Clearly, even if the table be isotropic it need not be normal, but at least the test for isotropy affords a rapid and simple means for excluding certain distributions which are not even remotely normal. Table II. of Chap. V. might possibly be regarded as a grouping of normally distributed frequency if re-arranged as suggested in § 10 of the same chapter—it would be worth the investigator's while to proceed further and compare the actual distribution with a fitted normal distribution—but Table IV. could not be regarded as normal, and could not be rearranged so as to give a grouping of normally distributed frequency.

13. If the frequencies in a contingency-table be not large, and also if the contingency or correlation be small, the influence of casual irregularities due to fluctuations of sampling may render it difficult to say whether the distribution may be regarded as essentially isotropic or no. In such cases some further con-densation of the table by grouping together adjacent rows and columns, or some process of "smoothing" by averaging the

frequencies in adjacent compartments, may be of service. The correlation-table for stature in father and son (Table III., Chap. IX.), for instance, is obviously not strictly isotropic as it stands: we have seen, however, that it appears to be normal, within the limits of fluctuations of sampling, and it should consequently be isotropic within such limits. We can apply a rough test by regrouping the table in a much coarser form, say with four rows and four columns : the table below exhibits such a grouping, the limits of rows and of columns having been so fixed as to include not less than 200 observations in each array.

TABLE I.—(condensed from Table III. of Chapter IX.).

Son's Stature (inches).	Father's Stature (inches).				
	Under 65·5.	65·5–67·5	67·5–69·5.	69·5 and over.	Total.
Under 66·5	97·5	74·25	34·75	10·5	217
66·5–68·5	76·5	108	85	52	321·5
68·5–70·5	33·25	64·75	95	84·5	277·5
70·5 and over	14·75	32 5	80·75	134	262
Total	222	279·5	295·5	281	1078

Taking the ratio of the frequency in col. 1 to the sum of the frequencies in cols. 1 and 2 for each successive row, and so on for the other pairs of columns, we find the following series of ratios :

TABLE II.—*Ratio of Frequency in Column m to Frequency in Column m + Frequency in Column (m + 1) in Table I.*

Row.	Columns		
	1 and 2.	2 and 3.	3 and 4.
1	0·568	0·681	0·768
2	0·415	0·560	0·620
3	0 339	0·405	0·529
4	0·312	0·287	0·376

These ratios decrease continuously as we pass from the top to the bottom of the table, and the distribution, as condensed, is therefore isotropic. The student should form one or two other condensations of the original table to 3- × 3- or 4- × 4-fold form : he will probably find them either isotropic, or diverging so slightly from isotropy that an alteration of the frequencies, well within the margin of possible fluctuations of sampling, will render the distribution isotropic.

14. Before concluding this chapter we may note briefly some of the principal properties of the normal distribution of frequency for any number of variables, referring the student for proofs to the original memoirs. Denoting the frequency of the combination of deviations x_1, x_2, x_3, . . . , x_n by $y_{12} \ldots _n$, we must have in the notation of Chapter XII., if the uncorrelated deviations x_1, $x_{2.1}$, $x_{3.12}$, etc. be completely independent (cf. § 3 of the present chapter),

$$y_{12 \, \cdots \, n} = y'_{12 \, \cdots \, n} \, e^{-\frac{1}{2}\phi(x_1 x_2 \, \cdots \, x_n)} \qquad . \qquad . \qquad (12)$$

where

$$\phi(x_1 x_2 \, \cdots \, x_n) = \frac{x_1^2}{\sigma_1^2} + \frac{x_{2.1}^2}{\sigma_{2.1}^2} + \frac{x_{3.12}^2}{\sigma_{3.12}^2} + \, \cdots \, + \frac{x_{n.1 \, \cdots \, (n-1)}^2}{\sigma_{n.1 \, \cdots \, (n-1)}^2} \qquad (13)$$

and

$$y'_{12 \, \cdots \, n} = \frac{N}{(2\pi)^{n/2} \sigma_1 \sigma_{2.1} \sigma_{3.12} \, \cdots \, \sigma_{n.1 \, \cdots \, (n-1)}} \qquad . \qquad (14)$$

The expression (13) for the exponent ϕ may be reduced to a general form corresponding to that given for two variables, viz.—

$$\phi = \frac{x_1^2}{\sigma_{1.23 \, \cdots \, n}^2} + \frac{x_2^2}{\sigma_{2.13 \, \cdots \, n}^2} + \, \cdots \, + \frac{x_n^2}{\sigma_{n.12 \, \cdots \, (n-1)}^2} \qquad . \qquad . \qquad . \qquad (15)$$

$$-2.r_{123 \, \cdots \, n} \frac{x_1 x_2}{\sigma_{1.23 \, \cdots \, n} \sigma_{2.13 \, \cdots \, n}} - \, \cdots \, - 2r_{(n-1)n.12 \, \cdots \, (n-2)} \frac{x_{n-1} x_n}{\sigma_{(n-1).1 \, \cdots \, (n-2)n} \sigma_{n.1 \, \cdots \, (n-1)}}.$$

Several important results may be deduced directly from the form (13) for the exponent. Clearly this might have been written in a great variety of ways, commencing with any deviation of the first order, allotting any primary subscript to the second deviation (except the subscript of the first), and so on, just as in § 3 we arrived at precisely the same final form for the exponent whether we started with the two deviations x_1 and $x_{2.1}$ or with x_2 and $x_{1.2}$. Our assumption, then, that the deviations x_1, $x_{2.1}$, $x_{3.12}$, etc. are normally distributed amounts to the assumption that all deviations of any order and with any suffixes are normally distributed, i.e. *in the general normal distribution for* n *variables every array of every order is a normal distribution*. It will also follow, generalising the deduction of § 6, that any linear function of x_1, x_2 . . . . x_n is normally distributed. Further, if in (13) any fixed values be assigned to $x_{3.12}$ and all the following deviations, the correlation between x_1 and x_2, on expanding $x_{2.1}$, is, as we have seen, normal correlation. Similarly, if any fixed values be assigned to x_1, to $x_{4.123}$, and all the following deviations, on reducing $x_{3.12}$ to the second order we shall find that the correlation between $x_{2.1}$ and $x_{3.1}$ is normal correlation, the correlation coefficient being $r_{23.1}$, and so on. That is to say, using k to denote any group of secondary suffixes, (1) *the correlation between any two deviations $x_{m.k}$ and $x_{n.k}$ is normal correlation*; (2) *the correlation between the said deviations is $r_{mn.k}$ whatever the particular fixed values assigned to the remaining deviations.* The latter conclusion, it will be seen, renders the meaning of partial correlation coefficients much more definite in the case of normal correlation than in the general case. In the general case $r_{mn.k}$ represents merely the average correlation, so to speak, between $x_{m.k}$ and $x_{n.k}$: in the normal case $r_{mn.k}$ is constant for all the sub-groups corresponding to particular assigned values of the other variables. Thus in the case of three variables which are normally correlated, if we assign any given value to x_3, the correlation between the associated values of x_1 and x_2 is $r_{12.3}$: in the general case $r_{12.3}$, if actually worked out for the various sub-groups corresponding, say, to increasing values of x_3, would probably exhibit some continuous change, increasing or decreasing as the case might be. Finally, we have to note that if, in the expression (15) for ϕ, we assign fixed values, say h_2, h_3, etc., to all the deviations except x_1, and then throw ϕ into the form of a perfect square (as in § 4 for the case of two variables), we obtain a normal distribution for x_1 in which the mean is displaced by

$$r_{12.34\ldots n}\frac{\sigma_{1.23\ldots n}}{\sigma_{2.13\ldots n}}h_2 + r_{13.24\ldots n}\frac{\sigma_{1.23\ldots n}}{\sigma_{3.12\ldots n}}h_3 + \ldots r_{1n.2\ldots(n-1)}\frac{\sigma_{1.23\ldots n}}{\sigma_{n.12\ldots(n-1)}}h_n.$$

But this is a linear function of h_2, h_3, etc., therefore in the case of normal correlation *the regression of any one variable on any or all of the others is strictly linear.* The expressions $r_{12.34\ldots n}$ $\sigma_{1.23\ldots n}/\sigma_{2.13\ldots n}$, etc. are of course the partial regressions $b_{12.34\ldots n}$, etc.

REFERENCES.

General.

(1) Bravais, A., "Analyse mathématique sur les probabilités des erreurs de situation d'un point," *Acad. des Sciences* : *Mémoires presentés par divers savants*, IIe série, ix., 1846, p. 255.

(2) Galton, Francis, "Family Likeness in Stature," *Proc. Roy. Soc.*, vol. xl., 1886, p. 42.

(3) Galton, Francis, *Natural Inheritance*; Macmillan & Co., 1889.

(4) DICKSON, J. D. HAMILTON, Appendix to (2), *Proc. Roy. Soc.*, vol. xl., 1886, p. 63.

(5) EDGEWORTH, F. Y., "On Correlated Averages," *Phil. Mag.*, 5th Series, vol. xxxiv., 1892, p. 190.

(6) PEARSON, KARL, "Regression, Heredity, and Panmixia," *Phil. Trans. Roy. Soc.*, Series A, vol. clxxxvii., 1896, p. 253.

(7) PEARSON, KARL, "On Lines and Planes of Closest Fit to Systems of Points in Space," *Phil. Mag.*, 6th Series, vol. ii., 1901, p. 559. (On the fitting of "principal axes" and the corresponding planes in the case of more than two variables.)

(8) PEARSON, KARL, "On the Influence of Natural Selection on the Variability and Correlation of Organs," *Phil. Trans. Roy. Soc.*, Series A, vol. cc., 1902, p. 1. (Based on the assumption of normal correlation.)

(9) PEARSON, KARL, and ALICE LEE, "On the Generalised Probable Error in Multiple Normal Correlation," *Biometrika*, vol. vi., 1908, p. 59.

(10) YULE, G. U., "On the Theory of Correlation," *Jour. Roy. Stat. Soc.*, vol. lx., 1897, p. 812.

(11) YULE, G. U., "On the Theory of Correlation for any number of Variables treated by a New System of Notation," *Proc. Roy. Soc.*, Series A, vol. lxxix., 1907, p. 182.

(12) SHEPPARD, W. F., "On the Application of the Theory of Error to Cases of Normal Distribution and Normal Correlation," *Phil. Trans. Roy. Soc.*, Series A, vol. cxcii., 1898, p. 101.

(13) SHEPPARD, W. F., "On the Calculation of the Double-integral express-ing Normal Correlation," *Cambridge Phil. Trans.*, vol. xix., 1900, p. 23.

Applications to the Theory of Attributes, etc.

(14) PEARSON, KARL, "On the Correlation of Characters not Quantitatively Measurable," *Phil. Trans. Roy. Soc.*, Series A, vol. cxcv., 1900, p. 1. (*Cf.* criticism in ref. 3 of Chap. III.)

(15) PEARSON, KARL, "On a New Method of Determining Correlation between a Measured Character A and a Character B, of which only the Percent-age of Cases wherein B exceeds (or falls short of) a given Intensity is recorded for each grade of A," *Biometrika*, vol. vii., 1909, p. 96.

(16) PEARSON, KARL, "On a New Method of Determining Correlation, when one Variable is given by Alternative and the other by Multiple Categories," *Biometrika*, vol. vii., 1910, p. 248.

See also the memoir (12) by Sheppard.

Various Methods and their Relation to Normal Correlation.

(17) PEARSON, KARL, "On the Theory of Contingency and its Relation to Association and Normal Correlation," *Drapers' Company Research Memoirs, Biometric Series I.* ; Dulau & Co., London, 1904.

(18) PEARSON, KARL, "On Further Methods of Determining Correlation," *Drapers' Company Research Memoirs, Biometric Series IV.* (Methods based on correlation of ranks : difference methods.) Dulau & Co., London, 1907.

(19) SPEARMAN, C., "A Footrule for Measuring Correlation," *Brit. Jour. of Psychology*, vol. ii., 1906, p. 89. (The suggestion of a "rank" method : see Pearson's criticism and improved formula in (18) and Spearman's reply on some points in (20).)

(20) SPEARMAN, C., "Correlation calculated from Faulty Data," *Brit. Jour. of Psychology*, vol. iii., 1910, p. 271.

(21) THORNDIKE, E. L., "Empirical Studies in the Theory of Measurement," *Archives of Psychology* (New York), 1907.

EXERCISES.

1. Deduce equation (11) from the equations for transformation of co-ordinates without assuming the normal distribution. (A proof will be found in ref. 10.)

2. Hence show that if the pairs of observed values of x_1 and x_2 are represented by points on a plane, and a straight line drawn through the mean, the sum of the squares of the distances of the points from this line is a minimum if the line is the major principal axis.

3. The coefficient of correlation with reference to the principal axes being zero, and with reference to other axes *something*, there must be some pair of axes at right angles for which the correlation is a maximum, *i.e.* is numerically greatest without regard to sign. Show that these axes make an angle of 45° with the principal axes, and that the maximum value of the correlation is—

$$\pm \frac{\Sigma_1^2 - \Sigma_2^2}{\Sigma_1^2 + \Sigma_2^2}.$$

4. (Sheppard, ref. 12.) A fourfold table is formed from a normal correlation table, taking the points of division between A and a, B and β, at the medians, so that $(A)=(a)=(B)=(\beta)=N/2$. Show that

$$r = \cos \left(1 - \frac{2(AB)}{N} \right) \pi.$$

CHAPTER XVII

THE SIMPLER CASES OF SAMPLING FOR VARIABLES : PERCENTILES AND MEAN.

1. In Chapters XIII.–XVI. we have been concerned solely with the theory of sampling for the case of attributes and the frequency-distributions appropriate . to that case. We now proceed to consider some of the simpler theorems for the case of variables (*cf.* Chap. XIII. § 2). Suppose that we have a bag containing a practically infinite number of tickets or cards bearing the recorded values of some variable X, and that we draw a ticket from this bag, note the value that it bears, draw another, and so on until we have drawn n cards (a number small compared with the whole number in the bag). Let us continue this process until we have N such samples of n cards each, and then work out the mean, standard-deviation, median, etc., for each of the samples. No one of these measures will prove to be absolutely the same for every sample, and our problem is to determine the standard-deviation that each such measure will exhibit.

2. In solving this problem, we must be careful to define precisely . the conditions which are assumed to subsist, so as to realise the limitations of any solution obtained. These conditions

were discussed very fully for the case of attributes (Chap. XIII. § 8), and we would refer the student to the discussion then given. Here it is sufficient to state the assumptions briefly, using the letters (a), (b) and (c) to denote the corresponding assumptions indicated by the same letters in the section cited.

(a) We assume that we are drawing from precisely the same record throughout the experiment, so that the chance of drawing a card with any given value of X, or a value within any assigned limits, is the same at each sampling.

(b) We assume not only that we are drawing from the same record throughout, but that *each of our cards* at each drawing may be regarded quite strictly as drawn from the same record (or from identically similar records): *e.g.* if our card-record is contained in a series of bundles, we must not make it a practice to take the first card from bundle number 1, the second card from bundle number 2, and so on, or else the chance of drawing a card with a given value of X, or a value within assigned limits, may not be the same for each individual card at each drawing.

(c) We assume that the drawing of each card is entirely independent of that of every other, so that the value of X recorded on card 1, at each drawing, is uncorrelated with the value of X recorded on card 2, 3, 4, and so on. It is for this reason that we spoke of the record, in § 1, as containing a practically infinite number of cards, for otherwise the successive drawings at each sampling would not be independent: if the bag contain ten tickets only, bearing the numbers 1 to 10, and we draw the card bearing 1, the average of the following cards drawn will be higher than the mean of all cards drawn ; if, on the other hand, we draw the 10, the average of the following cards will be lower than the mean of all cards—*i.e.* there will be a negative correlation between the number on the card taken at any one drawing and the card taken at any other drawing. Without making the number of cards in the bag indefinitely large, we can, as already pointed out for the case of attributes (Chap. XIII. § 3), eliminate this correlation by replacing each card before drawing the next.

Sampling conducted under these conditions we shall, as before, speak of as *simple sampling*. We do not, it should be noticed, make the further assumption that the sample is unbiassed, *i.e.* that the chance of inclusion in the sample is independent of the value of X recorded on the card (*cf.* the last paragraph in § 8, Chap. XIII., and the discussion in §§ 4–8, Chap. XIV.). This assumption is unnecessary. If it be true, the interpretation of our results becomes simpler and more straightforward, for we can substitute for such phrases as "the standard-deviation of X *in a very large sample*," "the form of the frequency-distribution *in a very large sample,*" the phrases "the standard-deviation of *X* in the original record," "the form of the frequency-distribution *in the original record*": but in very many, perhaps the majority of, practical cases the very question at issue is the nature of the relation between the distribution of the sample and the distribution of the record from which it is drawn. As has already been emphasised in the passages to which reference is made above, no examination of samples drawn under the same conditions can give any evidence on this head.

3. *Standard Error of a Percentile.*—Let us consider first the fluctuations of sampling for a given percentile, as the problem is intimately related to that of Chaps. XIII.–XIV.

Let X_p be a value of X such that pN of the values of X in an indefinitely large sample drawn under the same conditions lie above it and qN below it.

If we note the proportions of observations above X_p in samples of n drawn from the record, we know that these observed values will tend to centre round p as mean, with a standard-deviation $\sqrt{pq/n}$. If now at each drawing, as well as observing the proportion of X's above X_p, say $p + \delta$, for the sample, we also proceed to note the adjustment ϵ required in X_p to make the proportion of observations above $X_p + \epsilon$ in the sample pn, the standard-deviation of ϵ will bear to the standard-deviation of δ the same ratio that ϵ on an average bears to δ. But this ratio is quite simply determinable if the number of observations in the sample is sufficiently large to justify us in assuming that δ is small—so small that we may regard the element of the frequency curve (for a very large sample) over which $X_p + \epsilon$ ranges as approximately a rectangle. If this assumption be made, and we denote the standard-deviation of X in a very large sample by σ, and the ordinate of the frequency curve at X_p when drawn with unit area and unit standard-deviation by y_p,

$$\epsilon = \frac{\sigma}{y_p} \cdot \delta.$$

Therefore for the standard-deviation of ϵ or of the percentile corresponding to a proportion p we have

$$\sigma_{x_p} = \frac{\sigma}{y_p} \sqrt{\frac{pq}{n}} \quad . \quad . \quad . \quad . \quad (1)$$

4. If the frequency-distribution for the very large sample be a normal curve, the values of y_p for the principal percentiles may be taken from the published tables. A table calculated by Mr Sheppard (Table III., p. 9, in *Tables for Statisticians and Biomet-*

22

ricians, or Table IV., ref. 16, in Appendix I.) gives the values directly, and these have been utilised for the following : the student can estimate the values roughly by a combined use of the area and ordinate tables for the normal curve given in Chapter XV., remembering to divide the ordinates given in that table by $\sqrt{2\pi}$ so as to make the area unity—

Value of y_p

Median	0·3989423
Deciles 4 and 6 . . .	0·3863425
„ 3 and 7	0·3476926
„ 2 and 8	0·2799619
„ 1 and 9	0·1754983
Quartiles	0·3177766

Inserting these values of y_p in equation (1), we have the following values for the standard errors of the median, deciles, etc., and the values given in the second column for their probable errors (Chap. XV. § 17), which the student may sometimes find useful :—

	Standard error is $\sigma/\sqrt{n}$ multiplied by	Probable error is $\sigma/\sqrt{n}$ multiplied by
Median . . .	1·25331	0·84535
Deciles 4 and 6 .	1·26804	0·85528
„ 3 and 7 .	1·31800	0·88897
„ 2 and 8 .	1·42877	0·96369
„ 1 and 9 .	1·70942	1·15298
Quartiles . .	1·36263	0·91908

It will be seen that the influence of fluctuations of sampling on the several percentiles increases as we depart from the median : the standard error of the quartiles is nearly one-tenth greater than that of the median, and the standard error of the first or ninth deciles more than one-third greater.

5. Consider further the influence of the form of the frequency-distribution on the standard error of the median, as this is an important form of average. For a distribution with a given number of observations and a given standard-deviation the standard error varies inversely as y_p. Hence for a distribution in which y_p is small, for example a U-shaped distribution like that of fig. 18 or fig. 19, the standard error of the median will be relatively high, and it will, in so far, be an undesirable form of average to employ. On the other hand, in the case of a distribution which has a high peak in the centre, so as to exhibit a value of y_p large compared with the standard-deviation, the standard error of the median will be relatively low. We can create such a

"peaked" distribution by superposing a normal curve with a small standard-deviation on a normal curve with the same mean and a relatively large standard-deviation. To give some idea of the reduction in the standard error of ,the median that may be effected by a moderate change in the form of the distribution, let us find for what ratio of the standard-deviations of two such curves, having the same area, the standard error of the median reduces to $\sigma/\sqrt{n}$, where σ is of course the standard-deviation of the compound distribution.

Let σ_1, σ_2 be the standard-deviations of the two distributions, and let there be $n/2$ observations in each. Then

$$\sigma = \sqrt{\frac{\sigma_1^2 + \sigma_2^2}{2}} \qquad . \quad . \quad . \quad (a)$$

On the other hand, the value of y_p is—

$$\left\{ \frac{1}{2\sqrt{2\pi} . \sigma_1} + \frac{1}{2\sqrt{2\pi} . \sigma_2} \right\} \sqrt{\frac{\sigma_1^2 + \sigma_2^2}{2}} \quad . \quad . \quad (b)$$

Hence the standard error of the median is

$$\sqrt{\frac{2\pi}{n}} \frac{\sigma_1 \sigma_2}{\sigma_1 + \sigma_2} \qquad . \quad . \quad . \quad (c)$$

(c) is equal to $\sigma/\sqrt{n}$ if

$$\frac{(\sigma_1 + \sigma_2) \sqrt{\sigma_1^2 + \sigma_2^2}}{2\sqrt{\pi}\sigma_1\sigma_2^\bullet} = 1.$$

Writing $\sigma_2/\sigma_1 = \rho$, that is if

$$\frac{(1 + \rho) \sqrt{1 + \rho^2}}{2\sqrt{\pi\rho}} = 1$$

or

$$\rho^4 + 2\rho^3 + (2 - 4\pi)\rho^2 + 2\rho + 1 = 0.$$

This equation may be reduced to a quadratic and solved by taking $\rho + \dfrac{1}{\rho}$ as a new variable. The roots found give $\rho = 2\cdot2360$ .... or $0\cdot4472$ ...., the one root being merely the reciprocal of the other. The standard error of the median will therefore be $\sigma/\sqrt{n}$, in such a compound distribution, if the standard-deviation of the one normal curve is, in round numbers, about $2\frac{1}{4}$ times that of the other. If the ratio be greater, the standard error of the median will be less than $\sigma/\sqrt{n}$. The distribution for which the standard error of the median is exactly equal to $\sigma/\sqrt{n}$ is shown in fig. 53 : it will be seen that it is by no means a very striking form of distribution ; at a hasty glance it might almost be taken as normal: In the case of distributions of a form more or less similar to that shown, it is evident that we cannot at all safely estimate by eye alone the relative standard error of the median as compared with $\sigma/\sqrt{n}$.

6. In the case of a grouped frequency-distribution, if the number of observations is sufficient to make the class-frequencies run fairly smoothly, *i.e.* to enable us to regard the distribution

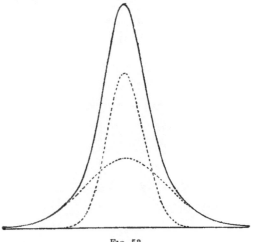

FIG. 53.

as nearly that of a *very large* sample, the standard error of any percentile can be calculated very readily indeed, for we can eliminate σ from equation (1). Let f_p be the frequency-per-class-interval at the given percentile—simple interpolation will give us the value with quite sufficient accuracy for practical purposes, and if the figures run irregularly they may be smoothed. Let σ be the value of the standard-deviation expressed in class-intervals, and let n be the number of observations as before. Then since y_p is the ordinate of the frequency-distribution when drawn with unit standard-deviation and unit area, we must have

$$y_p = \frac{\sigma}{n} f_p.$$

But this gives at once for the standard error *expressed in terms of the class-interval as unit*

$$\sigma_{x_p} = \frac{\sqrt{npq}}{f_p} \qquad . \qquad . \qquad . \quad (2)$$

As an example in which we can compare the results given by the two different formulæ (1) and (2), take the distribution of stature used as an illustration in Chaps. VII. and VIII. and in §§ 13, 14 of Chap. XV. The number of observations is 8585, and the standard-deviation 2·57 in., the distribution being approximately normal : $\sigma/\sqrt{n} = 0.027737$, and, multiplying by the factor 1·253 . . . . given in the table in § 4, this gives 0·0348 as the standard error of the median, on the assumption of normality of the distribution. Using the direct method of equation (2), we find the median to be 67·47 (Chap. VII. § 15), which is very nearly at the centre of the interval with a frequency 1329. Taking this as being, with sufficient accuracy for our present purpose, the frequency per interval at the median, the standard error is

$$\tfrac{1}{2}\frac{\sqrt{8585}}{1329} = 0.0349.$$

As we should expect, the value is practically the same as that obtained from the value of the standard-deviation on the assumption of normality.

Let us find the standard error of the first and ninth deciles as another illustration. On the assumption that the distribution is normal, these standard errors are the same, and equal to 0·027737 × 1·70942 = 0·0474. Using the direct method, we find by simple interpolation the approximate frequencies per interval at the first and ninth deciles respectively to be 590 and 570, giving standard errors of 0·0471 and 0·0488, mean 0·0479, slightly in excess of that found on the assumption that the frequency is given by the normal curve. The student should notice that the class-interval is, in this case, identical with the unit of measurement, and consequently the answer given by equation (2) does not require to be multiplied by the magnitude of the interval.

In the case of the distribution of pauperism (Chap. VII., Example i.), the fact that the class-interval is not a unit must be remembered. The frequency at the median (3·195 per cent.) is approximately 96, and this gives for the standard error of the median by (2) (the number of observations being 632) 0·1309 intervals, that is 0·0655 per cent.

7. In finding the standard error of the difference between two

percentiles in the same distribution, the student must be careful to note that the errors in two such percentiles are not independent. Consider the two percentiles, for which the values of p and q are $p_1 q_1$, $p_2 q_2$ respectively, the first-named being the lower of the two percentiles. These two percentiles divide the whole area of the frequency curve into three parts, the areas of which are proportional to q_1, $1 - q_1 - p_2$, and p_2. Further, since the errors in the first percentile are directly proportional to the errors in q_1, and the errors in the second percentile are directly proportional but of opposite sign to the errors in p_2, the correlation between errors in the two percentiles will be the same as the correlation between errors in q_1 and p_2 but of opposite sign. But if there be a deficiency of observations below the lower percentile, producing an error δ_1 in q_1, the missing observations will tend to be spread over the two other sections of the curve in proportion to their respective areas, and will therefore tend to produce an error

$$\delta_2 = -\frac{p_2}{p_1} . \delta_1$$

in p_2. If then r be the correlation between errors in q_1 and p_2, ϵ_1 and ϵ_2 their respective standard errors, we have

$$r\frac{\epsilon_2}{\epsilon_1} = -\frac{p_2}{p_1}.$$

Or, inserting the values of the standard errors,

$$r = -\sqrt{\frac{p_2 q_1}{q_2 p_1}}.$$

The correlation between the percentiles is the same in magnitude but opposite in sign : it is obviously positive, and consequently

$$\left.\begin{array}{c}\text{correlation between errors} \\ \text{in two percentiles}\end{array}\right\} = +\sqrt{\frac{p_2 q_1}{q_2 p_1}} \qquad . \qquad . \quad (3)$$

If the two percentiles approach very close together, q_1 and q_2, p_1 and p_2 become sensibly equal to one another, and the correlation becomes unity, as we should expect.

8. Let us apply the above value of the correlation between percentiles to find the standard error of the semi-interquartile range for the normal curve. Inserting $q_1 = p_2 = \frac{1}{4}$, $q_2 = p_1 = \frac{3}{4}$, we find $r = \frac{1}{3}$. Hence the standard error of the interquartile range is, applying the ordinary formula for the standard-deviation of a difference, $2/\sqrt{3}$ times the standard error of either quartile, or

the standard error of the *semi*-interquartile range $1/\sqrt{3}$ times the standard error of a quartile. Taking the value of the standard error of a quartile from the table in § 4, we have, finally,

$$\left.\begin{array}{l}\text{standard error of the semi-} \\ \text{interquartile range in a} \\ \text{normal distribution}\end{array}\right\} = 0\cdot78672\frac{\sigma}{\sqrt{n}} . \quad . \quad (4)$$

Of course the standard-deviation of the inter-quartile, or semi-interquartile, range can readily be worked out in any particular case, using equation (2) and the value of the correlation given above: it is best to work out such standard errors from first principles, applying the usual formula for the standard deviation of the difference of two correlated variables (Chap. XI. § 2, equation (1)).

9. If there is any failure of the conditions of simple sampling, the formulæ of the preceding sections cease, of course, to hold good. We need not, however, enter again into a discussion of the effect of removing the several restrictions, for the effect on the standard error of p was considered in detail in §§ 9–14 of Chap. XIV., and the standard error of any percentile is directly proportional to the standard error of p (*cf.* § 3). Further, the student may be reminded that the standard error of any percentile measures solely the fluctuations that may be expected in that percentile owing to the errors of simple sampling alone: it has no bearing, therefore, save on the one question, whether an observed divergence of the percentile, from a certain value that might be expected to be yielded by a more extended series of observations or that had actually been observed in some other series, might or might not be due to fluctuations of simple sampling alone. It cannot and does not give any indication of the possibility of the sample being biassed or unrepresentative of the material from which it has been drawn, nor can it give any indication of the magnitude or influence of definite errors of observation—errors which may conceivably be of greater importance than errors of sampling. In the case of the distribution of statures, for instance, the standard error almost certainly gives quite a misleading idea as to the accuracy attained in determining the average stature for the United Kingdom: the sample is not representative, the several parts of the kingdom not contributing in their true proportions. The student should refer again to the discussion of these points in §§ 4–8 of Chap. XIV. Finally, we may note that the standard error of a percentile cannot be evaluated unless the number of observations is fairly large—large enough to determine f_p (eqn. 2) with reasonable accuracy, or

to test whether we may treat the distribution as approximately normal (*cf.* also § 16 below).

(As regards the theory of sampling for the median and percentiles generally, *cf.* ref. 15, Laplace, Supplement II. (standard error of the median), Edgeworth, refs. 5, 6, 7, and Sheppard, ref. 27 : the preceding sections have been based on the work of Edgeworth and Sheppard.)

10. *Standard Error of the Arithmetic Mean.*—Let us now pass to a fresh problem, and determine the standard error of the arithmetic mean.

This is very readily obtained. Suppose we note separately at each drawing the value recorded on the first, second, third . . . . and *n*th card of our sample. The standard-deviation of the values on each separate card will tend in the long run to be the same, and identical with the standard-deviation σ of x in an indefinitely large sample, drawn under the same conditions. Further, the value recorded on each card is (as we assume) uncorrelated with that on every other. The standard-deviation of the sum of the values recorded on the n cards is therefore $\sqrt{n}.\sigma$, and the standard-deviation of the mean of the sample is consequently 1/nth of this ; or,

$$\sigma_m = \frac{\sigma}{\sqrt{n}} \quad . \quad . \quad . \quad . \quad (5)$$

This is a most important and frequently cited formula, and the student should note that it has been obtained without any reference to the size of the sample or to the form of the frequency-distribution. It is therefore of perfectly general application, if σ be known. We can verify it against our formula for the standard-deviation of sampling in the case of attributes. The standard-deviation of the number of successes in a sample of m observations is $\sqrt{m.pq}$: the standard-deviation of the total number of successes in n samples of m observations each is therefore $\sqrt{nm.pq}$: dividing by n we have the standard-deviation of the mean number of successes in the n samples, viz. $\sqrt{mpq}/\sqrt{n}$, agreeing with equation (5).

11. For a normal curve the standard error of the mean is to the standard error of the median approximately as 100 to 125 (*cf.* § 4), and in general the standard errors of the two stand in a somewhat similar ratio for a distribution not differing largely from the normal form. For the distribution of statures used as an illustration in § 6 the standard error of the median was found to be 0·0349 : the standard error of the mean is only 0·0277. The distribution being very approximately normal, the ratio of

the two standard errors, viz. 1·26, assumes almost exactly the theoretical magnitude. In the case of the asymmetrical distribution of rates of pauperism, also used as an illustration in § 6, the standard error of the median was found to be 0·0655 per cent. The standard error of the mean is only 0·0493 per cent., which bears to the standard error of the median a ratio of 1 to 1·33. As such cases as these seem on the whole to be the more common and typical, we stated in Chap. VII. § 18 that the mean is *in general* less affected than the median by errors of sampling. At the same time we also indicated the exceptional cases in which the median might be the more stable—cases in which the mean might, for example, be affected considerably by small groups of widely outlying observations, or in which the frequency-distribution assumed a form resembling fig. 53, but even more exaggerated as regards the height of the central "peak" and the relative length of the "tails." Such distributions are not uncommon in some economic statistics, and they might be expected to characterise some forms of experimental error. If, in these cases, the greater stability of the median is sufficiently marked to outweigh its disadvantages in other respects, the median may be the better form of average to use. Fig. 53 represents a distribution in which the standard errors of the mean and of the median are the same. Further, in some experimental cases it is conceivable that the median may be less affected by definite experimental errors, the average of which does not tend to be zero, than is the mean,—this is, of course, a point quite distinct from that of errors of sampling.

12. If two quite independent samples of n_1 and n_2 observations respectively be drawn from a record, evidently ϵ_{12}, the standard error of the difference of their means is given by

$$\epsilon_{12}^2 = \sigma^2\left(\frac{1}{n_1} + \frac{1}{n_2}\right) \qquad . \qquad . \qquad . \qquad . \qquad (6)$$

If an observed difference exceed three times the value of ϵ_{12} given by this formula it can hardly be ascribed to fluctuations of sampling. If, in a practical case, the value of σ is not known *a priori*, we must substitute an observed value, and it would seem natural to take as this value the standard-deviation in the two samples thrown together. If, however, the standard-deviations of the two samples themselves differ more than can be accounted for on the basis of fluctuations of sampling alone (see below, § 15), we evidently cannot assume that both samples have been drawn from the same record : the one sample must have been drawn from a record or ·a universe exhibiting a greater standard-deviation than the other. If two samples be drawn quite independently from different universes, indefinitely large samples from which exhibit the standard-deviations σ_1 and σ_2, the standard error of the difference of their means will be given by

$$\epsilon_{12}^2 = \frac{\sigma_1^2}{n_1} + \frac{\sigma_2^2}{n_2} \quad . \quad . \quad . \quad . \quad (7)$$

This is, indeed, the formula usually employed for testing the significance of the difference between two means in any case: seeing that the standard error of the mean depends on the standard-deviation only, and not on the mean, of the distribution, we can inquire whether the two universes from which samples have been drawn differ in mean *apart from any difference in dispersion.*

If two quite independent samples be drawn from the same universe, but instead of comparing the mean of the one with the mean of the other we compare the mean m_1 of the first with the mean m_0 of both samples together, the use of (6) or (7) is not justified, for errors in the mean of the one sample are correlated with errors in the mean of the two together. Following precisely the lines of the similar problem in § 13, Chap. XIII., case III., we find that this correlation is $\sqrt{n_1/(n_1 + n_2)}$, and hence

$$\epsilon_{01}^2 = \sigma^2 \frac{n_2}{n_1(n_1 + n_2)} \quad . \quad . \quad . \quad (8)$$

(For a complete treatment of this problem in the case of samples drawn from two different universes *cf.* ref. 22.)

13. The distribution of means of samples drawn under the conditions of simple sampling will always be more symmetrical than the distribution of the original record, and the symmetry will be the greater the greater the number of observations in the sample. Further, the distribution of means (and therefore also of the differences between means) tends to become not merely symmetrical but normal. We can only illustrate, not prove, the point here ; but if the student will refer to § 13, Chap. XV., he will see that the genesis of the normal curve in this case is in accordance with what we then stated, viz. that the distribution tends to be normal whenever the variable may be regarded as the sum (or some slightly more complex function) of a number of other variables. In the present instance this condition is strictly fulfilled. The mean of the sample of n observations is the sum of the values in the sample each divided by n, and we should expect the distribution to be the more nearly normal the larger n. As an illustration of the approach to symmetry even for small values

of n, we may take the following case. If the student will turn to the calculated binomials, given as illustrations of the forms of binomial distributions in Chap. XV. § 3, he will find there the distribution of the number of successes for twenty events when $q = 0.9$, $p = 0.1$: the distribution is extremely skew, starting at zero, rising to high frequencies for 1 and 2 successes, and thence tailing off to 20 cases of 7 successes in 10,000 throws, 4 cases of 8 successes and 1 case of 9 successes. But now find the distribution for the mean number of successes in groups of five throws, under the same conditions. This will be equivalent to finding the distribution of the number of successes for 100 such events, and then dividing the observed number of successes by five—the last process making no difference to the form of the distribution, but only to its scale. But the distribution of the number of successes for 100 events when $q = 0.9$, $p = 0.1$, is also given in Chap. XV. § 3, and it will be seen that, while it is appreciably asymmetrical, the divergence from symmetry is comparatively small : the distribution has gained, very greatly in symmetry though only five observations have been taken to the sample. We may therefore reasonably assume, if our sample is large, that the distribution of means is approximately a normal distribution, and we may calculate, on that assumption, the frequency with which any given deviation from a theoretical value or a value observed in some other series, in an observed mean, will arise from fluctuations of simple sampling alone.

The warning is necessary, however, that the approach to normality is only rapid if the condition that the several drawings for each sample shall be independent is strictly fulfilled. If the observations are not independent, but are to some extent positively correlated with each other, even a fairly large sample may continue to reflect any asymmetry existing in the original distribution (cf. ref. 32 and the record of sampling there cited).

If the original distribution be normal, the distribution of means, even of small samples, is strictly normal. This follows at once from the fact that any linear function of normally distributed variables is itself normally distributed (Chap. XVI. § 6). The distribution will not in general, however, be normal if the deviation of the mean of each sample is expressed in terms of the standard-deviation of that sample (cf. ref. 30).

14. Let us consider briefly the effect on the standard error of the mean if the conditions of simple sampling as laid down in § 2 cease to apply.

(a) If we do not draw from the same record all the time, but first draw a series of samples from one record, then another series from another record with a somewhat different mean and standard-deviation, and so on, or if we draw the successive samples from essentially different parts of the same record, the standard error will be greatly increased. For suppose we draw k_1 samples from the first record, for which the standard-deviation (in an indefinitely large sample) is σ_1, and the mean differs by d_1 from the mean of all the records together (as ascertained by large samples in numbers proportionate to those now taken); k_2 samples from the second record, for which the standard-deviation is σ_2, and the mean differs by d_2 from the mean of all the records together, and so on. Then for the samples drawn from the first record the standard error of the mean will be $\sigma_1/\sqrt{n}$, but the distribution will centre round a value differing by d_1 from the mean for all the records together : and so on for the samples drawn from the other records. Hence, if σ_m be the standard error of the mean, N the total number of samples,

$$N.\sigma_m^2 = \Sigma\left(k\frac{\sigma^2}{n}\right) + \Sigma(k.d^2).$$

But the standard-deviation σ_0 for all the records together is given by

$$N.\sigma_0^2 = \Sigma(k\sigma^2) + \Sigma(kd^2).$$

Hence, writing $\Sigma(kd^2) = N.s_m^2$,

$$\sigma_m^2 = \frac{\sigma_0^2}{n} + \frac{n-1}{n}s_m^2 \quad . \quad . \quad . \quad . \quad (9)$$

This equation corresponds precisely to equation (2) of § 9, Chap. XIV. The standard error of the mean, if our samples are drawn from different records or from essentially different parts of the entire record, may be increased indefinitely as compared with the value it would have in the case of simple sampling. If, for example, we take the statures of samples of n men in a number of different districts of England, and the standard-deviation of all the statures observed is σ_0, the standard-deviation of the means for the different districts will not be $\sigma_0/\sqrt{n}$, but will have some greater value, dependent on the real variation in mean stature from district to district.

(b) If we are drawing from the same record throughout, but always draw the first card from one part of that record, the second card from another part, and so on, and these parts differ more or less, the standard error of the mean will be decreased. For if, in large samples drawn from the subsidiary parts of the record from which the several cards are taken, the standard-deviations are $\sigma_1, \sigma_2, \ldots \sigma_m$ and the means differ by $d_1, d_2,$

. . . . d_n from the mean for a large sample from the entire record, we have

$$\sigma_0^2 = \frac{1}{n}\Sigma(\sigma^2) + \frac{1}{n}\Sigma(d^2).$$

Hence

$$\sigma_m^2 = \frac{1}{n^2}\Sigma(\sigma^2)$$

$$= \frac{\sigma_0^2}{n} - \frac{s_m^2}{n} \qquad . \quad . \quad . \quad . \quad (10)$$

The last equation again corresponds precisely with that given for the same departure from the rules of simple sampling in the case of attributes (Chap. XIV. § 11., eqn. 4). If, to vary our previous illustration, we had measured the statures of men in each of n different districts, and then proceeded to form a set of samples by taking one man from each district for the first sample, one man from each district for the second sample, and so on, the standard-deviation of the means of the samples so formed would be appreciably less than the standard error of simple sampling $\sigma_0/\sqrt{n}$. As a limiting case, it is evident that if the men in each district were all of precisely the same stature, the means of all the samples so compounded would be identical : in such a case, in fact, $\sigma_0 = s_m$, and consequently $\sigma_m = 0$. To give another illustration, if the cards from which we were drawing samples had been arranged in order of the magnitude of X recorded on each, we would get a much more stable sample by drawing one card from each successive nth part of the record than by taking the sample according to our previous rules—e.g. shaking them up in a bag and taking out cards blindfold, or using some equivalent process.

The result is perhaps of some practical interest. It shows that, if we are actually taking samples from a large area, different districts of which exhibit markedly different means for the variable under consideration, and are limited to a sample of n observations ; if we break up the whole area into n sub-districts, each as homogeneous as possible, and take a contribution to the sample from each, we will obtain a *more stable* mean by this orderly procedure than will be given, for the same number of observations, by any process of selecting the districts from which samples shall be taken by chance. There may, however, be a greater risk of biassed error. The conclusions seem in accord with common-sense.

(c) Finally, suppose that, while our conditions (a) and (b) of § 2 hold good, the magnitude of the variable recorded on one card drawn is no longer independent of the magnitude recorded on another card, *e.g.* that if the first card drawn at any sampling bears a high value, the next and following cards of the same sample are likely to bear high values also. Under these circumstances, if r_{12} denote the correlation between the values on the first and second cards, and so on,

$$s_m^2 = \frac{\sigma^2}{n} + 2\frac{\sigma^2}{n^2}(r_{12} + r_{13} + \ldots + r_{23} + \ldots).$$

There are $n(n-1)/2$ correlations; and if, therefore, r is the arithmetic mean of them all, we may write

$$\sigma_m^2 = \frac{\sigma^2}{n}[1 + r(n-1)] \qquad . \qquad . \qquad . \qquad (11)$$

As the means and standard-deviations of $x_1, x_2, \ldots x_n$ are all identical, r may more simply be regarded as the correlation coefficient for a table formed by taking all possible pairs of the n values in every sample. If this correlation be positive, the standard error of the mean will be increased, and for a given value of r the increase will be the greater, the greater the size of the samples. If r be negative, on the other hand, the standard error will be diminished. Equation (11) corresponds precisely to equation (6), § 13, of Chap. XIV.

As was pointed out in that chapter, the case when r is positive covers the case discussed under (*a*): for if we draw successive samples from different records, such a positive correlation is at once introduced, although the drawings of the several cards *at each* sampling are quite independent of one another. Similarly, the case discussed under (*b*) is covered by the case of negative correlation, for if each card is always drawn from a separate and distinct part of the record, the correlation between any two *x*'s will on the average be negative : if some one card be always drawn from a part of the record containing low values of the variable, the others must on an average be drawn from parts containing relatively high values. It is as well, however, to keep the cases (*a*), (*b*), and (*c*) distinct, since a positive or negative correlation may arise for reasons quite different from those considered under (*a*) and (*b*).

15. With this discussion of the standard error of the arithmetic mean we must bring the present work to a close. To indicate briefly our reasons for not proceeding further with the discussion of standard errors, we must remind the student that in order to express the standard error of the mean we require to know, in addition to the mean itself, the standard-deviation about the mean, or, in other words, the mean (deviation)^2 with respect to the mean.

Similarly, to express the standard error of the standard-deviation we require to know, in the general case, the mean (deviation)[4] with respect to the mean. Either, then, we must find this quantity for the given distribution—and this would entail entering on a field of work which hitherto we have intentionally avoided—or we must, if that be possible, assume the distribution to be of such a form that we can express the mean (deviation)[4] in terms of the mean (deviation)[2]. This can be done, as a fact, for the normal distribution, but the proof would again take us rather beyond the limits that we have set ourselves. To deal with the standard error of the correlation coefficient would take us still further afield, and the proof would be laborious and difficult, if not impossible, without the use of the differential and integral calculus. We must content ourselves, therefore, with a simple statement of the standard errors of some of the more important constants.

Standard-deviation.—If the distribution be normal,

$$\text{standard error of the} \atop \text{standard-deviation in} \atop \text{a normal distribution} \left.\right\} = \frac{\sigma}{\sqrt{2n}} \qquad . \qquad . \quad (12)$$

This is generally given as the standard error in all cases : it is, however, by no means exact : the general expression is

$$\text{standard error of the standard-} \atop \text{deviation in a distribution} \atop \text{of any form} \left.\right\} = \sqrt{\frac{\mu_4 - \mu_2^2}{4\mu_2 \, . \, n}} \qquad . \quad (13)$$

where μ_4 is the mean (deviation)[4]—deviations being, of course, measured from the mean—and μ_2 the mean (deviation)[2] or the square of the standard-deviation : n is assumed sufficiently large to make the errors in the standard-deviation small compared with that quantity itself. Equation (13) may in some cases give values considerably greater—twice as great or more—than (12). (*Cf.* ref. 17.) If, however, the distribution be normal, equation (12) gives the standard error not merely of standard-deviations of order zero, to use the terminology of Chap. XII., but of standard-deviations of any order (ref. 33). It will be noticed, on reference to equation (4) above, § 8, that the standard error of the standard-deviation is less than that of the semi-interquartile range for a normal distribution.

For a normal distribution, again, we have—

$$\text{standard error of the co-} \atop \text{efficient of variation } v \left.\right\} = \frac{v}{\sqrt{2n}} \left\{ 1 + 2\left(\frac{v}{100}\right)^2 \right\}^{\frac{1}{2}}. \quad (14)$$

The expression in the bracket is usually very nearly unity, for a normal distribution, and in that case may be neglected.

Correlation coefficient.—If the distribution be normal,

$$\left.\begin{array}{l}\text{standard error of the cor-}\\ \text{relation coefficient for}\\ \text{a normal distribution}\end{array}\right\} = \frac{1 - r^2}{\sqrt{n}} \qquad . \qquad . \quad (15)$$

This is the value always given : the use of a more general formula which would entail the use of higher moments does not appear to have been attempted. As regards the case of small samples, *cf.* refs. 10, 28, and 31. Equation (15) gives the standard error of a coefficient of any order, total or partial (ref. 33). For the standard error of the correlation-coefficient for a fourfold table (Chap. XI., § 10), see ref. 34 : the formula (15) does not apply.

Coefficient of regression.—If the distribution be normal,

$$\left.\begin{array}{l}\text{standard error of the co-}\\ \text{efficient of regression } b_{12}\\ \text{for a normal distribution}\end{array}\right\} = \frac{\sigma_1 \sqrt{1 - r_{12}^2}}{\sigma_2 \sqrt{n}} = \frac{\sigma_{1.2}}{\sigma_2 \sqrt{n}} \qquad . \quad (16)$$

This formula again applies to a regression coefficient of any order, total or partial : *i.e.* in terms of our general notation, k denoting any collection of secondary subscripts other than 1 or 2,

$$\left.\begin{array}{l}\text{standard error of } b_{12.k} \text{ for}\\ \text{a normal distribution}\end{array}\right\} = \frac{\sigma_{1.2k}}{\sigma_{2.k} \sqrt{n}}.$$

Correlation ratio.—The general expression for the standard error of the correlation-ratio is a somewhat complex expression (*cf.* Professor Pearson's original memoir on the correlation-ratio, ref. 18, Chap. X.). In general, however, it may be taken as given sufficiently closely by the above expression for the standard error of the correlation coefficient, that is to say,

$$\left.\begin{array}{l}\text{standard error of correlation-}\\ \text{ratio approximately}\end{array}\right\} = \frac{1 - \eta^2}{\sqrt{n}} \qquad . \qquad . \quad (17)$$

As was pointed out in Chap. X., § 21, the value of $\zeta = \eta^2 - r^2$ is a test for linearity of regression. Very approximately (Blakeman, ref. 1),

$$\text{standard error of } \zeta = 2 \sqrt{\frac{\zeta}{n}} \sqrt{(1 - \eta^2)^2 - (1 - r^2)^2 + 1} . \quad (18)$$

For rough work the value of the second square root may be taken as nearly unity, and we have then the simple expression,

$$\text{standard error of } \zeta \text{ roughly} = 2 \sqrt{\frac{\zeta}{n}} . \qquad (19)$$

To convert any standard error to the probable error multiply by the constant 0·674489 . . . .

16. We need hardly restate once more the warnings given in Chap. XIV., and repeated in § 9 above, that a standard error can give no evidence as to the biassed or representative character of a sample, nor as to the magnitude of errors of observation, but we may, in conclusion, again emphasise the warnings given in §§ 1–3, Chap. XIV., as to the use of standard errors when the number of observations in the sample is small.

In the first place, if the sample be small, we cannot in general assume that the distribution of errors is approximately normal : it would only be normal in the case of the median (for which p and q are equal) and in the case of the mean of a normal distribution. Consequently, if n be small, the rule that a range of three times the standard error includes the majority of the fluctuations of simple sampling *of either sign* does not strictly apply, and the "probable error" becomes of doubtful significance.

Secondly, it will be noted that the values of σ and y_p in (1), of f_p in (2), and of σ in (4) and (5), *i.e.* the values that would be given for these constants by an indefinitely large sample drawn under the same conditions, or the values that they possess in the original record if the sample is unbiassed, are assumed to be known *a priori*. But this is only the case in dealing with the problems of artificial chance : in practical cases we have to use the values given us by the sample itself. If this sample is based on a considerable number of observations, the procedure is safe enough, but if it be only a small sample we may possibly mis-estimate the standard error to a serious extent. Following the procedure suggested in Chap. XIV., some rough idea as to the possible extent of under-estimation or over-estimation may be obtained, *e.g.* in the case of the mean, by first working out the standard error of σ on the assumption that the values for the necessary moments are correct, and then replacing σ in the expression for the standard error of the mean by $\sigma \pm$ three times its standard error so obtained.

Finally, it will be remembered that unless the number of observations is large, we cannot interpret the standard error of any constant in the inverse sense, *i.e.* the standard error ceases to measure with reasonable accuracy the standard-deviation of true values of the constant round the observed value (Chap. XIV. § 3). If the sample be large, the direct and inverse standard errors are approximately the same.

REFERENCES.

The probable errors of various special coefficients, etc., are generally dealt with in the memoirs concerning them, reference to which has been made in the lists of previous chapters: reference has also been made before to most of the memoirs concerning errors of sampling in proportions or percentages. The following is a classification of some of the memoirs in the list below :—

General : 18, 20.

Theory of fit of two distributions: 9, 19, 23.

Averages and percentiles: 5, 6, 7, 30, 32, 35, 36.

Standard deviation : 17, 26.

Coefficient of correlation (product-sum and partial correlations): 10, 12, 13, 28, 31, 33, 34.

Coefficient of correlation, other methods, normal coefficient, etc. : 24, 29.

Coefficients of association : 34.

Coefficient of contingency : 2, 25.

As regards the conditions under which it becomes valid to assume that the distribution of errors is normal, *cf.* ref. 14.

(1) BLAKEMAN, J., "On Tests for Linearity of Regression in Frequency Distributions," *Biometrika*, vol. iv., 1905, p. 332.

(2) BLAKEMAN, J., and KARL PEARSON, "On the Probable Error of the Coefficient of Mean Square Contingency," *Biometrika*, vol. v., 1906, p. 191.

(3) BOWLEY, A. L., *The Measurement of Groups and Series* ; C. & E. Layton, London, 1903.

(4) BOWLEY, A. L., *Address to Section F of the British Association*, 1906.

(5) EDGEWORTH, F. Y., "Observations and Statistics: An Essay on the Theory of Errors of Observation and the First Principles of Statistics," *Cambridge Phil. Trans.*, vol. xiv., 1885, p. 139.

(6) EDGEWORTH, F. Y., "Problems in Probabilities," *Phil. Mag.*, 5th Series, vol. xxii., 1886, p. 371.

(7) EDGEWORTH, F. Y., "The Choice of Means," *Phil. Mag.*, 5th Series, vol. xxiv., 1887, p. 268.

(8) EDGEWORTH, F. Y., "On the Probable Errors of Frequency Constants," *Jour. Roy. Stat. Soc.*, vol. lxxi., 1908, pp. 381, 499, 651 ; and Addendum, vol. lxxii., 1909, p. 81.

(9) ELDERTON, W. PALIN, "Tables for Testing the Goodness of Fit of Theory to Observation," *Biometrika*, vol. i., 1902, p. 155.

(10) FISHER, R. A., "The Frequency Distribution of the Values of the Correlation Coefficient in Samples from an Indefinitely large Population." *Biometrika*, vol. x., 1915, p. 507.

(11) GIBSON, WINIFRED, "Tables for Facilitating the Computation of Probable Errors," *Biometrika*, vol. iv., 1906, p. 385.

(12) HERON, D., "An Abac to determine the Probable Errors of Correlation Coefficients," *Biometrika*, vol. vii., 1910, p. 411. (A diagram giving the probable error for any number of observations up to 1000.)

(13) HERON, D., "On the Probable Error of a Partial Correlation Coefficient," *Biometrika*, vol. vii., 1910, p. 411. (A proof, on ordinary algebraic lines, for the case of three variables, of the result given in (33).)

(14) ISSERLIS, L., "On the Conditions under which the 'Probable Errors' of Frequency Distributions have a real Significance," *Proc. Roy. Soc.*, Series A, vol. xcii., 1915, p. 23.

(15) LAPLACE, PIERRE SIMON, Marquis de, *Théorie des probabilités*, 2ᵉ édn., 1814. (With four supplements.)

(16) PEARL, RAYMOND, "The Calculation of Probable Errors of Certain Constants of the Normal Curve," *Biometrika*, vol. v., 1906, p. 190.

(17) PEARL, RAYMOND, "On certain Points concerning the Probable Error of the Standard-deviation," *Biometrika*, vol. vi., 1908, p. 112. (On the amount of divergence, in certain cases, from the standard error $\sigma/\sqrt{2n}$ in the case of a normal distribution.)

(18) PEARSON, KARL, and L. N. G. FILON, "On the Probable Errors of Frequency Constants, and on the Influence of Random Selection on Variation and Correlation," *Phil. Trans. Roy. Soc.*, Series A, vol. cxci., 1898, p. 229.

(19) PEARSON, KARL, "On the Criterion that a given System of Deviations from the Probable in the Case of a Correlated System of Variables is such that it can be reasonably supposed to have arisen from Random Sampling," *Phil. Mag.*, 5th Series, vol. l., 1900, p. 157.

(20) PEARSON, KARL, and others (editorial), "On the Probable Errors of Frequency Constants," *Biometrika*, vol. ii., 1903, p. 273, and vol. ix., 1913, p. 1. (Useful for the general formulæ given, based on the general case without respect to the form of the frequency-distribution.)

(21) PEARSON, KARL, "On the Curves which are most suitable for describing the Frequency of Random Samples of a Population," *Biometrika*, vol. v., 1906, p. 172.

(22) PEARSON, KARL, "Note on the Significant or Non-significant Character of a Sub-sample drawn from a Sample," *Biometrika*, vol. v., 1906, p. 181.

(23) PEARSON, KARL, "On the Probability that two Independent Distributions of Frequency are really Samples from the same Population," *Biometrika*, vol. viii., 1911, p. 250, and vol. x., 1914, p. 85.

(24) PEARSON, KARL, "On the Probable Error of a Coefficient of Correlation as found from a Fourfold Table," *Biometrika*, vol. ix., 1913, p. 22.

(25) PEARSON, KARL, "On the Probable Error of a Coefficient of Mean Square Contingency," *Biometrika*, vol. x., 1915, p. 590.

(26) RHIND, A., "Tables for Facilitating the Computation of Probable Errors of the Chief Constants of Skew Frequency-distributions," *Biometrika*, vol. vii., 1909-10, p. 127 and p. 386.

(27) SHEPPARD, W. F., "On the Application of the Theory of Error to Cases of Normal Distribution and Normal Correlation," *Phil. Trans. Roy. Soc.*, Series A, vol. cxcii., 1898, p. 101.

(28) SOPER, H. E., "On the Probable Error of the Correlation Coefficient to a Second Approximation," *Biometrika*, vol. ix., 1913, p. 91.

(29) SOPER, H. E., "On the Probable Error of the Bi-serial Expression for the Correlation Coefficient," *Biometrika*, vol. x., 1914, p. 384.

(30) "STUDENT," "On the Probable Error of a Mean," *Biometrika*, vol. vi., 1908, p. 1. (The standard error of the mean in terms of the standard error of the sample.)

(31) "STUDENT," "On the Probable Error of a Correlation Coefficient," *Biometrika*, vol. vi., 1908, p. 302. (The problem of the probable error with small samples.)

(32) "STUDENT," "On the Distribution of Means of Samples which are not drawn at Random," *Biometrika*, vol. vii., 1909, p. 210.

(33) YULE, G. U., "On the Theory of Correlation for any number of Variables treated by a New System of Notation," *Proc. Roy. Soc.*, Series A, vol. lxxix., 1907, p. 182. (See pp. 192-3 at end.)

(34) YULE, G. U., "On the Methods of Measuring Association between two Attributes," *Jour. Roy. Stat. Soc.*, vol. lxxvi., 1912. (Probable error of the correlation coefficient for a fourfold table, of association coefficients, etc.)

Reference may also be made to the following, which deal for the most part with the effects of errors other than errors of sampling:—

(35) Bowley, A. L., "Relations between the Accuracy of an Average and that of its Constituent Parts," *Jour. Roy. Stat. Soc.*, vol. lx., 1897, p. 855.

(36) Bowley, A. L., "The Measurement of the Accuracy of an Average," *Jour. Roy. Stat. Soc.*, vol. lxxv., 1911, p. 77.

EXERCISES.

1. For the data in the last column of Table IX., Chap. VI. p. 95, find the standard error of the median (154·7 lbs.).

2. For the same distribution, find the standard errors of the two quartiles (142·5 lbs., 168·4 lbs.).

3. For the same distribution, find the standard error of the semi-interquartile range.

4. The standard-deviation of the same distribution is 21·3 lbs. Find the standard error of the mean, and compare its magnitude with that of the standard error of the median (Qn. 1).

5. Work out the standard error of the standard deviation for the distribution of statures used as an illustration in § 6. (Standard-deviation 2·57 in. ; 8585 observations.) Compare the ratio of standard error of standard-deviation to the standard-deviation, with the ratio of the standard error of the semi-interquartile range to the semi-interquartile range, assuming the distribution normal.

6. Calculate a small table giving the standard errors of the correlation coefficient, based on (1) 100, (2) 1000 observations, for values of $r = 0$, 0·2, 0·4, 0·6, 0·8, assuming the distribution normal.

APPENDIX I.

TABLES FOR FACILITATING STATISTICAL WORK.

A. CALCULATING TABLES.

FOR heavy arithmetical work an arithmometer is, of course, invaluable; but, owing to their cost, arithmetic machines are, as a rule, beyond the reach of the student. For a great deal of simple work, especially work not intended for publication, the student will find a slide-rule exceedingly useful: particulars and prices will be found in any instrument maker's catalogue. A plain 25-cm. rule will serve for most ordinary purposes, or if greater accuracy is desired, a 50-cm. rule, a Fuller spiral rule, or one of Hannyngton-pattern rules (Aston & Mander, London), in which the scale is broken up into a number of parallel segments, may be preferred. For greater exactness in multiplying or dividing, logarithms are almost essential: five-figure tables suffice if answers are only desired true to five digits; if greater accuracy is needed, seven-figure tables must be used. It is hardly necessary to cite special editions of tables of logarithms here, but attention may perhaps be directed to the recently issued eight-figure tables of Bauschinger and Peters (W. Engelmann, Leipzig, and Asher & Co., London, 1910; vol. i. containing logarithms of all numbers from 1 to 200,000, price 18s. 6d. net.; vol. ii. containing logs. of trigonometric functions).

If it is desired to avoid logarithms, extended multiplication tables are very useful. There are many of these, and four of different forms are cited below. Zimmermann's tables are inexpensive and recommended for the elementary student, Cotsworth's, Crelle's, or Peters' tables for more advanced work. Barlow's tables are invaluable for calculating standard-deviations of ungrouped observations and similar work.

(1) BARLOW's *Tables of Squares, Cubes, Square-roots, Cube-roots, and Reciprocals of all Integer Numbers up to* 10,000; E. & F. N. Spon, London and New York; stereotype edition, price 6s.

(2) COTSWORTH, M. B., *The Direct Calculator*, Series O. (Product table to 1000 × 1000.) M'Corquodale & Co., London ; price with thumb index, 25s. ; without index, 21s.

(3) CRELLE, A. L., *Rechentafeln*. (Multiplication table giving all products up to 1000 × 1000.) Can be obtained with explanatory introduction in German or in English. G. Reimer, Berlin ; price 15s.

(4) ELDERTON, W. P. "Tables of Powers of Natural Numbers, and of the Sums of Powers of the Natural Numbers from 1 to 100" (gives powers up to seventh), *Biometrika*, vol. ii. p. 474.

(5) PETERS, J., *Neue Rechentafeln für Multiplikation und Division*. (Gives products up to 100 × 10,000 : more convenient than Crelle for forming four-figure products. Introduction in English, French or German.) G. Reimer, Berlin ; price 15s.

(6) ZIMMERMANN, H., *Rechentafel*, nebst Sammlung häufig gebrauchter Zahlenwerthe. (Products of all numbers up to 100 × 1000 : subsidiary tables of squares, cubes, square-roots, cube-roots and reciprocals, etc. for all numbers up to 1000 at the foot of the page.) W. Ernst & Son, Berlin ; price 5s. ; English edition, Asher & Co., London, 6s.

B. SPECIAL TABLES OF FUNCTIONS, ETC.

Several tables of service will be found in the works cited in Appendix II., *e.g.*, a table of Gamma Functions in Elderton's book (12) and a table of six-figure logarithms of the factorials of all numbers from 1 to 1100 in De Morgan's treatise (11). The majority of the tables in the list below, which were originally published in *Biometrika*, together with others, are contained in *Tables for Statisticians and Biometricians*, edited by Karl Pearson (Cambridge University Press, 1914, price 15s. net).

(7) DAVENPORT, C. B., *Statistical Methods, with especial reference to Biological Variation*; New York, John Wiley ; London, Chapman & Hall ; second edition, 1904. (Tables of area and ordinates of the normal curve, gamma functions, probable errors of the coefficient of correlation, powers, logarithms, etc.)

(8) DUFFELL, J. H., "Tables of the Gamma-function," *Biometrika*, vol. vii., 1909, p. 43. (Seven-figure logarithms of the function, proceeding by differences of 0·001 of the argument.)

(9) ELDERTON, W. P., "Tables for Testing the Goodness of Fit of Theory to Observation," *Biometrika*, vol. i., 1902, p. 155.

(10) EVERITT, P. F., "Tables of the Tetrachoric Functions for Four-fold Correlation Tables," *Biometrika*, vol. vii., 1910, p. 437, and vol. viii., 1912, p. 385. (Tables for facilitating the calculation of the correlation coefficient of a fourfold table by Pearson's method on the assumption that it is a grouping of a normally distributed table ; *cf.* ref. 14 of Chap. XVI.)

(11) GIBSON, WINIFRED, "Tables for Facilitating the Computation of Probable Errors," *Biometrika*, vol. iv., 1906, p. 385.

(12) HERON, D., "An Abac to determine the Probable Errors of Correlation Coefficients," *Biometrika*, vol. vii., 1910, p. 411. (A diagram giving the probable error for any number of observations up to 1000.)

(13) LEE, ALICE, "Tables of $F(r, \nu)$ and $H(r, \nu)$ Functions," *British Association Report*, 1899. (Functions occurring in connection with Professor Pearson's frequency curves.)

(14) LEE, ALICE, "Tables of the Gaussian 'Tail-functions,' when the 'tail' is larger than the body," *Biometrika*, vol. x., 1914, p. 208.

(15) RHIND, A., "Tables for Facilitating the Computation of Probable Errors of the Chief Constants of Skew Frequency-distributions," *Biometrika*, vol. vii., 1909-10, p. 127 and p. 386.

(16) SHEPPARD, W. F., "New Tables of the Probability Integral," *Biometrika*, vol. ii., 1903, p. 174. (Includes not merely table of areas of the normal curve (to seven figures), but also a table of the ordinates to the same degree of accuracy.)

(17) SHEPPARD, W. F., "Table of Deviates of the Normal Curve" (with introductory article on *Grades and Deviates* by Sir Francis Galton), *Biometrika*, vol. v., 1907, p. 404. (A table giving the deviation of the normal curve, in terms of the standard-deviation as unit, for the ordinates which divide the area into a thousand equal parts.)

APPENDIX II.

SHORT LIST OF WORKS ON THE MATHEMATICAL THEORY OF STATISTICS AND THE THEORY OF PROBABILITY.

THE student may find the following short list of service, as supplementing the lists of references given at the ends of the several chapters, the latter containing, as a rule, original memoirs only. The economic student who wishes to know more of the practical side of statistics may be referred to Mr A. L. Bowley's "Elements" (6 below), to *An Elementary Manual of Statistics* (Macdonald & Evans, London, 1910), by the same writer (useful as a general guide to English statistics), and to M. Jacques Bertillon's *Cours élémentaire de statistique* (Société d'éditions scientifiques, 1895: international in scope). Dr A. Newsholme's *Vital Statistics* (Swan Sonnenschein, 3rd edn., 1899) will also be of service to students of that subject.

The great majority of the works mentioned in the following list, with others which it has not been thought necessary to include, are in the library of the Royal Statistical Society.

(1) AIRY, Sir G. B., *On the Algebraical and Numerical Theory of Errors of Observations* ; 1st edn., 1861 ; 3rd edn., 1879.

(2) BERNOULLI, J., *Ars conjectandi, opus posthumum: Accedit traclatus de seriebus infinitis, et epistola gallicè scripta de ludo pilae reticularis,* 1713. (A German translation in Ostwald's *Klassiker der exakten Wissenschaften,* Nos. 107, 108.)

(3) BERTRAND, J. L. F., *Calcul des probabilités* ; Gauthier-Villars, Paris, 1889.

(4) BETZ, W., *Ueber Korrelation* ; Beihefte zur Zeitschrift für ang. Psych. und psych. Sammelforschung ; J. A. Barth, Leipzig, 1911. (Applications to psychology.)

(5) BOREL, É., *Éléments de la théorie des probabilités* ; Hermann, Paris, 1909.

(6) BOWLEY, A. L., *Elements of Statistics* ; P. S. King, London ; 1st edn., 1901 ; 3rd edn., 1907.

(7) BROWN, W., *The Essentials of Mental Measurement* ; Cambridge University Press, 1911. (Part 2 on the theory of correlation : applications to experimental psychology.)

(8) BRUNS, H., *Wahrscheinlichkeitsrechnung und Kollektivmasslehre* ; Teubner, Leipzig, 1906.

(9) COURNOT, A. A., *Exposition de la théorie des chances et des probabilités*, 1843.

(10) CZUBER, E., *Wahrscheinlichkeitsrechnung und ihre Anwendung auf Fehlerausgleichung, Statistik und Lebensversicherung* ; Teubner, Leipzig, 2nd edn., vol. i., 1908–10.

(11) DE MORGAN, A., *Treatise on the Theory of Probabilities* (extracted from the *Encyclopœdia Metropolitana*), 1837.

(12) ELDERTON, W. P., *Frequency Curves and Correlation* ; C. & E. Layton, London, 1906. (Deals with Professor Pearson's frequency curves and correlation, with illustrations chiefly of actuarial interest.)

(13) FECHNER, G. T., *Kollektivmasslehre* (posthumously published ; edited by G. F. Lipps) ; Engelmann, Leipzig, 1897.

(14) GALLOWAY, T., *Treatise on Probability* (republished from the 7th edn. of the *Encyclopœdia Britannica*), 1839.

(15) GAUSS, C. F., *Méthode des moindres carrés: Mémoires sur la combinaison des observations*, traduits par J. Bertrand, 1855.

(16) JOHANNSEN, W., *Elemente der exakten Erblichkeitslehre* ; Fischer, Jena, 2te Ausgabe, 1913. (Very largely concerned with an exposition of the statistical methods.)

(17) LAPLACE, PIERRE SIMON, Marquis de, *Essai philosophique sur les probabilités*, 1814. (The introduction to 18, separately printed with some modifications.)

(18) LAPLACE, PIERRE SIMON, Marquis de, *Théorie analytique des probabilités* ; 2nd edn., 1814, with supplements 1 to 4.

(19) LEXIS, W., *Abhandlungen zur Theorie der Bevölkerungs- und Moralstatistik* ; Fischer, Jena, 1903.

(20) POINCARÉ, H., *Calcul des probabilités* ; Gauthier-Villars, Paris, 1896.

(21) POISSON, S. D., *Recherches sur la probabilité des jugements en matière criminelle et en matière civile, précédées des règles générales du calcul des probabilités*, 1837. (German translation by C. H. Schnuse, 1841.)

(22) QUETELET, L. A. J., *Lettres sur la théorie des probabilités, appliquée aux sciences morales et politiques*, 1846. (English translation by O. G. Downes, 1849.)

(23) THORNDIKE, E. L., *An Introduction to the Theory of Mental and Social Measurements*, Science Press, New York, 1904.

(24) VENN, J., *The Logic of Chance : an Essay on the Foundations and Province of the Theory of Probability, with especial reference to its Logical Bearings and its Application to Moral and Social Science and to Statistics* ; 3rd edn., Macmillan, London, 1888.

(25) WESTERGAARD, H., *Die Grundzüge der Theorie der Statistik* ; Fischer, Jena, 1890.

SUPPLEMENTS.

I. DIRECT DEDUCTION OF THE FORMULÆ FOR REGRESSIONS.

(Supplementary to Chapters IX. and XII.)

To those who are acquainted with the differential calculus the following direct proof may be useful. It is on the lines of the proof given in Chapter XII. § 3.

Taking first the case of two variables (Chapter IX.), it is required to determine values of a_1 and b_1 in the equation

$$x = a_1 + b_1 \cdot y$$

(where x and y denote deviations from the respective means) that will make the sum of the squares of the errors like

$$u = x' - \overline{a_1 + b_1 \cdot y'}$$

a minimum, x' and y' being a pair of associated deviations.

The required equations for determining a_1 and b_1 will be given by differentiating

$$\Sigma(u^2) = \Sigma(x - \overline{a_1 + b_1 \cdot y})^2$$

with respect to a_1 and to b_1 and equating to zero.

Differentiating with respect to a_1, we have

$$\Sigma(x - \overline{a_1 + b_1 \cdot y}) = 0.$$

But
$$\Sigma(x) = \Sigma(y) = 0,$$

and consequently we have $\quad a_1 = 0.$

Dropping a_1, and differentiating with respect to b_1,

$$\Sigma(x - b_1 \cdot y)y = 0.$$

That is,
$$b_1 = \frac{\Sigma(xy)}{\Sigma(y^2)} = r\frac{\sigma_x}{\sigma_y},$$

as on p. 171.

Similarly, if we determine the values of a_2 and b_2 in the equation

$$y = a_2 + b_2 x$$

that will make the sum of the squares of the errors like

$$v = y' - \overline{a_2 + b_2 \cdot x'}$$

a minimum, we will find

$$a_2 = 0$$
$$b_2 = \frac{\Sigma(xy)}{\Sigma(x^2)} = r\frac{\sigma_y}{\sigma_x}.$$

If, as in Chapter XII. §§ 4 *et seq.* (*cf.* especially § 7), a number of variables are involved, the equations for determining the coefficients will be given by differentiating

$$\Sigma(x_1 - \overline{b_{12.34} \ldots \ldots n} \cdot x_2 + \ldots \ldots + \overline{b_{1n.23} \ldots \ldots (n-1)} \cdot x_n)^2$$

with respect to each coefficient in turn and equating the result to zero. This gives the equations of the form there stated. If a constant term be introduced, its "least square" value will be found to be zero, as above.

II. THE LAW OF SMALL CHANCES.

(*Supplementary to Chapter XV.*)

WE have seen that the normal curve is the limit of the binomial $(p+q)^n$ when n is large and neither p nor q very small. The student's attention will now be directed to the limit reached when either p or q becomes very small, but n is so large that either np or nq remains finite.

Let us regard the n trials of the event, for which the chance of success at each trial is p, as made up of $m + m' = n$ trials; then the probability of having at least m successes in the $m + m'$ trials is evidently the sum of the $m' + 1$ terms of the expansion of $(p+q)^n$ beginning with p^n. But this probability, which we may term P_m, can be expressed in another and more convenient form with the help of the following reasoning. The required result might happen in any one of $m' + 1$ ways. For instance :—

(*a*) Each of the first m trials might succeed; the chance of this is p^m.

(*b*) The first $m + 1$ trials might give m successes and 1 failure, the latter not to happen on the $(m+1)^{\text{th}}$ trial (a condition already covered by (*a*)). But the probability of m successes and 1 failure, the latter at a specified trial, is $p^m \cdot q$, and, as the failure might occur in any one of m out of $m + 1$ trials, the complete probability of (*b*) is $mp^m \cdot q$.

(*c*) The first $m + 2$ trials might give m successes and 2 failures, the $(m+2)^{\text{th}}$ trial not to be a failure (so as to avoid a repetition of either of the preceding cases); the probability of this is

$$\frac{m(m+1)}{2!} p^m q^2.$$

In a similar way we find for the contribution of $m + 3$ trials, giving m successes and 3 failures,

$$\frac{m(m+1)(m+2)}{3!} p^m q^3$$

Ultimately we reach

$$P_m = p^m \left[1 + mq + \frac{m(m+1)}{2!}q^2 + \ldots \frac{m \cdot (m+1) \ldots (m+m'-1)}{m'!}q^{m'} \right] \quad . \quad (7)$$

This expression is of course equivalent to the first $m'+1$ terms of the binomial expansion beginning with p^m, as the student can verify. For instance, if $m = n - 2$, so that $m' = 2$, we have

$$p^{n-2}\left[1 + (n-2)q + \frac{(n-2)(n-1)}{2!}q^2 \right]$$

$$= p^{n-2}(1-q)^2 + np^{n-2}(1-q)q + \frac{n(n-1)}{2!}p^{n-2}q^2$$

$$= p^n + np^{n-1}q + \frac{n(n-1)}{2!}p^{n-2}q^2.$$

Let us now suppose that q is very small, so that $\dfrac{m'}{n}$ = ratio of failures to total trials is also very small. Let us also suppose that n is so large that $nq = \lambda$ is finite. Writing $q = \dfrac{\lambda}{n}$ and putting $m = n - m'$, (7) becomes

$$\left(1 - \frac{\lambda}{n} \right)^n \left(1 - \frac{\lambda}{n} \right)^{-m'} \left[1 + \lambda + \frac{\lambda^2}{1.2} + \frac{\lambda^3}{3!} + \ldots \frac{\lambda^{m'}}{m'!} \right],$$

since $\dfrac{m'}{n}$ and smaller fractions can be neglected.

But $\left(1 - \dfrac{\lambda}{n} \right)^n$ is shown in books on algebra to be equal to $e^{-\lambda}$, where e is the base of the natural logarithms, when n is infinite and, under similar conditions,

$$\left(1 - \frac{\lambda}{n} \right)^{-m'} = 1.$$

Hence, if n be large and q small, we have

$$P_m = e^{-\lambda}\left(1 + \lambda + \frac{\lambda^2}{2!} + \frac{\lambda^3}{3!} + \ldots \frac{\lambda^{m'}}{m'!} \right) \quad . \quad . \quad (8)$$

If we put $m' = 0$, we have the chance that the event succeeds every time, and (8) reduces to $e^{-\lambda}$. Put $m' = 1$, and we get the chance that the event shall not fail more than once, $e^{-\lambda}(1+\lambda)$, so that $e^{-\lambda} \cdot \lambda$ is the chance of exactly one failure, and the terms within the bracket give us the proportional frequencies of 0, 1, 2, etc. failures. In other words, (8) is the limit of the binomial $(p+q)^n$ when q is very small but nq finite.

The investigation contained in the preceding paragraphs was published in 1837 by Poisson, so that (8) may be termed Poisson's limit to the binomial; but the result has been reached independently by several writers since Poisson's time, and we shall give one of the methods of proof adopted by modern statisticians, which the student may perhaps find easier to follow than that of Poisson (see ref. 19, p. 273).

$$(p+q)^n = (1-q+q)^n = (1-q)^{\frac{\lambda}{q}}\left(1+\frac{q}{1-q}\right)^{\frac{\lambda}{q}} \qquad . \qquad (9)$$

The first bracket on the right is equal to $e^{-\lambda}$ when q is indefinitely small. Expanding the second bracket, we have

$$1 + \frac{\lambda}{q}\cdot\frac{q}{1-q} + \frac{\frac{\lambda}{q}\left(\frac{\lambda}{q}-1\right)}{2!}\cdot\left(\frac{q}{1-q}\right)^2 + \ldots$$

The ratio of the $(r+1)^{\text{th}}$ to the rth term is

$$\frac{q}{1-q}\times\frac{\frac{\lambda}{q}-r+1}{r} \qquad . \qquad . \qquad . \qquad (9a)$$

which reduces to $\frac{\lambda}{r}$ when q is very small. The convergence of the series is seen from the fact that r cannot exceed $\frac{\lambda}{q}$, and the substitution of this value in $(9a)$ reduces it to

$$\frac{q^2}{(1-q)\lambda},$$

which vanishes with q.

Hence the second bracket on the right of (9) may be written

$$\left(1+\lambda+\frac{\lambda^2}{2!}+\frac{\lambda^3}{3!}\cdots\right)$$

and (9) is

$$e^{-\lambda}\left(1+\lambda+\frac{\lambda^2}{2!}+\frac{\lambda^3}{3!}+\ldots\right),$$

identical with (8).

The frequent rediscovery of this theorem is due to the fact that its value is felt in the study of problems involving small, independent probabilities. For instance, if we desired to find the distribution of n things in N pigeon-holes (all the pigeon-holes being of equal size and equally accessible), N being large, the distribution given by the binomial

$$N\left(\frac{1}{N} + \frac{N-1}{N}\right)^n .$$

would be effectively represented by (8), tables of which for different values of λ have been published by v. Bortkewitsch and others.

The theorem has also been applied to cases in which, although the actual value of q (or p) is unknown, it may safely be assumed to be very small. It should be noticed that, if (8) is the real law of distribution, certain relations must obtain between the constants of the statistics (see par. 12, Chapter XIII.). Using the method of par. 6, Chapter XV., we have for the mean

$$e^{-\lambda}\left(\lambda + \lambda^2 + \frac{\lambda^3}{2!} + \ldots\right)$$

$$= \lambda e^{-\lambda}\left(1 + \lambda + \frac{\lambda^2}{2!} + \ldots\right)$$

$$= \lambda$$

and for σ^2

$$e^{-\lambda}\left(\lambda + 2\lambda^2 + \frac{3\lambda^3}{2!} + \ldots\right) - \lambda^2$$

$$= e^{-\lambda}\lambda\left(1 + \lambda + \frac{\lambda^2}{2!} + \frac{\lambda^3}{3!} + \ldots\right) + e^{-\lambda}\lambda\left(\lambda + \frac{2\lambda^2}{2!} + \frac{3\lambda^3}{3!} + \ldots\right) - \lambda^2$$

$$= \lambda + e^{-\lambda}\lambda^2\left(1 + \lambda + \frac{\lambda^2}{2!} + \ldots\right) - \lambda^2$$

$$= \lambda + \lambda^2 - \lambda^2$$

$$= \lambda.$$

Hence any statistics produced by causes conforming to Poisson's limit should, within the limits of sampling, have the mean equal to the square of the standard deviation. For instance, in the statistics used in par. 12 of Chapter XIII., the mean is ·61, $\sigma = ·78$, $\sigma^2 = ·6079$.

If we now compute the theoretical frequencies from (8), putting $\lambda = {\cdot}61$, we have the following results :—

Deaths.	Actual Frequency.	Frequency assigned by Poisson's Limit.
0	109	108·7
1	65	66·3
2	22	20·2
3	3	4·1
4	1	·7 (4 and over)

The agreement here is excellent, but such a concordance is not very common in actual statistics. Cases do, however, occur in which the method is of service, and the advanced student will find that the reasoning illustrated is of value in many theoretical investigations.

III. GOODNESS OF FIT.

(Supplementary to Chapter XVII.)

In par. 15, Chapter XV. (p. 308), it was remarked that the general· treatment of the problem, whether the discrepancies between any system of observed frequencies and those postulated by a theoretical law might have arisen by the operation of random sampling, was beyond the scope of this work. As, however, the student will find in the course of his reading that a test of this character is often applied in practical problems, the following notes may be of service by way of comment on, or elucidation of, the highly technical papers in which the subject is fully discussed (see refs. 22 and 23, p. 315, and also additional refs. on p. 390).

The student who has followed the argument leading up to the table on p. 310 will have perceived that, when the frequency distribution of a variable is known, the probability that a set of observations departing from the most likely value would occur can be evaluated by comparing the portion of area bounded by the ordinate corresponding to the observed deviation with the whole area of the theoretical curve, and the work is illustrated in Examples i.-iv. of pp. 311-313. In this case there is only a single variable, and the test for goodness of fit is reduced to its simplest terms. But a consideration of Chapter XVI., and the

relation there shown to hold between the normal curve and the
surface of normal correlation, at once suggests that the same
principle will apply when there are two variables.

It was proved on pp. 319–321 that the contours of a normal
surface are a system of concentric ellipses. Now suppose we
have a normal system of frequency in two variables x and y,
then the chance that on random sampling we should obtain the
combination x' y' is measured by the corresponding ordinate of
the surface, and the feet of all ordinates of equal height will lie
upon an ellipse which will therefore be the locus of all combinations of x and y equally likely to occur as is x' y'. Any combination more likely to occur than x' y' will have a taller ordinate,
and as the locus of its foot must also be an ellipse, that ellipse
will be contained within the x' y' ellipse. Conversely, combinations less likely to occur than x' y' will be represented by
ordinates located upon ellipses wholly surrounding the x' y'
ellipse. Hence, if we dissect the surface into indefinitely thin
elliptical slices and determine the total volumes of the sum of
the slices from $x = x'$ and $y = y'$ down to $x = 0$ and $y = 0$, this
volume divided by the total volume of the surface will be the
probability of obtaining in sampling a result not worse than
x' y'; or, if we prefer, we may sum from $x = x'$, $y = y'$ to
$x = y = \infty$, and then the fraction is the chance of obtaining as
bad a result as x' y', or a worse result.

The reader who has compared the figures on p. 166 and
p. 246, and followed the algebra of pp. 331–332, will have no
difficulty in seeing that, when the number of variables is
3, 4 . . . . n, the above principle remains valid although it
ceases to be possible to give a graphic representation. With
three variables the contour ellipse becomes an ellipsoidal surface,
and the four-dimensioned frequency "volume" must be dissected
into tridimensional ellipsoids; with four variables another
dimension is involved, and so on; but throughout the equation
of the contour of equal probability is of the ellipse type (cf. the
generalisation of the theorems of Chapter IX. in Chapter XII.).
Let us now suppose that if a certain set of data is derived
from a statistical universe conforming to a particular law, these
data, N in number, should be distributed into $n + 1$ groups containing respectively n_0, n_1, n_2 . . . . n_n each. Instead of this
we actually find m_0, m_1, m_2 . . . . m_n, where

$$m_0 + m_1 + \ \ldots \ldots \ m_n = n_0 + n_1 + \ \ldots \ldots \ n_n = N.$$

The problem to be solved is whether the observed system of
deviations from the most probable values might have arisen in

random sampling. Since, N being given, fixing the contents of any n of the classes determines the $n+1^{th}$, there are only n independent variables. Let us now suppose that the distribution of deviations is normal. Then the equation of the frequency "solid" is of the type set out in equation (15) of p. 331, which we will write for the present in the form

$$\kappa e^{-\frac{1}{2}\chi^2}.$$

χ^2 = a constant, is then the equation of the "ellipsoid" delimiting the two portions of the "volume" corresponding to combinations more or less likely to occur than $m_0, m_1, m_2 \ldots . m_n$. Accordingly, to find the chance of a system of deviations as probable as or less probable than that observed, we have to dissect the frequency solid, adding together the elliptic elements from the ellipsoid χ^2 to the ellipsoid ∞, and to divide this summation by the total volume, i.e. the summation from the ellipsoid 0 to the ellipsoid ∞.

In this book we have been concerned with summations the elements of which were finite. The reader is probably aware that when the element summed is taken indefinitely small the summation is called an integration, the symbol $\int$ replacing Σ or S, and the infinitesimal element being written dx. In the present case we have to reduce an n-fold integral the summation relating to n elements dx_1, dx_2, etc. To reduce this n-fold integral to a single integral, the following method is adopted. In the first place the ellipsoid, referred to its principal axes, is transformed into a spheroid by stretching or squeezing, and the system of rectangular co-ordinates transformed into polar co-ordinates.

The reason for adopting the latter device is that, when two rectangular elements dx, dy are transformed to polar co-ordinates, we replace them by an angular element $d\theta$, a vectorial element dr, and a term in r, the radius vector. When n such elements are transformed, the integral vectorial factor is raised to the $n-1^{th}$ power and there is an infinitesimal vectorial element, dr, and a "solid" angular element. But as the limits of integration of the angular (not of the vectorial) element will be the same in the numerator and denominator, these cancel out, while χ may be treated as the vectorial element or ray. Hence the multiple integral reduces to a single integral and the expression becomes

$$\frac{\int_{\chi}^{\infty} e^{-\frac{1}{2}\chi^2} . \chi^{n-1} . d\chi}{\int_{0}^{\infty} e^{-\frac{1}{2}\chi^2} . \chi^{n-1} . d\chi},$$

24

the reduction of which, its integration, can be effected in terms of χ by methods described in text-books of the integral calculus. Everything turns, therefore, upon the computation of the function χ.

As we have seen, χ^2 is determined by evaluating the standard deviations of the n variables and their correlations two at a time (the higher partials being deducible if the correlations of zero order are known).

By an application of the method of p. 257, we have

$$\sigma_p = \sqrt{N\left(1 - \frac{n_p}{N}\right)\frac{n_p}{N}}$$

for the standard error of sampling in the content of the pth class; while by a similar adaptation of the reasoning on p. 342 we reach

$$r_{pq} = -\frac{n_p n_q}{N\sigma_p\sigma_q}$$

for the correlation of errors of sampling in the pth and q^{th} classes. With these data, χ^2 can be deduced (the actual process of reduction is somewhat lengthy, but the student should have no difficulty in following the steps given in pp. 370-2 of ref. 47, *infra*). Its value is

$$\chi^2 = \overset{n=n}{\underset{n=0}{S}}\frac{(m_n - n_n)^2}{n_n},$$

the summation extending to all $n+1$ classes of the frequency distribution.

Values of the probability that an equally likely or less likely system of deviations will occur, usually denoted by the letter P, have been computed for a considerable range of χ^2 and of $n' = n+1 = $ the number of classes, and are published in the *Tables for Statisticians and Biometricians* mentioned on p. 358.

The arithmetical process is illustrated upon the two examples of dice-throwing given on p. 258.

There are three points which the student should note as regards the practical application of the method. In the first place, the proof given assumes that deviations from the expected frequencies follow the normal law. This is a reasonable assumption only if no theoretical frequency is very small, for if it is very small the distribution of deviations will be skew and not normal. It is desirable, therefore, to group together the small frequencies in the "tail" of the frequency distribution, as is done in the second illustration below, so as to make the expected frequency a few units at least. In the case of the first illustration it might have been better to group the frequency of 0 successes with that of

Twelve Dice thrown 4096 times, a throw of 4, 5, or 6 points reckoned a success (p. 258).

No. of Successes.	Observed Frequency (m').	Expected Frequency (m) $4096(\frac{1}{2}+\frac{1}{2})^{12}$.	$(m'-m)^2$.	$\frac{(m'-m)^2}{m}$.
0	0	1	1	1·0000
1	7	12	25	2·0833
2	60	66	36	·5455
3	198	220	484	2·2000
4	430	495	4225	8·5354
5	731	792	3721	4·6982
6	948	924	576	·6234
7	847	792	3025	3·8194
8	536	495	1681	3·3960
9	257	220	1369	6·2227
10	71	66	25	·3788
11	11	12	1	·0833
12	0	1	1	1·0000
Totals	4096	4096	...	$34·5860 = \chi^2$

From the tables we find :—

n'.	χ^2.	P.
13	30	·002792
13	40	·000072

Hence, by interpolation for $\chi^2 = 34·5860$, $P = ·0015$.

Twelve Dice thrown 4096 times, a throw of 6 points reckoned a success.

No. of Successes.	Observed Frequency (m').	Expected Frequency (m) $4096(\frac{5}{6}+\frac{1}{6})^{12}$.	$(m'-m)^2$.	$\frac{(m'-m)^2}{m}$.
0	447	459	144	·3137
1	1145	1103	1764	1·5993
2	1181	1213	1024	·8442
3	796	809	169	·2089
4	380	364	256	·7033
5	115	116	1	·0086
6	24	27	9	·3333
7 and over	8	5	9	1·8000
Totals	4096	4096	...	$5·8113 = \chi^2$

From the tables we find :—

n'.	χ^2.	P.
8	5	·659963
8	6	·539750

Hence, by interpolation for $\chi^2 = 5·8113$, $P = ·5624$.

1 success, and the frequency of 12 successes with that of 11 successes.

In the second place, the proof outlined assumes that the theoretical law is known *a priori*. In a large number, perhaps almost the majority, of practical cases in which the test is applied this condition is not fulfilled. We determine, for example, the constants of a frequency curve from the observations themselves, not from *a priori* considerations : we determine the "independence values" of the frequencies for a contingency table from the given row and column totals, again not from *a priori* considerations. This general case is dealt with below, in the section headed "Comparison Frequencies based on the Observations."

Finally, attention should be paid to the run of the signs of the differences $m' - m$. The method used pays no attention to the order of these signs, and it may happen that χ^2 has quite a moderate value and P is not small when all the positive differences are on one side of the mode and all the negative differences on the other, so that the mean shows a deviation from the expected value that is quite outside the limits of sampling, or that the differences are negative in both tails so that the standard deviation shows an almost impossible divergence from expectation. In the first example on the preceding page all the differences are negative up to 5 successes, positive from 6 to 10 successes, and negative again for 11 and 12 successes. This is almost the first case supposed, and in fact we have already found (p. 267) that the mean deviates from the expected value by 5·1 (more precisely 5·13) times its standard error. From Table II. of Tables for Statisticians we have :—

Greater fraction of the area of a normal
  curve for a deviation 5·13 .   .   .   ·9999998551
Area in the tail of the curve .   .   .   ·0000001449
Area in both tails .   .   .   .   ·0000002898

so that the probability of getting such a deviation (+ or −) on random sampling is only about 3 in 10,000,000. The value found for P (·0015) by the grouping used is therefore in some degree misleading. If we regroup the distribution according to the signs of $m' - m$, we find

Successes.	Observed Frequency.	Expected Frequency.
0– 5	1426	1586
6–10	2659	2497
11–12	11	13
Total. .	4096	4096

For this comparison n' is 3, χ^2 is 26·96, or practically 27, and P is about ·000001—a value much more nearly in accordance with that suggested by the mean.

Such a regrouping of the frequency distribution by the runs of classes that are in excess and in defect of expectation would appear often to afford a useful and severe test of the real extent of agreement between observation and theory. In the second example the signs are fairly well scattered, and the regrouping has a comparatively small effect; the mean being in almost precise agreement with expectation. The regrouped distribution is :—

Successes.	Observed Frequency.	Expected Frequency.
0	447	459
1	1145	1103
2–3	1977	2022
4	380	364
5–6	139	143
7–8	8	5
Total. .	4096	4096

Here n' is 6, χ^2 is 5·52, and P 0·36, so that the deviations from expectation are still well within the range of fluctuations of sampling.

The value of P is the probability that a set of observations will occur giving a group of deviations from theory, $i.e.$ a value of χ^2, which is more improbable than that observed. If, to take the second illustration above, we were to repeat 4096 throws of twelve dice a large number of times, noting the throws of sixes, we should expect to get a worse fit to theory, $i.e.$ a value of χ^2 greater than 6·77, roughly speaking 56 times in every hundred trials.

The value of P corresponding to $\chi^2 = 0$ is necessarily unity, for it is certain that all values of χ^2 must exceed zero. If the value of P corresponding to $\chi^2 = 1$ is P_1, then $1 - P_1$ is the frequency of values of χ^2 between 0 and 1. Similarly, if the value of P corresponding to $\chi^2 = 2$ is P_2, then the frequency of values of χ^2 between 1 and 2 is $P_1 - P_2$, and so on. Thus, for 16 classes $(n' = 16)$, we find in the tables :—

χ^2.	P.	Differences of P.
0	1·	·007 873
5	·992 127	·172 388
10	·819 739	·368 321
15	·451 418	·279 486
20	·171 932	·171 932

We should expect, therefore, in, say, 1000 sets of random sampling with 16 classes, about 8 cases of χ^2 between 0 and 5, about 172 cases between 5 and 10, 368 between 10 and 15, 279 between 15 and 20, and 172 over 20. The following table shows the results obtained for the more modest number of 100 sets of trials, and gives very fair agreement with theory, especially considering that the assumption of normality can hardly be strictly true. The trials were carried out by throwing 200 beans into a revolving circular tray with sixteen equal radial compartments, and counting the number of beans in each compartment. The value of χ^2 was then computed, taking the expected frequency as $200/16 = 12\cdot5$.

χ^2.	Number of Tables giving a Value of χ^2 lying between the Limits on the Left.	
	Expected.	Observed.
0– 5	0·8	—
5–10	17·2	20
10–15	36·8	36
15–20	27·9	30·5
20 upwards	17·2	13·5

If we treat this in its turn as a comparison of observation with theory, we find, bracketing the first two groups together, so as to reduce the number of classes to four, $\chi^2 = 1\cdot28$, whence from the tables P is approximately 0·74. That is to say, we should expect a worse agreement with theory about three times out of four.

It follows from what was said above that, in any series of trials by simple sampling, equal numbers of cases should be found within equal intervals of P, e.g. from 1·0 to 0·9, from 0·9 to 0·8, from 0·8 to 0·7, and so on. The frequency distribution of P, that is to say, when we fulfil the conditions of simple sampling, is uniform over the whole range from 0 to 1. Thus for a rough grouping into four classes the above series of trials gave :—

P.	Number of Tables giving a Value of P lying between the Limits on the Left.	
	Expected.	Observed.
1·00–0·75	25	23
0·75–0·50	25	30
0·50–0·25	25	22
0·25–0	25	25

The value of χ^2 for this comparison is 1·52, giving $P = 0.68$, or we should expect a worse fit roughly twice in every three trials.

COMPARISON FREQUENCIES BASED ON THE OBSERVATIONS.

Contingency Tables.—Attention was specially directed above to the fact that the theoretical frequencies were assumed to be given *a priori*. The theory of the more general case, in which comparison is made with frequencies determined by the aid of the observations themselves, has only recently been fully worked out (Fisher, ref. 49). The most important practical case of the kind is that of association or contingency tables in which the observed frequencies are compared with the independence-values obtained from the totals of rows and columns—that is, the values

$$(A_m B_n)_0 = \frac{(A_m)(B_n)}{N}$$

of Chapter V. § 6, p. 64, and in which the differences

$$\delta_{mn} = (A_m B_n) - (A_m B_n)_0$$

are used as an indication of the divergence from independence. The rule to which the theory leads is a very simple one: the χ^2 method is still applicable, but the tables must be entered with n' equal to the number of algebraically independent frequencies (or values of δ) increased by unity, and not with n' equal to the number of compartments in the table. Now, if in any column of the contingency table we are given all the values of δ but one— say, the marginal value at the bottom,—the remaining one can be determined, because the sum of the δ's for every column must be zero. The same statement must hold good for every row. Hence, if r be the number of rows, c the number of columns, the number of algebraically independent values of δ is $(r-1)(c-1)$, and the tables must be entered with the value

$$n' = (r-1)(c-1)+1.$$

The student will realise that this is a reasonable rule if he considers that when we take n' as the number of classes, the comparison frequencies being given *a priori*, we are taking it as one more than the number of algebraically independent frequencies, since the total number of observations is fixed.

The following will serve as an illustration (Yule, ref. 5 of Chapter V.). Sixteen pieces of photographic paper were printed down to different depths of colour from nearly white to a very deep blackish brown. Small scraps were cut from each sheet and pasted on cards, two scraps on each card one above the other, combining scraps from the several sheets in all possible ways, so that there were 256 cards in the pack. Twenty observers then went through the pack independently, each one naming each tint either "light," "medium," or "dark."

TABLE *showing the Name (light, medium, or dark) assigned to each of two Pieces of Photographic Paper on a Card:* 256 *Cards and* 20 *Observers. Upper figure, observed frequency; central figure, independence frequency; bottom figure, difference* δ. (Yule, ref. 5 of Chap. V., Table XXI.)

Name assigned to Lower Tint on Card.	Name assigned to Upper Tint on Card.			Total.
	Light.	Medium.	Dark.	
Light . .	850 **785** + 65	571 **633** − 62	580 **583** − 3	2001
Medium . .	618 **653** − 35	593 **527** + 66	455 **486** − 31	1666
Dark . .	540 **570** − 30	456 **460** 4	457 **423** + 34	1453
Total . .	2008	1620	1492	5120

4225/785	. . .	5·38
3844/633	. .	6·07
9/583	.	·02
1225/653	. . .	1·88
4356/527	. . .	8 27
961/486	. . .	1·98
900/570	. .	1·58
16/460	. . .	·03
1156/423	. . .	2·73

Total χ^2		27·94
n'		5
P		·000012

The results are shown in the preceding table, the upper figure in
each compartment of the table being the observed frequency of
the corresponding pair of names. Below the observed frequency
are given the independence frequency $(A_m B_n)_0$ and the difference
δ_{mn}. It will be seen that the observed figures are not very close
to the independence-values, there being apparently a marked
tendency to give the same names to the two tints on any card, so
that all the diagonal frequencies are in excess of the independence-
values and all the others in defect.

Working out χ^2 as shown, the total comes to 27·94, or practically
28. Since r and c are both 3, n' must be taken as $(2 \times 2) + 1$—
that is, 5. Turning up the tables in the column $n' = 5$, we find
$P = ·000012$—that is to say, we would only expect to find so great
a divergence from independence, in random sampling, a little
more than once in 100,000 trials, so the result is certainly
significant.

Association Tables.—When we are dealing with an association
table there are only two rows and two columns, and consequently
n' must be taken as $(2 - 1)(2 - 1) + 1$—that is, 2. But no column
for $n' = 2$ is given in *Tables for Statisticians and Biometricians*, the
lowest value taken being $n' = 3$, and a supplementary table (XV. o)
is not sufficiently detailed: the necessary table, reprinted by
permission from the *Journal of the Royal Statistical Society*
(ref. 50), will be found at the end of this Supplement. As will
be seen from the following illustrations, the required probability
can also be determined from the table of areas of the normal
curve, but it is very convenient to keep the arithmetic in the
usual form.

Example i.—(Data from Chapter III., p. 37.) The following
data are there cited for colour of flower and prickliness of fruit in
Datura : the independence-frequencies have been entered below
the numbers of observations.

Flower.	Fruit.		Total.
	Prickly.	Smooth.	
Violet . . $\cdot\left\{\vphantom{}\right.$	47 48·337	12 10·663	59
White . . $\cdot\left\{\vphantom{}\right.$	21 19·663	3 4·337	24
Total	68	·15	83

Here δ is 1·337, and

$$\chi^2 = (1·337)^2\left\{\frac{1}{48·337} + \frac{1}{10·663} + \frac{1}{19·663} + \frac{1}{4·337}\right\}$$
$$= ·708.$$

Turning up this value of χ^2 in the table on p. 385, we find by interpolation $P = ·400$. As stated in the text, the association, negative in this case, is "so small that no stress can be laid on it as indicating anything but a fluctuation of sampling."

Precisely the same result can be arrived at by working out the standard error of the difference between the proportions of violet and of white flowers that have smooth fruits, taking the ratio of the difference to its standard error and then using the table of areas of the normal curve. Thus :—

Proportion of violet flowers that have smooth
fruits, 12/59 or . . . . . . ·2033
Proportion of white flowers that have smooth
fruits, 3/24 or . . . . . . ·1250
Difference 0783
Proportion of all flowers that have smooth fruits,
15/83 or . . . . ·1807

Standard error of the difference between proportions of smooth fruits in sampling from a universe in which the proportions are ·1807 and ·8193, and the numbers in the samples 59 and 24 respectively :—

$$\sqrt{·8193 \times ·1807\left(\frac{1}{59} + \frac{1}{24}\right)} = ·0932.$$

Hence the ratio of the observed difference to its standard error is ·0783/·0932 or ·840.

Interpolating in the table of areas of the normal curve on p. 310, or taking the required figure directly from Table II. of Tables for Statisticians, we have :—

Greater fraction of area for a deviation of ·84 in
the normal curve . . . . . . ·7995
Area in the tail . . . . . . ·2005
Area in both tails . . . . . . ·401

That is to say, the probability of getting a difference, of either sign, as great as or greater than that actually observed is ·401, agreeing, within the accuracy of the arithmetic, with the probability given by the χ^2 method.

The same result would again have been obtained had we worked from the columns instead of from the rows, and considered the difference between the proportions of white flowers for prickly and for smooth fruits respectively.

Example ii.—(Data from ref. 6 of Chapter III., Table XIV.) The following table shows the result of inoculation against cholera on a certain tea estate :—

	Not-attacked.	Attacked.	Total.
Inoculated . . .$\left\{\vphantom{\begin{matrix}a\\b\end{matrix}}\right.$	431 427·7	5 8·3	436
Not-inoculated . .$\left\{\vphantom{\begin{matrix}a\\b\end{matrix}}\right.$	291 294·3	9 4·7	300
Total	722	14	736

As in the last example, the independence-frequencies have been given below the numbers observed. The value of δ is 3·3, and

$$\chi^2 = (3\cdot3)^2\left\{\frac{1}{427\cdot7} + \frac{1}{8\cdot3} + \frac{1}{294\cdot3} + \frac{1}{4\cdot7}\right\} = 3\cdot27.$$

From the table on p. 386 P is ·0706.

Working from the proportions not-attacked, we can arrive at the same result.

Proportion not-attacked amongst   inoculated . ·01147
„   „   „   not-inoculated . ·03000
Difference . . . . ·01853

The standard error of the difference is

$$\sqrt{·98098 \times ·01902\left(\frac{1}{436} + \frac{1}{300}\right)} = ·01025.$$

The ratio of the difference to its standard error is therefore ·01853/·01025, or 1·808.

Greater fraction of normal curve for a deviation of 1·808 is ·96470
Fraction in tail . . . . ·03530
Fraction in the two tails . . . . . . ·07060

As before, both methods must lead to the same result.

An Aggregate of Tables.—It may often happen that we have formed a number of contingency or association tables—more often the latter than the former—for similar data from different fields. All may give, perhaps, a positive association, but the values of P may run so high that we do not feel any great confidence even in the aggregate result. The question then arises whether we cannot obtain a single value of P for the aggregate as a whole, telling us what is the probability of getting by mere random sampling a series of divergences from independence as great as or greater than those observed. The question is usually answered by pooling the tables; but, in view of the fallacies that may be introduced by pooling (*cf.* Chapter IV. §§ 6 and 7), this method is not quite satisfactory. A better answer is given by the application of the present general rule. Add up all the values of χ^2 for the different tables, thus obtaining the value of χ^2 for the aggregate, and enter the P-tables with a value of n' equal to the total of algebraically independent frequencies increased by unity: that is, take n' as given by

$$n' = 1 + \Sigma(r - 1)(c - 1).$$

For the association table there is only one algebraically independent value of δ. Hence if we are testing the divergence from independence of an aggregate of association tables, we must add together the values of χ^2 and enter the P-tables with n' taken as one more than the number of tables in the aggregate.

Thus from ref. 6 of Chapter III., from which the data of Example ii. were cited, we take the following values of χ^2 and of P for six tables that include that example. They refer to six different estates in the same group.

χ^2.	P.
9·34	·0022
6·08	·014
2·51	·11
3·27	·071
5·61	·018
1·59	·21
Total . . 28·40	

The association between inoculation and protection from attack is positive for each estate, but for only one of the tables is the value of P so small that we can say the result is *very* unlikely to have arisen as a fluctuation of sampling. Adding up the values of χ^2, the total is 28·40, and entering the column for $n' = 7$ (one more than the number of tables considered), we find

χ^2.	$P.$
28	·000094
29	·000061

whence by interpolation the value of P is ·000081, *i.e.* we should only expect to get a total of χ^2's as great as or greater than this, on random sampling, 81 times in 1,000,000 trials. We can therefore regard the results as significant with a high degree of confidence.

We may, I think, go further: for all the observed associations are positive, and in six cases there are 2^6 or 64 possible permutations of sign. We should therefore only expect to get an equal or greater total value of χ^2 *and tables all showing positive associa-tion*, not 81 times in 1,000,000 trials but 81/64 or, roundly, 1·3 times. P for the *observed event* ($\Sigma(\chi^2) = 28\cdot4$ and all associations positive) is therefore only ·0000013.

Experimental Illustrations of the General Case.—The formulæ for the general case, as for the special case in which the frequencies with which comparison is made are given *a priori*, can be checked by experiment.

The numbers of beans counted in each of the sixteen compart-ments of the revolving circular tray mentioned on p. 374 above were entered as the frequencies of a table (1) with 4 rows and 4 columns, (2) with 2 rows and 8 columns, and the value of χ^2 computed for each table for divergence from independence. For the two cases we have

$$n' = (3 \times 3) + 1 = 10$$

and

$$n' = (1 \times 7) + 1 = 8$$

respectively. Differencing the columns for P corresponding to these two values of n', we obtain the theoretical frequency-distri-butions given in the columns headed "Expectation" in Table A. The observed distributions of the values of χ^2 in 100 experimental tables are given in the columns headed "Observation." It will be seen that the agreement between expectation and observation is excellent for so small a number of observations. If the goodness of fit be tested by the χ^2 method, grouping together the frequencies from $\chi^2 = 15$ upwards, so that n' is 4, χ^2 is found to be 2·27 for the 4×4 tables and 4·36 for the 2×8 tables, giving $P = 0\cdot52$ in the first case and 0·22 in the second.

TABLE A.—*Theoretical Distribution of χ^2, calculated from Independence-values, in Tables with 16 Compartments, compared with the Actual Distributions given by 100 Experimental Tables. In the first case n' must be taken as 10, in the second as 8. (Ref. 50.)*

χ^2	4 Rows, 4 Columns.		2 Rows, 8 Columns.	
	Expectation.	Observation.	Expectation.	Observation.
0– 5	16·6	17	34·0	29·5
5–10	48·4	44	47·1	56·5
10–15	26·0	32	15·3	10
15–20	7·3	6	3·0	3
20–	1·8	1	0·6	1
Total	100·1	100	100·0	100

For tables with 2 rows and 2 columns 350 experimental tables of 100 observations each were available. The observed distribution of values of χ^2, calculated from the independence-frequencies, is shown in Table B, together with the theoretical distribution obtained by differencing the table on pp. 385–386. Testing goodness of fit on Table B as it stands, n' is 10, χ^2 works out at 7·53, and P is 0·583.

TABLE B.—*Theoretical Distribution of χ^2 for a Table with 2 Rows and 2 Columns, when χ^2 is calculated from the Independence-values, compared with the Actual Results for 350 Experimental Tables. (Ref. 50.)*

Value of χ^2.	Number of Tables.	
	Expected.	Observed.
0 –0·25	134·02	122
0·25–0·50	48·15	54
0·50–0·75	32·56	41
0·75–1·00	24.21	24
1 –2	56·00	62
2 –3	25·91	18
3 –4	13·22	13
4 –5	7·05	6
5 –6	3·86	5
6–	5·01	5
Total . .	349·99	350

The theorem last given for evaluating P for an aggregate of tables is illustrated by the experimental data of Tables C and D. The values of χ^2 for the 350 fourfold tables of Table B were added together in pairs, giving 175 pairs. According to theory the resulting frequency-distribution for the totals of pairs of χ^2's should be given by differencing the column of the P-table for $n' = 3$. The results of theory and observation are compared in the first pair of columns of Table C. Testing goodness of fit, grouping the values of χ^2 7 and upwards, n' is 8, χ^2 is 5·53, and P is 0·60.

Grouping the values of χ^2 for the 350 experimental tables similarly in sets of three and summing, we get the observed distribution on the right of Table C, and the theoretical distribution by differencing the column of the P-table for $n' = 4$. Grouping values of χ^2 8 and upwards, and testing goodness of fit between theory and observation, n' is 9, χ^2 is 2·18, and P 0·97.

TABLE C.—*Theoretical Distribution of Totals of χ^2 (calculated from Independence-values) for Pairs and for Sets of Three Tables with 2 Rows and 2 Columns, compared with the Actual Distributions given by Experimental Tables. n' must be taken as 3 in the first case, and 4 in the second.*

Sum of χ^2's.	Pairs of Tables.		Sets of 3 Tables.	
	Expectation.	Observation.	Expectation.	Observation.
0–1	68·9	67	23·1	21
1–2	41·8	46	26·5	26
2–3	25·3	22	21·0	22
3–4	15·4	19	15·1	19
4–5	9·3	7	10·4	9
5–6	5·6	3	7·0	7
6–7	3·4	6	4·6	4
7–8	2·1	3	3·0	4
8–	3·2	2	5·3	4
Total	175·0	175	116·0	116

Table D makes a similar comparison for the values of χ^2, calculated from independence, for 100 pairs of 4×4 tables. Here there are 9 algebraically independent δ's for each table of the pair, and consequently n' must be taken as 19. Differencing the P-table for $n' = 19$, the expected distribution is obtained, which is shown in the first column of Table D, the observed distribution being given in the second column. Taking the two groups at the bottom of the table together and testing goodness of fit, χ^2 is found to be 4·11, n' is 5, and P is 0·39.

TABLE D. — *Theoretical Distribution of Totals of χ^2 (calculated from Independence-values) for Pairs of Tables with 4 Rows and 4 Columns, compared with the Actual Distribution given by Experimental Tables.*

Sum of two χ^{2}'s.	Expectation.	Observation.
0–10	6·8	8
10–15	27·0	27
15–20	32·9	31
20–25	20·8	27
25–30	8·8	6
30–	3·7	1
Total . .	100·0	100

The general theorem that n' must be taken equal to the number of algebraically independent frequencies increased by unity applies not only to association and contingency tables, but to all cases in which the frequencies observed are connected with those expected by a number of linear relations, beyond their restriction to the same total frequency (Fisher, ref. 49). Thus, if a frequency curve has been fitted by the mean and standard deviation, n' should be taken as 2 less than the number of classes : if it has been fitted by the first four moments, n' should be taken as four less than the number of classes.

Table of the Values of P for Divergence from Independence in the
Fourfold Table.

A.—$\chi^2 = 0$ to $\chi^u = 1$ by steps of 0·01.

χ^2	P	Δ	χ^2	P	Δ
0	1·00000	7966	0·50	0·47950	436
0·01	0·92034	3280	0·51	0·47514	430
0·02	0·88754	2505	0·52	0·47084	423
0·03	0·86249	2101	0·53	0·46661	418
0·04	0·84148	1842	0·54	0·46243	411
0·05	0·82306	1656	0·55	0·45832	406
0·06	0·80650	1516	0·56	0·45426	400
0·07	0·79134	1404	0·57	0·45026	395
0·08	0·77730	1312	0·58	0·44631	389
0·09	0·76418	1235	0·59	0·44242	384
0·10	0·75183	1169	0·60	0·43858	379
0·11	0·74014	1111	0·61	0·43479	374
0·12	0·72903	1060	0·62	0·43105	369
0·13	0·71843	1015	0·63	0·42736	365
0·14	0·70828	974	0·64	0·42371	360
0·15	0·69854	938	0·65	0·42011	355
0·16	0·68916	905	0·66	0·41656	351
0·17	0·68011	874	0·67	0·41305	346
0·18	0·67137	845	0·68	0·40959	343
0·19	0·66292	820	0·69	0·40616	338
0·20	0·65472	795	0·70	0·40278	334
0·21	0·64677	773	0·71	0·39944	330
0·22	0·63904	752	0·72	0·39614	326
0·23	0·63152	731	0·73	0·39288	322
0·24	0·62421	713	0·74	0·38966	318
0·25	0·61708	696	0·75	0·38648	315
0·26	0·61012	679	0·76	0·38333	311
0·27	0·60333	663	0·77	0·38022	308
0·28	0·59670	648	0·78	0·37714	304
0·29	0·59022	634	0·79	0·37410	301
0·30	0·58388	620	0·80	0·37109	297
0·31	0·57768	607	0·81	0·36812	294
0·32	0·57161	595	0·82	0·36518	291
0·33	0·56566	583	0·83	0·36227	287
0·34	0·55983	572	0·84	0·35940	285
0·35	0·55411	560	0·85	0·35655	281
0·36	0·54851	551	0·86	0·35374	278
0·37	0·54300	540	0·87	0·35096	276
0·38	0·53760	530	0·88	0·34820	272
0·39	0·53230	521	0·89	0·34548	270
0·40	0·52709	512	0·90	0·34278	267
0·41	0·52197	503	0·91	0·34011	264
0·42	0·51694	495	0·92	0·33747	261
0·43	0·51199	487	0·93	0·33486	258
0·44	0·50712	479	0·94	0·33228	256
0·45	0·50233	471	0·95	0·32972	253
0·46	0·49762	463	0·96	0·32719	251
0·47	0·49299	457	0·97	0·32468	248
0·48	0·48842	449	0·98	0·32220	246
0·49	0·48393	443	0·99	0·31974	243
0·50	0·47950	436	1·00	0·31731	241

B.—$\chi^2=1$ to $\chi^2=10$ by steps of 0·1.

χ^2	P	Δ	χ^2	P	Δ
1·0	0·31731	2304	5·5	0·01902	106
1·1	0·29427	2095	5·6	0·01796	99
1·2	0·27332	1911	5·7	0·01697	94
1·3	0·25421	1749	5·8	0·01603	89
1·4	0·23672	1605	5·9	0·01514	83
1·5	0·22067	1477	6·0	0·01431	79
1·6	0·20590	1361	6·1	0·01352	74
1·7	0·19229	1258	6·2	0·01278	71
1·8	0·17971	1163	6·3	0·01207	66
1·9	0·16808	1078	6·4	0·01141	62
2·0	0·15730	1000	6·5	0·01079	59
2·1	0·14730	929	6·6	0·01020	56
2·2	0·13801	864	6·7	0·00964	52
2·3	0·12937	803	6·8	0·00912	50
2·4	0·12134	749	6·9	0·00862	47
2·5	0·11385	699	7·0	0·00815	44
2·6	0·10686	651	7·1	0·00771	42
2·7	0·10035	609	7·2	0·00729	39
2·8	0·09426	568	7·3	0·00690	38
2·9	0·08858	532	7·4	0·00652	35
3·0	0·08326	497	7·5	0·00617	33
3·1	0·07829	465	7·6	0·00584	32
3·2	0·07364	436	7·7	0·00552	30
3·3	0·06928	408	7·8	0·00522	28
3·4	0·06520	383	7·9	0·00494	26
3·5	0·06137	359	8·0	0·00468	25
3·6	0·05778	337	8·1	0·00443	24
3·7	0·05441	316	8·2	0·00419	23
3·8	0·05125	296	8·3	0·00396	21
3·9	0·04829	279	8·4	0·00375	20
4·0	0·04550	262	8·5	0·00355	19
4·1	0·04288	246	8·6	0·00336	18
4·2	0·04042	231	8·7	0·00318	17
4·3	0·03811	217	8·8	0·00301	16
4·4	0·03594	205	8·9	0·00285	15
4·5	0·03389	192	9·0	0·00270	14
4·6	0·03197	181	9·1	0·00256	14
4·7	0·03016	170	9·2	0·00242	13
4·8	0·02846	160	9·3	0·00229	12
4·9	0·02686	151	9·4	0·00217	12
5·0	0·02535	142	9·5	0·00205	10
5·1	0·02393	134	9·6	0·00195	11
5·2	0·02259	126	9·7	0·00184	10
5·3	0·02133	119	9·8	0·00174	9
5·4	0·02014	112	9·9	0·00165	8
5·5	0·01902	106	10·0	0·00157	8

For values of P corresponding to $\chi^2=11$ to $\chi^2=30$, by units, see Table XV. (c), p. 30 of *Tables for Statisticians and Biometricians*.

ADDITIONAL REFERENCES.

History of Official Statistics (p. 6).

(1) KOREN, J. (edited by), *The History of Statistics, their Development and Progress in many Countries*, New York, The Macmillan Co., 1918. (A collection of articles, mainly on the progress of official statistics, written by a specialist for each country.)

Contingency (p. 73).

(2) PEARSON, KARL, "On the General Theory of Multiple Contingency with Special Reference to Partial Contingency," *Biometrika*, vol. xi., 1916, p. 145. (An extension of the method of contingency coefficients to classification subjected to various conditions ; arithmetical examples are provided in the undermentioned paper.)

(3) PEARSON, KARL, and J. F. TOCHER, "On Criteria for the Existence of Differential Death-Rates," *Biometrika*, vol. xi., 1916, p. 159.

(4) RITCHIE-SCOTT, A., "The Correlation Coefficient of a Polychoric Table," *Biometrika*, vol. xii., 1918, p. 93. (Considers various methods of measuring association with special reference to 4×3-fold classifications.)

The Mode (p. 130).

(5) DOODSON, ARTHUR T., "Relation of the Mode, Median and Mean, in Frequency Curves," *Biometrika*, vol. xi., 1916–17, p. 429. (Gives a proof of the relation noted on p. 121.)

Index-numbers (p. 130).

There are useful discussions as to method in the following :—

(6) KNIBBS, G. H., "Prices, Price-Indexes, and Cost of Living in Australia," *Commonwealth of Australia, Labour and Industrial Branch, Report No. 1*, 1912.

(7) WOOD, FRANCES, "The Course of Real Wages in London, 1900–12," *Jour. Roy. Stat. Soc.*, vol. lxxvii., 1913–14, p. 1.

(8) WORKING CLASSES, COST OF LIVING COMMITTEE, 1918, *Report* (Cd. 8980, 1918), H.M. Stationery Office.

(9) BOWLEY, A. L., "The Measurement of Changes in Cost of Living," *Jour. Roy. Stat. Soc.*, vol. lxxxii., 1919, p. 343.

(10) BENNETT, T. L., "The Theory of Measurement of Changes in the Cost of Living," *Jour. Roy. Stat. Soc.*, vol. lxxxiii., 1920, p. 455.

(11) FLUX, A. W., "The Measurement of Price Changes," *Jour. Roy. Stat. Soc.*, vol. lxxxiv., 1921, p. 167.

(12) FISHER, IRVING, "The Best Form of Index-number," *Quart. Pub. Amer. Stat. Ass.*, March 1921, p. 533.

(13) PERSONS, W. M., "Fisher's Formula for Index-numbers," *Rev. Econ. Statistics*, vol. iii., 1921, p. 103.

(14) MARCH, L., "Les modes de mesure du mouvement général des prix," *Metron*, vol. i., No. 4, 1921, p. 40.

For the student of the cost of living in Great Britain the following are useful :—

(15) "Labour Gazette Index Number : Scope and Method of Compilation," *Lab. Gaz.*, March 1920 and Feb. 1921.

(16) "Final Report on the Cost of Living of the Parliamentary Committee of the Trades Union Congress" (The Committee, 32 Eccleston Sq., London, 1921); critical notices of the same in the *Labour Gazette* for Aug. and Sept. 1921 ; and review by A. L. Bowley, *Econ. Jour.*, Sept. 1921.

(17) BOWLEY, A. L., *Prices and Wages in the United Kingdom*, 1914-20, Oxford, 1920 (Clarendon Press).

Correlation : History (p. 188).

(18) PEARSON, K., "Notes on the History of Correlation," *Biometrika*, vol. xiii., 1920, p. 25.

Fit of Regression Lines (p. 209).

(19) PEARSON, KARL, "On the Application of Goodness of Fit Tables to test Regression Curves and Theoretical Curves used to describe Observational or Experimental Data," *Biometrika*, vol. xi., 1916-17, p. 237. (Criticises and extends the work of Slutsky.)

Correlation in Case of Non-linear Regression (p. 209).

(20) WICKSELL, S. D., "On Logarithmic Correlation, with an Application to the Distribution of Ages at First Marriage," *Meddelande fran Lunds Astronomiska Observatorium*, No. 84, 1917. Svenska Aktuarieforenings Tidskrift.

(21) WICKSELL, S. D., "The Correlation Function of Type A," *Kungl. Svenska Vetenskapsakademiens Handl.*, Bd. lviii., 1917.

(22) PEARSON, K., "On a General Method of Determining the Successive Terms in a Skew Regression Line," *Biometrika*, vol. xiii., 1921, p. 296.

Correlation : Effect of Errors of Observation, etc. (p. 225).

(23) HART, BERNARD, and C. SPEARMAN, "General Ability, its Existence and Nature," *Brit. Jour. Psychology*, vol. v., 1912, p. 51.

Correction or Standardisation of Death-rates (p. 226).

The term "standardisation" is now usually employed instead of "correction," and a "potential or standard death-rate" is termed an "index death-rate" : for the methods of standardisation in present use see—

(24) *Seventy-fourth Annual Report of the Registrar General of Births, Deaths, and Marriages in England and Wales* (1911). [Cd. 6578, 1913.]

Correlation : Miscellaneous (p. 226).

(25) HARRIS, J. ARTHUR. "The Correlation between a Component, and between the Sum of Two or More Components, and the Sum of the Remaining Components of a Variable," *Quart. Pub. American Stat. Ass.*, vol. xv., 1917, p. 854.

(26) YULE, G. U., "On the Time-correlation Problem," *Jour. Roy. Stat. Soc.*, vol. lxxxiv., 1921, p. 497.

(27) WICKSELL, S. D., "An Exact Formula for Spurious Correlation," *Metron*, vol. i., No. 4, 1921, p. 33.

Partial Correlation and Partial Correlation Ratio (p. 252).

(28) KELLEY, T. L., "Tables to facilitate the Calculation of Partial Coefficients of Correlation and Regression Equations," *Bulletin of the University of Texas*, No. 27, 1916. (Tables giving the values of $1/\sqrt{(1-r_{13}^2)(1-r_{23}^2)}$ and $r_{13}r_{23}/\sqrt{(1-r_{13}^2)(1-r_{23}^2)}$.)

(29) PEARSON, KARL, "On the Partial Correlation Ratio," *Proc. Roy. Soc.*, Series A, vol. xci., 1915, p. 492.

(30) ISSERLIS, L., "On the Partial Correlation Ratio; Part ii., Numerical," *Biometrika*, vol. xi., 1916–17, p. 50.

Sampling of Attributes (p. 273).

(31) DETLEFSEN, J. A., "Fluctuations of Sampling in a Mendelian Population," *Genetics*, vol. iii., 1918, p. 599.

The Law of Small Chances (p. 273).

(32) BORTKIEWICZ, L. VON, "Realismus und Formalismus in der mathematischen Statistik," *Allgemein. Stat. Arch.*, vol. ix., 1916, p. 225. (Continues the discussion initiated by the paper of Miss Whitaker, cited on p. 273.)

(33) GREENWOOD, M., and G. UDNY YULE, "On the Statistical Interpretation of some Bacteriological Methods employed in Water Analysis," *Journal of Hygiene*, vol. xvi., 1917, p. 36. (Applies a criterion developed from Poisson's limit to the discrimination of water analyses; numerous arithmetical examples.)

(34) "STUDENT," "An Explanation of Deviations from Poisson's Law in Practice," *Biometrika*, vol. x., 1919, p. 211.

(35) BORTKIEWICZ, L. VON, "Ueber die Zeitfolge Zufälliger Ereignisse," *Bull. de l'Institut Int. de Stat.*, tome xx., 2e livr., 1915.

(36) MORANT, G., "On Random Occurrences in Space and Time when followed by a Closed Interval," *Biometrika*, vol. xiii., 1921, p. 309.

See also reference 46.

Frequency Curves (p. 314).

(37) PEARSON, KARL, "Second Supplement to a Memoir on Skew Variation," *Phil. Trans. Roy. Soc.*, Series A, vol. ccxvi., 1916, p. 429. (Completes the description of type frequency curves contained in references (1) and (3) of p. 105.)

The advanced student who desires to compare the merits of different frequency systems proposed, should consult the following:—

(38) CHARLIER, C. V. L., Numerous papers issued from the Astronomical Department of Lund, 1906–12, especially "Contributions to the Mathematical Theory of Statistics" (1912).

(39) EDGEWORTH, F. Y., "On the Mathematical Representation of Statistical Data," *Jour. Roy. Stat. Soc.*, vol. lxxix., 1916, p. 456; lxxx., pp. 65, 266, 411; lxxxi., 1918, p. 322.

(These papers are concerned with the general theory of frequency systems; the undermentioned deal with the forms which are suitable for the representation of particular classes of data, especially statistics of epidemic disease.)

(40) BROWNLEE, J., "The Mathematical Theory of Random Migration and Epidemic Distribution," *Proc. Roy. Soc. Edin.*, vol. xxxi., 1910–11, p. 262.

(41) BROWNLEE, J., "Certain Aspects of the Theory of Epidemiology in Special Reference to Plague," *Proc. Roy. Soc. Medicine, Sect. Epidemiology and State Medicine*, vol. x. D, 1918, p. 85. (The appendix to this paper summarises the author's results and those of Sir Ronald Ross ; *vide infra.*)

(42) ROSS, Sir RONALD, "An Application of the Theory of Probabilities to the Study of a *priori* Pathometry," *Proc. Roy. Soc.*, A, vol. xcii., 1916, p. 204.

(43) ROSS, Sir RONALD, and HILDA P. HUDSON, "An Application of the Theory of Probabilities to the Study of a *priori* Pathometry," Pts. II. and III., *Proc. Roy. Soc.*, A, vol. xciii., 1917, pp. 212 and 225.

(44) KNIBBS, G. H., "The Mathematical Theory of Population," Appendix A to vol. i. of *Census of the Commonwealth of Australia.* (Contains a full discussion of the application of various frequency systems to vital statistics.)

(45) MOIR, H., "Mortality Graphs," *Trans. Actuarial Soc. America*, vol. xviii., 1917, p. 311. (Numerous graphs of mortality rates in different classes and periods.)

(46) GREENWOOD, M., and YULE, G. U., "An Enquiry into the Nature of Frequency Distributions representative of Multiple Happenings, with particular reference to the Occurrence of Multiple Attacks of Disease or of Repeated Accidents," *Journ. Roy. Stat. Soc.*, vol. lxxxiii., 1920, p. 255.

Goodness of Fit (p. 315 and p. 367).

(47) PEARSON, KARL, "On a Brief Proof of the Fundamental Formula for testing the Goodness of Fit of Frequency Distributions and on the Probable Error of P.," *Phil. Mag.*, vol. xxx. D (6th series), 1916, p. 369.

(48) PEARSON, KARL, "Multiple Cases of Disease in the same House," *Biometrika*, vol. lx., 1913, p. 28. (A modification of the goodness-of-fit test to cover such statistics as those indicated by the title.)

(49) FISHER, R. A., "On the Interpretation of χ^2 from Contingency Tables, and the Calculation of P," *Jour. Roy. Stat. Soc.*, vol. lxxxv., 1922, p. 87.

(50) YULE, G. U., "On the Application of the χ^2 Method to Association and Contingency Tables, with experimental illustrations," *Jour. Roy. Stat. Soc.*, vol. lxxxv., 1922, p. 95. (After correspondence with Mr Fisher I wish to withdraw the statement on p. 97 of this paper, that a full proof [of the general theorem as applied to contingency tables] seems still to be lacking : he has convinced me that his proof covers the case.)

See also reference 19.

Probable Errors: General References (p. 355).

(51) ISSERLIS, L., "On the Value of a Mean as calculated from a Sample," *Jour. Roy. Stat. Soc.*, vol. lxxxi., 1918, p. 75.

(52) SOPER, H. E., and Others, "On the Distribution of the Correlation Coefficient in Small Samples," *Biometrika*, vol. xi., 1916–17, p. 328.

(53) PEARSON, KARL, "On the Probable Error of Biserial η," *Biometrika*, vol. xi., 1916–17, p. 292.

(54) YOUNG, ANDREW, and KARL PEARSON, "On the Probable Error of a Coefficient of Contingency without Approximation," *Biometrika*, vol. xi., 1916–17, p. 215.

(55) Editorial, "On the Probable Errors of Frequency Constants," Pt. III., *Biometrika*, vol. xiii., 1920, p. 113.

(56) "STUDENT," "An Experimental Determination of the Probable Error of Dr Spearman's Correlation Coefficients," *Biometrika*, vol. xiii., 1921, p. 263.

(57) BISPHAM, J. W., "An Experimental Determination of the Distribution of the Partial Correlation Coefficient in Samples of Thirty," *Proc. Roy. Soc.*, A, vol. xcvii., 1920.

(58) TCHOUPROFF, A. A., "On the Mathematical Expectation of the Moments of Frequency Distributions," *Biometrika*, vol. xii., 1918–19, pp. 140 and 185, and vol. xiii., 1921, p. 283.

(59) FISHER, R. A., "On the Probable Error of a Coefficient of Correlation deduced from a Small Sample," *Metron*, vol. i., No. 4, 1921, p. 3.

Errors of Sampling in Agricultural Experiment.

A good deal of work has been done on this particular branch of the subject, and the following references may be useful :—

(60) BERRY, R. A., and O'BRIEN, D. G., "Errors in Feeding Experiments with Cross-bred Pigs," *Jour. Agr. Sci.*, vol. xi., 1921, p. 275.

(61) HARRIS, J. A., "On a Criterion of Substratum Homogeneity (or Heterogeneity) in Field Experiments," *Amer. Naturalist*, 1916, p. 430.

(62) HALL, A. D., E. J. RUSSELL, T. B. WOOD, S. U. PICKERING, S. H. COLLINS, "The Interpretation of the Results of Agricultural Experiments," *Journal of the Board of Agriculture*, Supplement 7, 1911. (Contains a collection of papers on error in field trials, feeding experiments, horticultural work, milk-testing, etc.)

(63) LYON, T. L., "Some Experiments to estimate Errors in Field Plat Tests," *Proc. Amer. Soc. of Agronomy*, vol. iii., 1911, p. 89.

(64) MERCER, W. B., and A. D. HALL, "The Experimental Error of Field Trials," *Jour. Agr. Science*, vol. iv., 1911, p. 107. (With an appendix by "Student" describing the chessboard method of conducting yield trials.)

(65) MITCHELL, H. H., and H. S. GRINDLEY, "The Element of Uncertainty in the Interpretation of Feeding Experiments," *Univ. of Illinois Agr. Exp. Station*, Bulletin 165, 1913.

(66) ROBINSON, G. W., and W. E. LLOYD, "On the Probable Error of Sampling in Soil Surveys," *Jour. Agr. Science*, vol. viii., 1915, p. 144.

(67) SURFACE, F. M., and RAYMOND PEARL, "A Method of Correcting for Soil Heterogeneity in Variety Tests," *Jour. Agr. Research*, vol. v., 1916, p. 1039.

(68) WOOD, T. B., and R. A. BERRY, "Variation in the Chemical Composition of Mangels," *Jour. Agr. Science*, vol. i., 1905, p. 16.

(69) WOOD, T. B., "The Feeding Value of Mangels," *Jour. Agr. Science*, vol. iii., 1910, p. 225.

(70) WOOD, T. B., and F. J. M. STRATTON, "The Interpretation of Experimental Results," *Jour. Agr. Science*, vol. iii., 1910, p. 417.

Works on Theory of Probability, etc. (App. II., p. 361).

(71) BACHELIER, L., *Calcul des probabilités*, tome i., Gauthier-Villars, Paris, 1912.

(72) BACHELIER, L., *Le jeu, la chance, et le hasard*, Flammarion, Paris, 1914,

(73) BOWLEY, A. L., *Elements of Statistics*, P. S. King, London, 4th ed., 1920. (This edition has been much extended in Part II., "Applications of Mathematics to Statistics" : the two Parts can now be purchased separately.)

(74) BRUNT, DAVID, *The Combination of Observations*, Cambridge University Press, 1917.

(75) CZUBER, E., *Die statistische Forschungsmethode*, L. W. Seidel, Wien, 1921.

(76) ELDERTON, W. PALIN, Addendum to *Frequency Curves and Correlation*, London, 1917 (Layton).

(77) FISHER, ARNE, *The Mathematical Theory of Probabilities and its Application to Frequency Curves and Statistical Methods*, vol. i., New York (Macmillan), 1915.

(78) FORCHER, HUGO, *Die statistische Methode als selbständige Wissenschaft*, Leipzig, 1913 (Veit).

(79) JONES, C., *A First Course in Statistics*, Bell & Sons, London, 1921.

(80) JULIN, A., *Principes de statistique théorique et appliquée* : tome i., *Statistique théorique*, Paris (Rivière), Bruxelles (Dewit), 1921.

(81) KEYNES, J. M., *A Treatise on Probability*, Macmillan, London, 1921.

(82) WEST, C. J., *Introduction to Mathematical Statistics*, Adams & Co., Columbus, 1918.

An inexpensive reprint of Laplace's *Essai philosophique* (ref. 17 on p. 361) has been published by Gauthier-Villars (Paris, 1921) in the · series entitled "Les maîtres de la pensée scientifique."

ANSWERS

CHAPTER I.

1.

N	26,287	(AB)	887
(A)	2,308	(AC)	374
(B)	2,853	(BC)	353
(C)	749	(ABC)	149

2.

(ABC)	156	(aBC)	179
$(AB\gamma)$	431	$(aB\gamma)$	1,249
$(A\beta C)$	272	$(a\beta C)$	163
$(A\beta\gamma)$	759	$(a\beta\gamma)$	20,504

3. The frequencies not given in the question itself are—

(a) (AB) 107 (AC) 405 (BC) 525.

(b) $(A\beta\gamma)$ 22,980 $(aB\gamma)$ 13,585 $(a\beta C)$ 96,478 $(a\beta\gamma)$ 28,868,495.

4. $$\frac{(AB)}{(A\beta)} > \frac{(B)}{(\beta)} \qquad \therefore \quad \frac{(AB)}{(AB)+(A\beta)} > \frac{(B)}{(B)+(\beta)},$$

that is $$\frac{(AB)}{(B)} > \frac{(A)}{N}, \text{ that is } \frac{(AB)}{(B)-(AB)} > \frac{(A)}{N-(A)}$$

that is $$\frac{(AB)}{(aB)} > \frac{(A)}{(a)}.$$

5. $(AB)+(BC)-(B)$, i.e., the sum of the excesses of (AB) and (BC) over $(B)/2$.

8. 160. Take A = husband exceeding wife in first measurement, B = husband exceeding wife in second measurement, and find $(a\beta)$.

CHAPTER II.

1. 80/263 or 304 per thousand.

2. 55/85 or 65 per cent.

3. 32 per cent. and 30 per cent.

4. 117.

5. 108.

8. $p \not> \frac{1}{4}(1-2q)$, $p \not< \frac{1}{4}(1+2q)$, i.e., p must lie between 0 and $\frac{1}{4}(1-2q)$ or between $\frac{1}{4}(1+2q)$ and $\frac{1}{2}$.

9. As a hint, remember the condition that—

$$(BC) \not< (B)+(C)-N.$$

CHAPTER III.

1. Deaf-mutes from childhood per million among males 222 ; among females 183 ; there is therefore positive association between deaf-mutism and male sex : if there had been no association between deaf-mutism and sex, there would have been 3176 male and 3393 female deaf-mutes.

2. (a) positive association, since $(AB)_0 = 1457$.
   (b) negative association, since $294/490 = 3/5$, $380/570 = 2/3$.
   (c) independence, since $256/768 = 1/3$, $48/144 = 1/3$.

3.

	Percentage of Plants above the Average Height.	
Parentage	Crossed.	Self-fertilised.
Ipomæa purpurea.	86 per cent.	25 per cent.
Petunia violacea .	79 ,,	17 ,,
Reseda lutea	78 ,,	34 ,,
Reseda odorata	71 ,,	45 ,,
Lobelia fulgens .	50 ,,	35 ,,

The association is much less for the species at the end than for those at the beginning of the list.

4. Percentage of dark-eyed amongst the sons of dark-eyed fathers 39 per cent.

Percentage of dark-eyed amongst the sons of not dark-eyed fathers 10 per cent.

If there had been no heredity, the frequencies to the nearest unit would have been $(AB)_0$ 18, $(A\beta)_0$ 111, $(aB)_0$ 121, $(a\beta)_0$ 750.

5. Percentage of light-eyed amongst the wives of light-eyed husbands 59 per cent.

Percentage of light-eyed amongst the wives of not light-eyed husbands 53 per cent.

If there had been no association : $(AB)_0 = 298$, $(A\beta)_0 = 225$, $(aB)_0 = 143$, $(a\beta)_0 = 108$.

6. The following are the proportions of the insane per thousand in successive age groups :—

In general population : 0·9, 2·3, 4·1, 5·7, 6·9, 7·5, 7·7, 6·8.
Amongst the blind : 20·1, 16·0, 16·3, 20·7, 18·3, 17·8, 11·4, 5·3.

Note the diminishing association, which is especially clear in the age-group 65—, and the negative association in the last age-group. The association coefficient gives the values below, which decrease continuously :—
   Association coefficient : +0·92, +0·75, +0·61, +0·57, +0·46, +0·41, +0·20, −0·13.

CHAPTER IV.

1.

$(D)/N$ = 6·9 per cent.	$(A)/N$ = 6·8 per cent.
$(AD)/(A)$ = 45·0 ,,	$(AD)/(D)$ = 44·6 ,,
$(\beta D)/(\beta)$ = 3·6 ,,	$(A\beta)/(\beta)$ = 4·7 ,,
$(A\beta D)/(A\beta)$ = 41·2 ,,	$(A\beta D)/(\beta D)$ = 54·9 ,,
$(BD)/(B)$ = 42·7 ,,	$(AB)/(B)$ = 29·2 ,,
$(ABD)/(AB)$ = 51·6 ,,	$(ABD)/(BD)$ = 35·3 ,,

The above give two legitimate comparisons. The general results are the same as for the boys, i.e. a very small association between development-defects and dulness amongst those exhibiting nerve-signs, as compared with those who do not exhibit nerve-signs, or with the girls in general. As the association amongst those who do not exhibit nerve-signs is quite as high as for the girls in general, the "conclusion" quoted does not seem valid.

2.

	(1) per thousand.	(2) per thousand.		(1) per thousand.	(2) per thousand.
$(B)/N$	3·2	7·5	$(A)/N$	0·9	4·0
$(AB)/(A)$	14·9	11·7	$(AB)/(B)$	4·0	6·3
$(BC)/(C)$	38·8	63·0	$(AC)/(C)$	6·6	18·8
$(ABC)/(AC)$	216	214	$(ABC)/(BC)$	36·8	63·8

The above give the two simplest comparisons, either of which is sufficient to show that there is a high association between blindness and mental derangement amongst the deaf-mutes as well as in the general population; amongst the old, the association is, in fact, small for the general population, but well-marked for deaf-mutes. This result stands in direct contrast with that of Qu. 1, where the association between the two defects A and D was much smaller in the defective universe β than in the universe at large. As previously stated, no great reliance can be placed on the census data as to these infirmities.

3. If the cancer death-rates for farmers over 45 and under 45 respectively were the same as for the population at large, the rate for all farmers 15— would be 1·11. This is *slightly* less than the actual rate 1·20, but the excess would not justify the statement that "farmers were peculiarly liable to cancer." It is, in point of fact, due to the further differences of age-distribution that we have neglected, *e.g.* amongst those over 45 there are more over 55 amongst farmers than amongst the general population, and so on.

4. 15 per cent.

6. If A and B were independent in both C and γ universes, we would have (AB) equal to

$$\frac{471 \times 419}{617} + \frac{151 \times 139}{383} = 374 \cdot 7.$$

Actually (AB) only $= 358$. Therefore A and B must be disassociated in one or both partial universes.

9. (1) 68·1 per cent. (2) 42·5 per cent. The fallacy discussed in § 2 is now avoided, and there seems no reason for declining to consider this as evidence of the effect of expenditure on election results.

10. The limits to y are—

$$y < \tfrac{1}{2}(3x - x^2 - 1)$$
$$> \tfrac{1}{2}(x + x^2),$$

subject to the conditions $y \not> x$, $y \not< 0$, $y \not< 2x - 1$. No inference of a positive association from two negatives is possible unless x lies between the limits ·382 . . . , ·618 . . . .

11. The limits to y are :—

(1)
$$y < \tfrac{1}{2}(6x - 6x^2 - 1)$$
$$> \tfrac{1}{2}(x + 6x^2),$$

subject to conditions $y \not< 0$, $\not< 4x - 1$, $\not> x$.

An inference is only possible from positive associations of AB and AC if $x \not> \tfrac{1}{6}$; an inference is only possible from two negative associations if x lies between ·211 . . . . and ·274 . . . . Note that x cannot exceed $\tfrac{1}{3}$.

(2)
$$y < \tfrac{1}{2}(6x - 3x^2 - 1)$$
$$> \tfrac{1}{2}(2x + 3x^2),$$

subject to conditions $y \not< 0$, $\not< 5x - 1$, $\not> x$.

No inference is possible from positive associations of AB and BC.
An inference is only possible from negative associations if x lie between
·183 . . . . and ·215 . . . . Note that x cannot exceed $\frac{1}{4}$.

(3)
$$y < \tfrac{1}{2}(6x - 2x^2 - 1)$$
$$> \tfrac{1}{2}(3x + 2x^2),$$

subject to the conditions $y \not< 0$, $\not< 5x - 1$, $\not> 0$.
As in (2), no inference is possible from positive associations of AC and BC;
an inference is possible from negative associations if x lie between ·177 . . . .
and ·224 . . . . Note that x cannot exceed $\frac{1}{4}$.

CHAPTER V.

1. A, 0·68. B, 0·36.

CHAPTER VI.

1. 1200 ; 200. 2. 100 ; 20. 3. 146·25. 4. 216·5.

CHAPTER VII.

2. Mean, 156·73 lb. Median, 154·67 lb. Mode (approx.) 150·6 lb. (Note
that the mean and the median should be taken to a place of decimals further
than is desired for the mode: the true mode, found by fitting a theoretical
frequency curve, is 151·1 lb.)
3. Mean, 0·6330. Median, 0·6391. Mode (approx.), 0·651. (True mode
is 0·653.)
4. £35·5 approximately.
5. (1) 116·0. (2) Means 77·4, 89·0, ratio 114·9. (3) Geometrical means 77·2,
88·9, ratio 115·2. (4) 115·2.
6. (1) 921,507. (2) 916,963.
7. 1st qual. 10s. 6$\frac{3}{4}$d. 2nd qual. 9s. 2$\frac{1}{4}$d.
8. $n.p.$ If the terms of the given binomial series are multiplied by 0, 1, 2, 3
. . . , note that the resulting series is also a binomial when a common factor
is removed. [The full proof is given in Chapter XV. § 6.]

CHAPTER VIII.

2. Standard deviation 21·3 lb. Mean deviation 16·4 lb. Lower quartile
142·5, upper quartile 168·4 ; whence $Q = 12·95$. Ratios: m.d./s.d. $= 0·77$,
Q/s.d. $= 0·61$. Skewness, 0·29.
3. Approximately lower quartile $= £26·1$, upper quartile $= £54·6$, ninth
decile $= £94$.
5. (1) $M = 73·2$, $\sigma = 17·3$. (2) $M = 73·2$, $\sigma = 17·5$. (3) $M = 73·2$, $\sigma = 18·0$.
(Note that while the mean is unaffected in the second place of decimals, the
standard deviation is the higher the coarser the grouping.)
6. $\sqrt{n.pq}$. The proof is given in Chapter XV. § 6.
7. The assumption that observations are evenly distributed over the

intervals does not affect the sum of deviations, except for the interval in which the mean or median lies: for that interval the sum is $n_2(0\cdot25+d^2)$, hence the entire correction is

$$d(n_1 - n_3) + n_2(0\cdot25 + d^2).$$

In this expression d is, of course, expressed as a fraction of the class-interval, and is given its proper sign. Notice that the n_1 and n_3 of this question are not the same as the N_1 and N_2 of § 16.

CHAPTER IX.

1. $\sigma_x = 1\cdot414$, $\sigma_y = 2\cdot280$, $r = +0\cdot81$. $X = 0\cdot5\,Y + 0\cdot5$. $Y = 1\cdot3X + 1\cdot1$.

2. Using the subscripts 1 for earnings, 2 for pauperism, 3 for out-relief ratio, $M_3 = 5\cdot79$, $\sigma_3 = 3\cdot09$: $r_{13} = -0\cdot13$, $r_{23} = +0\cdot60$.

CHAPTER XI.

1. $1\cdot232$ per cent. (against $1\cdot240$ per cent.) : $2\cdot556$ in. against $2\cdot572$ in.

2. The corrected standard-deviation is $0\cdot9954$ of the rough value.

3. Estimated true standard-deviation $6\cdot91$: standard-deviation of fluctuations of sampling $9\cdot38$. (The latter, which can be independently calculated, is too low, and the former consequently probably too high. *Cf.* Chap. XIV. § 10.)

4. $0\cdot43$.

5. 58 per cent.

6. $\sigma_2^2/\sqrt{(\sigma_1^2 + \sigma_2^2)(\sigma_2^2 + \sigma_3^2)}$.

7. $\dfrac{a\sigma_1}{\sqrt{a^2\sigma_1^2 + b^2\sigma_2^2}}$.

8. $0\cdot30$.

9. $r_{12} = \dfrac{1}{2ab\sigma_1\sigma_2}(-a^2\sigma_1^2 - b^2\sigma_2^2 + c^2\sigma_3^2)$.

The others may be written down from symmetry.

10. (1) No effect at all.   (2) If the mean value of the errors in variables is d, and in the weights e, the value found for the weighted mean is—

$$\text{The true value} + d - r.\sigma_x.\sigma w\frac{e}{\overline{w}(\overline{w}+e)}.$$

If r is small, d is the important term, and hence errors in the quantities are usually of more importance than errors in the weights. If r become considerable, errors in the weights may be of consequence, but it does not seem probable that the second term would become the most important in practical cases.

11. $Q = 2/3$.

12. $Q = 0\cdot77$.

CHAPTER XII.

1. $r_{23} = +0\cdot759$, $r_{13\cdot2} = +0\cdot097$, $r_{23\cdot1} = -0\cdot436$.
  $\sigma_{1\cdot23} = 2\cdot64$, $\sigma_{2\cdot13} = 0\cdot594$, $\sigma_{3\cdot12} = 70\cdot1$.
  $X_1 = 9\cdot31 + 3\cdot37\,X_2 + 0\cdot00364\,X_3$.

2. $r_{12\cdot34} = +0.680$, $r_{13\cdot24} = +0.803$, $r_{14\cdot23} = +0.397$.

$r_{23\cdot14} = -0.433$, $r_{24\cdot13} = -0.553$, $r_{34\cdot12} = -0.149$.

$\sigma_{1\cdot234} = 9.17$, $\sigma_{2\cdot134} = 49.2$, $\sigma_{3\cdot124} = 12.5$, $\sigma_{4\cdot123} = 105.4$.

$X_1 = 53 + 0.127\ X_2 + 0.587\ X_3 + 0.0345\ X_4$.

3. The correlation of the pth order is $r/(1+pr)$. Hence if r be negative, the correlation of order $n-2$ cannot be numerically greater than unity and r cannot exceed (numerically) $1/(n-1)$.

4. $-r_{12}$.

5. $r_{12\cdot3} = -1$, $r_{13\cdot2} = r_{23\cdot1} = +1$.

6. $r_{12\cdot3} = r_{13\cdot2} = r_{23\cdot1} = -1$.

CHAPTER XIII.

1. Theo. $M=6$, $\sigma=1.732$: Actual $M=6.116$, $\sigma=1.732$.
2. (a) Theo. $M=2.5$, $\sigma=1.118$: Actual $M=2.48$, $\sigma=1.14$.
   (b) ,, $M=3$, $\sigma=1.225$: ,, $M=2.97$, $\sigma=1.26$.
   (c) ,, $M=3.5$, $\sigma=1.323$: ,, $M=3.47$, $\sigma=1.40$.
3. Theo. $M=50$, $\sigma=5$: Actual $M=50.11$, $\sigma=5.23$.
4. The standard deviation of the proportion is 0.00179, and the actual divergence is 5.4 times this, and therefore almost certainly significant.
5. The standard deviation of the number drawn is 32, and the actual difference from expectation 18. There is no significance.
6. $p=1-\sigma^2/M$, $n=M/p$: $p=0.510$, $n=12.0$: $p=0.454$, $n=110.4$.
8. Standard deviation of simple sampling 23.0 per cent. The actual standard-deviation does not, therefore, seem to indicate any real variation, but only fluctuations of sampling.
9. Difference from expectation 7.5 : standard error 10.0. The difference might therefore occur frequently as a fluctuation of sampling.
10. The test can be applied either by the formulæ of Case II. or Case III. Case II. is taken as the simplest.

(a) $(AB)/(B)=69.1$ per cent.: $(A\beta)/(\beta)=80.0$ per cent. Difference 10.9 per cent. $(A)/N=71.1$ per cent. and thence $\epsilon_{12}=12.9$ per cent. The actual difference is less than this, and would frequently occur as a fluctuation of simple sampling.

(b) $(AB)/(B)=70.1$ per cent.: $(A\beta)/(\beta)=64.3$ per cent. Difference 5.8 per cent. $(A)/N=67.6$ per cent., and thence $\epsilon_{12}=3.40$ per cent. The actual difference is 1.7 times this, and might, rather infrequently, occur as a fluctuation of simple sampling.

CHAPTER XIV.

1.

Row.	σ_p.	Group of Rows.	σ_p.
1	3.1	5, 6, and 7	2.1
2	2.1	8, 9, 10, and 11	1.6
3	1.7	12, 13, and 14	1.2
4	2.7	15 and upwards	1.1

σ_p is given in units per 1000 births, as s and s_0.

2. $s_0=7.02$, and $\sigma_p=2.5$ units.
3. $\sigma^2=n.pq$ as if the chance of success were p in all cases (but the mean is $n/2$ not $p.n$).
4. Mean number of deaths per annum $=\sigma_0^2=680$,

$$\sigma^2=566,582. \qquad r=0.000029.$$

CHAPTER XV.

1.

(1)				
	0	í	7	792
	1	12	8	495
	2	66	9	220
	3	220	10	66
	4	495	11	12
	5	792	12	1
	6	924		

Total, 4096

(2)				
	0	459·4	5	116·4
	1	1102·6	6	27·2
	2	1212·8	7	4·7
	3	808·6	8	·6
	4	363·9		

Total, 4096·2

(3)		
	0	192
	1	288
	2	144
	3	24

Total, 648

2. The frequency of r successes is greater than that of $r-1$ so long as $r < np + p$: if np is an integer, $r = np$ gives the greatest term and also the mean.

3. This follows at once from a consideration of the Galton-Pearson apparatus.

4.

Binomial.	Normal curve.
1	1·7
10	10·5
45	42·7
120	116·1
210	211·5
252	258·4
210	211·5
etc.	etc.

5. The data are $M = 68·855$, $\sigma = 2·56$, $y_0 = 155·8$.

6. (1) United Kingdom—direct 1·75, from standard-deviation 1·73.

(2) Cambridge students—direct 1·68, from standard-deviation 1·73.

7. 70·6 per cent. **8.** 27 per cent.

9. (1) In a 12·4 per cent., b 1·0 per cent. of the trials, assuming normality, but the assumption is hardly quite valid. (2) a about 13 times in 100,000 trials; b practically impossible, being a deviation of over 7 times the standard error.

10. 853. **11.** Mean 74·3, standard-deviation 3·23.

CHAPTER XVI.

3. From equations (10) and (11) replace σ_1 and σ_2 by Σ_1 and Σ_2 in equation (9). Regarding this as an equation for r, note that r^2 is a maximum when $\tan 2\theta$ is infinite, or $\theta = 45°$.

4. In fig. 50, suppose every horizontal array to be given a slide to the right until its mean lies on the vertical axis through the mean of the whole distribution : then suppose the ellipses to be squeezed in the direction of this vertical axis until they become circles. The original quadrant has now become a sector with an angle between one and two right angles, and the question is solved on determining its magnitude.

CHAPTER XVII.

1. Estimated frequency 1554, standard error 0·28 lb. 2. Lower Q, frequency 1472, standard error 0·26 lb. ; upper Q, frequency 1116, standard error 0·34 lb. 3. 0·18 lb. 4. 0·24 lb., 17 per cent. less than the standard error of the median. 5. 0·0196 in. or 0·76 per cent. of the standard-deviation : the standard error of the semi-interquartile range is 1·23 per cent. of that range.

6.

r.	$n = 100$.	$n = 1000$.
0·0	0·1	0·0316
0·2	0·096	0·0304
0·4	0·084	0·0266
0·6	0·064	0·0202
0·8	0·036	0·0114

INDEX.

—∗∗—

[The references are to pages. The subject-matter of the Exercises given at the ends of the chapters has been indexed only when such exercises (or the answers thereto) give the constants for statistical tables in the text, or theoretical results of general interest; in all such cases the number of the question cited is given. In the case of authors' names, citations in the text are given first, followed by citations of the authors' papers or books in the lists of references.]

ABILITY, general, refs., 388.
Accident, deaths from (law of small chances), 265–266.
Achenwall, Gottfried, *Abriss der Staatswissenschaft*, 2.
Ages, at death of certain women (table), 78; of husband and wife (correlation), 159; diagram, 173; constants (qu. 3), 189.
Aggregate, of classes, 10–11.
Agricultural labourers' earnings. *See* Earnings.
Agriculture, experiment, errors in, refs., 391.
Airy, Sir G. B., use of terms " error of mean square " and " modulus," 144. Refs., *Theory of Errors of Observation*, 360.
Ammon, O., hair and eye-colour data cited from, 61.
Anderson, O., correlation difference method, 198; refs., 208.
Annual value of dwelling-houses (table), 83; of estates in 1715, table, 100; diagram, 101.
Arithmetic mean. *See* Mean, arithmetic.
Array, def., 164; standard-deviation of, 177, 204–205, 236–237, in normal correlation, 319–321.
Association, generally, 25–59; def., 28; degrees of, 29–30; testing by

comparison of percentages, 30–35; constancy of difference from independence values for the second-order frequencies, 35–36; coefficients of, 37–39; illusory or misleading, 48–51; total possible number of, for n attributes, 54–56; case of complete independence, 56–57; use of ordinary correlation-coefficient as measure of association, 216–217; Pearson's coefficient based on normal correlation (refs.), 40, 333; refs., 15, 39–40, 333.
Association, partial, generally, 42–59; the problem, 42–43; total and partial, def., 44; arithmetical treatment, 44–48; testing, in ignorance of third-order frequencies, 51–54; refs., 57.
——examples: deaths and sex, 32–33; deaths and occupation, 52–53; deaf-mutism and imbecility, 33–34; eye-colour of father and son, 34–35; eye-colour of grandparent, parent, and offspring, 46–48, 53–54; colour and prickliness of *Datura* fruits, 36–37, 377–378; defects in school-children, 45–46; inoculation, 379–381.
Asymmetrical frequency-distributions, 90–102; relative positions

26

efficient, partial association and partial correlation, 252 ; partial correlation in case of normal distribution of frequency, 331–332. Refs. 252–253, 332–333, 389.

Correlation ratio, 204–207 ; standard error, 352 ; refs., 209 ; partial, 252, and refs., 252, 389.

Cosin, values of estates in 1715, 100.

Cost of living, refs., 387–388.

Cotsworth, M. B., refs., multiplication table, 358.

Cournot, A. A., refs., theory of probability, 361.

Crawford, G. E., refs., proof that arithmetic mean exceeds geometric, 130.

Crelle, A. L., refs., multiplication table, 358.

Crops and weather, correlation, 196–197.

Cunningham, E., ref., omega-functions, 314.

Czuber, E., refs., *Wahrscheinlichkeitsrechnung*, 361 ; *Die statistische Forschungsmethode*, 392.

DARBISHIRE, A. D., data cited from, 128, 265. Refs., illustrations of correlation, 188, 273.

Darwin, Charles, data cited from, 269–270.

Datura, association between colour and prickliness of fruit, 37, 38, (qu. 10) 275, 378.

Davenport, C. B., data as to *Pecten* cited from, 158. Refs., statistical tables, 358.

Deaf-mutism, association with imbecility, 33–34, 38 ; frequency amongst offspring of deaf-mutes, table, 104.

Deaths, death-rates, association with sex, 32–33 ; with occupation (partial correction for age-distribution), 52–53 ; in England and Wales, 1881–1890, table, 77 ; from diphtheria, table, 98, diagram, 97 ; infantile and general, correlation of movements, 197–199 ; correction of, for age and sex-distribution, 52–53, 223–225, refs., 226, 388 ; applications of theory of sampling—deaths from accident,

265–266, deaths in childbirth, 282–284, deaths from explosions in mines, 287–288 ; inapplicability of the theory of simple sampling, 260–261, 282–284, 285–286, 287–288 ; criteria (refs.) 387.

Deciles, 150–152 ; standard error of, 337–341.

Defects : in school children, association of, 12, 45–46, refs., 15 ; census tabulation of, 14–15.

De Morgan, A., refs., *Formal Logic*, 23 ; *Theory of Probabilities*, 361.

Detlefsen, J. A., refs., fluctuations of sampling in Mendelian population, 389.

Deviation, mean, 134 ; generally, 144–147 : def., 144; is least round the median, 144–145 ; refs., 154 ; calculation of, 145–146, (qu. 7) 155–156 ; comparison of advantages with standard-deviation 146 ; of magnitude with standard-deviation, 146–147 ; of normal curve, 304.

Deviation, quartile. *See* Quartiles.

—— root-mean-square. *See* Deviation, standard.

—— standard, 134–144 ; def. 134 ; relation to root-mean-square deviation from any origin, 134–135 ; is the least possible root-mean-square deviation, 135 ; little affected by small errors in the mean, 135 ; calculation for ungrouped data, 135–137, for a grouped distribution, 138–141 ; influence of grouping, 140, 211–212 ; range of six times the s.d. contains the bulk of the observations, 140–142, 309 ; of a series compounded of others, 142–143 ; of N consecutive natural numbers, 143 ; of rectangle, 143 ; of arrays in theory of correlation, 177, 204, 205, 319–320 ; of generalised deviations (arrays), 234, 236–237 ; other names for, 144 ; of a sum or difference, 210–211 ; effect of errors of observation on, 211 ; of an index, 214–215 ; of binomial series, 299–300. For standard-deviations of sampling, *see* Error, standard.

De Vries, H., data cited from, 102.

PRINTED IN GREAT BRITAIN BY NEILL AND CO., LTD., EDINBURGH.